The Old Regime and the Haitian Revolution

The Haitian Revolution (1789–1804) was an epochal event that galvanized slaves and terrified planters throughout the Atlantic world. Rather than view this tumultuous period solely as a radical rupture with slavery, Malick W. Ghachem's innovative study shows that emancipation in Haiti was also a long-term product of its colonial legal history. The key to this interpretation lies in the Code Noir, the law that regulated master-slave relations in the French empire. The Code's rules for the freeing and punishment of slaves were at the center of intense eighteenth-century debates over the threats that masters – not just freedmen and slaves – posed to the plantation order. Ghachem takes us deep into this volatile colonial past, digging beyond the letter of the law and vividly reenacting such episodes as the extraordinary prosecution of a master for torturing and killing his slaves. This book brings us face to face with the revolutionary invocation of Old Regime law by administrators seeking stability, but also by free people of color and slaves demanding citizenship and an end to brutality. The result is a subtle yet dramatic portrait of the strategic stakes of colonial governance in the land that would become Haiti.

Malick W. Ghachem is associate professor of law at the University of Maine School of Law. A historian and lawyer, he has held a Chateaubriand Fellowship from the French government; a senior fellowship at the Gilder Lehrman Center for the Study of Slavery, Resistance, and Abolition at Yale University; and the Charles Hamilton Houston Fellowship in Law Teaching at Harvard Law School. His articles and reviews have appeared in *Law and History Review*, *The William and Mary Quarterly*, *Historical Reflections/Réflexions Historiques*, and *The Los Angeles Times Book Review*.

The Old Regime and the Haitian Revolution

MALICK W. GHACHEM

University of Maine School of Law

CAMBRIDGE
UNIVERSITY PRESS

CAMBRIDGE UNIVERSITY PRESS
Cambridge, New York, Melbourne, Madrid, Cape Town,
Singapore, São Paulo, Delhi, Mexico City

Cambridge University Press
32 Avenue of the Americas, New York, NY 10013-2473, USA

www.cambridge.org
Information on this title: www.cambridge.org/9780521545310

First published 2012

Printed in the United States of America

A catalog record for this publication is available from the British Library.

Library of Congress Cataloging in Publication data
Ghachem, Malick W. (Malick Walid)
The Old Regime and the Haitian Revolution / Malick W. Ghachem.
p.   cm.
Includes bibliographical references and index.
ISBN 978-0-521-83680-7 (hardback) – ISBN 978-0-521-54531-0 (paperback)
1. Law – Haiti – History.   2. Haiti – Politics and government – 1791–1804.
3. France. Code noir.   I. Title.
KGS294.G48   2012
349.7294–dc23   2011038739

ISBN 978-0-521-83680-7 Hardback
ISBN 978-0-521-54531-0 Paperback

For Faisal and Ayanna,
my free spirits

Contents

Figures

Acknowledgments

I had the idea for this book long before I knew what form its argument would ultimately take and where its narrative thread would lead. I am deeply grateful for the patience and encouragement of those who kept me at the task when other demands – most notably, those of the clients I served for about five years in the practice of law – forced me to put this work aside. Frank Smith took this book on at Cambridge University Press, and Eric Crahan took it over after Frank assumed the directorship of the press's New York office. I thank Frank and Eric for standing by with such forbearance and equanimity while I sought to shape and then reshape the contours of the manuscript until it became the book I had envisioned.

That it now appears in this form is due in very large measure to my friend and colleague Rebecca Scott, whose learning and counsel have been major blessings in my intellectual life. Rebecca generously read and commented on nearly every part of this book and was entirely indispensable to my ability to see it through to completion, even as she worked to finish her own study that travels through some of these same waters. Her sheer enthusiasm for legal-historical scholarship and her determination to recover lost stories of slavery and emancipation repeatedly reinforced me during some of my most trying moments with this endeavor. I could write whole paragraphs about everything else she has done to improve the final product, but I will content myself by saying simply: Thank you, Rebecca, for bringing me back to what I had started.

Laurent Dubois has brought tremendous energy and insight to the field of Haitian history; my debts to him are particularly great. The sharp critiques of two anonymous readers of an earlier version of this manuscript – one of whom I believe I have just thanked – were indispensable. Chris Desan's perceptive reading of the introduction helped me clear some of my last remaining hurdles, and I am enormously thankful for her many other acts of support during the preparation of this work. Vince Brown's gentle impatience to see this book between covers was heartening.

This book began life as a dissertation at Stanford University, and the three scholars who served on my thesis committee, Keith Baker, Jack Rakove, and Peter Sahlins, deserve special mention. Keith Baker's brilliance made Tocqueville's vision of French history come alive for me, and motivated me to rethink that vision in the context of the Haitian experience. To work with him was one of the great privileges of my academic career, which he has done much to advance. Jack Rakove's superb example in the field of American revolutionary history has also been vitally important to me; I am particularly indebted to him for sacrificing time during a sabbatical year to comment on my thesis (and for lugging the cumbersome text all the way to Eastern Europe and back). Peter Sahlins warmly welcomed an interloper to his wonderful seminar on the legal history of early modern France at the University of California at Berkeley, where I first began exploring in depth the material that forms the basis of this book. I remember the fresh excitement and intensity of those seminar meetings, to which my colleague Gillian Weiss introduced me. My longtime friend and mentor Dan Gordon read the completed dissertation and helped me imagine how its argument might be developed into a book.

At various stages in the preparation of this work, I received generous fellowship support from the following sources: the Stanford University Department of History, the John Carter Brown Library, the French government's Chateaubriand Fellowship program, the International Center for Jefferson Studies (funded by the Coca-Cola Company), the Stanford Humanities Center, the W. E. B. Du Bois Institute for African and African American Research, the Charles Hamilton Houston Fellowship at Harvard Law School, and the Gilder Lehrman Center for the Study of Slavery, Resistance, and Abolition at Yale. For this support, and for associated acts of kindness undertaken while I worked under the aegis of these institutions, I thank Norman Fiering, Karen DeMaria, Dany Gentilt, Michel Troper, Jim Horn, Peter Onuf, Joe Miller, Jim Caesar, Theodore and Frances Geballe, Peter Stansky, Susie Dunn, Susan Sebbard, Gwen Lorraine, Debra Pounds, Rania Hegazi, Randall Kennedy, Robert Clark, Morton Horwitz, Ellen Adolph, Henry Louis Gates, Jr., Karen Dalton,

David Brion Davis, and Rob Forbes. I miss my friend Lara Moore, whose example and sense of purpose remain with me.

This study would not have been possible without the assistance of archivists and librarians at the following institutions: in France, the Archives nationales d'outre-mer, the Archives nationales, the Bibliothèque nationale de France, the Bibliothèque Historique de la Ville de Paris, the Bibliothèque Cujas, the Bibliothèque de l'Ordre des Avocats (particularly Yves Ozanam); in Haiti, the Bibliothèque haïtienne des Pères du Saint-Esprit (where Patrick Tardieu was my host); and in the United States, the John Carter Brown Library (especially Lynne Harrell and Susan Danforth), Stanford's Green Library (where thanks are due to Sonia Moss, Mary Munill, Mary Jane Parrine, and the staff of the Department of Special Collections), and Harvard's Widener Library.

Along the way, I presented bits and pieces of this project at various conferences, workshops, lectures, seminars, and presentations, of which I must single out several highly congenial and inspiring rounds of Bernard Bailyn's Atlantic History Seminar at Harvard. For their feedback and presence at these gatherings, and for other assorted odds and ends, I thank Bernard Bailyn, Pat Denault, Ed Cox, Ron Hoffman, Philip Morgan, Robert Gross, Fredrika Teute, Ron Schechter, Richard Dunn, John Smolenski, Michael Zuckerman, Sally Gordon, Aron Rodrigue, Karen Offen, Julie Saville, Max Edelson, Randy Sparks, Rosemary Brana-Shute, John Garrigus, Seymour Drescher, Hubert Gerbeau, Lou Roberts, Colin Jones, James Sheehan, Tim Brown, Richard Ross, William Forbath, Amy Upgren, John Wirth, Sheryl Kroen, David Bell, Joyce Chaplin, Paul Robinson, Sarah Sussman, Brian Vick, Ken Moss, Gillian Weiss, Amalia Kessler, Walter Johnson, Emma Rothschild, David Todd, Mary Lewis, Morton Horwitz, and Alan Dershowitz. A colloquium marking the 200th anniversary of the death of Toussaint Louverture, held in Port-au-Prince in 2003, taught me to appreciate the significance of the Haitian Revolution for contemporary Haitians; thank you to Carole Berotte Joseph and Marie Lourdes Elgirus for that memorable occasion. I twice presented draft sections of this book at the University of Michigan Law School. For those rewarding experiences and the insights that flowed from them, I thank Rebecca Scott and the students in her "Law in Slavery and Freedom" seminar, Martha Jones, Jean Hébrard, Tom Green, Bill Novak, and the students in the Green/Novak legal history colloquium. A version of Chapter 4 appeared in the November 2011 issue of *Law and History Review* by permission of Cambridge University Press.

Within the community of slavery and Haitian revolutionary studies, I must acknowledge a special debt to David Brion Davis, whose profound and searching commitment to this field of history has been important to me for more than a decade. David Geggus bestowed on me the benefits of his vast erudition on numerous occasions; his assistance in matters large and small over the years is much appreciated. Jeremy Popkin, Alyssa Sepinwall, Domingue Rogers, Miranda Spieler, John Garrigus, and Louis Sala-Molins answered my calls for help when I sounded them and generously shared their work with me. I have also learned a great deal from Gene Ogle's incisive writings on Saint-Domingue.

At the University of Maine School of Law, deans Peter Pitegoff, Jenny Wriggins, and Chris Knott were solicitous of my needs beyond the call of duty. Christine Hepler generously helped to obtain permissions for the various images that appear in this book. Sherry McCall answered my seemingly endless requests for interlibrary loan materials with unfailing good cheer and resourcefulness. Fran Smith's patient and kind soul kept me from discombobulating when this work overlapped with a hectic transition to law teaching.

Years ago, I saw a reproduction of the great Haitian artist Ernst Prophète's wonderful painting of the Haitian declaration of independence, and it has remained in my mind ever since. Heartfelt thanks to Ernst, Jack Rosenthal, and Holly Russell for permission to use the image that appears on this book's cover, and to David Fechheimer for enabling me to reach its creator. I am grateful as well to Abby Zorbaugh and Aishwarya Daksinamoorty for help with the production process and to John McWilliams for his copyediting. Christine Hoskin prepared a superb index.

My parents, Said and Khedija Ghachem, made many sacrifices for my education and raised me with an openness to the world beyond that enabled me to follow my interests where they led. This book is also the product of their faith and efforts. My four siblings – Sofia, Samy, Karim, and Leila – stepped into roles that needed filling when our separate boats started to drift apart; they assisted me in staying the course. June Cargile and Lori James were unstinting in their support of my family; Kieren James-Lubin helped me prepare for new responsibilities.

My wise and brilliant wife, Erica James, gave me the time I needed to bring this project to a close. But her contributions have been much more extensive than this. A Haiti scholar herself, she has been asking me good questions about this book since the day I first met her – a most fortuitous encounter prompted, as it happens, by the almost certainly unfounded suspicion that I was trying to recall all of the Haitian history books she had checked out at the local library. (How we got from there to our wedding day is a long and somewhat contested but nonetheless romantic affair.) Her own perseverance and drive to make sense of Haiti's troubles were an inspiration to me, as well as a humbling reminder of what suffering and courage still obtain in the contemporary world. More than anyone, she persuaded me that I had a story worth telling here and, through her love and compassion, helped me to bring it to fruition.

This book is dedicated to Faisal and Ayanna, my two beloved and exuberant children. I hope that in reading it someday, they will recall that their story, too, travels through Haiti.

North Hampton, New Hampshire
June 2011

Introduction

"What is a Revolution?" asked a *Revolutionary Catechism* published in year two of the French Republican calendar (1793–1794). Came the answer: "It is a violent passage from a state of slavery to a state of liberty."[1] The Jacobin ideology encapsulated in this formulation was no less heartfelt or effective for its metaphorical character. The use of the word slavery to evoke the oppressions of a despotic form of government was common to classical republicans of both the American and French revolutions.[2] Yet the late eighteenth century also witnessed a more literal example of the catechistic definition of a revolution.

On a strict construction of the catechism, the Haitian Revolution of 1789–1804 was the quintessential revolution of the "Age of Revolutions." Even today, it stands as the only instance of a victorious war of slave

---

[1] *Catéchisme révolutionnaire, ou L'histoire de la Révolution française, par demandes et par réponses: à l'usage de la jeunesse républicaine, et de tous les peuples qui veulent devenir libres* (Paris: Debarle, 1793–1794), 3, also quoted in Michel Vovelle, *La mentalité révolutionnaire: Société et mentalités sous la Révolution française* (Paris: Éditions sociales, 1985), 103. Unless otherwise noted, all translations in this book are my own.

[2] On the equation of British imperial rule with slavery in radical Whig pamphlets of the American Revolution, see Bernard Bailyn, *The Ideological Origins of the American Revolution*, enl. ed. (Cambridge, MA: Harvard University Press, 1992), 119–120, 122, 232–234. The paradigmatic example on the French revolutionary side is Jean-Paul Marat's *The Chains of Slavery*, originally published in English in 1774 and republished in French in 1793. See Keith M. Baker, "Transformations of Classical Republicanism in Eighteenth-Century France," *Journal of Modern History* 73 (2001): 43–44; idem, "Political languages of the French Revolution," in *The Cambridge History of Eighteenth-Century Political Thought*, ed. Mark Goldie and Robert Wokler (New York: Cambridge University Press, 2006), 643.

liberation on a national scale.[3] In 1804, the leaders of the formerly enslaved population of Saint-Domingue announced the independence of Haiti, ending more than a century of French colonial rule in the Caribbean territory and creating the first independent black state. The Haitian Revolution forever transformed New World slavery and the Atlantic world more generally, providing the single most important inspiration for slave resistance and abolitionism in the modern era.[4] Moreover, by driving Napoleon to abandon his dream of restoring the French Caribbean empire and to sell Louisiana to the United States in 1803, the Haitian Revolution initiated a long-term shift in the geopolitical orientation of the French empire.[5] It also greatly facilitated the westward expansion and rise of the cotton-plantation economy of the United States, with consequences that can be most clearly seen in the events of the American Civil War. Indeed, the distinctive imprint of Haitian revolutionary ideology can be seen as far down as the litigation that produced the Supreme Court's 1896 decision in *Plessy v. Ferguson*. The notion of "public rights" that Homer Plessy embraced in that case to challenge (unsuccessfully) Louisiana's railway-car segregation law was the outgrowth of an Atlantic tradition of anti-caste activism engendered by free people of color who emigrated from Saint-Domingue to Louisiana during and after the Haitian Revolution.[6]

Such considerations underscore the inherent drama of the Haitian Revolution as a (violent) passage from slavery to freedom. For many late-eighteenth- and early-nineteenth-century observers, including erstwhile planters and others writing from a proslavery or reactionary perspective,

---

[3] The eighteenth-century maroon wars of Jamaica and Suriname succeeded in ending slavery in parts of those colonies, but only in Saint-Domingue did slaves manage to eliminate colonial slavery throughout the entire territory in which it had taken root. On the Jamaican and Surinamese maroons, see Richard Price, ed., *Maroon Societies: Rebel Slave Communities in the Americas*, 3rd ed. (Baltimore, MD: The Johns Hopkins University Press, 1996), 227–311.

[4] Even scholars who take a relatively modest view of the impact of the Haitian Revolution agree that its success almost certainly made it much easier for Britain to end involvement in the slave trade in 1807 and then to abolish plantation slavery in 1833 without concern that these measures would advantage its longtime political and commercial rival, France. See David Geggus, "The Caribbean in the Age of Revolution," in *The Age of Revolutions in Global Context, ca. 1760–1840*, ed. David Armitage and Sanjay Subrahmanyam (New York: Palgrave Macmillan, 2010), 91.

[5] On this shift, see David Todd, "A French Imperial Meridian, 1814–1870," *Past and Present* 210, no. 1 (Feb. 2011): 155–186.

[6] Rebecca J. Scott, "The Atlantic World and the Road to Plessy v. Ferguson," *Journal of American History* 94, no. 3 (2007): 726–733; idem, "Public Rights, Social Equality, and the Conceptual Roots of the Plessy Challenge," *Michigan Law Review* 106 (2008): 784–786.

that narrative of rupture was tragic in nature: a story of loss and catastrophe fueled by images of retributive black-on-white violence. Indeed, for much of the outside world until well into the twentieth century, "[t]he enduring memory of the Haitian Revolution was ... [Jean-Jacques] Dessalines," who as emperor of Haiti ordered the 1805 massacre of most of the whites then remaining in the former slave colony.[7] The American historian Ulrich Bonnell Phillips, for example, subsumed the Haitian Revolution under the rubric of "slave crime" in his 1918 study, *American Negro Slavery*.[8] For others, most notably the descendants of free people of color and slaves in nineteenth-century Haiti and elsewhere in the Atlantic world, the operative tale was progressive and heroic. Many contemporary Haitians remember the violence of their revolutionary heritage as an inspirational display of physical courage and perseverance in the face of great and long-standing suffering.

From its origins in the early nineteenth century to our own day, the rupture narrative that is shared by these competing images has served to suppress other kinds of stories that can be told about the Haitian Revolution: stories of continuity rather than change, of irony and unintended consequences rather than catastrophe or emancipation. The task of understanding the Haitian Revolution *as* a revolution, in other words, has proven to be a deceptively simple one. The dramatic discontinuity effected by the events of 1789–1804 has obscured critical aspects of their genesis and, thus, also their character. In this book, I set aside the still resonant image of the Haitian Revolution as a violent and sudden passage from slavery to freedom in favor of a different motif. Simply put, my thesis is that emancipation in Haiti was also a long-term product of its colonial history. For the Haitian revolutionaries, like all other revolutionaries before and since, did not succeed altogether in their effort to

[7] David Brion Davis, *Inhuman Bondage: The Rise and Fall of Slavery in the New World* (New York: Oxford University Press, 2006), 172. See also Malick W. Ghachem, "The Colonial Terror," paper read at the Wednesday colloquium of the Dubois Institute for African and African American Research, Harvard University, December 10, 2003; and Laurent Dubois, "Avenging America: The Politics of Violence in the Haitian Revolution," in *The World of the Haitian Revolution*, ed. David Patrick Geggus and Norman Fiering (Bloomington: University of Indiana Press, 2009), 111–124.

[8] Ulrich Bonnell Phillips, *American Negro Slavery: A Survey of the Supply, Employment and Control of Negro Labor As Determined by the Plantation Regime* (New York: D. Appleton, 1918), 467–469, also quoted in Vincent Brown, "A Vapor of Dread: Observations on Racial Terror and Vengeance in the Age of Revolution," in *Revolution! The Atlantic World Reborn*, ed. Thomas Bender, Laurent Dubois, and Richard Rabinowitz (New York: D. Giles, for the New York Historical Society, 2011), 198 n.32.

"sever their past from their future, as it were, and hollow out an abyss between what they had been and what they wished to become." Thus, to borrow Tocqueville's words again, if we want to understand what happened in Haiti between 1789 and 1804, we must close our eyes periodically to the Haiti of those years, and of the years that have passed since, and "begin our investigation at the tomb of the [Haiti] that is no more."[9]

As its title suggests, this book seeks to interrogate the relationship between the Old Regime and the Haitian Revolution, and in doing so frames a long eighteenth-century continuity between the colonial and revolutionary periods of Haitian history. Within that historical frame, the law of slavery was a profoundly important factor. Between the Code Noir of 1685 – which laid the foundations of the law of slavery in Saint-Domingue – and the declaration of Haitian independence in 1804, a world of violent and persistently evocative collective memories was formed. That world has been largely divided into separate compartments of "colonial" and "revolutionary" history, at significant cost to our understanding of both. The Haitian Revolution was undeniably a "violent passage from a state of slavery to a state of liberty," but violence was not the only means of the revolution, and the revolutionary era is not the only time frame relevant to understanding how and why the passage occurred as it did.

Indeed, where the colony's free people of color were concerned, the revolutionary period was the end, rather than the beginning, of a process of liberation from slavery. The manumission of slaves was already a practice of long-standing pedigree in Saint-Domingue by 1789, fuelling a dramatic growth in the size of the free colored population that had few parallels in the colonial Americas (although freed persons continued to face a daunting array of discriminatory measures well after they were freed, particularly in the aftermath of the Seven Years' War of 1754–1763.)[10] Moreover, the servitude of slaves itself underwent significant changes over the course of the colonial period – at the level of both experience and representation – which helped determine the manner in which slavery was eventually abolished.[11]

---

[9] Alexis de Tocqueville, *The Ancien Régime and the French Revolution*, ed. Jon Elster, trans. Arthur Goldhammer, Cambridge Texts in the History of Political Thought (New York, NY: Cambridge University Press, 2011), 1.

[10] Carolyn E. Fick, "The French Revolution in Saint Domingue: A Triumph of a Failure?" in *A Turbulent Time: The French Revolution and the Greater Caribbean*, ed. David Patrick Geggus and David Barry Gaspar (Bloomington: Indiana University Press, 1997), 55.

[11] For a tentative discussion of changes in the conditions of enslavement in Saint-Domingue during the late colonial period, see David Geggus, "Saint-Domingue on the Eve of Revolution," in Geggus and Fiering, *The World of the Haitian Revolution*, 9–12.

In emphasizing the role of the law of slavery in Haiti's long-term, eighteenth-century transformation, my purpose is to highlight how the outer boundaries of an oppressive legal system – in this case, the regime of the Code Noir – can be refashioned, over time and through the combined efforts of often conflicting groups and individuals, into a source of emancipation. In this reading of the law of slavery, slaves and free people of color were, to be sure, actors and not merely subjects: They proactively engaged with the law of slavery and eventually transformed it, even as the law of slavery consistently operated on them, often with a disturbing ruthlessness.[12] However, I equally show that planters, the kingpins of this world, were subjects of and not merely agents in the legal universe that Atlantic slavery created. The author of an anonymous 1847 pamphlet, seeking to demonstrate the assimilability of colonial law into a metropolitan framework, observed that the Code Noir was "no less the code of the whites than that of the blacks."[13] We need not go this far to recognize that the law of slavery sought to control the actions of masters as well as slaves, whites and persons of African descent (both slave and free) alike.

The Code Noir (or "Black Code") was a system of tremendously invidious racial domination, but its maintenance required different forms of control at different times, particularly with respect to the regulation of manumission and planter brutality. These methods of control sometimes pitted the colonial administration against those very persons whose interests are often identified with the law of slavery: the planters, a group that, in Saint-Domingue, included both whites and significant numbers of free people of color. The law of slavery evolved over the course of the colonial period as a result of many different individual interactions and contests between administrators, jurists, white planters, free people of color, and slaves. At a number of its most critical turning points – including the free colored movement for political rights in 1789–1792 and the abolition of slavery in 1793 and 1794 – the Haitian Revolution reflects the unintended legacies of these colonial conflicts and collaborations. In its most general form, this is the story I tell in the following pages.

There are lessons to be found here for other experiences of legal oppression and transformation, both earlier and later, colonial and noncolonial, in the Atlantic world and elsewhere. Few laws are so immaculately designed, few decisional principles so clearly drawn, as to leave

---

[12] Cf. Robert Olwell, *Masters, Slaves, & Subjects: The Culture of Power in the South Carolina Low Country, 1740–1790* (Ithaca, NY: Cornell University Press, 1998), 6–10.
[13] *De la représentation des colonies dans le parlement* (Paris: Librairie d'Amyot, 1847), 10.

no room at all for creative tinkering with their margins, for indirect critiques, unintended applications, and reinterpretations that can eventually circle back to draw in question the premises that underlie those laws and principles. The story of the Code Noir showcases the imaginative opportunities that exist for disenfranchised persons and their advocates to reconfigure the cards they have been dealt and to arrange them in a hand that comes closer to justice. I hope that this message, in the unromantic form of a study in legal continuities, will reach such individuals.

This is, however, first and finally a book about Haiti, a nation that, to an uncommon degree, was long entrapped in the categories imposed on its own passage out of slavery. As historians of the French Revolution have recognized, the question of the *Revolutionary Catechism* was not an innocent or abstract one. By answering that a revolution entails the violent replacement of slavery with liberty, the *Catechism* sought to justify the use of the guillotine to eliminate the political enemies of Robespierre and his fellow Jacobin revolutionary leaders during the so-called Reign of Terror. Since the time of its unfolding, the Haitian Revolution has been questioned, if not indicted, for its complicity with this understanding of violence as a natural and necessary means of revolutionary change. Unlike the Haitian revolutionaries, however, the Jacobins in France did not themselves have to labor under the special burdens that racial subordination imposes.[14] The dilemma of the Haitian Revolution has always been that of a "no-win" situation, in David Brion Davis's words.[15] It requires a great deal of idealism, racism, or both to believe that liberation from slavery in Saint-Domingue could have come without the willingness of slaves to use physical force against their oppressors. Yet the roots of Haiti's no-win dilemma were far deeper and more complex than the competing versions of the rupture thesis and their extant manifestations suggest, for those roots involved problems of law as well as violence. Colonial law set many of the terms of the Haitian Revolution, including the terms by which violence was or was not used. Whatever we may conclude about the Haitian Revolution, we cannot think of it solely in

---

[14] In 1817, Germaine de Staël contrasted the relative tranquility of the seventeenth-century English revolution with the fourteen months of the Reign of Terror in France. She concluded from this comparison that "no people had ever been as fortunate for a hundred years as the French people. If the Negroes of Saint-Domingue have committed even more atrocities, it is because they had been all the more oppressed." "It does not flow from these reflections," she continued, "that the crimes [of the Terror] merit less hatred." Germaine de Staël, *Considérations sur la Révolution française*, ed. Jacques Godechot (Paris: Tallandier, 2000), 303–304.

[15] Davis, *Inhuman Bondage*, 172.

relation to itself; rather, we must consider it as part and parcel of the larger human tragedy that was Atlantic slavery.

The Code Noir occupies center stage in this account. But what exactly was the Code Noir? In the narrowest sense, the phrase served (as of the early eighteenth century) to denote the text of Louis XIV's 1685 edict itself: fifty-nine articles that spanned the gamut of topics ranging from religion and marriage to punishment, property, and manumission. More broadly, it also signified the full array of eighteenth-century laws, regulations, and judicial decisions concerning the relationship between masters, slaves, and free people of color in the French colonies.[16] If the emancipation of Saint-Domingue took place through law as well as violence, and over a period of many more years than the fifteen we associate with the Haitian Revolution per se, it is at least in part because the Code Noir was transformed over this long period in ways that its framers did not always intend or even imagine. This transformation, in turn, suggests a third meaning of the phrase "Code Noir." More than a corpus of free-standing legal texts, the Code Noir was the subject of a permanent debate in colonial and revolutionary Haiti, a debate that was a key part of the colony's overall culture and the very essence of its legal culture. To recapture the terms of that debate is to grasp some of the more covert mechanisms of Haiti's long passage from slavery to freedom.

This is not, however, a story of total transformation, for there are tantalizing clues in the prehistory of the Code Noir indicating that the dilemma of how to maintain stability in a slave society was already recognized as an old one by 1685. The nature of this dilemma was such that it generated a special kind of concern about the radical tendencies of slave societies, a concern that, similarly, is much older than (if distinguishable from) the antislavery and abolitionist thought we associate with the revolutionary era. The law of slavery in Saint-Domingue posited a state of chronic danger that flowed naturally from the forms of domestic license and coercion at work in plantation society. The strategic ethics of this regime were shaped by many factors, but most prominently and persistently by an ambivalent preoccupation with manumission and planter brutality: the polar extremes of slave society. That same ambivalent anxiety later structured the encounters between leading free people of color, slave insurgents, and successive French revolutionary governments in the contingent course of events that was the Haitian Revolution.

---

[16] As in the title of this 1743 compilation, for example: *Code noir, ou Recueil d'édits, déclarations et arrêts concernant les esclaves nègres de l'Amérique* (Paris: Libraires associés, 1743).

By the "strategic ethics" of slavery, I understand a mode of legality that is essentially instrumental or pragmatic in its orientation, and a style of criticism that is concerned primarily with the stability and efficacy of slavery as opposed to its injustice. A strategic ethics is an ethics of prudence: It seeks to avoid reckless conduct that threatens the ship of state. Moreover, it embraces "prudent government" in the further sense that it is distinct from (although not incompatible with) humanitarian concerns.[17] A strategic ethics embodies, first and foremost, the seemingly neutral calculation of aggregate social welfare – understood in this context to mean the well-being of the plantation order – rather than a set of normative commitments to individual human rights.[18]

Such a pragmatic orientation toward political and social institutions does not decide the substantive content of one's views about those institutions. Instrumentalism has no necessary or inherent normative implications, but is rather a highly malleable, open-ended style of thought.[19] As an abstract matter, it can and does swing either for or against the status quo. However, in early modern slave societies such as Saint-Domingue – and perhaps in Saint-Domingue above all – the subtext of this ethics of prudence was hardly an abstract matter. The tactical deliberations of those who participated in the regime of the Code Noir revolved around a set of quite specific practices that were believed to pose "systemic" risks to the survival of the plantation economy. It was the concrete implications of these practices – not merely a strategic or instrumental attitude per se – that influenced the relative balance between change and continuity in the eighteenth-century Atlantic world. Yet the ideological scaffolding that grew up around the practices and institutions of slavery was inseparable from their real-world consequences.

---

[17] For the use of this phrase, see Chapter 3.

[18] Gordon Lewis discusses the "policy of prudence" that informed attitudes toward plantation slavery in the French colonies and elsewhere. He connects this policy to proslavery ideology rather than to the critique of slavery, and emphasizes its limitations in the face of a "policy of terror" to which prudence was opposed. Gordon K. Lewis, *Main Currents in Caribbean Thought: The Historical Evolution of Caribbean Society in its Ideological Aspects, 1492–1900* (Lincoln: University of Nebraska Press, 2004), 165–168. According to Lewis, "[t]he arguments of the reformers in favor of better treatment of the slaves – more protection, for example, in the courts – were in themselves proslavery, since better treatment was seen as weakening the case for early emancipation." Ibid., 168. As I will explain further, the experience of Saint-Domingue suggests a messier, less coherent relationship between prudence and proslavery ideology than this.

[19] Cf. Morton Horwitz, *The Transformation of American Law, 1780–1860* (Cambridge, MA: Harvard University Press, 1979), 1–2 (identifying the rise of an instrumental conception of American law in the late eighteenth and early nineteenth centuries with the rise of a market economy and the judicial promotion of economic development).

Put differently, the law of slavery in Saint-Domingue was both highly imaginative and mundane: It conjured up ancient images of slaves even as it called on the contemporaneous power of local intuitions and everyday experiences, in a manner that recalls Clifford Geertz's definition of law as a "complex of characterizations and imaginings [and] stories about events cast in imagery about principles."[20] French colonial slave law was just such a complex of characterizations, imaginings, and stories, translated insistently by administrators, jurists, and planters into a set of formal principles concerning the maintenance of what Jean Bodin called "the well-ordered commonwealth" ("la république bien ordonnée"). The concept of the well-ordered commonwealth, as it was reflected in both doctrinal and administrative writings of the early modern French empire, runs throughout the narrative arc of this book.

The motif of the well-ordered commonwealth resonated in Saint-Domingue largely because of its relationship to a second motif that runs through the life of the Code Noir: an anxiety about the retributive impulses of slaves as the "natural enemies of society" (to use Montesquieu's phrase).[21] The merger of these two themes is perhaps best reflected in Bodin's discussion of the dangers of slavery to a stable polity in his *Six Books of a Commonwealth* (first published in 1576). There, Bodin invoked what he called an "ancient proverb" – "*So many slaves, so many enemies in a man's house*" – to sum up the lessons of four thousand years of historical experience with slaves.[22] This was not merely a political-theoretical hypothesis. As the governor of Saint-Domingue warned his metropolitan superior in 1685, the year of the Code Noir, "In our slaves we have domestic enemies."[23]

French colonial slave law, above all as applied in Saint-Domingue, took shape against the backdrop of this powerful image of slaves and of the nature of master-slave relations. Almost by its very nature, that image served to conjure up, at the social level, the prospect of a slave

---

[20] Clifford Geertz, *Local Knowledge: Further Essays in Interpretive Anthropology* (New York: Basic Books, 1983), 215.

[21] Charles-Louis de Secondat, Baron de Montesquieu, *The Spirit of the Laws*, trans. Anne M. Cohler et al., Cambridge Texts in the History of Political Thought (Cambridge, UK: Cambridge University Press, 1989), 256.

[22] Jean Bodin, *The Six Bookes of a Commonweale: A Fascimile reprint of the English translation of 1606 Corrected and supplemented in light of a new comparison with the French and Latin texts*, trans. Richard Knolles trans., ed. Kenneth Douglas McRae (Cambridge, MA: Harvard University Press, 1962), 45 (emphasis in the original). I have modernized the spelling of this translation throughout.

[23] Report of Pierre-Paul Tarin de Cussy, governor, to Jean-Baptiste Colbert de Seignelay, naval minister, 18 Oct. 1685, Archives nationales d'outre-mer [hereafter ANOM], Correspondance générale Saint-Domingue [hereafter CGSD], C/9A/1, fol. 250.

...olution. Future-oriented speculation about the fate of colonial slavery; predictions of the turbulence that would flow from a failure to heed the warnings of administrators attuned to the inherent instabilities of slave society; prophecies of racial violence on a greater or lesser scale – these were significant aspects of the political and legal culture of Saint-Domingue well before the French and Haitian Revolutions.[24] The colonial imagination was broad enough to associate such prospects with a revealingly wide range of events, behaviors, and worldviews. Although the fear of violent slave unrest was pervasive in the eighteenth-century Atlantic world, the preoccupation with analyzing and counteracting its putative sources was especially pronounced in colonial Haiti.[25] French colonial administrators and planters identified the specter of black revolt with everything from earthquakes and famines to Jesuit proselytism, freemasonry, and vodou. The British were among the usual suspects, but so too were the Spanish, the maroons (fugitive slaves) of Jamaica, and the maroons of Saint-Domingue. Even the sound of slaves drumming and dancing at night in the countryside and the boisterous communing of slaves and free people of color alike in the colony's urban taverns evoked genuine alarm.

Over the course of the eighteenth century, however, two potential sources of the downfall of the colonial commonwealth stood out with a special consistency in the minds of administrators, jurists, and commentators: manumission and planter brutality. In order to guard against the threat of a slave revolution, administrators sought to impose effective restraints on these two seemingly contradictory tendencies of France's flagship colony in the New World. The site of rampant brutality, Saint-Domingue also offered slaves access to manumission at higher rates than any other plantation society before or since.[26] Under the original terms of the Code Noir, masters were at liberty, during their lifetimes or at the

---

[24] For a stimulating discussion of an analogous strain in eighteenth-century metropolitan French political culture emphasizing the relationship between public debt and the militarization of the state, see Michael Sonenscher, *Before the Deluge: Public Debt, Inequality, and the Intellectual Origins of the French Revolution* (Princeton, NJ: Princeton University Press, 2007).

[25] Cf. Geggus, "Saint-Domingue on the Eve of the Haitian Revolution," 3–5, which seems to me to go too far in the direction of making this question of political and legal culture a strictly empirical matter of the actual incidence of slave rebellion in the colonial era.

[26] Fick, "The French Revolution in Saint-Domingue," 55–56; John D. Garrigus, *Before Haiti: Race and Citizenship in French Saint-Domingue* (New York: Palgrave Macmillan, 2006), 4–5. For the population growth rates in Saint-Domingue, see Jean Meyer, "Des origines à 1763," in Jean Meyer, Annie Rey-Goldzeiguer, and Jean Tarrade, *Histoire de la France coloniale*, vol. 1, *La conquête*, (Paris: Armand Colin, 1991), 136.

time of death, to manumit their slaves for any reason or no reason at all, and many did so.[27] This combination of emancipative and repressive policies created a complex and unique political culture, one whose ironies were fully reflected in the law of slavery. Chief among these ironies was the role played by slave law in the governance of masters no less than slaves, for the conduct of the slave master in Saint-Domingue turned out – not entirely unexpectedly – to be a major theme in the eighteenth-century implementation of the Code Noir.

The freeing of slaves by individual masters was seen by turns as both a cause of and a remedy for possible slave unrest. Early in the eighteenth century, in the name of containing "disorder," colonial administrators began taking steps to set limits on this prerogative granted slaveholders under the Code Noir (and exercised mainly in favor of the planters' own children, born of interracial unions and coercive encounters with women slaves). However, by the end of the colonial period, manumission, in connection with military service, had also come to be seen as an effective strategy for co-opting the energies of potentially rebellious slaves, a kind of safety valve for the release of pent-up hostilities. The coexistence of these two understandings of manumission – instigator of disorder and antidote for subversion – during the eighteenth century helped inform the ambivalent, sometimes zigzagging debates of the revolutionary period over the rights of free people of color and, later, slaves.[28]

Planter brutality was susceptible to the same kind of Janus-faced manipulation. Like manumission, the radical abuse of slaves by masters and overseers was alternately viewed as both an impetus for slave revolt and a necessary means of discouraging black insubordination. Whereas planters often interpreted the resort to brutal forms of discipline and punishment as an extension of their ownership rights over the slave, administrators identified a kind of collective-action problem: The costs of brutality would inevitably be imposed on the system as a whole by way of a slave reaction that threatened to travel far beyond the boundaries

---

[27] Code Noir (1685), art. 55.

[28] Orlando Patterson justly observes that "it is incorrect to expect that a slave system with a high rate of manumission was in any way on the path to abolition." On the other hand, it probably goes too far to say, as Patterson does, that "manumission had little to do with the abolition of slavery." Orlando Patterson, "Three Notes of Freedom: The Nature and Consequences of Manumission," in *Paths to Freedom: Manumission in the Atlantic World*, ed. Rosemary Brana-Shute and Randy J. Sparks (Charleston: University of South Carolina Press, 2009), 20. There was undoubtedly a relationship, albeit one that was neither unilinear nor predictable, between manumission and abolition in Saint-Domingue.

of any one individual plantation. By the end of the colonial period, the abuse and torture of "domestic enemies" had become a central concern for the Old Regime bureaucrats and lawyers whose job it was to keep the colonial enterprise going.

To avert the prospect of a coordinated slave uprising, French colonial law navigated between the hazards associated with the large-scale emancipation of individual slaves as a result of individual owners' choices and the dangers attendant with allowing masters to impose an unremittingly harsh system of slave punishment and discipline. The administrators charged with maintaining the stability of the plantation system came eventually to look on the slaveholder's long-term economic interests (understood to encompass his physical safety) as a way of containing his self-destructive passions.[29] For their part, the planters of Saint-Domingue vigorously resisted such regulatory designs, which they were not embarrassed to describe (along with other policies of the colonial administration) as the workings of ministerial "despotism." Even as they did so, Saint-Domingue continued to foster ever greater numbers of free people of color and ever higher rates of slave abuse.

To fully understand the relationship between the Old Regime and the Haitian Revolution, we must complicate the argument of certain historians that the "true" or "essential" function of the law of slavery was to legitimate the sovereignty of masters over slaves.[30] The story of the Code Noir's journey over time was thoroughly inflected by racialist assertions of the profligate libertinism of freed persons and the violent predisposition of slaves. However, colonial slave law was not merely the rhetorical veneer of a hypocritical effort to cast the exploitations and brutalities of life under slavery in a more generous and humane light. To be sure, legitimating planter hegemony over slaves was a core objective of the law of slavery. It was not the slave code's only pursuit, however, and may not even have been its dominant purpose. Precisely in order to maintain the

---

[29] Cf. Albert O. Hirschman, *The Passions and the Interests: Political Arguments for Capitalism before Its Triumph* (Princeton, NJ: Princeton University Press, 1977).

[30] Louis Sala-Molins describes the Code Noir as an instrument for "the legitimation of a practice ... of torture" and the regulation of "utilitarian genocide." Louis Sala-Molins, *Le code noir, ou le calvaire de Canaan*, 6th ed. (Paris: Presses universitaires de France, 1998) viii. Colin Dayan characterizes the Code Noir as part of a broader "language" of slave law that "offered protection and normalized abuse." Colin Dayan, *The Story of Cruel and Unusual* (Cambridge, MA: MIT Press, 2007), 10–11. See also Nick Nesbitt, *Universal Emancipation: The Haitian Revolution and the Radical Enlightenment* (Charlottesville: University Press of Virginia, 2008). (observing that "New World slave owners ... quite actively tortured and bestialized as a colonial power whose actions were defended by the state and rule of law that promulgated the *Code Noir*").

stability of the social order, colonial administrators found it necessary not only to reinforce the grip of plantation discipline, but also to set meaningful limits on the institutions and practices of planter sovereignty.[31]

The demographic dimension of this balancing act was unavoidable, if rarely discussed in explicit terms. When the French Revolution began, the official population of Saint-Domingue consisted of about 465,000 slaves, 30,000 whites, and at least 28,000 (and probably many more) free blacks and free people of color (*affranchis* and *gens de couleur libres*). These racial categories ought not to be taken at face value. There were significant divisions within all three groups, and the terms used to describe these communities were mutable artifacts of colonial law that masked complexities not always captured in either eighteenth-century or contemporary usage. For example, the phrase *gens de couleur* is a late colonial legal category sometimes used today to group together both manumitted black slaves – designated as *affranchis* or *nègres libres* by way of two other official colonial terms – and free people of color. By contrast, beginning in about 1770, the term *affranchis* was increasingly used to describe free people of color, so as to emphasize the ex-slave aspect of their biographies. The colonial census of 1782, however, distinguished the category of *gens de couleur* from that of (emancipated) "free blacks" (*nègres libres*), in a reflection of the growing economic power of free people of color. Yet the lines between these groups were not as clear as colonial policy suggested: Some "free blacks" were themselves born into freedom, and the free people of color included persons no more than one generation removed from slavery. Indeed, the labels "slave" and "white" are themselves convenient shorthands for groups that encompassed a broad range of persons.[32]

[31] On the relationship between planter brutality and "domestic sovereignty" in the French Caribbean colonies, see Yvan Debbasch, "Au coeur du 'gouvernement des esclaves': La souveraineté domestique aux Antilles françaises (XVIIᵉ – XVIIIᵉ siècles)," *Revue française d'histoire d'outre-mer* 72, no. 266 (1985): 31–54. In the endnotes to his essay, Debbasch announced a successor article on Pierre-Victor Malouet that seems never to have appeared. See also Debbasch's important study of the *gens de couleur* in the French Caribbean between 1635 and 1833: *Couleur et liberté: Le jeu du critère ethnique dans un ordre juridique esclavagiste* (Paris: Librairie Dalloz, 1967).

[32] Using the term *affranchis* as a synonym for free blacks, therefore, can be potentially misleading in certain circumstances. This is to say nothing of the distinctions drawn in the late colonial period between freed blacks and free people of color based on different degrees of European ancestry. There were no less than eleven such racial gradations (of which mulatto [*mulâtre*] was only one). See John Garrigus, "Blue and Brown: Contraband Indigo and the Rise of a Free Colored Planter Class in French Saint-Domingue," *The Americas* 50, no. 2 (1993): 259–260; idem, *Before Haiti*, 167; Laurent Dubois, *Avengers of the New World: The Story of the Haitian Revolution* (Cambridge, MA: Harvard University

These caveats notwithstanding, the racial imbalances of Saint-Domingue may well have been the most extreme of any New World society at the time, and the security risk they represented in a society based on the antagonisms of chattel slavery was not lost on contemporaries.[33] By the same token, administrators and white planters were not alone in perceiving and responding to the hazards of life in the tinderbox atmosphere of France's leading slave colony.

Free people of color and slaves also lived in worlds structured by their own perceptions of danger, very different from those that informed white elite understandings, and just as important for understanding how slave law unfolded over the course of the eighteenth century. As owners of coffee, indigo, and cotton plantations, the wealthier *gens de couleur* certainly had interests in common with white slaveholders. Particularly in the period after the Seven Years' War, however, *affranchis* and free people of color also confronted hazards unique to their community, encompassing everything from a return to slavery to the many insecurities and insults of second-class citizenship. Saint-Dominguan slaves, for their part, were engaged in a constant struggle for physical survival against the elements of nature and the dehumanizing forces of chattel bondage, including the not-infrequent prospect of abuse and neglect that sometimes took the form of outright torture. Insofar as they can be gleaned with relative confidence from the archival and published sources I have consulted, the responses of freed persons and slaves to the risks that attended their respective experiences of plantation society also inform the interpretation set forth here.

In the end, it was the interactions between administrators, jurists, planters, free people of color, and slaves that gave the law of slavery in

Press, 2004), 70; and David Nicholls, *From Dessalines to Duvalier: Race, Colour and National Independence in Haiti*, rev. ed. (New Brunswick, NJ: Rutgers University Press, 1996), 25. For a useful summary of the divisions within each of the three major populations of Saint-Domingue, see David Geggus, *Haitian Revolutionary Studies* (Bloomington: Indiana University Press, 2002), 6–7. I address these matters further in Chapters 1 and 2.

[33] Jamaica's demography was closely comparable. As of 1788–1789, the enslaved of both Jamaica and Saint-Domingue counted for nearly 90% of the overall population, and in both colonies about 93% of the inhabitants were identifiably of African descent. By contrast, the slave population of the so-called Lesser Antilles islands of the eastern Caribbean, such as Barbados, Martinique, and Guadeloupe, comprised 75 to 85% of the total population. In the Southern states of the newly independent United States, slaves were only 40% of the population, and in Brazil the figure was closer to 50%. Jean Meyer, "Des origines à 1763," 136; Vincent Brown, *The Reaper's Garden: Death and Power in the World of Atlantic Slavery* (Cambridge, MA: Harvard University Press, 2008), 15; Garrigus, *Before Haiti*, 5–6.

Saint-Domingue its distinctively calculative and anxious character. Viewing the law of slavery as a product of the collisions between individual members of all of these groups over time – as the subject of a permanent debate over the nature of legal authority in Saint-Domingue – bridges the conventional gap between the Old Regime and the Haitian Revolution. The story of the Code Noir, broadly understood in this dynamic and interactive sense, carried forward into the revolutionary period. For the quasi-existential anxiety about the unintended consequences of manumission and the radical abuse of slaves that imbued the ambivalent and malleable administrative culture of Saint-Domingue did not suddenly dissipate with the end of the Old Regime. The revolutionary drama was, in significant part, the continuation of the colonial search for a well-ordered commonwealth in Saint-Domingue by other means. How best to contain, if not break, the perceived vicious cycle of brutality and revenge turned out to be a central problem of the entire revolutionary period. It was a problem handled partly through further (private) violence and partly through law, including tactics that blurred the boundary between the coercive power of colonial administrators and the appeal to legal norms.

From 1789 to the abolition of slavery in 1793–1794, the Code Noir continued to serve, as it had under the Old Regime, both as a source of legal authority and as the locus of an ongoing contest over how best to manage relations between white planters, free people of color, and slaves. Yet the understanding of who was authorized to speak in its name – to invoke the Code's authority in the court of public opinion and to trade its currency in the marketplace of revolutionary ideas – changed dramatically during these years. To an extent that would have been unimaginable in 1685 or indeed at any other point in the colonial era, free people of color and slave insurgents now took control of these interpretive activities to serve their own strategic needs and goals. In a time of revolution, they invoked the letter or spirit of those provisions of the Code Noir that best suited what they believed was their rightful place in the new colonial order to come, as events and experience gave them to see that order. In so doing, they transformed the permanent debate over the Code Noir in eighteenth-century Haiti.

Metropolitan legislators, colonial administrators, and white planters did not, of course, cede this terrain lightly or voluntarily. Violence was an ever-present reality and instrument of the revolutionary conflicts; and the policies of successive French revolutionary governments reenacted, on a colonywide basis, the repressive measures that planters had adopted to deal with slave resistance on individual plantations during the colonial period. Appeals to law and legal authority were nonetheless an essential element of the human rights advances that we associate with the Haitian Revolution. Historians have often cast these appeals in the starkly opposed guises of royalism and republicanism. They are more accurately described as extensions and transformations of the debate over the Code Noir that constituted the legal culture of Saint-Domingue.

In seeking to elucidate these legacies, I focus on three pivotal developments of the Haitian revolutionary era: the free colored movement for political rights in 1789–1792; the dialogue in 1791–1792 between key leaders of the slave insurgency in the north and the French civil commissioners sent to subdue the "troubles" of Saint-Domingue; and the abolition of slavery in 1793–1794. The free people of color who invoked the Code Noir's guarantee of equal citizenship to manumitted slaves – as a way of shaming the French National Assembly into living up to its revolutionary ideals – suggest an especially concrete and vivid example of the revolutionary metamorphosis of colonial law. The case for fully enfranchising free people of color during the early years of the Revolution relied in part on their critical strategic role in manning the colony's military defenses and policing its fugitive slave population. Even as free people of color and metropolitan abolitionists evoked the specter of a slave revolt to advocate for an end to racial discrimination in the colony, planters and merchants (with strong support in administrative circles) used that same threat to argue that erasing the color line would usher in the colony's total ruin.

The leaders of the slave insurgency in the north, who so pragmatically reappropriated Louis XIV's 1685 edict so as to denounce their former masters' violations of its protective provisions, are an even more dramatic illustration of the tactical and ironic revenge of the Code Noir. The documentation of this point is far less generous than in the case of the free people of color, and my conclusions are accordingly tentative. There are nonetheless revealing indications that a concern with planter brutality shaped the critical early dialogue between the insurgent leaders Jean-François Papillon and Georges Biassou and the French civil commissioners in late 1791 and 1792.

The pre-revolutionary critique of manumission and plantation discipline found further expression in the close connection that emerged between abolition and military strategy – the emancipation and arming of slaves – as methods of containing the threat of black insurgence.[34] The abolition of slavery in Saint-Domingue in 1793–1794, amidst a dire need for military manpower to counter the invading forces of Britain and Spain, is a signature moment in a broader history of strategic abolitionism in the Atlantic world.[35] A less familiar and visible although equally important aspect of the policies that the French civil commissioners Léger Félicité Sonthonax and Etienne Polverel pursued during this period is their articulation of standards for the governance of nominally free plantation workers. These standards drew explicitly on the text of the Code Noir and implicitly on various late colonial administrative schemes for the reform – rather than abolition – of plantation slavery. (To a lesser though still recognizable extent, so too did Toussaint Louverture's projects for the revival of plantation agriculture and the inculcation of a rule of law in Saint-Domingue at the turn of the nineteenth century.)

The proclamations of Sonthonax and Polverel suggest that abolitionism itself was propelled by a precautionary, strategic ethics not unlike that which pervaded the governance of slavery in colonial Haiti. Thus the story of the Code Noir ultimately becomes one about the instrumental and strategic roots of certain key strands of antiracist and antislavery thought.[36] For some, the lessons of that story arrived too late. Napoleon's

---

[34] On this subject, see Christopher Leslie Brown and Philip D. Morgan, eds., *Arming Slaves: From Classical Times to the Modern Age* (New Haven: Yale University Press, 2006).

[35] In this way, the Haitian Revolution, although driven by forces specific to its colonial formation, also speaks to some classic episodes in American history, such as Lord Dunmore's invitation to the slaves of revolutionary Virginia to join the British side in exchange for their manumission and Lincoln's 1863 proclamation of freedom at a particularly desperate moment for the Union forces. On the 1793–1794 French abolition, see Dubois, *Avengers of the New World*, 152–170; Robert Louis Stein, *Léger Félicité Sonthonax: The Lost Sentinel of the Republic* (Rutherford, NJ: Fairleigh Dickinson University Press, 1985); and Jeremy D. Popkin, *You Are All Free: The Haitian Revolution and the Abolition of Slavery* (New York: Cambridge University Press, 2010). On Lord Dunmore's campaign, see Benjamin Quarles, *The Negro in the American Revolution* (Chapel Hill: University of North Carolina Press, 1996), 19–32; Simon Schama, *Rough Crossings: Britain, the Slaves, and the American Revolution* (London: BBC Books, 2005), 72–91. On the military context of Lincoln's proclamation, see James M. McPherson, *Tried by War: Abraham Lincoln as Commander in Chief* (New York: Penguin Press, 2008), 149–160.

[36] Christopher Leslie Brown usefully distinguishes between three concepts that are generally merged under the broader rubric of the "antislavery campaign" in Britain: antislavery thought (or the "development of ideas and values hostile to slavery and the slave trade"); abolitionism (or the "crystallization of programs to reform or transform imperial and colonial policy"); and the actual achievement of abolition and emancipation. Abolitionism, he argues, represents a type of antislavery initiative, that is, an effort to translate the complex of antislavery sentiments and ideas into active reform programs.

bid to crush the slave revolution and formally reinstitute the rule of the
Code Noir in 1802–1803, following earlier efforts at a more moderate
and conciliatory approach, reflected a nexus between colonial-era planter
brutality and revolutionary policies of attempted racial extermination.
The result was one that Napoleon would later rue from a position of exile
in Saint Helena: "I have to reproach myself for the attempt at the colony
during the Consulate; it was a great mistake to have wanted to subdue it
by force," he wrote. "I should have contented myself to govern it through
the intermediary of Toussaint [Louverture]," continued Napoleon, who
had fatefully narrowed his options even prior to the invasion by earlier ordering the capture and deportation of the Haitian revolutionary
leader.[37] (Louverture perished on April 7, 1803, in a French prison in the
Jura mountains bordering present-day Switzerland.)

   As this confession suggests, even Napoleon would eventually, if
begrudgingly, recognize the power of the strategic case for ending (or
at least recasting under Toussaint Louverture's leadership) plantation
slavery. Moreover, long after Napoleon had departed from the scene, the
strategic critique of slavery continued to run like a vein through the geo-
logical underpinnings of the French antislavery movement, especially in
its more moderate, bureaucratic wing, culminating in 1848 with the final
abolition of the Code Noir.[38] These moderate critics of slavery believed
that, although sudden abolition would have destructive results for plantation economies, emancipation was, in the end, the only way for France
to hold on to its colonies.[39]

Christopher Leslie Brown, *Moral Capital: Foundations of British Abolitionism* (Chapel
Hill: University of North Carolina Press, 2006), 17–18. With some slight modifications,
this framework is also useful for understanding the history of French abolitionism, which
has tended to center on the antagonism between the planter lobby and the revolutionary
abolitionist group known as the Society of the Friends of the Blacks, founded in 1788
by the journalist Jacques-Pierre Brissot de Warville. See Marcel Dorigny, "La Société des
Amis des Noirs: antiesclavagisme et lobby colonial à la fin du siècle des Lumières (1788–
1792)," in Marcel Dorigny and Bernard Gainot, *La Société des Amis des Noirs, 1788–
1799: Contribution à l'histoire de l'abolition de l'esclavage* (Paris: Éditions UNESCO,
1998), 13–57; and Dubois, *Avengers of the New World*, 72–76.

[37] Quoted in Madison Smartt Bell, *Toussaint Louverture: A Biography* (New York:
Pantheon, 2007), 270.

[38] Seymour Drescher distinguishes between three different wings of the French abolitionist
movement: a moderate wing that included Alexis de Tocqueville, Victor de Broglie, and
Odilon Barrot; a more "polemical and strident radical side" headed by Victor Schoelcher;
and a conservative wing associated with François Guizot. Seymour Drescher, *Dilemmas
of Democracy: Tocqueville and Modernization* (Pittsburgh, PA: University of Pittsburgh
Press, 1968), 161–162.

[39] Ibid., 156, 159, 181, 187–188, 190. On the 1848 abolition, see also Nelly Schmidt,
Réformateurs coloniaux et abolitionnistes de l'esclavage, 1820–1851 (Paris: Karthala,
2000); Lawrence C. Jennings, *French Anti-Slavery: The Movement for the Abolition*

Outside of revolutionary France and the French empire, a precautionary vision of abolition also materialized wherever the threats associated with the Haitian Revolution were most keenly felt, such as the early American republic. The "lessons" of Haiti took different forms in the broader Atlantic world, including a reactionary bunker mentality in the Southern U.S. states. Yet a distinctive strand of American abolitionist thought, in both the North and South, maintained that ending slavery was necessary to avert widespread bloodshed between whites and blacks. Not coincidentally, this strand appealed first and foremost to the "disastrous" experience of Haiti's recently completed revolution.

In these ways and more, the legacies of the Old Regime helped shape many of the events, themes, and outcomes of the Haitian Revolution and its aftermath. For the most part, however, historians of colonial and revolutionary Haiti have had little to say to each other, their chronological subfields treated as separate domains of research in much the way that Old Regime France and the French Revolution have come to be seen as "distinct, separate entit[ies]."[40] The title of this book echoes Alexis de Tocqueville's classic account of *The Old Regime and the Revolution* (1856), which attributed to the French Revolution an exceptional role in continental history analogous to the part played by Haiti in Atlantic history. As its title implies, Tocqueville's is a history neither of the Old Regime nor the French Revolution but rather an interpretation of the relationship between the two. Driven by a struggle to understand the failure of four successive revolutions in France – 1789, 1830, 1832, and 1848 – and the

of *Slavery in France, 1802–1848* (New York: Cambridge University Press, 2000); and Laurent Dubois, "The Road to 1848: Interpreting French Anti-Slavery," *Slavery and Abolition* 22, no. 3 (2001): 150–157.

[40] Lynn Hunt, "Forgetting and Remembering: The French Revolution Then and Now," *American Historical Review* 100, no. 4 (1995): 1125. For a recent statement of this commitment to "chronological caesurae," see Jean-Daniel Piquet, *L'émancipation des Noirs dans la Révolution française (1789–1795)* (Paris: Éditions Karthala, 2002), 15. Two important exceptions are Garrigus, *Before Haiti* and Debbasch, *Couleur et liberté*, both of which focus on the free people of color. On the historiography of the Haitian Revolution generally (with some discussion of the colonial scholarship as well), see John D. Garrigus, "White Jacobins/Black Jacobins: Bringing the Haitian and French Revolutions together in the Classroom," *French Historical Studies* 23, no. 2 (Spring 2000): 259–275; David Geggus, "Thirty Years of Haitian Revolution Historiography," *Revista Mexicana del Caribe* 3, no. 5 (1998): 179–197; idem, *Haitian Revolutionary Studies*, 33–42; idem, "The Caribbean in the Age of Revolution," 83–100; Michel-Rolph Trouillot, *Silencing the Past: Power and the Production of History* (Boston: Beacon Press, 1995), 95–107; and Robin Blackburn, "Haiti, Slavery, and the Age of the Democratic Revolution," *The William and Mary Quarterly* 63, no. 4 (2006): 643–674. Geggus's review essay in the *Revista Mexicana del Caribe* includes a useful bibliography.

inability of a liberal political system to take root, Tocqueville found the explanation in continuities between the administrative centralization of Old Regime absolutism and the post-revolutionary authoritarianism of Napoleon Bonaparte and his successors. In contrast to the Anglo-Americans, wrote the author of *Democracy in America*, the French had managed only to invent "new forms of servitude."[41]

Notwithstanding his reductive reading of French colonial history as a microcosm of these same metropolitan trends, Tocqueville was the first historian to lay out in detail the kind of argument about revolutionary change that underlies the present work.[42] (It is fitting for this purpose that he was also one of the leaders of the distinctly moderate branch of French abolitionists who helped end French colonial slavery in 1848.)[43] Although it has sometimes weighed too heavily over the historiography of the French Revolution, Tocqueville's book has yet to influence in any significant or sustained way the interpretation of the Haitian Revolution.[44] As Robin Blackburn has written, with the wave of new studies that appeared around the time of the bicentennial of Haitian independence in 2004 and in the years since, the "silencing" of Haiti's past has now ended.[45] I am

---

[41] Tocqueville, *The Ancien Régime and the French Revolution*, 251, also quoted in Seymour Drescher, "Tocqueville and the Revolution of 1848," in *Profiles of Revolutionaries in Atlantic History, 1700–1850*, ed. R. William Weisberger et al. (Boulder, CO: Social Science Monographs, 2007), 298.

[42] In an endnote concerning French North America in the age of Louis XIV, Tocqueville argued that "[i]t was in the colonies that it was possible to judge the character of metropolitan government most accurately because there, the features of that government were magnified and thus easiest to see." Thus Canada provided a "microscope" through which to observe the "flaws" and "deformity" of Louis XIV's administration. Tocqueville, *The Ancien Régime and the French Revolution*, 225. The French colonies, in effect, were significant primarily for purposes of confirming what Tocqueville believed could already be gleaned from the metropolitan record: namely, that administrative centralization in the absence of a strong aristocracy or clergy would inevitably lead to tyranny. In all of his writings, Tocqueville seems to have mentioned Saint-Domingue itself only once, in the context of a more contemporary interest in French Algeria. See Alexis de Tocqueville, *Writings on Empire and Slavery*, ed. and trans. Jennifer Pitts (Baltimore, MD: The Johns Hopkins University Press, 2001), 48.

[43] A series of articles that Tocqueville published in 1843 on the emancipation of slaves in the French empire is translated in Tocqueville, *Writings on Empire and Slavery*, 199–226.

[44] The modern revival of Tocqueville in French revolutionary scholarship, prompted by François Furet's 1978 book, *Interpreting the French Revolution*, did little to redress that scholarship's general neglect of the Atlantic world. The school of French revolutionary historiography associated with Tocqueville and Furet is hardly alone in this respect. See Lynn Hunt, "The French Revolution in Global Context," in Armitage and Subrahmanyam, *The Age of Revolutions in Global Context*, 23–24.

[45] Robin Blackburn, "Epilogue," in Geggus and Fiering, *The World of the Haitian Revolution*, 393. Blackburn is here referencing the powerful and influential argument

deeply indebted to, and have drawn much inspiration from, this exciting and outstanding new body of scholarship, which informs my own understanding of the revolutionary period. Even as scholars have drawn the events and consequences of the Revolution to the attention of a wider public during the last decade or so, however, the relationship between Haiti's colonial and revolutionary stories remains relatively cloudy.

Historians have tended to focus instead on the more synchronic task of identifying the distinctive characteristics of the Haitian Revolution against the backdrop of the Atlantic revolutionary age in which it was once submerged.[46] There is, to begin with, the question of how to understand its relationship to the French Revolution, with which it was so closely linked by the bonds of imperial administration. Whether a Haitian slave uprising would have occurred in the absence of a metropolitan revolution has become one of the more belabored (and less interesting) questions that historians of this subject have tried to address. Short of such a hypothetical dead end, much of the debate over the origins and unfolding of the Haitian Revolution has focused on how best to make sense of the many complicated interconnections between local happenings in Saint-Domingue and events in the metropole – that is, calculating the relative weight to ascribe to Caribbean versus "French" factors.[47] This is a challenge endemic to the field of Atlantic history generally, and in recent years has led some particularly enterprising scholars to consider the reverse scenario of the Haitian Revolution's impact on the French Revolution.[48]

of Trouillot, *Silencing the Past*, which may yet have some purchase where contemporary French scholarship on colonialism is concerned. See, for example, Jean-Pierre Rioux, *Dictionnaire de la France coloniale* (Paris: Flammarion, 2007), which manages to overlook entirely the Haitian Revolution.

[46] The classic English-language writings on the Atlantic revolutions are Robert Palmer's two-volume *The Age of the Democratic Revolution: A Political History of Europe and America, 1760–1800* (Princeton, NJ: Princeton University Press, 1959, 1964); and Eric Hobsbawm, *The Age of Revolution, 1780–1848* (London: Weidenfeld & Nicholson, 1962; reprinted New York: Vintage, 1996). For more recent and inclusive accounts of the Age of Revolutions, encompassing both the Haitian and the early-nineteenth-century Spanish-American revolutions, see Armitage and Subrahmanyam, *The Age of Revolutions in Global Context*; Wim Klooster, *Revolutions in the Atlantic World: A Comparative History* (New York: New York University Press, 2009); and Lester D. Langley, *The Americas in the Age of Revolution, 1750–1850* (New Haven, CT: Yale University Press, 1996). The radicalism of the Haitian Revolution vis-à-vis the other Atlantic revolutions is stressed in Dubois, *Avengers of the New World*, 3; and Nesbitt, *Universal Emancipation*.

[47] See, most recently, Geggus, "The Caribbean in the Age of Revolution," 83–100.

[48] See, for example, Yves Benot, *La Révolution française et la fin des colonies* (Paris: Éditions la Découverte, 1989); and Jeremy D. Popkin, "The French Revolution's Other Island,"

Other interpretive problems going to the distinctive character of the Haitian Revolution abound. Historians are still in the early stages of understanding how the white planters, free people of color, and slaves of Saint-Domingue perceived the precedent of the American Revolution.[49] The role of African (particularly Congolese) political and religious practices in the unfolding of the slave revolution in Haiti has begun to generate some significant, if contested, research; and more is on the way, notwithstanding the limitations inherent in the source materials bearing on this issue.[50] Further, the Haitian Revolution's impact, both domestically and internationally, has developed into a topic of considerable complexity. Thus historians have vigorously debated whether the new nation resurrected slave labor under a new guise or guaranteed a new regime of universal liberty,[51] whether it engendered republican or authoritarian political traditions,[52] and whether its creation did more to help or to hinder the cause of slave emancipation elsewhere in the Atlantic world.[53]

in Geggus and Fierings, *The World of the Haitian Revolution*, 199–222. Lynn Hunt addresses this issue in her essay "The French Revolution in Global Context," 20–36. See also Laurent Dubois, "An Atlantic Revolution," *French Historical Studies* 32, no. 4 (2009): 659–661.

[49] See John D. Garrigus, "Catalyst or Catastrophe? Saint-Domingue's Free Men of Color and the Battle of Savannah, 1779–1782," *Revista/Review Interamericana* 22, nos. 1–2 (1992): 109–125; Malick W. Ghachem, "Sovereignty and Slavery in the Age of Revolution: Haitian Variations on a Metropolitan Theme" (PhD Diss., Stanford University, 2002), 172–217; Charles Frostin, *Les révoltes blanches à Saint-Domingue aux XVIIe et XVIIIe siècles: Haïti avant 1789* (Paris: Éditions de l'École, 1975); Geggus, *Haitian Revolutionary Studies*, 8–9. Gary Nash strikes a highly skeptical note about the American Revolution's impact on Saint-Domingue in "Sparks from the Altar of '76: International Repercussions and Reconsiderations of the American Revolution," in Armitage and Subrahmanyam, *The Age of Revolutions in Global Context*, 3.

[50] Trouillot, *Silencing the Past*, 40–44, 66–69; John K. Thornton, "'I am the Subject of the King of Congo': African Ideology in the Haitian Revolution," *Journal of World History* 4 (1993): 181–214; idem, "African Soldiers in the Haitian Revolution," *Journal of Caribbean History* 25 (1993): 59–80. Vincent Brown is at work on a study of the relationship between slave revolts in the Americas and concurrent political developments in Africa.

[51] For a subtle discussion of the distinction between "individual" and "general" liberty in Toussaint Louverture's thought, see Claude Moïse, *Le projet national de Toussaint Louverture et la Constitution de 1801* (Montréal: Éditions du Cidihca, 2001), 61–81.

[52] See Geggus, "The Caribbean in the Age of Revolution," 95–100; and Robert Fatton Jr., *The Roots of Haitian Despotism* (Boulder, CO: Lynne Rienner, 2007), 60.

[53] Two recent works that take a cautious approach to Haiti's overseas reverberations during the revolutionary era are Seymour Drescher, *Abolition: A History of Slavery and Antislavery* (New York: Cambridge University Press, 2009), 180; and David Geggus,

The present work touches only briefly (and sometimes only indirectly) on these important issues in the historiography of the Haitian Revolution, although many of them might usefully be approached more diachronically, as unfolding developments of preexisting dynamics that reached back far into the colonial world from which the Haitian Revolution emerged.[54] My primary historiographical goal – in addition to situating Haiti's revolutionary experience in a more diachronic, eighteenth-century perspective – is to supplement the narratives that frame the vast scholarship on antislavery and abolitionism, whether in the French[55] or British/Anglo-American contexts.[56]

ed., *The Impact of the Haitian Revolution in the Atlantic World* (Charleston: University of South Carolina Press, 2001). See also Davis, *Inhuman Bondage*, 172–174 (suggesting that "as a model of liberation, the Haitian Revolution suffered from inherent liabilities" and "probably reinforced the conviction ... that free blacks were incapable of governing themselves in a civilized state").

[54] In contrast, the scholarship on Spanish-speaking Latin America has long been dominated by a preoccupation with the freight imposed by the colonial past. See Jeremy Adelman, ed., *Colonial Legacies: The Problem of Persistence in Latin American History* (New York: Routledge, 1999). To be clear, although I believe that Haiti's colonial heritage continues to weigh heavily on it today, I am not primarily concerned in this book with the influence of slavery on Haiti's contemporary situation. The most careful and influential such analyses are probably Michel-Rolph Trouillot, *Haiti: State against Nation: The Origins and Legacy of Duvalierism* (New York: Monthly Review Press, 1989); and Nicholls, *From Dessalines to Duvalier*.

[55] For a short and lucid synopsis of the rise of antislavery and abolitionism in France, see Marcel Dorigny, *Anti-esclavagisme, abolitionnisme, et abolitions: Débats et controverses en France de la fin du XVIIIe siècle aux années 1840* (Québec: Les Presses de l'Université Laval, 2008). See also, *inter alia*, Benot, *La Révolution française et la fin des colonies*; Robin Blackburn, *The Overthrow of Colonial Slavery, 1776–1848* (New York: Verso, 1988), 161–211, 473–515; David Brion Davis, *The Problem of Slavery in the Age of Revolution, 1770–1823* (Ithaca, NY: Cornell University Press, 1975); Gabriel Debien, *Les colons de Saint-Domingue et la Révolution: Essai sur le Club Massiac (Août 1789 – Août 1792)* (Paris: Armand Colin, 1953); Geggus, *Haitian Revolutionary Studies*, 157–170; Jean Tarrade, "Les colonies et les principes de 1789: les Assemblées révolutionnaires face au problème de l'esclavage," in *La Révolution française et les colonies*, ed. Jean Tarrade (Paris: Librairie l'Harmattan, 1989), 9–33; Dorigny, "La Société des Amis des Noirs," 13–57; Drescher, *Abolition*, 146–180, 281–282; Jennings, *French Anti-Slavery*; and Marcel Dorigny, ed., *Les abolitions de l'esclavage: De L. F. Sonthonax à V. Schoelcher, 1793–1794–1848* (Paris: Presses Universitaires de Vincennes et Éditions UNESCO, 1995).

[56] Claudia Fergus argues for the significance of insurrectionary fears (and of the Haitian Revolution more specifically) in the path to British abolition in "'Dread of insurrection': Abolitionism, Security, and Labor in Britain's West Indian Colonies, 1760–1823," *The William and Mary Quarterly* 66, no. 4 (Oct. 2009): 759–761, 772–775. Cf. Seymour Drescher, "History's Engines, British Mobilization in the Age of Revolution," *The*

Many of those narratives emphasize the role of Enlightenment moralism and religiosity, the rise of capitalism and free labor, imperial or nationalist rivalry, and the mobilizing power of transnational networks of activists and intellectuals. In the French case, a dialectical dance of antislavery and proslavery (or racist) Enlightenment theses has developed.[57] Certainly there have been some efforts to complicate these mirror images.[58] Scholars such as Michèle Duchet, moreover, have identified something like what I am calling strategic antislavery in the writings of figures such as the Abbé Raynal, Condorcet, and Mercier.[59]

William and Mary Quarterly 66, no. 4 (Oct. 2009): 745–748. For cogent summaries and critiques of the profuse historical literature on the British antislavery debate, see Thomas Bender, ed., *The Antislavery Debate: Capitalism and Abolitionism as a Problem in Historical Interpretation* (Berkeley: University of California Press, 1992); Thomas C. Holt, *The Problem of Freedom: Race, Labor, and Politics in Jamaica and Britain, 1832–1938* (Baltimore, MD: Johns Hopkins University Press, 1991), 21–33; Davis, *Inhuman Bondage*, 231–249; and Brown, *Moral Capital*, 3–22. Brown argues that British antislavery thought and abolitionism were rooted in the preoccupation of the 1760s and 1770s with "the moral character of colonial institutions and imperial practices." Brown, *Moral Capital*, 27. There are traces of strategic antislavery in the literature Brown discusses. Ibid., 237 (discussing the "persisting concern for stability, commerce, and civic harmony" that characterized British concepts of emancipation in the era of the American Revolution, particularly the belief that emancipated "slave labor would transform mutual contempt and violence among black and white in British America into a perpetual, fraternal peace"). However, the focus on the *morality* of slavery still distinguishes this pattern of thought from the French antislavery variant that I discuss here. Margaret Abruzzo documents the tactical commitment of antislavery rhetoric in the antebellum United States to highlighting the immoral cruelty of southern slavery in *Polemical Pain: Slavery, Cruelty, and the Rise of Humanitarianism* (Baltimore, MD: The Johns Hopkins University Press, 2011).

[57] For a polemical critique of the philosophes for their purported failure to castigate the Code Noir and New World slavery generally, see Sala-Molins, *Le code noir*; idem, *Dark Side of the Light: Slavery and the French Enlightenment*, trans. John-Conteh Morgan (Minneapolis: University of Minnesota Press, 2006). For more optimistic interpretations of Enlightenment views on empire and slavery, see Jean Ehrhard, *Lumières et esclavage: L'esclavage colonial et la formation de l'opinion publique en France au XVIIIe siècle* (Brussels: Éditions Andre Versaille, 2008); and Sankar Muthu, *Enlightenment against Empire* (Princeton, NJ: Princeton University Press, 2003). An oft-cited early study of the antislavery Enlightenment is Edward D. Seeber's largely bibliographical *Anti-Slavery Opinion in France during the Second Half of the Eighteenth Century* (Baltimore, MD: Johns Hopkins University Press, 1937).

[58] Ehrhard's study seeks to claim this territory, but functions essentially as a "pleading in defense" of the Enlightenment against the "denigrations" and "calumnies" of Sala-Molins. Ehrhard, *Lumières et esclavage*, 17, 25–32, 214.

[59] Michèle Duchet, *Anthropologie et histoire au siècle des lumières* (Paris: Albin Michel, 1995. I discuss this important work in greater detail in Chapter 3. Laurent Dubois provides a useful critique of the scholarship on the Enlightenment and slavery in "An enslaved Enlightenment: Rethinking the Intellectual History of the French Atlantic," *Social History* 31, no. 1 (2006): 1–14. On Mercier's and Raynal's prophecies of slave

Nonetheless, I think it is still the case that, in its colonial setting, the ○ Enlightenment was much more ambivalent and far more juristic and administrative in character than has been generally perceived, as a reading of Montesquieu's subtle and highly influential chapters on the social hazards of slavery in *The Spirit of the Laws* (1748) suggests.[60] Viewed holistically, it is possible to see in the eighteenth-century Haitian experience, as through a microscope, that intermingling and overlay of pragmatic and humanitarian impulses that was such a striking feature of the colonial Enlightenment.[61] *The Old Regime and the Haitian Revolution* emphasizes the relatively neglected role of this moderate, strategic, and prudential vision of slavery in the rise and fall of the first French empire. For although the strategic ethics of slavery have sometimes figured in our understanding of the ideological roots of abolitionism generally, their foundation in the world of the law and their place in the unfolding of the Haitian Revolution have not yet crystallized in the historical literature.

The phrase "strategic antislavery" must be handled with some care. Eighteenth-century moral revulsion at slavery could and often did fall well short of abolitionism.[62] There is also an important distinction to be made between those critics of the plantation regime who sought to preserve the institution of slavery and those who sought to undermine it.[63] The vocabulary of the "strategic ethics" or "strategic morality" of slavery is thus more appropriate than "strategic antislavery," pure and simple. However, I do want to insist that, although not foundationally opposed to slavery or the slave trade *tout court*, the strategic ethics of slavery in

revolution in the New World, see also Dorigny, *Anti-esclavagisme, abolitionnisme, et abolitions*, 20–23; Ehrhard, *Lumières et esclavage*, 202–203; and Dubois, *Avengers of the New World*, 57–59.

[60] This is not to deny the powerful and long-recognized role of irony in Montesquieu's antislavery vision. See, for example, Dorigny, *Anti-esclavagisme, abolitionnisme, et abolitions*, 15–16.

[61] My interest here is in certain key threads of late-eighteenth-century colonial administrative and legal thought that partake both of antislavery values and of abolitionism (to follow Brown's analytical framework, see Brown, *Moral Capital*, 17 n.14). On the idea of a "colonial Enlightenment," see Gene Ogle, "'The Eternal Power of Reason' and 'The Superiority of Whites': Hilliard d'Auberteuil's Colonial Enlightenment," *French Colonial History* 3 (2003): 35–50; and Malick W. Ghachem, "Montesquieu in the Caribbean," in *Postmodernism and the Enlightenment: New Perspectives in Eighteenth-Century French Intellectual History*, ed. Daniel Gordon (New York: Routledge, 2001), 183–210. A very different and more contemporary reading of the "colonial Enlightenment" can be found in David Scott, *Conscripts of Modernity: The Tragedy of Colonial Enlightenment* (Durham, NC: Duke University Press, 2004).

[62] Dorigny, *Anti-esclavagisme, abolitionnisme, et abolitions*, 7.

[63] Ibid., 8–9.

Saint-Domingue ultimately fed into the projects of abolitionism.[64] The ambiguous role of manumission in colonial administration and the portrayal of planter brutality as an uninsured risk to the survival of colonial society brought the antislavery movement in France one critical step closer to the view that slavery could, in fact, be abolished – and that it might need to be, if only to protect the plantation economy from itself.

It is easy in retrospect for us to look back on this social ethics of prudence and regard it as amoral or insipid, lacking in the clear-cut, principled, and robust qualities that we associate with a modern, rights-based opposition to slavery and racism. I am not so certain that our own approaches to questions of social justice in the contemporary world are morally superior.[65] The story of Haiti's passage from slavery to freedom is in part a reminder that legal and moral progress travel through complicated, unintended, and lengthy byways.[66] That realization ought to arrest rather than reassure us in our everyday complacency. There are many forms of injustice in today's world that do not lend themselves to a straightforward, sharply normative, rights-based approach to ethical evaluation and reform. In the eighteenth century, those who fixed attention on the pervasive violence of slave societies did not necessarily object to slavery as such. Yet nor did they forego engagement with the task

---

[64] Philip Morgan describes the forces giving rise to the abolition of Britain's slave trade in 1807 as an "entangled world of pragmatism and principle." Morgan notes that "by their commitment to improvement," British and Danish Caribbean planters "paradoxically found some compatibility with abolitionist aims, even as those commitments arose out of defensiveness and political weakness." Philip D. Morgan, "Ending the Slave Trade: A Caribbean and Atlantic Context," in *Abolitionism and Imperialism in Britain, Africa, and the Atlantic*, ed. Derek R. Peterson (Athens: Ohio University Press, 2010), 121. Cf. Winthrop Jordan, *White Over Black: American Attitudes Toward the Negro, 1550–1812* (Baltimore, MD: Penguin Books, 1969), 368. Jordan sketches the rise of a humanitarian reform movement in the late-eighteenth-century American South that sought, among other things, to alleviate brutality in the management of slave plantations. Yet Jordan notes a "supreme irony" in this development: "As slavery became less brutal there was less reason why it should be abolished." The critique of planter brutality, in other words, made slavery "more tolerable for the slaveowner and even for the abolitionist" (ibid.). There is some validity to this alarming insight even as parallel developments in the French and British Caribbean are concerned. Jordan does not comment in this passage on the French slave colonies or their impact on the United States but observes that in the British Caribbean, unlike in the mainland, "slavery ... helped doom itself by its notorious cruelty" (ibid.).

[65] Cf. Amartya Sen's discussion of the "plural grounding" of ethical argument in *The Idea of Justice* (Cambridge, MA: Harvard University Press, 2009), 2.

[66] Jeremy Popkin offers some kindred reflections in *You Are All Free*, 382–385, emphasizing the significance of the events of June 20, 1793 – when Sonthonax and Polverel first offered freedom to the slaves of Cap Français in exchange for military support – rather than the long-term context of abolition in Saint-Domingue. For further discussion of this work, see Chapter 6.

of trying to understand slavery's pathological violence and its relationship to law simply because they lacked access to our modern-day moral
vocabulary. They tapped into the vocabulary that was available to them
at the time, and that seemed most likely to persuade others that something was not quite right in the practices of everyday life. From those
circumstances, some kind of justice eventually flowed.

I stumbled quite unexpectedly on the riches of this subject some years ago
when I came across a reference to the career of the great Saint-Domingue
jurist Moreau de Saint-Méry. Moreau's *Loix et constitutions des colonies françaises*, published in six volumes between 1784 and 1790, is an
indispensable resource for the study of the colonial Old Regime.[67] (An
unpublished seventh volume is at the Bibliothèque Haïtienne des Pères
du Saint-Esprit in Port-au-Prince, which collapsed days after the January
2010 earthquake, although the archivists succeeded in savings its collections.) From there it was on to the inexhaustible trove of eighteenth-
century archival sources located in the French Colonial Archives in
Aix-en-Provence: a vast corpus of administrative correspondence, judicial records, and notarial papers, many of which Moreau himself played
a large part in creating and preserving. Those records provide the central basis for the research reflected in this book. I have also relied extensively on the wonderful colonial and revolutionary pamphlet collections
of the John Carter Brown Library in Providence, Rhode Island, and the
Bibliothèque Nationale de France.[68] The pioneering use that French and

---

[67] Médéric-Louis-Elie Moreau de Saint-Méry, *Loix et constitutions des colonies françaises
de l'Amérique sous le vent* (Paris: by the author, 1784–90) (hereafter cited as "LC").
On Moreau's life, see Anthony Louis Elicona, *Un colonial sous la Révolution en France
et en Amérique: Moreau de Saint-Méry* (Paris: Jouve et Compagnie, 1934); Augustin
François, baron de Silvestre, *Notice biographique de M. Moreau de Saint-Méry … lue
à la Société royale d'agriculture* (Paris: Imprimerie de Mme. Huzard, 1819); Blanche
Maurel and Étienne Taillemite, introduction to *Description topographique, physique,
civile, politique et historique de la partie française de l'isle Saint-Domingue*, by Médéric-
Louis-Elie Moreau de Saint-Méry (Paris: Librairie Larose for the Société de l'histoire des
colonies françaises, 1958), 1:vii–xxxvi; Ghachem, "Montesquieu in the Caribbean"; and
Dubois, *Avengers of the New World*, 8–11. Moreau's strenuous efforts during the 1790s
to construct an historical identity for Saint-Domingue were motivated at least in part by
a reactionary hope that the colony's old order would one day be restored. His exhaustive
archival project anticipated the more scientific efforts of nineteenth-century archivists
to elaborate a system of authentic French national history. See the brilliant work by
Lara Jennifer Moore, *Restoring Order: The École des Chartes and the Organization of
Archives and Libraries in France, 1820–1870* (Duluth, MN: Litwin Books, 2008).
[68] For the JCBL's revolutionary collection, see Malick W. Ghachem, *The Haitian
Revolution, 1789–1804: An Exhibition at the John Carter Brown Library (May to*

Francophone scholars of a previous generation (such as the indefatigable Gabriel Debien) made of these sources continues to light the path for all who travel in this field.[69]

The remainder of this work proceeds as follows: Chapter 1 considers the relationship between the political theory of slavery and its institutionalization in Saint-Domingue by way of a thematic overview of the Code Noir and French colonial administration. Chapters 2 and 3 trace the eighteenth-century development of the law of manumission and planter brutality, respectively. Chapter 4 is an essentially narrative account of the prosecution of a master for the torture of two female slaves – the so-called Lejeune affair of 1788 – that draws together the major strands of the law of slavery in Saint-Domingue on the eve of the French and Haitian Revolutions. In Chapters 5 and 6, I look at some of the major turning points of the Haitian Revolution in light of what the Old Regime teaches us about the strategic dynamics of regulating the master-slave relationship in Saint-Domingue. The conclusion briefly traces the story of those dynamics under Toussaint Louverture's leadership, and then follows them outside of Haiti proper and into the broader Atlantic world of the late eighteenth and early nineteenth centuries, when the Haitian revolutionary experience was used (among other purposes) to channel Bodin's old anxiety about the dangers of slavery in a well-ordered commonwealth into a concrete symbol of the precautionary case for abolition.

September 2004) (Providence, RI: The John Carter Brown Library, 2004). Both the JCBL and the BNF have now made their entire Saint-Domingue/Haïti print collections available online: in the JCBL's case, via the Internet Archive, at http://www.archive.org/details/JohnCarterBrownLibrary (last accessed June 7, 2010); in the BNF's case, via the Gallica digital library, at http://gallica.bnf.fr/. The University of Florida at Gainsville's Digital Library of the Caribbean also includes an important Saint-Domingue collection: http://dloc.com/.

[69] On Debien's contributions to this subject, see David P. Geggus, "Gabriel Debien (1906–1990)," *Hispanic American Historical Review* 71, no. 1 (1991): 140–142.

I

Domestic Enemies

[F]or that the whole world is full of Slaves, excepting certain countries
in Europe (which since also by little and little receive them) it is needful
here to reason of the power of Lords and Masters over their Slaves, and
of the profits and disprofits which may redound unto a Commonwealth,
if slavery should again be called into use: a question of great moment
not for Families and societies only, but for all Commonwealths also in
general.

    – Jean Bodin, *The Six Books of a Commonwealth* (1606)[1]

The "power of Lords and Masters over their Slaves" is a classic topic
of political theory, but the sources of the strategic (or commonwealth)
ethics of slavery in Saint-Domingue do not lie in political theory alone.
To be sure, some of these sources were indeed legal and intellectual in
nature: the law of slavery (including ancient Roman antecedents), early
modern French concepts of absolute sovereignty and private property,
and the mythologies of racial hierarchy. Yet the brute forces of demography and geography also had their part, for they gave rise to the world
of gaping racial "imbalances" and isolated settler and slave communities
within which the formal letter of the Code Noir became practical law.
All of these factors played a role in laying the groundwork for the kind
of society that Saint-Domingue had become on the eve of the Haitian
Revolution: a society divided not only by racial animosities between
groups of different skin color, but also by conflicts that cut across racial

---

[1] Bodin, *The Six Bookes of a Commonweale*, 32.

lines and pitted certain colonial interests against others. The racialized power struggles that unfolded on the plantations were accompanied by internecine rivalries between imperial administrators and merchants, merchants and plantation owners, plantation owners and managers, and so forth.

In this respect, at least, Saint-Domingue differed little from metropolitan France. Since at least the time of Louis XIV's reign, conflicts between various factions of elite society – the royal court versus the provincial aristocracy, cardinals versus the nobility of the sword (*noblesse de l'épee*), financiers versus speculators, and so on – had become entrenched.[2] Overseas, however, political conflict generally took place against an institutional backdrop that had far fewer antecedents in the Old Regime. The map of royal authority in Saint-Domingue was still largely uncharted at the time of the promulgation of the Code Noir, for the central institution of colonial society, the plantation (*habitation*), was not for the most part an institution of the absolute monarchy.[3] An early modern commercial invention, the plantation did not owe its existence to the king, even though the king, in a sense, guaranteed the social order that was embodied on the plantation in the form of Code Noir, and even though various forms of royal legislation bore on the legal status of the *habitations*. The plantation did not exist to buttress or glorify the authority of the absolute monarch. In many ways, the reverse was closer to the mark: Colonial absolutism existed to ensure that the plantations would thrive. However, in an enclave of France based on novel concepts of social order, the task of making the plantations work was never transparent or straightforward.

In particular, plantation governance was complicated through and through by a pair of strategic dilemmas that stood at opposite poles of the spectrum of colonial behavior: manumission and the brutalization of slaves. Manumission made the line between slave and free a permeable and constantly shifting one, which explains why so much effort was invested in the task of policing that line. In retrospect, it may seem logical that a practice identified with the prerogative of the individual master would find itself increasingly subject to the regulatory discipline

---

[2] See, e.g., Alfred Cobban, *A History of Modern France*, vol. 1, *Old Régime and Revolution: 1715–1799* (New York: Pelican Books, 1957; reprint, New York: Penguin Books, 1990), 9–27.

[3] For an institutional survey of the Old Regime, see the classic work of Roland Mousnier, *Les institutions de la France sous la monarchie absolue, 1598–1789*, vol. 2, *Les organes de l'État et la Société* (Paris: Presses Universitaires de France, 1980).

of the imperial administrators. Yet this movement was by no means inevitable: It was shaped by legal and demographic contingencies that were still in flux as of 1789.

The second dilemma, which stood in a covert relationship with the first, was whether and how to contain the self-aggrandizing tendency of the master (and his disciplinary extensions, the plantation manager and foreman) to render slavery increasingly harsh in the interests of making it ever more profitable. This, too, was an intractable regulatory conundrum in Saint-Domingue, one that raised a host of simultaneously moral and instrumental questions that were far from resolved by the time the French Revolution began.

THE WORLD OF THE CODE NOIR

The lines of continuity that limned these two developments were formed in the late seventeenth century, in which Tocqueville began (and in some respects ended) his portrait of the Old Regime. Although he frames the larger story told here, Tocqueville is not the best of guides to the demographic and institutional thicket of Saint-Domingue. In a diary entry dated May 24, 1841, that Tocqueville recorded during one of his trips to Algeria, he protested "that *none of our colonies* has ever at *any* time been treated like Algiers. All, in one form or another, have allowed the local population some say or at the very least have allowed local authorities to administer local revenues. Algiers is singularly bad, even without our detestable system of colonization. Find out more exactly what Canada and Saint-Domingue used to be like and how the Antilles were ten years ago."[4]

Tocqueville never got around to writing the book that might have resulted from this curiosity about how the French colonies once "were." That might be just as well, for the implication that Saint-Domingue at the time of French colonization still retained a meaningful "local population" in the manner of North Africa or Canada would not have been an auspicious beginning.

Historians are still coming to terms with the fate of the indigenous population of Hispaniola. Some argue that the Columbian encounter with the island's Indians amounts to an unrecognized campaign of genocide, whereas others emphasize the unintended role of disease on top of

---

[4] Tocqueville, *Writings on Empire and Slavery*, 48. Emphasis in the original.

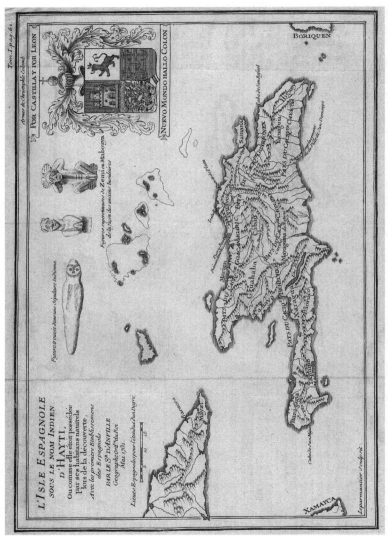

FIGURE 1.1. This 1731 map of Hispaniola (or Hayti, as the Taíno Indians called it) by the French royal geographer Jean-Baptiste Bourguignon d'Anville shows the island's indigenous populations at the time of the Columbian conquest. As Columbus had landed first on Hispaniola, his coat-of-arms featuring a map of the Caribbean was included. First published in Pierre-François-Xavier de Charlevoix, *Histoire de l'isle espagnole ou de S. Domingue* (Paris: François Didot, 1731). Courtesy of the Osher Map Library, University of Southern Maine.

the many brutalities inflicted by the Spanish conquistadors.[5] It is nonetheless clear that, within a century of the European invasion, the Taino
population of Hispaniola had ceased to exist.[6]

The Spanish maintained nominal control over Hispaniola for more
than two hundred years following the arrival of Columbus in 1492, but
an inability to attract significant numbers of settlers forced Spain to leave
almost the entire island deserted. Toward the end of the sixteenth century,
this social and political vacuum began to be filled by French privateers
(known as *flibustiers*) and buccaneers, who used the small island of Tortuga
just off Hispaniola's northwestern coast as a base from which to launch
raids and to promote small-scale tobacco cultivation.[7] Commissioned by
the French merchant marine, the *flibustiers* gradually established strong-
holds on the northern and western shores of Hispaniola, where they and
the buccaneers formed the beginnings of an unruly settler society in the
seventeenth century bolstered by the importation of indentured servants
from the metropole.

In 1664, the chief minister to the King of France, Jean-Baptiste Colbert,
created the joint-stock Compagnie des Indes Occidentales (West India
Company) to assume control of the metropolitan monopoly on trade with
the French Antilles as a whole.[8] The Company's first governor, Bertrand
d'Ogeron, took possession of Tortuga and managed to assert some degree
of control over the buccaneers of Saint-Domingue.[9] However, settler
opposition to the Company's prohibition on trade with Dutch and other
non-French (as well as with independent French) merchants resulted
in an uprising in 1670, the first of many white planter rebellions that
would complicate French rule over Saint-Domingue throughout the colony's history. The Company managed to put down the 1670 uprising
only with the aid of a French naval detachment stationed elsewhere in the
Caribbean.[10] In 1674, the Company was suppressed, and Saint-Domingue
was absorbed into the royal domain along with the monarchy's other

---

[5] For the genocide argument, see David E. Stannard, *American Holocaust: The Conquest
of the New World* (Oxford: Oxford University Press, 1992). An example of the more
conservative position is J. H. Parry, *The Spanish Seaborne Empire* (New York: Alfred
Knopf, 1981; reprint, Berkeley: University of California Press, 1990), 213–220.

[6] Parry, *The Spanish Seaborne Empire*, 213.

[7] Meyer, "Des origines à 1763," 96.

[8] Robin Blackburn, *The Making of New World Slavery: From the Baroque to the Modern,
1492–1800* (New York : Verso , 1997), 282.

[9] Pierre Pluchon, ed., *Histoire des Antilles et de la Guyane* (Toulouse: Privat, 1982),
470–471. Pluchon's book includes a useful chronology, on which I have relied for various
details in this chapter.

[10] Blackburn, *The Making of New World Slavery*, 283.

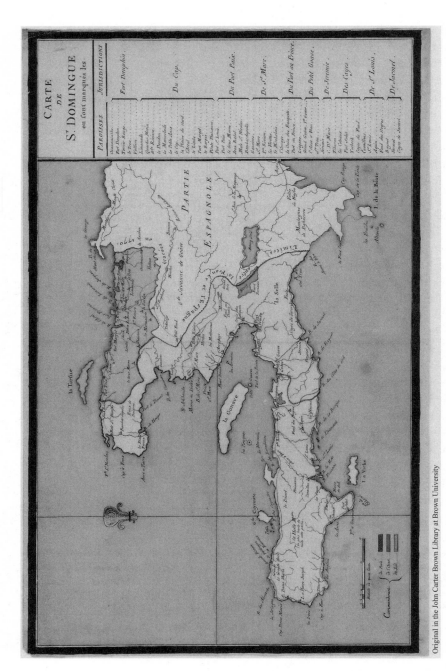

FIGURE 1.2. This 1770 map of Saint-Domingue shows the division of the colony into three administrative departments (north, west, and south). At the right-hand side is a list of Saint-Domingue's parishes and the ten lower-court jurisdictions into which they were grouped. Courtesy of the John Carter Brown Library at Brown University.

Caribbean colonies – the so-called Leeward Islands, or Lesser Antilles of Saint-Christophe, Martinique, and Guadeloupe – all of which had been acquired and settled during the third and fourth decades of the seventeenth century. With the Treaty of Ryswick in 1697, which ended the War of the League of Augsburg, Spain formally granted France sovereignty over the western third of Hispaniola. However, this step did not prevent the two sides of the island from engaging in near continuous eighteenth-century conflict over the control of resources and the movement of escaped slaves from one side of the border to the other.[11] Nor did it stop the *flibustiers* from remaining a powerful force in Saint-Domingue until as late as 1713, when the colony was split off from the administration of the Lesser Antilles and placed under the direct control of a separate royal governor. The separation of Saint-Domingue from the Leeward Islands would prove to be of great consequence for the colony's development of a distinct "provincial" identity in subsequent decades. In the meantime, this French "province" in the making was divided for administrative purposes into three departments: northern, western (a somewhat confusing label for the middle region of Saint-Domingue), and southern.

As this gradual shift from corporate to royal administrative sovereignty was unfolding, Saint-Domingue was also undergoing a profound demographic transformation – one never far from the surface of later efforts to control manumission and planter brutality in the colony. The dwindling supply of white indentured servants (known as *engagés*) from the metropole during the late seventeenth century went hand in hand with a rapid increase in the importation of African slaves.[12] Thus in 1681, Saint-Domingue had a total population of 6,648, 65 percent of which was white, 31 percent slave, and 3 percent free black or mulatto. Less than two decades later, these proportions were almost exactly reversed, with whites constituting only 29 percent of a population of 13,656, slaves 66 percent, and free blacks and mulattos 3.6 percent. The colony's racial imbalance (as well as its total population) would continue to grow dramatically during the eighteenth century, and most especially during the "boom" years of Saint-Domingue's sugar-exporting economy in the aftermath of the Seven Years' War. In 1764, out of a total population of

---

[11] Ibid., 293. Indeed, the border question and its related issues of control over resources and the movement of peoples remain a source of dispute between Haiti and the Dominican Republic even today. See Michele Wucker, *Why the Cocks Fight: Dominicans, Haitians, and the Struggle for Hispaniola* (New York: Hill and Wang, 1999).

[12] For more on this transition, see Gabriel Debien, *Les engagés pour les Antilles (1634–1715)* (Paris: Société de l'histoire des colonies françaises, 1952), 247–261.

227,000, whites made up 7 percent, slaves 90.7 percent, and free blacks and mulattos 2.3 percent. On the eve of the French Revolution, the official census reported 30,826 whites in the colony (5.8 percent of a total of 523,803),[13] 465,429 slaves (88.8 percent), and 27,548 free blacks and mulattos (5.2 percent).[14] Striking as these figures are, however, they do not reveal the colony's extremely high slave mortality rate relative to other New World slave societies. During their first three to five years of labor in Saint-Domingue, newly purchased Africans died on average at a rate of 50 percent.[15] Never was slave mortality higher than during the 1780s. During that decade, the importation of Africans to Saint-Domingue served not to augment the total number of slaves but rather to replace those who perished as a result of overwork, neglect, and abuse on the colony's plantation fields. This is to say nothing of the deaths that were caused by the Middle Passage itself: On the basis of the best available figures, it has been established that during the last quarter of the eighteenth century, the French slave trade mortality rate was 13 percent.[16]

The plantation system to which these lives were lost had its origins in the small-scale tobacco-growing operations of the seventeenth-century buccaneers. In the years after the West India Company was chartered in 1664, the buccaneers saw their profits siphoned off by their mercantilist rivals and successors. The Company was able to generate as much as 2.5 million livres worth of tobacco in 1674, but the formation of a

[13] The white population of Saint-Domingue was divided into an elite of *grand blanc* planters and a much larger community of *petit blanc* artisans, engineers, and plantation overseers. Given that many of the colony's estates were owned by persons residing in France, the role of the *petits blancs* in managing day-to-day plantation activities was highly significant.

[14] Meyer, "Des origines à 1763," 136. These figures likely underestimate the true numbers, given that masters were taxed on the basis of the number of slaves they owned and so had an incentive to underreport that information. The true number was likely closer to half a million. Dubois, *Avengers of the New World*, 30.

[15] Carolyn E. Fick, *The Making of Haiti: The Saint Domingue Revolution from Below* (Knoxville: The University of Tennessee Press, 1990), 26. For this figure, Fick cites Gabrien Debien's vast study of plantation documents and colonial correspondence in *Les esclaves aux Antilles françaises (XVIIᵉ-XVIIIᵉ siècles)* (Basse-Terre: Société d'histoire de la Guadeloupe, 1974), 83–84, 343–347; as well as the estimate of the eighteenth-century French antislavery advocate Frossard.

[16] During this period, the crossing from Africa to the French Caribbean took an average of seventy days. The peak in the French slave trade mortality rate (17 percent) came during the period between 1701 and 1725, when transatlantic voyages generally took about seventy-four days. During the second and third quarters of the eighteenth century, the Middle Passage required eighty-six to eighty-seven days on average, with slave mortality at 12 to 14 percent. See David Geggus, "The French Slave Trade: An Overview," *William and Mary Quarterly* 58, no. 1 (Jan. 2001): 136.

tobacco monopoly in France stifled what chance there may have been for the development of an economy along the lines of the Chesapeake system in North America (where planters were not constrained to sell to a single centralized buyer in their home country's market).[17] Indeed, the dramatic "success" of Virginia's tobacco-distribution network in the Old World itself served to convince French planters that their future lay in the cultivation of other crops. As tobacco production declined in Saint-Domingue during the last two decades of the seventeenth century, sugar and indigo (and later coffee) plantations began their long and spectacular rise.[18] Initially, indigo appeared to be on a path toward becoming the colony's leading export: In 1713, there were 1,182 indigo works in Saint-Domingue as compared to 138 sugar plantations (*sucreries*). The number of indigo estates continued to grow steadily over the ensuing decades, reaching a total of 3,445 in 1739. Around the middle of the eighteenth century, coffee exports also began to take off, climbing from 12 million livres in 1767 to 72 million livres in 1788–1789.[19] Yet it was sugar cultivation above all, with its unparalleled profit margins, that became the basis of eighteenth-century French colonial opulence. Between 1700 and 1760, raw sugar-cane exports from the French Caribbean islands as a whole rose eightfold, from 10,000 to 81,000 tons per year. In the aftermath of the Seven Years' War, the monarchy began allowing the planters of Saint-Domingue to refine their own sugar. As a result, by 1775, 250 out of 459 *sucreries* in the colony were capable of producing refined sugar; and at the end of the Old Regime, no less than 431 out of 739 sugar estates could boast of refining facilities.[20] The sugar plantations

---

[17] In 1674, the French livre tournois traded at a rate of about thirteen to one against the English pound sterling. A century later, in 1775, it would take about twenty-four livres tournois to buy a pound sterling. The colonial exchange rates differed dramatically. In 1775, the British pound sterling was worth roughly thirty-eight French livres. See John J. McCusker, *Money and Exchange in Europe and America, 1600–1775* (Chapel Hill: University of North Carolina Press, for the Institute of Early American History and Culture, 1978), 307, 312, 321.

[18] Blackburn, *The Making of New World Slavery*, 283–284.

[19] Ibid., 433–434. Especially in the period after the Seven Years' War, many of the coffee and indigo estates in the southern and western departments of Saint-Domingue were owned by *gens de couleur* rather than whites. See Garrigus, "Blue and Brown," 233–263.

[20] Blackburn, *The Making of New World Slavery*, 403, 433. The figures cited by Blackburn may underestimate the total number of sugar plantations in Saint-Domingue in the post–Seven Years' War period. Jean Tarrade gives a total of 541 *sucreries* for the year 1766 and 717 for 1778 (of which 269 possessed refining facilities). Jean Tarrade, "De l'apogée économique à l'effrondrement du domaine colonial (1763–1830)," in Meyer, Rey-Goldzeiguer, and Tarrade, *Histoire de la France coloniale*, vol. 1, *La conquête*, 334.

of Saint-Domingue were vast and complex operations: On the basis of a sample of 100 estates, David Geggus has found that between 1745 and 1792 the average labor force numbered 177 slaves.[21] Thanks to such sizable work regiments, toward the end of this period total sugar exports from the French Caribbean had jumped to 125,000 tons per year, 87,000 of which were exported from Saint-Domingue alone.[22] It was partly this expansion that explains the colony's extremely high slave mortality rate: The methods used to harvest and refine sugar cane were physically taxing to a degree that could not compare with those employed for any other crop. Not surprisingly, the disciplinary measures that managers and overseers developed to keep slaves working at a relentless pace, beginning at dawn and sometimes ending only late at night, were geared toward maximizing total yield regardless of the human costs.[23]

The rise of the Saint-Domingue plantation complex was fortuitously aided by the colony's peculiar geography. The coastline of the western third of Hispaniola is characterized by a seemingly endless run of nooks and crannies, which made possible the convenient and expeditious transfer of cargoes between the colony and other destinations (both legal and illicit). Even more significantly, Saint-Domingue was endowed with four large plains conducive to the sort of large-scale, intensive cultivation required by sugar plantations.[24] One of these plains radiated inland from Cap Français (also known as Le Cap) in the northern department, where the largest and most profitable sugar plantations were located, and another stretched outward from Les Cayes in the southern department. In the colony's western department, the Artibonite River plain and the plain of Cul de Sac served to spread around some of the wealth that derived from the *sucreries* of Saint-Domingue. The hills that rose behind

---

[21] David P. Geggus, "Sugar and Coffee Cultivation in Saint Domingue and the Shaping of the Slave Labor Force," in *Cultivation and Culture: Labor and the Shaping of Slave Life in the Americas*, ed. Ira Berlin and Philip D. Morgan (Charlottesville: University Press of Virginia, 1993), 74; also cited in Blackburn, *The Making of New World Slavery*, 434.

[22] Blackburn, *The Making of New World Slavery*, 433. These figures pertain to the year 1787. Blackburn (at 431) notes that Saint-Domingue's economy experienced its greatest growth during the years 1713–1740 and 1765–1790. Not coincidentally, of course, both of these periods were extended interwar eras.

[23] C. L. R. James, *The Black Jacobins: Toussaint L'Ouverture and the San Domingo Revolution*, 2nd ed. (New York: Random House, 1963), 10. Robin Blackburn's account emphasizes the proto-industrial character of the New World slave plantations in general and the Caribbean sugar plantations in particular. He argues that Atlantic slavery made a vital contribution to the rise of British industrialization. Blackburn, *The Making of New World Slavery*, 509–580. Whether and how the French Caribbean plantation economy fits into his framework is unclear, however.

[24] Blackburn, *The Making of New World Slavery*, 432.

each of these four level areas provided convenient sites for the layered terraces on which coffee beans could be grown. Further behind these hills ascended the numerous mountain ranges that cut across the colony's entire landscape, enabling groups of escaped slaves (or *marrons*) to hide away for indefinite periods of time throughout the eighteenth century. In addition to facilitating slave resistance, the mountains enclosed valleys of varying sizes that remained unsettled on the whole but also gave rise to an isolated plantation here and there. Finally, an elaborate network of rivers and streams, flowing down from the mountains and further channeled where necessary by the most advanced irrigation system in the Western hemisphere, ensured that the plantations of Saint-Domingue would rarely lack for the extensive water resources they required to outproduce the British and Spanish Caribbean colonies.

The colony's irrigation system was merely one of many institutions that the French monarchy managed to introduce into the Caribbean through the mediation of its local governmental apparatus. After 1699, that apparatus came under the jurisdiction of the Naval Ministry in Versailles. In 1710, the monarchy created a special division within the ministry, known as the Colonial Bureau, to assist with the increasingly important and lucrative business of administering France's Caribbean possessions.[25] Two officials, both appointed directly by the king and overseen by his naval minister, were responsible for running the wheels of government in Saint-Domingue. Modeled respectively on their counterparts in the *généralités* and provinces of the metropole,[26] the colonial intendants and governors[27] were given jurisdiction over distinct areas of

[25] Ibid., 294. Colonial finances were separated from those of the Navy beginning in 1750. By the 1780s the Colonial Bureau was itself divided into subdepartments, and in 1783 the Bureau was renamed the *Intendance Générale*. D. K. Fieldhouse, *The Colonial Empires: A Comparative Survey from the Eighteenth Century* (London: Weidenfeld and Nicolson, 1966), 36–37. On the reform of French colonial administration in the post-Seven Years' War period, see Jean Tarrade, "L'administration coloniale en France à la fin de l'Ancien Régime: Projets de réforme," *Revue historique* 229 (Jan.-March 1963): 103–122.

[26] D. K. Fieldhouse observes: "[T]he colonies were treated as provinces of metropolitan France[,] and their internal administration appropriately followed the French provincial pattern.... [The intendant's] office was a microcosm of French administrative history transferred from the provinces of the metropolis to the colonies." Fieldhouse, *The Colonial Empires*, 37. This view of French colonial administration is echoed in James E. McClellan III, *Colonialism and Science: Saint Domingue in the Old Regime* (Baltimore, MD: The Johns Hopkins University Press, 1992), 9–10, 40.

[27] As noted above, after the West India Company was dissolved in 1674 until 1713, Saint-Domingue was controlled out of Saint-Christophe by the Intendant and *Gouverneur-Général des Isles*. During these years a subordinate governor based in Saint-Domingue nonetheless reported directly to the naval minister in Versailles. After 1713 the colony was given a separate government.

policy and thereby were forced to check and balance each other's powers. In theory, this centerpiece of absolutist administrative strategy also
applied to the relationship between the intendants and governors of
France. As Toqueville famously observed, however, in the metropolitan
provinces "[a]ll the reality of government was vested in the intendant."[28]
In the colonies, on the other hand, the traditional designs of absolutism
retained a much greater hold on institutional practices.[29] The intendant,
who was generally a lawyer, controlled finance, taxation, the administration of justice, and the colonial police. He also had the power to make
appointments to minor governmental posts and to issue administrative
ordinances valid throughout the colony, a prerogative that was shared
by the governor. Typically a member of the *noblesse d'épée* (or military
nobility), for his part, the governor was given control over an especially
important sphere of colonial authority: the armed regiments. In addition,
he was charged with monitoring and punishing violations of the mercan-
tile regulations as well as hearing appeals of capital sentences handed
down by either of the colony's two high courts.[30]

The first of these courts was established in 1685 in Petit Goâve, the
initial capital of Saint-Domingue, located on the northern coast of the
southern department.[31] Initially known as a Conseil Souverain (sovereign court) before the monarchy decided to change its name to Conseil
Supérieur, the court was moved back and forth between Petit Goâve and
nearby Léogane in the early eighteenth century in response to military
conflicts in the surrounding region. In 1750, the colony's capital and
the Conseil Supérieur were both transferred (permanently, as it would
turn out) from Léogane to the newly founded town of Port-au-Prince.[32]
The second of the high courts was established (with the label Conseil

---

[28] Tocqueville, *The Ancien Régime and the French Revolution*, 41.
[29] Already by the mid-seventeenth century, writes Fieldhouse, provincial governorships in
France had become "largely honorific" titles. By contrast, the rivalry between the colonial
intendants and governors remained a constant feature of French imperial governance
until 1816, when the governors were granted complete control of overseas administration. Fieldhouse, *The Colonial Empires*, 37–38. For one example of the competitive
tensions that sometimes characterized relations between intendants and governors in
the Caribbean, see the letter from Louis XIV to Governor-General de Blénac, April 30
[date unclear], 1681, LC, 1:351 (concerning the "importance of the alliance between the
Governor-General and the Intendant" and the "subordination" of the latter's opinion in
the event of a disagreement).
[30] Fieldhouse, *The Colonial Empires*, 37–38.
[31] "Édit portant établissement d'un Conseil Souverain ... à Saint-Domingue," August 1685,
LC, 1:428.
[32] "Ordre du Roi pour la translation du Conseil Supérieur de Léogane au Port-au-Prince,"
October 23, 1750, LC, 4:34.

Supérieur) in Cap Français in June 1701,[33] and it remained there throughout the rest of the colonial period, with the exception of a brief interlude
just two years prior to the outbreak of the French Revolution.[34]

In the earliest days of its existence the Conseil in Cap Français issued
several acts bearing the ambitious qualification "Parlement," but this
practice was soon discontinued.[35] Despite their apparent similarities to
the *parlements* of France and to the Parlement of Paris in particular – the
colonial high courts were required to base their judgments on the *coutume
de Paris* (Parisian customary law) where it was applicable – the colonial
Conseils Supérieurs differed in important respects from their metropolitan counterparts. Most significantly, the colonial tribunals were nonvenal,
thus they were prevented from establishing the kind of *parlementaire*
family traditions that underwrote the development of judicial resistance
to the monarchy in eighteenth-century France.[36] This did not mean that
the colonial Conseils became docile partners of the royal administration; on the contrary, when the occasion called for it they exercised their
presumed *droit de remontrance* (right of protestation) with every bit as
much vigor as the Parlement of Paris at its most obstreperous.[37] However,

---

[33] "Édit de création et établissement du Conseil Supérieur du Cap Français," June 1701,
LC, 1:666.

[34] During that brief interlude, the Cap Français high court was suppressed and merged with
its counterpart in Port-au-Prince, an event that caused an uproar among the colonists in
the northern department; the decision was soon reversed.

[35] "Arrêt du Conseil du Cap," November 21, 1701, LC, 1:679. See Moreau de Saint-Méry's
note at the end of this document.

[36] An even closer source of comparison to the colonial high courts than the traditional
parlements can be found in the Conseils Souverains established in the provinces that
were conquered by Louis XIV, such as Roussillon, Flanders, and Alsace. In these provinces on the fringes of the early modern French state, the high courts were also initially
nonvenal. This changed in the 1690s when the monarchy introduced venality into all
of the Conseils Souverains except that of Roussillon. Marquis de Roux, *Louis XIV et
les provinces conquises: Artois, Alsace, Flandres, Roussillon, Franche-Comté* (Paris: Les
Éditions de France, 1938), 179. It is quite likely that Roussillon and the other conquered
provinces provided the actual precedent for the Conseils Supérieurs of the Caribbean,
although further research would be needed to confirm this point.

[37] The *parlements* of Old Regime France did not allow the king's ordinances to become law
in their jurisdictions without first registering them. The metropolitan high courts – and,
by virtue of their own sense of analogy, the Conseils Supérieurs of the colonies – used
what they considered to be their *droit de remontrance* to influence the shape of royal
legislation. Although they did not possess an absolute right to refuse registration, the
parlements did enjoy a de facto power of judicial review. The king could override the veto
by means of a *lit de justice* or by informal pressure short of that extraordinary ceremony.
See R. C. van Caenegem, *An Historical Introduction to Western Constitutional Law*
(Cambridge, UK: Cambridge University Press, 1995), 101–102. Despite the pretensions
of the Conseils Supérieurs, it was unclear whether the colonial high courts could insist on
the requirement of registration in the manner of the metropolitan *parlements*.

the power to name new members to the courts rested in the hands of the Crown. In addition to the intendant (who presided over the tribunals' proceedings), governor, and a handful of other senior military and civilian officials, six judges usually drawn from among the colony's leading resident planters were named to serve on each of the Conseils of Saint-Domingue.[38] The resulting imbrication of judicial and planter elites was one of the most notable characteristics of creole politics in the eighteenth century. The overlap between the two was never complete enough to make the Conseils Supérieurs simple pawns in the hands of the wealthiest and most influential sugar growers, but it was sufficiently large to rule out the alternative possibility that the tribunals would become mere oracles of and apologists for the royal will.[39]

Below the Conseils in terms of hierarchy were ten local trial courts (known as *sénéchaussées*), distributed throughout each of the colony's three departments. Beginning in 1717, admiralty tribunals (*amirautés*) were established in the port towns of Saint-Domingue to hear cases involving maritime trade and the discipline of sailors.[40] The decisions of these lower courts in matters both criminal and civil were subject to appellate review by the Conseils Supérieurs. In turn, those appellate decisions could be revised or quashed by the Conseil d'État in Versailles, which had final say over all the *parlements* of the kingdom by virtue of the principle of the royal *justice retenue* ("justice retained").[41] In actual fact, however, this extraordinary appellate jurisdiction was exercised only in the rarest of colonial cases. For the most part, the Conseils Supérieurs were left to go about their adjudicative business, which was supplemented by a variety of administrative responsibilities. These included the supervision of special ad hoc tribunals and the regulation of the colony's unruly, constantly growing legal profession: barristers, notaries, clerks, and (most especially) the powerful royal prosecutors and their substitutes.[42]

In addition, by registering (or refusing to register) royal ordinances according to their compatibility with the "local" conditions and interests

[38] Henri Joucla, *Le Conseil Supérieur des Colonies et ses Antécédents* (Paris: Les Éditions du Monde Moderne, 1927), i; Fieldhouse, *The Colonial Empires*, 38.

[39] Unlike the judges of the Conseils Supérieurs, the governor and intendant were barred by royal edict from owning plantations in Saint-Domingue. Many administrators nonetheless became plantation owners in the course of their tenure in the colony. Blackburn, *The Making of New World Slavery*, 298.

[40] Gene Ogle, "Policing Saint Domingue: Race, Violence, and Honor in an Old Regime Colony" (PhD Diss., University of Pennsylvania, 2003), 170. Ogle (at 171–173) provides a very useful chart summarizing the history and structure of Saint-Domingue's court system.

[41] Caenegem, *An Historical Introduction to Western Constitutional Law*, 99.

[42] Fieldhouse, *The Colonial Empires*, 38.

of elite creole society, the high courts exercised an essential "quasi-legislative" role on behalf of the colony.[43] In the vast majority of instances, the *droit de remontrance* was not invoked, whether for prudential or more straightforward reasons. Even more typically, however, the courts' quasi-legislative function and its judicial role merged imperceptibly into one another, as the Conseils heard cases that required them to interpret the provisions of royal law so as to avoid a conflict with competing provisions of Parisian customary law or colonial administrative policy.[44] Not surprisingly, that interpretive role – part legislative, part judicial – was never exercised with greater frequency or political and social impact than in the context of cases involving the Code Noir, the foundation of the French colonial law of slavery.

BODIN'S VISION

Louis XIV promulgated the Code Noir in March 1685, seven months after the revocation of the edict of Nantes (which had guaranteed toleration of Protestants within the borders of Catholic France) and eighteen months after the death of the king's illustrious chief minister, Colbert.[45] The last of the landmark royal ordinances of the late seventeenth century, the Code Noir brought to an unanticipated culmination the absolutist revolution in French law overseen by Colbert.[46] As a gesture to the deceased

---

[43] Ibid.

[44] On this subject, see especially Edith Géraud-Lloca, "La coutume de Paris outre-mer: l'habitation antillaise sous l'Ancien Régime," *Revue historique de droit français et étranger* 60, no. 2 (1982): 207–259.

[45] Officially titled "Édit servant de Règlement pour le Gouvernement et l'Administration de la Justice et de la Police des Isles Françoises de l'Amérique, et pour la Discipline et le Commerce des Nègres et Esclaves dans ledit Pays," the Code Noir did not become known as such until the eighteenth century. Brett Rushforth touches briefly on this point in his forthcoming *Bonds of Alliance: Indigenous and Atlantic Slaveries in New France* (Chapel Hill: University of North Carolina Press, for the Omohundro Institute of Early American History and Culture, 2012), chapters 2 and 6.

[46] The earlier highlights of Colbert's campaign to unify the laws of France included the 1667 *Ordonnance civile*, the 1670 *Ordonnance criminelle*, and the 1673 *Ordonnance commerciale*. See Duane Anderson, "The Legal History of the Reign," in *The Reign of Louis XIV: Essays in Celebration of Andrew Lossky*, ed. Paul Sonnino (Atlantic Highlands, NJ: Humanities Press International, 1990), 79–84. Anderson's essay is typical of the scholarship on French and European legal historiography generally in omitting any mention of the Code Noir. For two additional examples, see the discussion of the Colbertian ordinances in R. C. van Caenegem, *An Historical Introduction to Private Law*, trans. D. E. L. Johnston (Cambridge: Cambridge University Press, 1992), 91–93; and Mousnier, *Les institutions de la France sous la monarchie absolue*, 2: 380–397. François Olivier-Martin makes a very brief reference to the Code Noir in his *Histoire du droit français*

controller-general's role in unifying the hodgepodge, unruly legal systems of both an established European monarchy and a fledgling Caribbean empire, the king signed Colbert's name after his own at the end of the Code Noir. With this stroke of the royal pen, seconded by the formal imprimatur of the chancellor, Michel Le Tellier, France became the first European colonial power to codify African slavery in law. With the exception of an eight-year revolutionary hiatus (1794 to 1802), the Code Noir remained on the statute books of France until it was eventually abrogated on April 27, 1848, as a result of the abolitionist campaign spearheaded by Victor Schoelcher and actively supported by Tocqueville (among others).[47]

Since 1685, the place of colonial slavery in France's national memory has been irrevocably identified with Louis XIV, Colbert, and the Code Noir. As an institutional matter, French colonial slavery was first embodied in royal law, and it survived in that form for more than a century and a half, only to be terminated by the official act of a provisional republican government. For nearly its entire career, in other words, French colonial slavery bore the stamp of sovereignty. The abolitionist movement drew a great deal of its moral and political energy from this link between the nearby French state and the faraway realms of plantation governance.[48] However, the relationship between slavery and sovereignty (in its pre-revolutionary, absolutist manifestations) is far more complicated than this straightforward, abolitionist reading of the matter would suggest. The Code Noir, and the French law of slavery more generally, cannot be understood simply as the royal legitimation of a social institution or practice.[49] In Saint-Domingue, the legitimation of slavery by

---

des origines à la Révolution (Paris: Domat Montchrestien, 1948; reprint, Paris: CNRS Éditions, 1995), 355.

[47] Drescher, *Dilemmas of Democracy*, 151–195.

[48] Ibid., 189–191. See also Pitts, introduction to Tocqueville, *Writings on Empire and Slavery*, xxx.

[49] Sala-Molins describes the promulgation of the Code Noir in the following terms: "*The French monarchy establishes in law the non-right of black slaves to the state of law, whose juridical inexistence constitutes [their] sole and unique legal definition.*" ("*La monarchie française fonde en droit le non-droit à l'État de droit des esclaves noirs, dont l'inexistence juridique constitue la seule et unique définition légale.*") Sala-Molins, *Le code noir*, 24. Emphasis in original. However, this assertion of the "juridical inexistence" of the slave is plainly incorrect, given that the slave had a very definite legal existence as the property of his master (as Sala-Molins would surely concede). Whether the slave had any existence as a "legal" or "moral person" is a different and more controversial matter; strictly as a matter of law, however, the Code Noir clearly provided that slaves were to be treated as subjects of the Catholic Church.

LE CODE NOIR

O U

EDIT DU ROY,

SERVANT DE REGLEMENT

POUR le Gouvernement & l'Adminiftration de Juftice & la Police des Ifles Françoifes de l'Amerique, & pour la Difcipline & le Commerce des Negres & Efclaves dans ledit Pays.

Donné à Verfailles au mois de Mars 1685.

A V E C

L'EDIT du mois d'Aouft 1685. portant établiffement d'un Confeil Souverain & de quatre Sieges Royaux dans la Cofte de l'Ifle de S. Domingue.

A PARIS, AU PALAIS,

Chez CLAUDE GIRARD, dans la Grand'Salle, vis-à-vis la Grand'Chambre : Au Nom de JESUS.

M. DCC. XXXV.

FIGURE 1.3. Title page of the 1685 Code Noir, as Louis XIV's edict had come to be known by the time of this 1735 republication. Courtesy of the John Carter Brown Library at Brown University.

EDIT DU ROY,

TOUCHANT la Police des Isles de l'Amerique
Françoise.

Du mois de Mars 1685.

OUIS, par la grace de Dieu, Roy de France & de
Navarre : A tous presens & à venir : SALUT, comme
nous devons également nos soins à tous les Peuples que
la Divine Providence a mis sous notre obéïssance, Nous
avons bien voulu faire examiner en notre presence les
mémoires qui nous ont été envoyez par nos Officiers de
nos Isles de l'Amerique, par lesquels ayant été informé
du besoin qu'ils ont de notre Autorité & de notre Justice pour y mainte-
nir la discipline de l'Eglise Catholique, Apostolique & Romaine, & pour
y regler ce qui concerne l'Etat & la qualité des Esclaves dans nosdites
Isles ; & désirant y pourvoir & leur faire connoître qu'encore qu'ils
habitent des climats infiniment éloignez de notre séjour ordinaire, nous
leur sommes toujours present, non seulement par l'étenduë de notre puissance, mais encore par la promptitude de notre application à les secourir
dans leurs nécessités. A CES CAUSES, de l'avis de notre Conseil & de
notre certaine science, pleine puissance & autorité Royale, nous avons
dit, statué & ordonné, disons, statuons & ordonnons, voulons & nous
plaît ce qui ensuit.

ARTICLE I. Voulons & entendons que l'Edit du feu Roy de glo-
rieuse mémoire notre très-honoré Seigneur & Pere du 23 Avril 1615.

A ij

FIGURE 1.4. Opening paragraphs of the 1685 Code Noir, as republished in the
same 1735 edition displayed in the previous figure. Courtesy of the John Carter
Brown Library at Brown University.

the administrative monarchy must be set alongside the recurring tensions
that characterized relations between two forms of absolutism: colonial
and metropolitan.

Jean Bodin's *Les six livres de la république*, first published in French
in 1576, is an ideal philosophical guide to these tensions.[50] Bodin was
both the most important theorist of sovereignty in early modern France[51]
and – not coincidentally – one of the first opponents of slavery in the
European intellectual tradition.[52] His defense of absolute sovereignty and
his critique of slavery went hand in hand, and the reasons for this compatibility tell us as much about the nature of slavery as a form of government as they do about the theoretical identity of French absolutism.

Bodin's opposition to slavery had essentially to do with his conception
of the "well ordered Commonwealth" (*la République bien ordonnée*).
The phrase appeared in the very title of Bodin's chapter on slavery in the
Six livres de la république: "Of the power of a Lord or Master over his
Slaves (*De la puissance seigneuriale*), and whether Slaves are to be suffered in a well ordered Commonwealth." This chapter was the third of
three in the opening book to deal with the institutions of "household" or
"family" government, a category that also included the rule of husbands
over wives and fathers over children.[53] Yet Bodin insisted that slavery was
a "question of great moment not for Families and societies only, but for
all Commonwealths also in general."[54] Indeed, never "has there been any
Commonwealth in the world, which has not had slaves in it."[55] In short,
slavery mattered everywhere, first because slaves were everywhere to be
found, and second because no "well ordered Commonwealth" could
afford to ignore the question of how much "seigneurial power" it should
tolerate within its borders.

[50] The *Six livres* was also published in a French edition of 1583, a 1586 Latin translation by
Bodin himself, and another French edition of 1593. The 1577 French edition published
in Geneva was unauthorized and criticized by Bodin for its amendments. In preparing
his 1606 translation, upon which I partly rely here, Richard Knolles worked from both
the 1576 French and the 1586 Latin versions. David Brion Davis notes that the Latin
edition was even more critical of slavery than the 1576 French original. The Latin version strongly condemned the Spanish, as well as pirates and brigands, for their role in the
slave trade. See David Brion Davis, *The Problem of Slavery in Western Culture* (Ithaca,
NY: Cornell University Press, 1966), 122 n. 43.

[51] Julian H. Franklin, *Jean Bodin and the Rise of Absolutist Theory* (Cambridge, UK:
Cambridge University Press, 1973), vii.

[52] Davis, *The Problem of Slavery in Western Culture*, 111–114.

[53] "Government of the household" is a more accurate translation of Bodin's phrase
"gouvernement des ménages" than is Knolles's expression "government of the family."

[54] Bodin, *The Six Bookes of a Commonweale*, 32.

[55] Ibid., 34.

Once introduced into a commonwealth, Bodin explained, slavery tempted masters to push at the boundaries of their authority. The despotism of masters had predictable consequences for the treatment and status of the slaves themselves, and the result was a situation in which both masters and slaves had to fear for their lives.

[T]he cruelty and license of the lords and masters increased. [And yet] the state of Families and Commonwealths is always in danger of trouble and ruin, by the conspiracy of slaves combining themselves together: all Histories being full of servile rebellions and wars.[56]

The social instability produced by slavery was not all that different from the conditions that characterized the age of religious warfare through which Bodin lived and to which his treatise was a response.[57] In both contexts, the diversion of (private) loyalties away from a single unitary sovereign and toward other points of authority (whether religious or secular, voluntary or coercive) produced a crisis in the social order. In the case of slavery, Bodin pointed to the annals of classical Rome for evidence of the inevitability of servile uprisings. Yet Rome was hardly the only point of reference here. Four thousand years of history, wrote Bodin, provided all the illustration one might have needed for the "pernicious" effects of slavery, for all of the "murders, cruelties, and detestable villainies to have been committed upon the persons of slaves by their lords and masters."[58]

Bodin summed up the lessons of this history with reference to an "ancient proverb" – "*So many slaves, so many enemies in a man's house*" – that "shows right well what friendship, faith, and loyalty a man may look for of his slaves."[59] He then narrated a horror tale from Roman times about a slave who dropped his master's three children from the top of a house, killing all three. Bodin was clearly willing to make use of long-standing stereotypes about the diabolical and traitorous character of slaves to fortify his case against slavery, but the primary emphasis in

---

[56] Ibid., 38. I have slightly modified Knolles's translation here to better reflect the 1593 French text.

[57] Julian Frankin argues that the St. Bartholomew's Day massacre in 1572 was instrumental in triggering a new and more "absolutist" understanding of sovereignty in Bodin. Franklin, *Jean Bodin*, vii. This distinction between an earlier and later Bodin is questioned in the acknowledgments of Preston King, *The Ideology of Order: A Comparative Analysis of Jean Bodin and Thomas Hobbes* (London: George Allen & Unwin, 1974).

[58] Bodin, *The Six Bookes*, 44.

[59] Ibid., 45. Emphasis in the original. The original wording of this "ancient proverb" is "autant d'ennemis que d'esclaves."

this chapter of the *Six livres* was on the villainy of masters rather than slaves. Thus whereas slavery corrupted the hearts of both masters and slaves, only the former possessed the "seigneurial" authority to do something about the system as a whole. If the cycle of "murders, cruelties, and detestable villainies" threatened to continue unabated, it was because the slaveholders placed their own interests above the broader welfare of the republic. They would continue to do so until the slaves decided to take matters into their own hands and overthrow the status quo. For this reason, in Bodin's view, republics based on slavery were destined to be short lived.[60]

Bodin's case against slavery, at least up to this point, was one of expediency more than anything else. In order to survive, the republic had to take decisive action against the threat that self-interested nobles posed to the social order. This was where Bodin's theory of sovereignty entered the picture. At first glance, the doctrine of absolute sovereignty would seem to be entirely compatible with the prudential agenda of setting limits on the authority of masters in a slave-based republic. "[T]he main point of sovereign majesty and absolute power consists of giving the law to subjects in general without their consent," Bodin wrote in book 1, chapter 8.[61] All of the other marks of sovereignty – the power to declare war or make peace, the right to decide appeals in the last instance, the privilege of granting pardons, and so forth – were "comprehended" within this "first prerogative,"[62] which "cannot be shared with subjects."[63] Preventing the dispersion of this primary power was dictated by secular, prudential concerns rather than by divine law (as would be the case for the theologian

---

[60] Bodin bears comparison here with the thought of Machiavelli and other classical republican thinkers of the Renaissance period, as analyzed by J. G. A. Pocock in *The Machiavellian Moment: Florentine Political Thought and the Atlantic Republican Tradition* (Princeton, NJ: Princeton University Press, 1975). One of the chief characteristics of the Florentine tradition was its belief in the inevitably short-lived nature of all republics. It would be interesting to consider the extent to which slavery played a role in this belief about the time-dependent nature of republics. Bodin himself was a republican only in the strictest sense of the term, but it might be useful to think of him as translating the classical republican tradition into absolutist terms.

[61] Jean Bodin, *On Sovereignty: Four Chapters from "The Six Books of the Commonwealth,"* ed. and trans. Julian Franklin (Cambridge, UK: Cambridge University Press, 1992), 23. This chapter was entitled simply "On sovereignty." I have used Franklin's partial and more recent translation (based on the 1583 Paris edition) for the chapters on sovereignty, noting in parentheses the equivalent page numbers in the Knolles/McRae translation (K/M, 98).

[62] Ibid., 58–59 (K/M, 162–63). This passage is from book 1, chapter 10, titled "On the true marks of sovereignty."

[63] Ibid., 58 (K/M, 162).

Bossuet later in the seventeenth century). "The best expedient for preserving the state," Bodin observed, "is never to grant a prerogative of
sovereignty to any subject, much less a stranger, for it is a stepping stone
to sovereignty."[64]

If the "only hope of averting [the] disaster" of social disintegration
"lay in subjecting the nobles to the royal administration in all public
matters" – as Edward Whiting Fox has usefully summarized Bodin's
theory[65] – then the principle of sovereignty had much to commend itself
to a republic facing the kinds of troubles described in book 1, chapter 3
of the *Six livres*. The only trouble was that the doctrine of absolute sovereignty was also a doctrine of *limited* sovereignty,[66] and limited specifically
in a way that posed a serious and intractable challenge to the sovereign of
a republic where slavery prevailed. For just as the prince lacked the power
to violate the commands of natural (or divine) law, so too did he lack the
ability to interfere with the private property of his subjects "without just
and reasonable cause."[67] As Fox correctly notes, Bodin "understood that
the only possibility of having the monarchical state accepted by these
powerful and reluctant subjects [i.e., nobles] depended on the sovereign's
recognition of their right to enjoy their property freely and fully."[68] Thus
just as Bodin's opposition to slavery was (partly) grounded in the need
to preserve the republic from internal dissolution, so too was his support
of private property conditioned by pragmatic considerations about the
survival of the state.

Slavery as a form of property ownership both mimics and challenges
the Bodinian theory of sovereignty, which held that "the main point of
sovereign majesty and absolute power consists of giving the law to subjects
in general without their consent." If the "murders, cruelties, and detestable villainies"[69] that Bodin decried in the *Six livres* were about anything,
they were about masters "giving the law" to their slaves "without their
consent."[70] If not absolute sovereignty itself, in the Bodinian worldview

---

[64] Ibid., 71 (K/M, 170–71).

[65] Edward Whiting Fox, *History in Geographic Perspective: The Other France* (New York:
W. W. Norton, 1971), 74.

[66] Keith Michael Baker, "Enlightenment and Revolution in France: Old Problems, Renewed
Approaches," *Journal of Modern History* 53, no. 2 (June 1981): 287 ("[I]t was central
to the traditional notion of absolute power that, while incontestable, it was nevertheless
limited – by divine precept and natural law, as by the conviction that it formed part of a
constituted order of things which it existed to sustain").

[67] Bodin, *On Sovereignty*, 39 (K/M, 109).

[68] Fox, *History in Geographic Perspective*, 74.

[69] Bodin, *The Six Bookes*, 44.

[70] Bodin, *On Sovereignty*, 23 (K/M, 98).

slavery was at the very least a significant "stepping stone to sovereignty,"[71] which is another way of stating why Bodin identified slavery with the threat of social disorder. For the better part of four thousand years, seigneurial power (*la puissance seigneuriale*) over slaves and servants was based precisely on the free exercise of a right to property in humans.[72] The protection of that right formed the basis of the tacit social compact between sovereigns and nobles. It was not by accident that Bodin subsumed slavery under the broader category of "household" (or "family") "government."[73]

The parallel between the absolutism of the prince and the absolutism of the master was therefore both a social and a constitutional problem for Bodin's republic, and the two problems were linked. In their respective spheres, neither could tolerate the sharing of power with a rival form of government, but in practice it was impossible to keep those spheres entirely separate from one another. The prince might succeed in guarding his monopoly over the specific "rights of sovereignty" that Bodin considered essential to the preservation of the state, and yet fail to prevent masters from nibbling away at the "first prerogative of sovereignty": the power of "giving law or issuing commands to all in general and to each in particular."[74] In the long run, Bodin's proposed recipe for the republic – namely, to insulate the spheres of princely and aristocratic power completely from one another – was therefore untenable in the context of a slave society. If slavery was to be prevented from threatening social stability, it had to be either regulated or eliminated; in either case, this required interference with the property rights of nobles.

Yet slavery was not just any form of property: It served to create pockets of sovereignty within the state. The difference between these pockets of sovereignty and those associated with the power of lords over wives and children was a matter of degree rather than kind, but that difference was large enough to single out the case of slavery for special concern. And because the sovereignty of masters over bondsmen and bondswomen

---

[71] Ibid., 71 (K/M, 171).

[72] In defining "seigneurial power" in the very first sentence of book 1, chapter 3, Bodin mentioned both slaves (*esclaves*) and servants (*serviteurs*). However, the entirety of the chapter was devoted to the case of slaves throughout world history rather than to the case of servants or serfs. Bodin's use of the phrase seigneurial power was thus intended to describe the prerogatives of the lord (*Seigneur*) or master (*maître*) over slaves and should not be confused with the medieval institutions of feudal lordship or manorial jurisdiction.

[73] Bodin, *The Six Bookes*, 32.

[74] Bodin, *On Sovereignty*, 58 (K/M, 162).

tended naturally and inevitably toward despotism and the fomenting of revolution, Bodin's theory could not countenance slavery's unregulated existence within the republic.[75]

Two qualifications to this analysis are worth noting. The first concerns what might be called the "escape clause" in Bodin's definition of private property as a sacrosanct institution. The prince could carve out an exception to the general rule against taking the property of others in cases where there was "just and reasonable cause," that is:

> as by purchase, exchange, lawful confiscation, or in negotiating terms of peace with an enemy, if it cannot otherwise be concluded than by taking the property of private individuals for the preservation of the state. Many [commentators] are not of this opinion. But natural reason would have the public [interest, *le public*] preferred over the private [*particulier*], and have subjects not only pass over their injuries and desires for revenge, but give up their possessions also for the welfare of the commonwealth, as is ordinarily done by one public toward another public, and by one individual toward another.[76]

Bodin does not tell us whether this "escape clause" would have covered both human and nonhuman forms of property. However, his suggestion that in certain circumstances the unrestricted ownership of private property could threaten the "preservation of the state" and the "welfare of the commonwealth" resonates perfectly with his portrayal of the unstable slave society in book 1, chapter 3. Just as Bodin's doctrine of absolute sovereignty was also a doctrine of limited sovereignty, so too was his endorsement of the subjects' right to enjoy their property fully and freely a limited one (even if it was unclear how the limits were supposed to apply to different forms of property, as in the case of slavery).

A second qualification concerns the nature of Bodin's opposition to slavery. It bears repeating that in book 1 of the *Six livres*, Bodin arrived at his conclusions about the dangers of slavery and the proper organization of the state for strategic rather than religious or moral reasons. Yet there was another dimension to Bodin's vision of the "well-ordered commonwealth" that was also responsible for his critique of slavery. This other

---

[75] Fox argues that the "absolute separation of public and private business" was implicit in Bodin's use of the term *res publica* for his new state. "Translated into modern terms and concepts, however, this means that the sovereign was only one of two or more powers within France. The King could not be challenged in his realm, but that clearly did not include the totality of France. The state that Bodin helped revive was the first and most important, but not the only, power within the country." Fox, *History in Geographic Perspective*, 74.

[76] Bodin, *On Sovereignty*, 39–40 (K/M, 109).

dimension was expressed not in the pragmatic terms that characterized Bodin's discussion of the threat of a slave revolution but rather in a more moralistic language. In book 3, chapter 8, Bodin discussed "the orders and degrees of Citizens." Here he asked whether slaves, granted that they "be indeed of the basest sort of men," did not "deserve to be termed by the name of citizens."[77] Bodin's answer was striking for the corporeal description of society with which it began:

There be in man's body some members, I may not call them filthy (for that nothing can be so which is natural) but yet so shameful, as that no man except he be past all shame, can without blushing reveal or discover the same: and do they for that cease to be members of the whole body?[78]

Bodin went on to provide as an example of these "shameful" members "the feet themselves, which with perpetual labour hold up and carry about the whole bulk of the body." The indignities visited upon the feet in the course of undertaking a person's labor needs were no reason to excommunicate that particular anatomical part from the rest of the human body. Having introduced the theme of labor and dishonor, it was but a short and logical transition to the situation of slaves, who served the same purpose for societies as a whole that feet served in the lives of individuals. Yet just as feet were to be considered part of the human body, so too were slaves – "who are still pressed and kept under with the most heavy burdens and commands of the other citizens" – to be deemed constitutive features of the social body. As "subjects and not strangers, [slaves] must needs make up a part of the citizens, and be accounted in the number of them."[79] Bodin thus complemented his strategic case against slavery with a claim that, although cast in rigorously secular and physiological terms, was arguably rooted in the ideals of Christian universalism and the brotherhood of humankind.

Bodin went on to make clear that this argument in favor of incorporating slaves into the body of the citizenry was not to be mistaken for a call to reintroduce slavery into France, a nation from which it had "long since [been] taken away." On the other hand, the question of the civil status of slaves in France was not entirely a theoretical matter, for Bodin went on to warn that "servitude and slavery by little and little" are

---

[77] Bodin, *The Six Bookes*, 387, also quoted in part in Davis, *The Problem of Slavery in Western Culture*, 112.

[78] Bodin, *The Six Bookes*, 387.

[79] Ibid. As this sentence makes clear, in book 3, chapter 8 Bodin was indeed talking about slaves in the legal sense and not simply laborers generally.

beginning to "creep in, and to return again" to "our Commonwealth."[80]
This may have been a reference to the presence of a small number of
African and other slaves on French metropolitan territory in the late sixteenth century.[81] Bodin used the reappearance of slavery in the kingdom
as a reminder of the importance of treating slaves as well as was compatible with the requirements of "the state and condition of man"; and
he reiterated that slaves ought to be considered as having "their certain
place and order in the city."[82]

Considered as a whole, Bodin's antislavery views thus raise a set of
vexing questions: What is the relationship between strategic and moral
or humanitarian concerns in his critique? Are the two in tension or do
they coexist peacefully with one another? Does it matter whether one
takes precedence over the other, and if so, can the degree of precedence
be established? Following on the heels of these initial questions are others that might be raised to tease out the Machiavellian and prescriptive
dimensions of Bodin's writings on slavery. Why would a prince take
action to improve the condition of slaves or to remove slavery entirely
from the body politic? Why should he place a cap on the number of slaves
freed by their masters or insist, on the contrary, that not all slaves be kept
in servitude forever? Why would a master agree to accept laws limiting
the authority he exercises over his slaves? Why should one master consider it necessary to criticize the way other masters treat their own slaves?
Merely by posing these questions, one begins to touch upon some of the
fundamental ambiguities in Bodin's ideas about sovereignty, slavery, and
the relationship between the two.

---

[80] Ibid., 388.

[81] At least a few such cases are recorded. Sue Peabody cites the example of a Norman
slave merchant who arrived in Bordeaux in 1571 with a cargo of slaves. When he eventually tried to sell the slaves, the merchant was arrested and the slaves freed by virtue
of a declaration of the Parlement of Guyenne that slavery was intolerable in France, the
"mother of liberty." Sue Peabody, *"There Are No Slaves in France": The Political Culture
of Race and Slavery in the Ancien Régime* (New York: Oxford University Press, 1996),
12, 29. This case is also discussed in Blackburn, *The Making of New World Slavery*,
61; Davis, *The Problem of Slavery in Western Culture*, 130; and Ilona Vernez Johnson,
"The Reinvention of Slavery in France: From the Jean Boucaux Affair to the Eve of the
Haitian Revolution" (Ph.D. Diss., Pennsylvania State University, 1999), 47. Davis notes
that Bodin was actually in Toulouse in 1571 when the Parlement's decision was handed
down. For other examples of cases involving slaves in France during this period, see Léon
Vignols, *Les esclaves coloniaux en France au XVIIe et XVIIIe siècles et leur retour aux
Antilles* (Rennes: Oberthur, 1927), 2.

[82] Bodin, *The Six Bookes*, 388.

BALANCING "CRIME" AND PUNISHMENT

For all his awareness of slavery's "creeping" return to France in the late sixteenth century, Bodin could not have anticipated the rise of a slave system that would begin to develop only several decades after his death, and at a distance of several thousand miles from metropolitan absolutism. In this "other France" of the Caribbean, and in Saint-Domingue particularly, new forms of princely and aristocratic sovereignty – and of the relationship between them – would take root. The 1685 Code Noir is a concentrated repository of the tensions created by these new forms of sovereignty. Although there was always a significant chasm between the letter and the practice of law in Saint-Domingue, the making of the Code Noir is an indispensable point of departure for understanding how a precautionary concern with the risks of unregulated slavery shaped the colonial Old Regime.

Indeed, the Code Noir was itself the product of a kind of preemptive strategy. Seen from the perspective of its own time, before the massive rise of African slavery on a systematic basis in eighteenth-century Saint-Domingue, the Code Noir was an effort to grapple with a world of slave unrest and planter brutality that had not yet crystallized but was still coming into view. Part of the challenge of reconstituting the anxious politics of the slave-based colonial commonwealth – which Bodin envisioned on a largely theoretical plane – involves rewinding the tape to an anomalous, pre-eighteenth-century world in which whites still outnumbered blacks. In such a world, the task of explaining why the law of slavery should seek to regulate the conduct of masters as much as slaves becomes less anomalous than it may seem in hindsight. In significant respects, the Code Noir was closer to the pre-Atlantic slavery worldview of Bodin than it was to the full-fledged plantation society that Saint-Domingue had become by 1789.

On October 18, 1685, about seven months after the Code Noir was promulgated, the governor of Saint-Domingue, Pierre-Paul Tarin de Cussy, wrote a report to the French naval minister, Jean-Baptiste Colbert de Seignelay, son of the deceased controller-general. Among his other objectives, Cussy's goal was to convince Seignelay to issue an order prohibiting each colonist from having more (black) slaves than (white) indentured servants. The *engagés* had made possible the establishment of Saint-Domingue as a colony, he suggested, and if their numbers were allowed to diminish the colony as a whole would soon follow in decline as well. That servants from the metropole were far more expensive than African slaves meant that the administration had only to stand by and watch as the latter increasingly replaced the former. The risks associated with having a larger number of slaves than servants were particularly worrisome, Cussy argued, in light of the vulnerable military position of Saint-Domingue vis-à-vis rival Spanish powers on the other side of the island and elsewhere in the Caribbean, not to mention the other European powers with establishments in the region.[83]

The governor proceeded next to complain about the increasing numbers of "Negroes, Indians, and mulattos" (both male and female) who had made their way over to the Spanish side of the island, where they had "contracted" a spirit of "libertinage" and a "horror" of French manners. These runaway slaves (known as *marrons* or maroons) were seized by French military expeditions and returned to the French side of the island. By that time, Cussy suggested, they had experienced what it meant to enjoy a period of freedom, and colonial planters and administrators were finding it next to impossible to inculcate the habits of obedience and docility upon which the stability of a slave society was held to depend. Cussy alleged that several of these slaves – one hundred of them had escaped to the Spanish side in the past year, he noted – were responsible for the assassinations of white colonists. The lesson from all of these developments was clear: "In our slaves we have domestic enemies."[84] The governor closed his report with a request for approval and "the means" to evacuate part of the "troublesome" elements of the colony's African population (including a group of "mulatto and quadroon Indian" women whom he charged with infecting the young male pirate population of the colony with the vice of "concubinage").[85]

Cussy used an almost identical characterization of slaves as domestic enemies in a later report to the minister, dated August 27, 1687. There, the governor resumed his discussion of the threat that "free Spanish mulattos and blacks" – women as well as men, he noted once again – purportedly posed to the stability of Saint-Domingue. All of these individuals were described as "so many enemies that we keep among us." Cussy then reverted to the imagery of "infection," "libertinage," and "desertion": Each of the vices reflected in the behavior of these freed persons was likely to make its way to the slave population and would

---

[83] Report of Cussy to Colbert de Seignelay, October 18, 1685, ANOM, CGSD, C/9A/1, fol. 250.

[84] Ibid., fol. 252 ("Nous avons dans les esclaves des ennemis domestiques").

[85] Ibid. A quadroon was the child of one white parent and one mulatto parent.

probably spread to the colony's whites as well. For the second time in the space of two years, the governor called for the deportation of the (freed) slaves in question to other islands elsewhere in the Caribbean.[86]

As we have seen, at the time Cussy wrote these reports, the nature of the French Caribbean labor supply was in the midst of a gradual shift from white indentured servitude to African slavery. Throughout the first three or four decades of French settlement in western Hispaniola (roughly 1660 to 1700), administrators such as Cussy repeatedly voiced concern about the demographic balance of the colony, fearing that the pressures leading colonists to rely on slaves rather than indentured servants would introduce a security risk far greater than the supposed gains in productivity. In response to those concerns, the monarchy issued an ordinance on September 30, 1686, providing that the number of blacks in the colony not exceed the total *engagé* population; any excess in slave imports was to be confiscated (and presumably deported to other areas of the Caribbean).[87] In 1698, the king issued an order specifying the numbers of *engagés* that ships of various sizes were required to import into the ports of Saint-Domingue.[88] In subsequent years, similar requirements (as well as some incentives) were approved in an effort to maintain a basic level of racial equilibrium in the colony.[89]

Cussy's references to slaves as "domestic enemies" (or simply "enemies") are significant not only because they echoed the formulations of such early modern commentators on slavery as Bodin, Locke, and Montesquieu.[90] For Cussy, the slave had become the kind of immediate threat that these authors, writing in a historical and philosophical

---

[86] Report of Pierre-Paul Tarin de Cussy, governor, to Jean-Baptiste Colbert de Seignelay, naval minister, August 27, 1687, ANOM, CGSD, C/9A/1, fol. 386.

[87] "Ordonnance du Roi," September 30, 1686, LC, 1:434.

[88] "Ordre du Roi," February 19, 1698, LC, 1:581.

[89] Such measures were quite clearly the product of racism and racial anxieties, but they seem also to have implicated the colonists' sense of national belonging. Cussy's suggestion in his 1685 report that an "excess" of black slaves over white servants posed a security threat to the colony, that is, may have reflected a conviction that Saint-Domingue should be or become a *French* society. If that hypothesis is correct, then the colony's identity as an offshoot of the kingdom, and its concerns about the dangers posed by introducing a population of "domestic enemies" in the midst of the white settlers, were related to one another.

[90] In the *Second Treatise on Government*, Locke had characterized civil slavery as a state of war. John Locke, *Two Treatises of Government*, ed. Peter Laslett, Cambridge Texts in the History of Political Thought (Cambridge, UK: Cambridge University Press, 1988), 284. See also Peter S. Onuf, *Jefferson's Empire: The Language of American Nationhood* (Charlottesville: University Press of Virginia, 2000), 149. In *The Spirit of the Laws*,

rein about both ancient and "modern" institutions, did not have to confront in their own social contexts.[91] Yet the label "domestic enemies" also
served to justify an array of harsh punishments for slaves, including but
not limited to those who had been returned from the Spanish side of the
island as fugitives. To define slaves as enemies was to place them even further outside the protection of the law than they already were.

The attitude reflected in Cussy's reports to Versailles would find its
way into the Code Noir of 1685. More than any other, the question of
how best to deter and punish slave "crime"[92] preoccupied the handful of
colonial administrators who worked, at Colbert's behest, on the codification of existing slave-law policies and practices in the French Caribbean.
The monarchy's intentions in this endeavor were not limited to criminal law, but rather extended to the entire range of laws that a sovereign
power could use to determine the status of slaves. The primary question
posed by the drafting of the new code was whether slaves were to be
considered "subjects" of the Crown or merely domestic enemies. (Bodin
had raised and answered the same question in a way that would clearly
find little welcome in French colonial circles.) The authors of the Code
Noir aimed to strike a balance between the view of the slave as outside the bounds of sovereign authority and an alternative view of the
slave as a subject (however disfavored and mistreated) of the absolute
monarchy. Central to that balance was the question of where to draw
the line between "high" and "low" (*haute* and *basse*) justice in regulating the punishment of slaves.[93] In determining the location of that line,
the Code's drafters followed the precedents set by earlier colonial court

---

Montesquieu observed that slaves will always constitute the "natural enemies of society."
Montesquieu, *The Spirit of the Laws*, 256.

[91] Locke did play a significant role in British New World colonization as the author of
South Carolina's first constitution, but he performed that role from a purely metropoli-
tan vantage point, never venturing onto the territory of South Carolina. For a discussion
of the influence of Locke on the drafting of the South Carolina constitution and on
Locke's own theory of property, see David Armitage, "John Locke, Carolina, and the
Two Treatises of Government," *Political Theory* 32, no. 5 (2004): 602–627.

[92] I place this term in quotation marks to indicate that the concept of slave crime is an ideo-
logically loaded one.

[93] Under the feudal law of the Old Regime, *haute justice* denoted the range of "major"
crimes that could be adjudicated only by magistrates appointed by the king. *Basse justice*,
by contrast, encompassed the "minor" crimes that a lord or master could try in his personal capacity, provided those crimes occurred on lands directly under his domestic sovereignty. The actual justice (or justices) might be the same in both of these types of cases, but
the source of their judicial authority differed depending on the nature and circumstances
of the crime. See Marc Bloch, *La société féodale*, vol. 2, *Les classes et le gouvernement des*

rulings,[94] but they also replaced those precedents with a model that borrowed from metropolitan traditions.

On May 20, 1682, Jean-Baptiste Patoulet and the Comte de Blénac, the intendant and governor-general of the French Caribbean colonies, composed a *mémoire* to the king concerning "the guardianship [*conservation*], regulation [*police*], trial, and punishment of his subject's slaves in America."[95] With the exception of the first of these subjects, everything in the title of the *mémoire* pointed to the subjects of "crime" and punishment. The opinions of the three Conseils Supérieurs then in existence in the French Caribbean (those of Martinique, Saint-Christophe, and Guadeloupe) had been solicited on these questions. The *mémoire* was essentially a distillation of the precedents of all three courts, supplemented by the opinions of the two chief administrators. Although it is difficult to determine which parts of the document came directly from the court precedents and which came from Patoulet and Blénac, it is safe to say that the *mémoire* constituted a summary or partial codification of local practice in the Caribbean. As such, the proposal suggests not only the trends that characterized the "criminal" punishment of slaves prior to 1685 (and that would continue to characterize it even after), but also the nature of the reforms sought by leading members of French colonial society.

The administrators' stated concern with the defects in the status quo focused on the inability of individual planters to deal effectively with what Patoulet and Blénac described as a matter of systemic crime: crime not

---

hommes (Paris: Éditions Albin Michel, 1968), 502–508; and Robert Chesnais, introduction to *Le Code Noir*, ed. Robert Chesnais (Paris: L'Esprit frappeur, 1998), 11.

[94] "Arrêt du Conseil de la Martinique, contre un Particulier mauvais Mari et Maître cruel," October 20, 1670, LC, 1:203 (impeaching a militia lieutenant for mutilating his slaves); "Arrêt du Conseil de la Martinique, contre un Maître cruel," May 10, 1671, LC, 1:225–226 (imposing a fine on a colonist for burning the genitals of and excessively whipping his female slave). Throughout this book, as in this footnote, I will make selective use of a practice employed in legal scholarship to summarize the holdings of judicial decisions. That practice relies on the use of shorthand phrases enclosed within parentheses immediately following the case reference.

[95] "Projet de règlement de Mrs. de Blénac et Patoulet sur les Esclaves des Isles de l'Amérique," May 20, 1682, ANOM, F/3/90, fol. 1. As the title of this document indicates, the *mémoire* was in fact a draft proposal for what would become the Code Noir. See Vernon Valentine Palmer, "The Origins and Authors of the Code Noir," *Louisiana Law Review* 56, no. 2 (Winter 1995): 363–407; and Bernard Vonglis, "La double origine du Code noir", in *Les Abolitions dans les Amériques*, ed. Liliane Chauleau (Fort-de-France: Société des amis des archives et de la recherche sur le patrimoine culturel des Antilles, 2001), 101–107.

limited to a single plantation or two. This perception of uncontrollable slave "crime" figured centrally in the *mémoire*:

[A]ll of the regulations thus far issued to put a stop to the libertinage, thefts, and pernicious practices of the slaves of this place [have] failed to produce any effect, notwithstanding the various severe punishments that have been designed; on the contrary it is apparent that the slaves continue, and increase their thefts, acts of insolence, and other practices, including their habit of running away, to the extent of forming dangerous cabals, such that the public is greatly disturbed, with many poor families leaving and abandoning the island in order to avoid the losses with which they meet.[96]

The view that slave "crime" stemmed from "insolence" was reflected in both pre- and post-1685 judicial decisions that sought to limit the abusive treatment of slaves and indentured servants.[97] Those decisions aimed to discredit the argument that restraining the exercise of radical abuse would only encourage slaves and servants in their "disobedience." More importantly for our present purposes, the *mémoire* suggests the administrators' sense that slave "crime" – particularly theft, *marronage*, and libertinage, all three of which would remain fundamental to the colonists' perceptions of both slaves and *gens de couleur* throughout the eighteenth century – threatened the ability of the colony to attract and maintain a viable white population.

One way of interpreting the impetus behind the Code Noir, then, is in terms of an effort to salvage France's Caribbean dominion. That effort consisted of providing settlers, both actual and potential, with evidence of the Crown's determination to guarantee safety to the white population. The centrality of slave crime in the administrators' *mémoire*, in other words, can be understood as an attempt to justify the extension of absolutism abroad, a justification triggered by the putative tendency of many families to abandon the colony for other destinations.[98]

In their proposal, Patoulet and Blénac also invoked another theme central to the developments leading up to the promulgation of the Code Noir:

---

[96] "Projet de règlement," May 20, 1682, fol. 2.

[97] See, for example, the case references in note 94.

[98] The *mémoire*'s allusion to "poor families" as the category most affected by the supposed prevalence of slave "crime" is a little unclear. This allusion may have to do partly with the fact that a wealthy planter elite had not yet developed in Saint-Domingue, unlike in the other French colonies, where an elite had established itself several decades earlier and had already had time to generate a prosperous plantation economy. The destinations to which these "poor families" had recourse may have included not only the other French Caribbean colonies, but also non-French colonies elsewhere in the region.

the extent to which the colonists were themselves to blame for the ⟨
tion in which they found themselves. In developing this theme, the admiɴ
istrators reproduced in their *mémoire* an *arrêt* (or holding) of the Conseil
Supérieur of Saint-Christophe handed down only five months before. That
holding had expressed frustration with "all of the prohibitions, decisions,
and regulations that have been hitherto rendered, as much against the
slaves as against private persons (*particuliers*)" in the aim of restricting
slave crime.[99] However, the Conseil proceeded to place responsibility for
this situation on the masters rather than the slaves. The alleged instances
of theft (including stealing from sugar canes) could only be seen as "the
fault of the masters and patrons of the said slaves, who are not fed as God
and the law ordain."[100] If only the colonists had bothered to follow the
courts' other ordinances and regulations providing for the proper feeding
and clothing of slaves, so the argument went, there would have been no
need to promulgate so many (unenforceable) rules of criminal law.

The colonists were blameworthy in other respects as well. The *arrêt*
of the Saint-Christophe high court went on to note that certain colonists
were responsible for actually buying stolen goods from the slaves themselves.[101] It was therefore all the more necessary for an outside authority – whether judicial, in the form of the Conseils Supérieurs, or statutory,
in the form of royal legislation – to step in and regulate the status and
condition of slavery in the French colonies.

The situation that obtained in Saint-Christophe held also in Martinique
and Guadeloupe, where the high courts had been forced to render the
same diverse array of decisions, regulations, and other decrees bearing on
slave crime. In the *mémoire* that he signed with Blénac, Patoulet noted
that because these other documents were so similar to those rendered by
the high court of Saint-Christophe, it was not even necessary to reproduce them in the proposal. The more important task, he felt, was to set
out principles for the punishment of slaves and for the proper organization of colonial society in accordance with the logic of the *mémoire*. To
this end, Patoulet went on to state as his first principle, concerning adju-
dication, that the slaves "must be judged by ordinary magistrates, and by
appeal to the Sovereign Councils, and the [same] formalities that respect
a free person [must be] observed."[102]

---

[99] "Arrêt du Conseil de St. Christophe," January 12, 1682, in "Projet de règlement," May
20, 1682, fol. 3.
[100] Ibid.
[101] Ibid., fols. 3–4.
[102] "Projet de règlement," May 20, 1682, fol. 4.

This principle was striking first and foremost because it purported to place slaves on the same legal level as free persons; that is, slaves would deserve the same protections and legal formalities that applied to the trials of whites accused of committing crimes. That policy, the *mémoire* went on to note, was in conformity with the holdings of the colonial high courts. The principle of adjudicative parity is also worth underlining because it provided a supplementary justification for the extension of judicial authority over matters that had previously been left to independent planter authority.

As to specific methods of punishment, Patoulet and Blénac prohibited masters from inflicting either mutilation or torture "without the authority of justice" (thus implying that both could lawfully be administered in the colonial courts).[103] The administrators' proposal made only the following allowance to masters: "[I]t will be lawful ... to enchain, place in bars, and whip the slaves with canes."[104] The overall trend leading up to the Code Noir, then, was clear: It was necessary to set limits on the punitive discretion of masters and, in so doing, to create the conditions that would make the overall project of French colonization in the Caribbean feasible. The criminal law of slavery was the means by which this agenda could be carried forward.

Consistent with these themes, the Code Noir established a body of law that, along with the vast array of implementing regulations that followed in the Code's wake, would become known as the "civil law" of the colony. Articles 22 through 27 of the Code Noir set forth rules for the nourishment, clothing, and medical care of slaves. And article 42, most notably, provided that masters could chain and beat their slaves with twine or cane, but upon penalty of the confiscation of the slaves, they were prohibited from using torture or mutilation as instruments of punishment.[105] This latter restriction did little to prevent masters from actually torturing and mutilating their slaves, of course. The Code Noir's prohibitions were largely ineffectual absent the enforcement mechanisms that would have been necessary to oversee the distant and essentially autonomous plantations of the Caribbean colonies. Yet even though it was very rarely enforced, article 42 marked out the lines of authority that divided (in formal if not in practical terms) planter discretion from the

[103] Ibid., fol. 5.
[104] Ibid. I have used the phrase "place in bars" for the French expression "mettre à la boîte."
[105] Code Noir, arts. 22–27, 42 (1685).

prerogatives of the colonial judicial and administrative powers. Indeed, article 42 went so far as to call for special prosecutions of masters who violated the ban on torture and mutilation. Further, article 43 of the Code provided that masters or slave drivers who killed slaves under their authority would be punished "according to the circumstances of the atrocity."[106] A few planters were in fact prosecuted and fined for exceeding the limits on their authority. Whether their slaves were actually confiscated from them in those instances is not clear. Yet the legal principle that property held in slaves was not held in absolute dominion would find its way into subsequent cases involving the brutalization of slaves in Saint-Domingue.[107]

The problem of the radical abuse of slaves thus provided the colonial authorities with the justification they needed to set limits on private magisterial authority. Despite the fact that such limits were rarely observed or enforced, they established a framework of risk and responsibility that would help to define who was "barbaric" and who was "legitimate" by the standards of eighteenth-century Saint-Domingue.[108] In so doing, the Code Noir initiated the fateful process of assigning and managing risk in the strategic business of eighteenth-century plantation management.

At the level of political theory, Bodin's prescient vision set the stage for this process. Yet it was Montesquieu's reflections on the necessity for *balance* in slave societies that would frame the arguments in the colonial debate and provide an unmistakable point of departure for the positions advanced on both sides. For colonial purposes, perhaps the single most important passage in all of Montesquieu is the definition of "civil slavery" that opens book 15, chapter 1 of *The Spirit of the Laws*: "Slavery

---

[106] Ibid., arts. 42–43. On the Roman law antecedents for article 43, see Vonglis, "La double origine du Code noir," 104.

[107] See Chapter 3 and the account of the Lejeune prosecution in Chapter 4. One other provision of the Code Noir is worth highlighting in connection with the formal definition of sovereignty over the slave. Article 26 provided that slaves who were not nourished, clothed, and "maintained" by their masters, in accordance with the standards set out elsewhere in the Code, would be allowed to bring forth a complaint to the royal prosecutor. As a result of such complaints, the masters in question could be brought to trial. Article 26 further specified that prosecution was particularly necessary in situations involving the "barbarous and inhumane treatment of slaves by their masters." Code Noir, art. 26 (1685). On the Roman law precedent for this article, see Vonglis, "La double origine du Code noir," 106.

[108] Cf. the brief discussion of the North American slave codes in Hendrik Hartog, *Man and Wife in America: A History* (Cambridge, MA: Harvard University Press, 2000), 166.

in its proper sense is the establishment of a right which makes one man so much the owner of another man that he is the absolute master of his life and of his goods."[109] This understanding of slavery as absolute mastery – an echo of the Roman law doctrine of *patria potestas*, which accorded fathers and husbands supreme authority over everyone in their households – formed the basis on which Montesquieu proceeded to condemn the institution as "not good by its nature" and "useful neither to the master nor to the slave."[110]

Far from adopting the absolutist slaveholder's view that no civil laws could be allowed to extend to a relationship that was fundamentally beyond the purview of external surveillance, Montesquieu went on to argue that the law must serve the essential purpose of balancing between the twin dangers of slavery. In a chapter entitled "what the laws ought to do in relation to slavery," he wrote, "[b]ut whatever the nature of slavery, [the] civil laws must seek to remove, on the one hand, its abuses, and on the other, its dangers."[111] In other words, slavery generated side effects (or externalities, to use the modern economic language), and it was the job of the legislator to take these into account on behalf of society. This observation about the need for a "balancing act" of sorts constituted the entirety of Montesquieu's chapter on the responsibilities of the law of slavery, but in the subsequent two chapters he clarified his notion of "abuses" and "dangers." In the case of the former, Montesquieu singled out the problem of sexual corruption for special attention: Slavery allowed masters to assert their dominion not only over the labor but also the "virtue and honor" of their slaves.[112] This resulted in a culture of "voluptuousness" with effects equally harmful for masters and slaves alike. The provision of Roman law that barred slaves from marrying one another, in Montesquieu's view, was guilty of promoting the corruption that the master-slave relationship tended to produce of its own absolute accord.[113]

Under the rubric of "dangers," Montesquieu highlighted the problem of having too many slaves in a moderate or republican state. In such states, political and civil liberty were intimately related, and the presence

---

[109] Montesquieu, *The Spirit of the Laws*, 246. In the following discussion, I have made slight modifications to this translation, indicated by means of brackets.

[110] Ibid.

[111] Ibid., 254.

[112] Montesquieu's primary frame of reference here was Islamic slavery, in a return to one of the principal themes of his *Persian Letters* (1721).

[113] Montesquieu, *The Spirit of the Laws*, 255.

of slaves in any considerable degree (civil slavery) could only frustrate the efforts of legislators to guard against the onset of political slavery or tyranny. In an echo of Bodin's formulation, Montesquieu further observed that slaves would always constitute the "natural enemies of society."[114] Minimizing their numbers in any polity was a matter of strategic interest and common sense. The other principal "danger" to which Montesquieu drew attention followed logically from the first: the problem of having an armed slave population. Here again, the danger was one to which republican or moderate polities would be more vulnerable than monarchies. In republics, "men who are citizens will scarcely be able to contain people who, bearing arms, are the equals of the citizens."[115]

As a result of this combination of abuses and dangers, a legislative balancing act was necessary. The law had to restrain the prerogatives of masters sufficiently to allow a republican society to maintain itself, but not so far as to render masters incapable of believing they exercised that "absolute" power over their property that Montesquieu posited as the essence of slavery. The tension between his natural law condemnation of slavery – which appeared almost as a corollary of the opening definition of slavery as absolute dominion – and his prudential or strategic arguments in favor of limiting the will of the master was representative of a broader tension in Montesquieu's thought, and formed a striking parallel to the legal culture and dilemmas of pre-revolutionary Saint-Domingue.

The rest of Montesquieu's analysis of slavery was largely devoted to a description of the "precautions to [be taken] in moderate governments." He observed that men will become accustomed to the most penurious burdens, even slavery, provided that the master is not "[even] harsher" than the servitude itself.[116] Yet slavery proved difficult to contain within the limits first set out for it. When Rome expanded, legislators found it necessary to promulgate "terrible laws in order to establish security for these cruel masters who lived among their slaves as if among their enemies."[117] The characterization of slaves as enemies, another echo of Bodin, was one of the keys to understanding why Montesquieu believed the task of the legislator was so difficult to extricate from the position of the slaveholders. Before it could become possible for legislators to restrain masters from abusing their slaves, laws had to be passed that would give the masters an official justification for their high-handed behavior. After

[114] Ibid., 256.
[115] Ibid.
[116] Ibid., 258.
[117] Ibid.

mentioning several examples of Roman laws that exemplified the cruel treatment of slaves, Montesquieu wrote that "[b]ecause the slaves among the Romans could have no trust in the law, the law could have no trust in them."[118]

All of this was by way of prelude to the gist of Montesquieu's policy recommendations. Given that slave societies, and particularly those characterized by a republican form of government, tended toward anarchy, cruelty, and militarization, regulations were needed to govern relations between masters and slaves. For Montesquieu, the most important of these regulations were those that required the magistrate to verify that the slave had adequate food and clothing, and that care was taken of elderly and enfeebled slaves. In addition, if the law was going to go so far as to permit the master to take the life of his slave, it was a right that he should be allowed to exercise only as judge and not as master. Legislators should enact formalities to ward off what Montesquieu described as "the suspicion of a violent action."[119] Montesquieu went on to develop these principles with reference to various ancient and biblical laws that in his view did not do enough to protect slaves from the domestic severity of their masters. The upshot was a prescription for a balancing act: a concerted effort by lawmakers to ensure that the "abuses" and "dangers" of slavery were kept in balance, and that the master-slave relationship consisted of *relative* rather than absolute domination. The circulation of these and other ideas about slavery on both sides of the French Atlantic would make Montesquieu the veritable philosopher of the Code Noir and its precautionary spirit.

To take one particularly important example from near the end of the Old Regime, consider the articles on "slavery" and "negroes" in Guyot's *Répertoire universel et raisonné de jurisprudence*, an exhaustive encyclopedia of articles on every aspect of French law, the first volumes of which appeared in 1784. The article on slavery opened with the following definition, only slightly modified from the language of *De l'esprit des lois*: "the state of a person who is in servitude and under the absolute power of a master." Even more striking and familiar, however, was the article's explanation of the kind of government and laws necessary to sustain a slave society. In a moderate government, only the exercise of humanity could prevent the dangers that accompany a society with a large number of slaves. Men would accustom themselves to servitude provided that the

---

[118] Ibid., 259.
[119] Ibid.

master was more bearable than the institution over which he presided.[120] As for African slaves in particular, the article on "Negroes" instructed readers that their "nature" required one not to be too severe with them. "Moderate punishment" encouraged them to work, but "excessive rigor" led them to take refuge with "fugitive or savage negroes," who in turn threatened the stability of colonial society by creating pockets of collective resistance.[121] These articles were but two of many discussions of eighteenth-century French colonial slavery that would borrow heavily from both the details and the overall thrust of Montesquieu's vision.

THE "PREDICAMENT" OF MANUMISSION

The Code Noir provisions regarding the discipline and treatment of slaves point toward a dilemma that contemporary political theorists call a "collective action" problem: a situation in which the uncoordinated actions of individual "players" may lead to "suboptimal" outcomes for a group as a whole.[122] Although it would be many years before the systemic character of this risk would materialize, the phenomenon of planter brutality was a fundamental source of the strategic ethics of colonial administration in Saint-Domingue. However, that phenomenon was only one end of a polarity that defined the law of slavery and shaped the colony's political culture. The opposing pole conjured up a very different portrait of slave society, one seemingly inconsistent with, if not antithetical to, the practices and values of the colonial economy. Here, too, the Code Noir framed the terms of the eighteenth-century debates to follow, for it not only institutionalized slavery in Saint-Domingue and the other French Caribbean colonies, but it also made possible the rise of one of the largest communities of free persons of color in the New World.[123]

---

[120] "Esclavage," in *Répertoire universel et raisonné de jurisprudence civile, criminelle, canonique et bénéficiale*, ed. Joseph Nicolas Guyot (Paris: Visse, 1784), 7:71–72.

[121] "Nègres," in Guyot, *Répertoire universel*, 12:57. For more on French definitions of "blacks" in the eighteenth century, see William B. Cohen, *The French Encounter with Africans: White Response to Blacks, 1530–1880* (Bloomington: Indiana University Press, 1980), 132; and Simone Delesalle and Lucette Valensi, "Le mot 'nègre' dans les dictionnaires français d'Ancien Régime: histoire et lexicographie," *Langue française* 15 (Sept. 1972): 79–104.

[122] See, e.g., Richard Tuck, *Free Riding* (Cambridge, MA: Harvard University Press, 2008), 24. Tuck here considers the familiar form of a collective-action problem known as the prisoner's dilemma.

[123] Throughout the remainder of this book, I will use the expression "free persons of color" or "free colored community" as a convenient (if imperfect) shorthand for both mulattos and free blacks in Saint-Domingue, recognizing that mulattos constituted

Article 55 of the Code provided that masters aged twenty years and older (whether or not under parental control) could manumit their slaves either during the life of the owner or as a result of his death, without being required to provide a reason for the manumission.[124] Bernard Vonglis has pointed out that this latter proviso was a tacit rejection of the rule under the lex Aelia Sentia (4 A.D.), whereby masters who had attained the age of twenty could manumit slaves only if a tribunal had approved the owner's rationale.[125] That implicit trace of Roman influence probably explains one part of the mystery of article 55. Yet it remains something of a puzzle why the drafters of the Code Noir believed it necessary to include a basic authority to manumit in the text of the royal edict. If the objective of codification was to guarantee the property rights of masters and the criminal punishment of slaves, the articles designed to further these specific ends would presumably have sufficed.

Once the provisions concerning religious instruction and minimal subsistence for the slaves are taken into account, however, the problem appears more complicated, and for reasons that have little to do with the putatively humanitarian nature of those provisions. Bodin's analysis correctly foretold that there would be more to the creation of a slave jurisdiction than the establishment of a framework for the legalization and discipline of property held in the form of persons. The law of slavery served two additional purposes – justification and stabilization – without which the Code Noir and the subsequent history of Saint-Domingue make only partial sense.

The first of these purposes, justification, was primarily a problem for the monarchy in the early stages of colonization and enslavement, and most specifically at the moment of the Code Noir's promulgation.[126]

---

the vast majority (although not the entirety) of the colony's free nonwhite population. Occasionally I will also employ the expression *gens de couleur* with the same understanding in mind. Where necessary or useful as a reminder, I will refer separately to both free blacks and mulattos. It should be noted that, as it was used in the eighteenth century, the phrase *gens de couleur libres* generally connoted the mulatto rather than free black populations of the French colonies. The term *affranchis* was also used in the eighteenth century to refer to free persons of color; here again, the persons connoted were primarily of mixed-race background. On the use of these terms, see the sources cited at p. 13, n. 32.

[124] Code Noir, art. 55 (1685). Article 55 reads: "Masters twenty years and above may manumit their slaves by means of all acts *inter vivos* or by reason of death, without being required to give a reason for the manumission, nor to seek the advice of parents, even if they are minors twenty-five years of age."

[125] Vonglis, "La double origine du Code noir," 106.

[126] On this theme, see especially Sala-Molins, *Le code noir*.

The rise of state-sponsored colonial slavery had to be translated in ideological terms as an "exception" to the French freedom principle. As Sue Peabody explains in her study of this doctrine, since at least 1571, French tribunals – particularly the Parlement of Paris – consistently upheld the claims of slaves to be free by virtue of having touched the soil of France. The decisions upholding those claims regularly invoked the authority of earlier royal legislation that, over time, had supposedly eliminated all forms of servitude in the realm as contrary to the monarchy's guarantee of freedom to its (French) subjects. Henry II's 1556 edict enfranchising all the serfs in the Dauphiné – a territory of the Holy Roman Empire ruled since 1349 by the king's eldest son or, in the absence of a male heir, by the king himself – was one of the most commonly cited pieces of this legislation.[127] As a result of the French tribunals' vigilance in enforcing the freedom principle, any deviation from the policy of forbidding the presence of slaves on lands ruled over by the king, even lands that lay across the Atlantic Ocean, had to be rationalized in one way or another.

In the Code Noir, this rationalization took the form of a requirement that slaves undergo conversion and receive instruction in the Catholic sacraments.[128] Other provisions that touched indirectly on religion, such as the prohibition on masters working their slaves on Sundays, were no less important in terms of the need to justify a system of forced labor. From the monarchy's perspective, whether these requirements were enforced was less important than their mere existence in statutory law, there for all to see. Throughout the colonial period, administrators and the high courts occasionally pursued violations of these provisions of the Code Noir,[129] and there were many points during the eighteenth century when the monarchy felt obliged to justify its role in the maintenance of colonial slavery. Yet it was the initial encounter between French law and

---

[127] Peabody, *"There Are No Slaves in France,"* 5, 21; Johnson, "The Reinvention of Slavery in France," 47.

[128] The precedent of Louis XIII appears to have been decisive in this regard. Montesquieu cites the account of a Jesuit missionary and traveler in the Caribbean, Father Labat, concerning the "extreme difficulty" that Louis XIII underwent in approving the very first law making slaves of blacks in the French colonies. After the king was told that enslaving the Africans was the "surest path" to their conversion to Christianity, he consented to the law. Montesquieu, *The Spirit of the Laws,* 249. In its very first article, the Code Noir invoked Louis XIII and called for the enforcement of his 1615 edict. Code Noir, art. 1 (1685).

[129] See, for example, "Arrêt du Conseil du Petit-Goâve," September 29, 1688, LC, 1:476 (ordering publication and public Sunday reading of the Code Noir in all the colony's parishes, and citing violations of the Code).

the law of slavery in 1685 that stood most in need of explanation. By the end of the seventeenth century, the Catholic components of the Code Noir had become largely meaningless formalities, lacking in the ideological urgency that brought them into being.[130]

The same could not be said for those elements of the law of slavery that served the purpose of controlling the extremes to which slave society was prone, including, as we have already seen, by preventing "excesses" on the part of either masters or slaves. The need to balance between the "abuses" and "dangers" of slavery (to invoke Montesquieu's terms again)[131] not only persisted throughout the Old Regime but actually grew stronger with time, in large measure because the ratio of slaves to whites itself increased with each passing decade. The enforcement of judicial limits on the punishment of slaves was one strategy available to colonial administrators concerned with the overall stabilization of plantation society. Another was the use and regulation of manumission.

Historians of slavery now commonly observe that manumission was useful as a way of releasing pressure on the system. Manumission provided slaves with an incentive to conduct themselves in ways that were compatible with the smooth functioning of the plantation economy. By

---

[130] On the significance of the Catholic elements of the Code Noir, see George Breathett, "Catholicism and the Code Noir in Haiti," *The Journal of Negro History* 73, no.1 (1988): 10; and Frank Tannenbaum, *Slave and Citizen* (New York: Knopf, 1946; reprint, Boston: Beacon Press, 1992), 65, 97–103. For criticisms of Tannenbaum's thesis that the Catholic colonies cultivated a concern for the moral personality of the slave absent from Protestant colonial cultures, see David Brion Davis, *The Problem of Slavery in Western Culture* (Ithaca, NY: Cornell University Press, 1966), 223–261; idem, "The Comparative Approach to American History: Slavery," in *Slavery in the New World: A Reader in Comparative History*, ed. Laura Foner and Eugene D. Genovese (Englewood Cliffs, NJ: Prentice-Hall, 1969), 60–68; idem, *Slavery and Human Progress* (New York: Oxford University Press, 1984), 11–12; Carl N. Degler, *Neither Black nor White: Slavery and Race Relations in Brazil and the United States* (New York: Macmillan, 1971; reprint, Madison: University of Wisconsin Press, 1986), 19–47. The disregard shown violations of the Code Noir's religious provisions was not as pronounced with respect to the provisions concerning fed slave rations, probably because an inadequately fed slave population implicated the stability of the colony, whereas the absence of religious instruction did not. For two examples of an effort to enforce the alimentary provisions, see "Règlement du Conseil de Léogane," May 3, 1706, LC, 2:70 (ordering habitants to plant food for the subsistence of slaves as well as to "prevent all the accidents that might happen in this colony"; complains of slaves running away for lack of food and others found dead or mistreated for stealing food from neighboring plantations); and "Ordonnance du Roi," December 30, 1712, LC, 2:337 (an antitorture ordinance issued in the context of slaves deserting and causing "a great disorder in the said islands"; slaves were to be fed and maintained in accordance with the royal ordinances).

[131] Montesquieu, *The Spirit of the Laws*, 254.

holding out freedom as a possible reward for good behavior, planters hoped to minimize the scope for resistance, even if good behavior was rarely, if ever, the actual reason why slaves were granted their freedom.[132] By contrast, the incentive for resistance would be much greater in a situation where slaves were left to labor under the impression that there was no escape from their condition. From this perspective, the legalization of manumission was as crucial to the maintenance of plantation society as any other aspect of the law of slavery.[133] Something like the "safety-valve" theory was expressed by Moreau de Saint-Méry in a 1789 pamphlet on the rights of the *gens de couleur*: Manumission is "useful" to the master, he wrote, because it "offers a precious hope to his other slaves."[134] However, there is little evidence that the drafters of the Code Noir had such psychological strategic considerations in mind when they decided to legalize the act of private manumission. The draft proposal of Blénac and Michel Bégon (a former magistrate on the presidial court at Blois, who succeeded Patoulet as the colonial intendant in 1683) stated simply that masters would be allowed to free their slaves, and that slaves would enjoy the rights of all other free persons without needing to acquire letters of naturalization "even if they were born in foreign lands."[135]

In accounting for the origins of article 55, it seems relatively clear that the framers of the Code Noir incorporated the preexisting practice of French Caribbean planters in Martinique, Guadeloupe, and Saint-Christophe to provide for the manumission of their slaves.[136] Manumission was also

---

[132] See, for example, Orlando Patterson, *Slavery and Social Death: A Comparative Study* (Cambridge, MA: Harvard University Press, 1982), 205; idem, "Three Notes of Freedom," 17–18; Robin Blackburn, introduction to Brana-Shute and Sparks, *Paths to Freedom*, 4–5; William D. Phillips, Jr., "Manumission in Metropolitan Spain and the Canaries in the Fifteenth and Sixteenth Centuries," in Brana-Shute and Sparks, *Paths to Freedom*, 32.

[133] Patterson, "Three Notes of Freedom," 18, 20 (describing manumission as an "integral" and "necessary" part of slavery).

[134] Manumission also serves "the state," Moreau continued, because "it adds to the political constituency" and permits "an intermediate state between slavery and freedom." Médéric Louis Elie Moreau de Saint-Méry, *Observations d'un habitant des colonies sur le mémoire en faveur des gens de couleur, ou sang-mêlés, de Saint-Domingue et des autres Isles françaises de l'Amérique, addressé a l'Assemblée nationale, par M. Grégoire* (N.p.: n.p., 1789), 19.

[135] "Projet de Règlement de Messieurs de Blenac et Bégon sur la police et autres matières concernant les Esclaves des îsles de l'Amérique," February 13, 1683, ANOM, F/3/90, fol. 17. For Bégon's background, see Vonglis, "La double origine du Code noir," 105.

[136] Palmer, "The Origins and Authors of the Code Noir," 389–390 ("an initial policy of free manumission came from the Caribbean, and the Roman flourishes are a secondary dimension, refining that policy"). Palmer's article is a rebuttal of Alan Watson, *Slave*

codified in the Roman law of slavery, however, and given the Code Noir's substantial debt to any number of Roman slave law provisions, it is likely that manumission was part of a more general borrowing from ancient precedents.[137] Manumission by testament was one of three methods by which a slave could obtain freedom under classical Roman law.[138] The other two methods involved the registration of a slave as a free person in the census and a legal fiction known as *vindicta*, whereby a master, in the presence of a magistrate, granted his slave freedom on the pretence that the slave was actually a free person wrongfully held in bondage.[139] That the Code Noir provided for the enfranchisement as well as the freedom of manumitted slaves is also consistent with the Roman law of slavery.[140] According to the *Institutes* of Gaius (161 A.D.), "[h]e becomes a Roman citizen in whom these three elements concur: he is over thirty years old; he was held by his owner in full Roman ownership; and he is freed by a statutorily recognized mode of manumission."[141]

Law in the Americas (Athens: The University of Georgia Press, 1989), 85–86, which argues for the primacy of Roman law influences on the Code Noir. Watson responded to Palmer's criticism in "The Origins of the Code Noir Revisited," *Tulane Law Review* 71, no. 4 (March 1997): 1053–1055. Bernard Vonglis stakes out a compromise position between these localist/customary and Romanist poles (albeit one that veers rather more toward Watson's than Palmer's conclusion). As Vonglis puts it, the Code Noir is best understood not as an adaptation of Roman law to local contexts, but rather as the result of a "grafting of an ancient antecedent onto a recent subject." Vonglis, "La double origine du Code noir," 107.

[137] This accords with Alan Watson's argument in his debate with Vernon V. Palmer. Contrary to Palmer, it is difficult to believe that the similarities between classical Roman slave law and the Code Noir were merely coincidences. See Pierre Jaubert, "Le Code noir et le droit romain," in *Histoire du droit social: mélanges en homage à Jean Imbert*, ed. Jean-Louis Harouel (Paris: Presses Universitaires de France, 1989), 321–331; and Vonglis, "La double origine du Code noir." Jaubert (at 323) argues that the Code Noir retained all of the essential elements of the Roman law of slavery except the principle of *favor libertatis*, which granted a newborn free status if the mother was free at any moment during the period of her pregnancy, even if she was a slave at the moment of giving birth. Jaubert's article, a critique of Sala-Molins's book *Le code noir*, goes too far in the opposite direction of downplaying the customary influences on the Code.

[138] Watson, *Roman Slave Law*, 23–25.

[139] Ibid., 24–25. By the time of the Justinian codifications in the sixth century A.D., there were several additional means by which a slave might gain freedom. Watson, *Slave Law in the Americas*, 30.

[140] Code Noir, art. 57 (1685). Article 57 reads: "We declare that manumissions undertaken in our islands substitute for birth in our islands, and that freed slaves have no need of letters of naturalization to enjoy the advantages of our natural subjects in our kingdom, dominions, and lands under our allegiance, even if they were born in foreign lands."

[141] Gaius's *Institutes* 1.17, quoted in Watson, *Roman Slave Law*, 24. The drafters of the Code Noir had access to Justinian's Institutes (533 A.D.) rather than those of Gaius

So the sheer weight of an ancient legal tradition, combined with the customs of French Caribbean planters in the decades preceding the promulgation of the Code Noir, provide the most convincing explanation for the availability of manumission in the French law of slavery. The safety-valve theory helps explain why the Roman law of slavery itself allowed for manumission, but the drafters of the Code Noir were borrowing from the text of Roman law, not from its historical context, of which they may well have been entirely ignorant.[142] That said, the context of Roman manumission has an intriguing bearing on the experience of eighteenth-century Saint-Domingue. Indeed, the history of manumission in the French colony in part replicated the Roman legislative experience with freed slaves. For more than a century after the "constitutional" moment of 1685, article 55 of the Code Noir would have consequences for Saint-Domingue that its authors could not have anticipated, rooted as their experiences were in the very different slave societies of Martinique, Saint-Christophe, and Guadeloupe.

Manumission was, in effect, a second kind of collective-action problem for slave society.[143] Here, too, Montesquieu showed the way. In a revealing chapter of *The Spirit of the Laws*, on the problem of manumission under the Roman Republic, Montesquieu clarified why slaveholders and public administrators could agree on the importance of maintaining the overall stability of a slave society while disagreeing as to how manumission could best serve that goal. Montesquieu began his chapter by observing that a republican state with a large number of slaves would find it necessary to emancipate many of its bondsmen. Keeping too many slaves would pose a problem of "containment," by which Montesquieu seems to have meant the threat of a slave revolution.[144] On the other hand, it was

(written in the late second century A.D.), but the former were modeled on the latter (Watson, *Roman Slave Law*, 6).

[142] Bernard Vonglis notes the paucity of trained jurists in the French Caribbean islands at the time of the preparation of the draft of the Code Noir. On the other hand, as Vonglis argues, the colonial notables and Catholic priests whose views would have been consulted in the preparation of the Code were likely familiar with classical literary culture, with its many references and allusions to slavery. The redaction of the Code Noir itself (in contrast to the consultation process that produced the draft) was strictly the work of Roman-law-educated royal lawyers. Vonglis, "La double origine du Code noir," 105.

[143] Cf. Patterson, "Three Notes of Freedom," 16 (describing manumission as "a private act with immediate social and public consequences").

[144] Montesquieu, *The Spirit of the Laws*, 261 ("[I]f there are too many slaves, they cannot be contained; if there are too many freed men, they cannot survive and they become a burden to the republic; moreover, the republic can be equally endangered by too many freed men and by too many slaves").

equally important not to go too far in the opposite direction by freeing too many slaves. Not only would such a policy impose an excessive burden of welfare on the republic by reason of the inability of freed slaves to care for themselves, it would also foster the same type of security risk posed by an overly large slave population, as the latter would conspire with their manumitted counterparts to overthrow the state. The task of the lawmaker was to keep an eye on both "drawbacks" at once, thereby arriving at that prudent balance between slavery and freedom that would preserve the tranquility of the republic.[145]

That was the theory. When Montesquieu proceeded to consider the actual legislation promulgated by the Roman republic to promote this moderate and considered end, he found only indecision and disarray:

> The various laws and the senatus-consults made in Rome for and against slaves, sometimes to hamper, sometimes to facilitate, the freeing of slaves, make their uneasiness in this regard easy to see. There were even times when one did not dare make laws.[146]

As an example of the occasional tendency to refrain from legislating at all on the question of manumission, Montesquieu cited Tacitus on the emperor Nero. Rebuffing a private petition to the Roman senate that would have allowed patrons to reenslave their former bondsmen for "ingratitude," Nero had declared that it was necessary to judge specific cases on their own terms and to avoid the temptation of a uniform rule. This exercise of executive restraint Montesquieu adopted for his own more intellectual purposes, claiming ignorance as to the course of action a "good republic" should take with respect to manumission. The answer was too dependent on "circumstances" to suggest otherwise, although Montesquieu did advise against manumissions en masse by means of "general laws" (the inverse of the policy vetoed by Nero). Whenever "new citizens" were to be introduced into a republic, their arrival should be achieved as far as possible by "imperceptible" means.[147]

Montesquieu went on to make a number of other recommendations about the treatment to be accorded freed persons and the duties for which they should be held responsible. Yet the central point of his analysis remained the "predicament" (*embarras*) that manumission posed to the essential structure of a slave society. Connoting awkwardness, confusion,

[145] Ibid.
[146] Ibid.
[147] Ibid.

and difficulty, Montesquieu's choice of term here suggested not merely a practical or policy dilemma but also a more deeply rooted, perhaps even psychological quandary. The vacillations of the Roman lawmakers, alternately widening and narrowing the path to manumission, bespoke a sense of strategic paralysis and indirection that seemed to spring from the sheer coexistence of freedom and slavery in the same society. Paradoxical though it may seem, prohibiting manumission threw a slave society into crisis: By closing off any chance of escaping from servitude, such a policy would leave slaves with no other way of improving their lot than outright rebellion. (This, in essence, is the contemporary historians' safety-valve thesis in eighteenth-century form.)[148] Yet the opposite approach – unlimited manumission – was equally subversive, because it so clearly undermined the hierarchy and labor supply without which a slave society could not continue to exist. To this extent, the problem of manumission was a logical one that transcended the practical issue of how to preserve an ideal ratio of slaves to freed persons. Yet at the same time, Montesquieu's belief in the importance of context and "circumstances" in determining the appropriate legislative approach to manumission suggested a faith in the capacity of law to find the elusive but necessary balance.

The result, then, appeared to be a halfway position, one that recognized the conceptual and structural difficulties posed by manumission to a slaveholding regime, but that also acknowledged the role of context and of contingency. Consistent with his more general philosophy of law, Montesquieu implied that whereas too much legislative tinkering in too many different directions would end in stalemate, the right sort of intervention at the right moments, which balanced the civil against the political status of freed persons, would enable a republican slave society to avoid both the danger of revolution and the burden of a welfare state. There was an ideal median, one that the Roman republic at its best managed to achieve.

By its own terms, Montesquieu's analysis applied only to republican governments generally, and to the classical Roman republic in particular. Yet here as elsewhere in the section on slavery, and indeed throughout *De l'esprit des lois* as a whole, one wonders whether Montesquieu had more contemporary forms of experience covertly in mind, in keeping with the underlying thrust of classical republican thought in eighteenth-century France. For the story of manumission in France's then-greatest

---

[148] Indeed, the theory goes back further than the eighteenth century, as the quotation from Bodin that serves as the epigraph to this chapter suggests.

colony suggests that the Roman legal "predicament" anticipated the dilemma French colonial administrators would face centuries later. The experience of freed persons in Saint-Domingue also points toward the same need to balance considerations of historical contingency and social structure, practical policy and psychological or conceptual tension, that Montesquieu identified in his analysis of the slaveholding republic of ancient Rome.

Planter brutality and the proliferation of individual manumissions on a large scale: These were the two great policy dilemmas that increasingly confronted the slave society of Saint-Domingue as it consolidated and then expanded in the eighteenth century. The philosophical disquisitions of Bodin and Montesquieu, and the ambiguous but suggestive context surrounding the formation of the Code Noir, open a window onto a burgeoning world of risk management that was at once familiar and novel. In time, the challenges posed by the harsh treatment of slaves and the control of manumission would come to take on a distinctive character in Saint-Domingue. In this remote outpost of the French monarchy, the extremes of slavery generated strategic anxieties that find echoes in but were also more radical and pervasive than those experienced elsewhere in the Atlantic world. Ultimately, the source of those anxious commonwealth stirrings must be traced to the stories of individual masters and slaves, whose daily interactions over the course of the colonial period created a complex matrix of risks and responses that found expression in both apologetic and critical accounts of the slave system.

2

Manumission was the Means

Manumission was the means formerly retained all over Europe to obviate
[slave] rebellions.

        – Jean Bodin, *Les six livres de la république* (1593)[1]

The dramatic rise of a free colored population in eighteenth-century
Saint-Domingue is one of the more remarkable stories of early modern Atlantic history.[2] From a figure of 500 (or 3.6 percent of the colony's total population) in 1700, the *gens de couleur* population grew
to 1,573 (3 percent) in 1715, about 5,500 (2.4 percent) in 1764, and
no less than 27,548 (5.2 percent) on the eve of the French Revolution.
More revealing are the figures for the growth of the free colored community relative to the size of the white population. The *gens de couleur*
community was a mere 4.8 percent of the size of the white population in
1681, 12.3 percent in 1700, 33.5 percent in 1764, and 89.4 percent in
1789. (When the French Revolution broke out, the slave population of
Saint-Domingue stood at 465,429 and the white population at 30,826.)[3]

---

[1] Jean Bodin, *Les six livres de la république*, 6 vols. (Lyon: G. Cartier, 1593; reprint, Paris:
Fayard, 1986), 1:106. Curiously, this one sentence does not appear in the 1606 translation
by Knolles, though the rest of the passage in which it was situated shows up in both the
1593 French text and the English translation.

[2] See Fick, "The French Revolution in Saint-Domingue", 55.

[3] Meyer, "Des origines à 1763," 136. Like all other demographic figures for Saint-Domingue,
these numbers appear to be based on the estimates provided by Moreau de Saint-Méry's
Description topographique, 1: 84–85. These numbers almost certainly underestimate the
actual number of freed persons in the French colony, because Moreau relied on official
census figures and therefore did not include those who were manumitted informally by

It was not simply the growth in absolute and relative terms of the *gens de couleur* population that set Saint-Domingue apart, however, but also the concomitant rise in their economic and political power, particularly in the three decades between the end of the Seven Years' War and the onset of the Revolution.[4] Only Jamaica and Brazil compare in the extent to which they fostered a significant community of wealthy planters of African descent.[5]

The story told by these numbers and by the politicization of the *gens de couleur* in the pre-revolutionary period is a relatively familiar one, at least within the confines of Caribbean history.[6] By contrast, the legal and administrative struggles that went on in the background of this long eighteenth-century story – the Old Regime battles over the regulation of manumission – are much less well known. Set against its colonial administrative backdrop, the narrative of the rise of the *gens de couleur* appears much less inevitable, and far more paradoxical, than it seems from our post-revolutionary point of view. The effect of the revolution was to make freedom the ideological norm and slavery the exception to the rule. From an eighteenth-century point of view, by contrast, freedom was the "problem" that needed to be explained, the truth that had not yet (at least in this corner of the Atlantic world) become self-evident.[7]

Rather than following a unilinear path toward a predefined end, until near the very end of the colonial period, manumission policy in Saint-Domingue navigated between the horns of a strategic dilemma. Beginning as early as the Code Noir, and supported by a tradition

---

their masters (the so-called *libres de savane*) to avoid payment of a freedom tax. Because the latter were freed via unofficial means, we do not have any reliable estimates for their numbers. See Debien, *Les esclaves aux Antilles françaises*, 380–381; and Blackburn, *The Overthrow of Colonial Slavery*, 168.

[4] Fick, "The French Revolution in Saint-Domingue," 55–56.

[5] Garrigus, *Before Haiti*, 4–5. On the complexities of manumission in Jamaica and Brazil, see, most recently, the essays by John F. Campbell (Jamaica) and Mariana L. R. Dantas and Keila Grinberg (Brazil) in Brana-Shute and Sparks, *Paths to Freedom*.

[6] The most significant of recent contributions to this subject is Garrigus, *Before Haiti*. See also Domingue Rogers, "Les Libres de couleur dans les capitales de Saint-Domingue: Fortune, mentalités et intégration à la fin de l'Ancien Régime (1776–1789)," (Doctoral Thesis, Université de Bordeaux, 1999); idem., "On the Road to Citizenship: The Complex Route to Integration of the Free People of Color in the Two Capitals of Saint-Domingue," in Geggus and Fiering, *The World of the Haitian Revolution*, 65–78; and Stewart R. King, *Blue Coat or Powdered Wig: Free People of Color in Pre-Revolutionary Saint-Domingue* (Athens: University of Georgia Press, 2001).

[7] See generally Davis, *The Problem of Slavery in Western Culture*.

(common to all of the world's great religions) that saw manumission as an act of piety,[8] the French law of slavery authorized private manumissions. The institutional weight of royal authority was placed behind the individual master's decision to free his slave (who, in the typical situation, was also the master's son or daughter). Yet manumission was also an inherently public act, because it served to admit the formerly enslaved into the formal community of royal subjects and commanded equality of treatment therein, subject only to a duty of respect toward the former master and his family.[9] Article 57 of the Code Noir relieved freed persons, even those born in "foreign lands," of the need to obtain letters of naturalization in order to enjoy the "advantages" of natural-born royal subjects.[10] Further, article 59 granted to freed persons "the same rights, privileges, and immunities enjoyed by free-born persons."[11]

In his history of the Haitian Revolution, published in 1853 and written from a perspective very sympathetic to the free people of color, Beaubrun Ardouin argued that the framers of the Code Noir drew these provisions from Spanish colonial legislation of the sixteenth and early seventeenth centuries.[12] The notion of equal rights for the freed person, according to Ardouin, was already long at work in Hispaniola prior to the assumption of French sovereignty. Yet the Spanish law of manumission, like the French, was itself a throwback to the essentially nonracial Roman law of slavery. However important the Spanish precedents may have been, the egalitarian mandates of the Code Noir promised a dramatic expansion of absolutist citizenship (or subjecthood) in a code otherwise designed to sustain the emerging racial hierarchy of French Caribbean society.[13]

---

[8] Patterson, "Three Notes of Freedom," 21.

[9] The duty of respect was enshrined in Code Noir, art. 58 (1685).

[10] Ibid., art. 57. By "foreign lands" the Code seems to have meant non-French territories in the New World, although this provision would also have applied to non-French territory in Europe.

[11] Ibid., art. 59.

[12] Beaubrun Ardouin, *Études sur l'histoire d'Haïti; suivies de la vie du général J.-M. Borgella* (Paris: Dézobry and E. Magdeleine, 1863), 1:76.

[13] Watson, *Slave Law in the Americas*, 76, 127, 130–133; Davis, *The Problem of Slavery in Western Culture*, 49–50; A. Leon Higginbotham, foreword to Watson, *Roman Slave Law*, ix–xi; and Watson, *Roman Slave Law*, 3. Davis notes that although "slaves in most ancient societies were not distinguishable by skin color or other racial characteristics, their masters often marked them with visible symbols of their lowly status" (48–49). He

Multiplied on a wide scale, as it soon was in the years after 1685, manumission came to be perceived by colonial administrators as one of the central regulatory problems of slave society, a prime source of the destabilizing influence that a well-ordered plantation colony needed to contain. The essence of that supposed influence was the fear that freed persons would conspire with the still enslaved to commit various acts of resistance, culminating ultimately in rebellion.[14] The task of the administrator, then, was to look beyond the immediate interests of the slaveholder and deter the demographic and political disaster that lay down the path of manumission. In short, manumission law, like the law of slavery more generally, was part of a politics of risk management, closely bound up with dueling notions of sovereignty over the slave.[15]

The regulatory tug-of-war that paved the way for the rise of the *gens de couleur* began with the Code Noir. By legalizing manumission and promising equal citizenship to the freed person, the Code Noir created a gap between legal norms and lived experience that would never close. In the early eighteenth century, administrators began to reverse the course announced in 1685, making manumission available only upon the consent of the colonial regime and limiting the application of articles 57 and 59 of the Code. Between 1711 and the 1770s, there followed a series of contests over who properly controlled the gates of freedom. These legal maneuverings, in which slaves and freed persons were themselves intimately involved, centered on phenomena such as the taxation and registration of manumission acts, reenslavement proceedings, naming practices, the passing of slaves as free, and the nature of the "respect" owed by freed persons to their former patrons (in accordance with article 58 of the Code Noir). In each of these cases, not surprisingly, the

also observes that black slaves were not entirely absent from the Roman Empire (50). On Old Regime concepts of citizenship and naturalization, see Peter Sahlins, *Unnaturally French: Foreign Citizens in the Old Regime and After* (Ithaca, NY: Cornell University Press, 2004).

[14] Cf. Robin Blackburn, introduction to Brana-Shute and Sparks, *Paths to Freedom*, 5.

[15] Ibid., 9. A useful point of comparison can be found in Gregory Alexander, *Commodity and Propriety: Competing Visions of Property in American Legal Thought, 1776–1970* (Chicago: The University of Chicago Press, 1999). Alexander (at 1) contrasts a view of property as absolute commodity – a means of creating individual wealth for its owner – and a view of property as "proprietary," as "the material foundation for creating and maintaining the proper social order, the private basis for the public good." In the first view, any "external" regulation of the owner's property rights is seen as an illegitimate invasion of those rights; in the second view, regulation is considered not only valid but even indispensable for the purpose of promoting the well-ordered society.

perception of the risks of manumission was closely related to questions of race and sex. What was the colony's capacity to absorb free persons of color? What status would they occupy? What did the prevalence of interracial sexual unions portend for the boundary between "white" and "black," slave and free? Such were the cultural anxieties, both conscious and subliminal, associated with manumission. The task of managing the hazards of freedom in Saint-Domingue reflected these anxieties and entailed regulation not only of manumission per se, but also of the rights and conduct of the *gens de couleur* population.[16]

The administrators' preoccupation with the excesses of large-scale manumission and the dangers of racial parity never fully receded during the colonial period; indeed, it reasserted itself a few years before the Revolution began. In the period after the Seven Years' War, however, a shift took place: Manumission came to be seen not only as a threat to the colonial order, but also as one of its greatest potential bulwarks. There were inklings of such a shift in thinking earlier in the colonial period, but only in the 1770s did administrators and planters alike begin looking regularly to manumission to contain rather than stoke the prospect of slave resistance and rebellion. At that time, freedom became conditioned on a lengthy term of service in the fugitive slave police, whose task it was to apprehend maroons ensconced in the colony's isolated mountain regions. The long-term political significance of this shift is somewhat obscured by the racially charged campaign mounted by white elites, in the patriotic climate of the post–Seven Years' War period, to marginalize and segregate the free colored community of Saint-Domingue.[17] Indeed, one of the unintended consequences of that campaign may have been to exacerbate an underlying movement in the strategic ramifications of colonial manumission policy. The curbing of manumission as a collective-action problem thus morphed into a similarly pragmatic, but tactically polar, strategy of enabling enfranchisement for purposes of stabilizing slave society in the pre-revolutionary period. The revolutionary co-optation of emancipation as an instrumental tactic in the imperial military battles for control of Saint-Domingue was an extension of this prior colonial experience.

[16] Whereas Orlando Patterson is correct that "there is no necessary relationship between manumission rates and the status of freedmen," there was, in Saint-Domingue at least, a very close relationship between the *regulation* of manumission (based in part on perceived rates of manumission) and the status of freed persons. See Patterson, "Three Notes of Freedom," 23–24.

[17] On this subject see generally Garrigus, *Before Haiti*, chs. 4–5.

So too was the politicization of the *gens de couleur* and their perception that the rights accorded to them long ago by Louis XIV and the colonial law of slavery were due to be enforced in an age no longer friendly to kings. For the free people of color were never merely passive objects of the precautionary strategies described in this chapter. Instead, they responded to those strategies by developing their own, often equally legalistic, means of securing the benefits promised by the Code Noir. The law of manumission was a product not only of white elite perceptions of risk, but also of the very different threats that freed persons correctly perceived to be attached to their vulnerable status in a world increasingly drawn along color lines. In their efforts to make sense of and manage those dangers, free people of color helped to shape the story of eighteenth-century manumission policy and lay the ground for revolution.[18]

THE MOVE TO REGULATION

The first hint that manumission in Saint-Domingue might involve something more complicated than the exercise of a master's sovereign will over his slave appeared in the Code Noir itself. In granting masters at least twenty years of age the right to manumit, article 55 specified that they would not be held to account for their motivation in freeing a slave.[19] Indeed, both the act and the consequences of freeing a slave were self-executing under the Code: Neither justification by the master nor naturalization of the freed person was required for the latter to enjoy all of the advantages of natural-born subjects of the king. However, in the very act of bestowing on slaveholders and freed persons these privileges, the Code Noir implied the possibility of their revocation. Paul Veyne's observation about Roman slaveholders – "The pleasure that a master takes in manumitting [his slave] confirms the authority by virtue of which he might equally well not do so" – applies with equal force to the position of the monarch in the scheme of authority envisioned by the French law of slavery.[20] Similarly, a king who could forego the need for letters of naturalization was also a king who had the power to mandate them.

---

[18] Cf. Blackburn, introduction to Brana-Shute and Sparks, *Paths to Freedom*, 12 (noting that although "manumission was quite different from emancipation … the enslaved and their supporters did eventually find a way of linking the one to the other").

[19] Code Noir, art. 55 (1685) ("sans qu'ils soient tenus de rendre raison de leur affranchissement").

[20] Paul Veyne, "Les esclaves," in *Historie de la vie privée*, ed. Phillipe Ariès and Georges Duby, vol.1, *De l'empire romain à l'an mil*, ed. Paul Veyne (Paris: Éditions du Seuil, 1985), 74.

In the years after 1685, masters freely exercised the liberties granted by the Code Noir. In 1711, however, colonial administrators took their first step toward scaling back the unlimited power of manumission granted to slaveowners in article 55. Pending a royal decision on manumission policy in the Caribbean colonies, the ordinance banned all further grants of freedom made without the written permission of the administrators. The move toward regulation was portrayed as a response to a breakdown in the moral and social order of Saint-Domingue: "The vast majority of the disorders that occur among the slaves in the French islands stems from the ease with which the planters grant them freedom [in exchange] for sums of money."[21] In order to pay for these socially destabilizing manumissions, the ordinance claimed, slaves had been taking to the taverns (*cabarets*) of the colony and plying their "infamous and lewd trade": a thinly veiled euphemism for prostitution, indicating that slave women were the primary target of the regulation. The 1711 act further alleged that *gens de couleur* were instrumental in facilitating the efforts of their enslaved counterparts to corrupt the morals and line the pockets of planters.[22]

This accusation stood at the beginning of a persistent eighteenth-century colonial tradition that suspected *gens de couleur* in general, and women of color in particular, of conspiring to various undesirable ends with the supposedly otherwise quiescent slave population of Saint-Domingue. In the view of colonial administrators, the commercialization of manumission and the rise of interracial sexual relations were two sides of the same coin. The growth of a free colored community entailed the formation of another kind of enemy within: a collection of individuals formally belonging to the free population, but whose origins and suspected racial sympathies linked them irrevocably to slaves on the plantations. The primal character of these anxieties helps account for the relative suddenness of the shift from a policy of laissez-faire to one of full-fledged regulation.

In requiring masters to seek the written approval of royal agents in the colony, however, the 1711 ordinance accomplished something more complicated than a straightforward repeal of article 55 of the Code Noir. Somewhat paradoxically, once masters were deprived of a final and absolute say on the question of manumission, their grip on the institution of slavery was weakened. The decision of colonial administrators to assume control over the dispensation of freedom was also a decision

---

[21] "Ordonnance des Administrateurs-Généraux des Isles," August 5, 1711, LC, 2:272.
[22] Ibid.

to insert themselves into a central, previously sacrosanct aspect of the master-slave relationship: the conditions under which the master's proprietary rights could be terminated. Beginning in 1713, when the monarchy ratified the 1711 ordinance with an equivalent regulation of its own, those conditions became a matter for determination at the level of colonial-administrative rather than domestic sovereignty. In the space of roughly twenty-five years, manumission lost its initial status as an aspect of the private ordering of racial and sexual relations in Saint-Domingue, and instead became one of the principal tools of collective governance in the colony.

The 1713 ordinance continued the emphasis on the link between paid manumissions and the collapse of social order in Saint-Domingue. Putting a price on freedom only encouraged slaves to have recourse to "[t]he most illicit of means in order to procure themselves the sums necessary for obtaining [their] liberty."[23] The new law required masters both "mercenary" and otherwise to obtain the joint written permission of both the intendant and governor-general of the colony, both of whom would be responsible for evaluating the "legitimacy" of the reasons for manumission. Not surprisingly, the requirement of justification had a parallel in Roman law: the lex Aelia Sentia of 4 A.D. required masters who wished to manumit slaves under the age of thirty to provide a "just cause" for doing so.[24]

The new standard left colonial administrators with a great deal of discretion, but it was not wholly devoid of content. As early as the 1720s, administrators in Saint-Domingue began to realize that manumission could be a tool of considerable strategic value. In 1721, in a special case involving the slave of the recently deceased intendant of Saint-Domingue, the governor and acting intendant granted freedom to the slave as a way of memorializing his owner and as a reward for good service.[25] In 1726, the Conseil of Petit Goâve held that freedom should be offered to any slave who captured dead or alive any of several slaves wanted as "thieves

---

[23] "Ordonnance du Roi," October 24, 1713, LC, 2:398.

[24] Watson, *Roman Slave Law*, 29; Vonglis, "La double origine du Code noir," 106. The impact of these Saint-Domingue developments was perhaps most clearly felt in Louisiana, where a new version of the Code Noir was promulgated in 1724 that prohibited manumissions without the prior permission of the Conseil Supérieur of that colony. Code Noir, art. 50 (1724). The full text of both versions can be found in Sala-Molins, *Le code noir*; and Robert Giacomel, *Le code noir: autopsie d'un crime contre l'humanité* (Nîmes: C. Lacour, 2003).

[25] "Ordonnance de l'Intendant en Fonctions et Ratification du Général," October 10 and 11, 1721, LC, 2:784.

and assassins." The value of the manumitted slaves was to be reimbursed to their masters.[26] Although this was not a ruling involving administrative oversight of a master's private decision to free his slave, it suggests an early awareness that admission to the ranks of the free could be used as an effective weapon in the effort to contain slave resistance. Regulating conduct at the limits of slavery, in effect, was seen as a method of controlling behavior at slavery's core.

When strategic purposes such as these were not involved, however, administrators relied on the just-cause standard to prevent masters from freeing their slaves during the second and third decades of the eighteenth century. In response, the planters eventually managed to make their concerns about regulated manumission known to the naval minister in Versailles. In a letter of March 29, 1735, the minister instructed the governor and intendant of Saint-Domingue to be more flexible when applying the just-cause standard in cases involving mixed-race persons rather than blacks.[27] The impetus to give mixed-race slaves preferential treatment over their black counterparts was a function of the lopsided male-female ratio in the colonies. On the whole, planters were more likely to resent the regulatory arm of the colonial administrators where the slaves in question were their own children. Because slavery in the French Caribbean was determined by the status of the mother,[28] the *affranchis* of Saint-Domingue could only have been the children of mixed-race unions between enslaved women and (free) white males. (Women slaves were distinctly more likely to be emancipated than their male counterparts, not simply because of demographic imbalances in the white sex ratio, but also because of various incentives and opportunities created by the Code Noir itself.)[29] Although planters were not the only free white males in the

---

[26] "Arrêt du Conseil du Petit Goâve," May 6, 1726, LC, 3:166–169.

[27] Minister to the Marquis de Fayet, March 29, 1735, LC, 3:420.

[28] Article 13 of the Code Noir reads: "If a slave marries a free woman, both the male and the female children shall follow the condition of their mother and shall be free like her notwithstanding the servitude of their father; and if the father is free and the mother enslaved, the children shall similarly be slaves." Code Noir, art. 13 (1685). The Roman law expression for this principle was *partus sequitur ventrem*.

[29] As Sue Peabody notes in this connection, article 9 of the Code rewarded free men who agreed to a Catholic marriage with their slave concubines by automatically manumitting the women and freeing and legitimizing their children. By contrast, free men who declined this offer were subject to fines and confiscation of the slaves. Article 56, moreover, automatically freed slaves named as beneficiaries of a will – a status more likely to fall to women than men. Sue Peabody, "Négresse, Mulâtresse, Citoyenne: Gender and Emancipation in the French Caribbean, 1650–1848," in *Gender and Slave Emancipation in the Atlantic World*, ed. Pamela Scully and Diana Paton (Durham, NC: Duke

colony – the *petit blanc* (or poor and middling white) population occupied positions ranging everywhere from vagabond to lawyer in the towns of Saint-Domingue[30] – only property owners had the influence necessary to affect the contours of policy in the metropole.

Many planters evidently acted as if the 1713 royal ordinance had never been passed, for in 1736, the monarchy issued another ordinance on the subject, highlighting the tendency of masters to free their slaves without the permission of the administrators. In addition to this method of evading the 1713 law, planters also had recourse to another, less egregious strategy: manumission through baptism of the children of slave mothers.[31] There was no authority in the Code Noir for this second strategy, which depended on the cooperation of colonial clerics. On the contrary, by requiring that all slaves on the island be baptized, article 2 effectively neutralized the potential for baptism to be used as a justification for manumission.[32] That planters went ahead and tried to take advantage of religion to circumvent the royal ordinance exposes a tension in the relationship between Catholicism and the slave regime in Saint-Domingue. Against the Code Noir's effort to harmonize the two, the behavior of planters and slaves in using baptism as an exit from slavery suggests that the politics of Catholic conversion in the colony were more complicated than the statutory text alone would suggest. There was clearly an instrumental character to this way of lending moral sanction and prestige to the (now) illegal act of private manumission. The cooperation of clerics in this endeavor was indispensable, as baptismal certificates could issue from their hands alone. However, religion would only have been useful in this instrumental way if baptism were held to contradict or at least subvert the institution of legalized slavery. Long-standing historical associations between Christianity and freedom were thus inseparable from the type of extralegal maneuvering reflected in the 1736 ordinance.[33] Those

University Press, 2005), 57. Cf. Rosemary Brana-Shute, "Sex and Gender in Surinamese Manumissions," in Brana-Shute and Sparks, *Paths to Freedom*, 175–190. Although emphasizing that women had far greater access to manumission than men, Brana-Shute argues that a desire to recognize the children created by sexual relations between masters and women slaves accounted for only a minority of the manumissions in Dutch colonial Suriname.

[30] Fick, *The Making of Haiti*, 17.

[31] "Ordonnance du Roi," June 15, 1736, LC, 3:453–454.

[32] Code Noir, art. 2 (1685).

[33] On the association between freedom and Christian doctrine, see Orlando Patterson, *Freedom*, vol. 1, *Freedom in the Making of Western Culture* (New York: Basic Books, 1991), 293–344.

associations clearly did not suffice in the eyes of colonial administrators to legitimate the use of baptism by planters and slaves as a substitute for official manumission; but the emancipative connotations of Christian status and identity help account for the difficulty administrators faced in establishing their power to control the line between slavery and freedom. Whether for instrumental or idealistic reasons, or a complicated combination of the two, in the aftermath of the 1713 ordinance, masters came to realize that religion could be enlisted in the effort to promote the sanctity of their domestic sovereignty over slaves.

The 1736 regulation tacitly repealed article 55 of the Code Noir by imposing a fine, set at the full value of the slave, on both unauthorized secular manumissions and manumissions by baptism. The new law also mandated the confiscation of any slaves – adult or child – whose manumission had not been ratified via the official mechanisms. Such a combination of penalties indicated that colonial administrators were willing to go to unusual lengths to put a lid on the proliferation of unofficial manumissions. This message was further reinforced in the late 1730s or early 1740s, when the administrators began imposing a head tax on manumissions.[34] The effect of the head tax, however, was directly opposite to that of the 1736 penalties. Rather than raising the costs of flouting the administrative ordinances, the tax increased the incentives for unofficial manumission.

Despite these measures, there is reason to believe that many planters still found the incentives more compelling than the costs. Indeed, unapproved manumissions became so regular and commonplace in the eighteenth century as to inspire the creation of a distinctive lexicon. *Liberté de savane* ("Savanna freedom") was a term of colonial usage for freedom granted unofficially by masters at the plantation level to slaves who generally remained in some capacity on their former owners' estates. In his 1974 study, Gabriel Debien distinguishes between this and *liberté régulière*, that is, freedom conferred via the formal channels of the colonial administrative state. Masters perceived the formal requirements of *liberté régulière* as an injury to their absolute right of property in slaves. In response to this perceived injury, and as a means of avoiding payment

---

[34] The exact date is unclear, and according to Gabriel Debien the tax was ordered without the backing of the monarchy. Debien's source for this tax is a passage from Dessalles' *Annales* of the Conseils Souverains of Martinique, but we know that the tax was applied to Saint-Domingue as well (although not necessarily at the same time) based on documents from the 1760s to which reference is made later in this chapter. See Debien, *Les esclaves aux Antilles françaises*, 374.

of the head tax imposed on manumissions as of the 1740s, French colonial planters increasingly resorted to the extralegal device of *liberté de savane*.[35] Most of the slaves who achieved their freedom via this device enjoyed conditions barely distinguishable from outright slavery.[36] As that reality suggests, the controversy occasioned by unofficial manumission was stoked in good measure by perceptions of the balance of power between masters and administrators. Yet there is also evidence that some free persons of color who remained on the plantations used their freedom to communicate with slaves and *gens de couleur* on neighboring plantations and with fugitive slaves in the mountainous areas of the colony. Thus even Savanna freedom cannot have been an object of total indifference to the governing authorities.

Although it may have been the most pervasive strategy for evading the administrative ordinances and head tax on manumission, *liberté de savane* was not the only such method. The perceived risks of decentralized manumission were especially conspicuous in the colony's many urban centers, where masters freed a significant number of domestic slaves who tended to the maintenance of their townhouses.[37] Here in the urban milieu, the distinction between slavery and freedom would have been harder for masters to obscure, even if all former slaves were required to demonstrate loyalty and respect to their former patrons in accordance with article 58 of the Code Noir (a policy enshrined in Roman law).[38] Indeed, the "libertinage" associated with unrestricted manumission was seen as an essentially urban phenomenon, to judge from the content of various regulations passed over the course of the eighteenth century.[39] The presence of formally free but substantively enslaved blacks on the plantations would have been harder for administrators to monitor, and there may have

---

[35] Ibid., 380.

[36] Ibid., 386–387. See also Debien's earlier study of the Maulévrier coffee plantation in Saint-Domingue, in his *Études antillaises (XVIIIᵉ Siécle)* (Paris: Armand Colin, 1956), 116–118.

[37] Many if not all of the ordinances governing the status and conduct of free blacks and mulattos in Saint-Domingue concerned those residing in urban areas, as will be discussed further. Debien also refers to free blacks and mulattos living in the *bourgs* (or small market towns), although his reference here is to Martinique. Debien, *Les esclaves aux Antilles françaises*, 377.

[38] Although article 58 was directly inspired by Roman law, it departed from classical precedent in declining to require that the freed person either perform services for or bequeath assets to the former master. Vonglis, "La double origine du Code noir," 106.

[39] The mingling of whites and free persons of color in the taverns of colonial towns was a repeated target of colonial administrators and judges. See, for example, "Ordonnance du Juge de police du St. Marc," December 5, 1766, ANOM, F/3/273, fols. 119–120. Note the etymological connection of the term "libertinage" to the French word for "freedom."

been a tacit agreement between planters and administrators that *libertés de savane* were acceptable so long as planters maintained the peace on their plantations. Whatever the relative balance of concern between town and plantation, masters persisted in finding new ways around the restrictions placed in their path. A few months after the 1736 ordinance was passed, the high court of Cap Français fined a master for leaving his slave "libre de sa personne" ("free in his person") in exchange for a daily remittance from the slave.[40]

The colonial regulation of manumission anticipated (and may even have stimulated) parallel efforts to control the status of blacks in the metropole. Only two years after the monarchy's ordinance calling for the stricter application of manumission controls in Saint-Domingue, a similar policy, which involved slaves brought by their masters to metropolitan France, was adopted. Louix XV's 1738 declaration addressed the persistent violation of an earlier edict requiring masters to register the entry of all slaves brought from the colonies to the metropole with the clerk of the admiralty court at the port of entry. This earlier measure, issued in 1716,[41] provided that slaves could not automatically claim to be free simply on the basis of having entered the territory of metropolitan France. It also stipulated that slaves could only accompany their masters for purposes of religious instruction or training in a useful craft, for a period of not more than three years. The 1738 declaration reiterated this policy and ordered the confiscation and deportation of all slaves whose masters failed to follow the formalities of the 1716 edict. The only freedom claims that would be considered valid were those resulting from the express testamentary will of the slave's owner, provided also that the master died within the three-year period, after which the slave was required to return to the colonies.[42]

---

[40] "Arrêt du Conseil du Cap Français," September 3, 1736, LC, 3:458. It is unclear whether the remittance was paid in the form of cash or in kind. The phrase "libre de sa personne" could also have meant "free of [the master's] person," implying that slavery was not only a legal relationship but also a personal attachment between master and slave. If this was in fact the intended meaning, it would seem likely that an urban domestic servant was involved in this case, as the notion of personal supervision would have been out of place in the context of a plantation work force consisting of numerous slaves, generally overseen by a manager (or *économe*) rather than by the master himself.

[41] This date is also potentially significant, coming three years after the 1713 royal ordinance concerning colonial manumissions.

[42] "Déclaration du Roi," December 15, 1738, LC, 3:547–550. See Peabody, *"There Are No Slaves in France,"* 37–39; and Johnson, "The Reinvention of Slavery in France," 86–95. For the 1716 edict, see LC, 2:525; Peabody, *"There are No Slaves in France,"* 15–22; and Johnson, "The Reinvention of Slavery in France," 49–51.

In the metropolitan and colonial contexts alike, the monarchy invoked a felt need to preserve a certain level of social stability as justification for intervening in the master-slave relationship. In the words of the 1738 declaration, slaves who came to France acquired "habits and a spirit of independence that could have unfortunate consequences."[43] Whether these consequences would take hold first and foremost in the metropole or colonies was not specified. Subsequent regulations on this subject made clear that administrators were concerned about both sides of the Atlantic, and that their concerns took the form of an anxiety about racial "impurity."[44] In any case, as early as 1738, the colonial monarchy was consumed with the perceived link between unregulated manumissions and slave resistance, and was willing to resort to the confiscation of slave property in order to break that link.[45]

The 1736 and 1738 measures did not mean that the monarchy was uniformly opposed to manumission. Nor was a failure to observe the formalities of manumission always an insuperable bar to freedom. In 1740, the king ratified the manumission of a female mulatto slave whose owner had subsequently returned to France and died there, even though the manumission was procedurally defective.[46] Moreover, as we have seen, there were numerous instances in which the public welfare of Saint-Domingue led colonial administrators and judicial authorities on their own account to manumit slaves. In 1750, the high court of Léogane freed a slave who had helped save all the slaves of his master's plantation from enemy invasion. The master was reimbursed for the price of the freed bondsman.[47] The same year the Conseil Supérieur of Cap Français

---

[43] "Déclaration du Roi," December 15, 1738, LC, 3:547.

[44] See Guillaume Aubert, "'The Blood of France': Race and Purity of Blood in the French Atlantic World," *The William and Mary Quarterly* 61, no. 3 (July 2004): 439–78.

[45] The connections between colonial and metropolitan manumission policy deserve further exploration. The language and policies of the relevant ordinances, their coexistence in the same documentary collection of colonial legislation, as well as their chronological proximity, indicate that something more than coincidence may have been involved here. Perhaps images of a racially "impure" and politically destabilized Saint-Domingue served to feed metropolitan fears of slaves in France, fears that produced the kind of racial policy reflected in the 1738 declaration and subsequent royal pronouncements on the subject. Conversely, it may be that restrictions against slaves and free persons of color in the metropole, as well as the ideology of racial purity that lay behind those restrictions, fed back into the design and enforcement of manumission policy in the colonial arena.

[46] "Ordre du Roi," January 25, 1740, LC, 3:589–590.

[47] "Arrêt du Conseil de Léogane," March 25, 1750, ANOM, CSD, F/3/271, fol. 701. The "enemy invasion" here could refer to an invasion either by British forces from Jamaica or by Spanish forces from the other side of Hispaniola.

provided that masters would receive one thousand livres for each slave manumitted by the government in exchange for denouncing "assassins" (a term that may have served as a euphemism for slaves suspected of using poison).[48] In two unusual cases, administrators took steps to free slaves in connection with either a contractual promise or the provisions of the law of nations.[49] In 1752, the Conseil of Cap Français manumitted a female slave who had been "unduly branded" by her master.[50]

On the whole, however, the trend was in the direction of magnifying rather than minimizing the risks of manumission: closing off doors rather than opening them. The 1736 ordinance turned out to be only the first demonstration of the colonial authorities' inability to stamp out – let alone keep track of – illegal manumission. Thus in 1758, the high court of Le Cap issued an *arrêt* requiring manumitted blacks and mulattos to register their freedom and baptisms with clerks of the court within three months of the date of manumission. The decision also prohibited lower-level judges (*sénéchaux*), clerks, and notaries from recognizing as free those who failed to comply with the registration requirement.[51] The implication was that informally freed slaves were using the local tribunals to gain at least some level of official recognition of their free status. Freed persons were unlikely to receive such favor from the Conseils Supérieurs, which were presided over by the same intendant who was responsible (with the governor) for judging the legitimacy of individual manumission petitions.

The 1758 decision reflected the wide array of legal consequences that flowed from free or unfree status in Saint-Domingue, notwithstanding the elaborate system of racial discriminations that developed over the course of the eighteenth century to limit the political, social, and economic opportunities of the *gens de couleur*.[52] A freed slave who had

---

[48] "Arrêt du Conseil du Cap Français," July 9, 1750, LC, 4:23.

[49] "Ordonnance des Administrateurs," February 18, 1751, LC, 4:51 (manumitting a slave taken from the coast of Guinea on condition of being returned to his father after eight years of service); "Ordonnance des Administrateurs," April 15, 1751, LC, 4:63 (freeing two blacks taken from Brazil who claimed to have been born free and were enslaved in violation of the *droit des gens*, or law of nations). For another example of the invocation of the law of nations for the same purpose, see "Arrêt du Conseil du Cap Français," July 18, 1771, ANOM, CSD, F/3/273, fol. 459 (concerning a mulatto defending his freedom with reference to the *droit des gens*).

[50] "Arrêt du Conseil du Port-au-Prince," September 9, 1752, ANOM, CSD, F/3/271, fol. 853.

[51] "Arrêt de Règlement du Conseil du Cap," April 7, 1758, LC, 4:225–229.

[52] On Old Regime discriminatory legislation targeting *gens de couleur*, see Auguste Lebeau, *De la condition des gens de couleur libres sous l'Ancien Régime* (Poitiers: A. Masson,

business before a court of first instance, or who had been sued in one of these local courts by another party, had certain rights and responsibilities before the court system (even if not every right granted to him or her by article 57 of the Code Noir was actually enforced). The mere act of participating in litigation (whether on the defensive or offensive end) could serve, intentionally or not, to reinforce the personal status of the parties whose specific legal claims were at issue. Judges as well as clerks and notaries were responsible for issuing documents (*actes*) in connection with court cases. In the instance of notaries, these documents did not even necessarily involve actual litigation, as it was common for residents of the colony to approach notaries for various certifications. As John Garrigus has shown, free people of color in Saint-Domingue were both assiduous and meticulous in using notaries and notarized documents to protect their status and pursue their commercial interests.[53] The notary was thus a critical intermediary in negotiating conflicts between the *gens de couleur* and white elites. In its 1758 *arrêt*, the high court of Cap Français effectively conceded that the cooperation (whether forced or voluntary) of notaries and other lower-level legal officials would be needed in order to contain the risks believed to accompany unregulated manumission.[54]

1903), 17 ff. The earliest evidence Lebeau cites of an administrative ban on *gens de couleur* serving in public functions is the "Lettre de M. le Général au Gouverneur du Cap," December 7, 1733, LC, 3:382. On October 13, 1766, Naval Minister César-Gabriel de Choiseul de Praslin (the cousin of his more famous namesake and predecessor, Choiseul de Stainville) wrote to the intendant of French Guiana that permitting the *gens de couleur* to acquire "positions and dignities" would be "absolutely contrary to the constitutions of the colonies" (quoted in Lebeau, 17). See also Debbasch, *Couleur et liberté*, 49–50, which cites a 1734 letter from the governor of Saint-Domingue requesting the king to prohibit persons of mixed racial background ("mésalliés") from holding any office and from serving in the white militia. In 1706, the Conseil of Cap Français permitted a "bastard mulatto" to exercise the office of royal prosecutor, although not without a protest from the court's senior magistrate. Debbasch, *Couleur et liberté*, 50 n. 1. Debbasch argues that it was not until the 1760s and the end of the Seven Years' War that administrators put in place a system of strict racial segregation in Saint-Domingue and elsewhere in the French Antilles.

[53] Garrigus, *Before Haiti*, 86–95. See also Rogers, "On the Road to Citizenship."

[54] By the beginning of the 1760s, the concern over the relationship between notaries and free people of color was widespread and extended beyond the phenomenon of illegal manumission. In 1761, the Port-au-Prince Council prohibited notaries and priests from registering contracts, marriages, and other legal acts for persons of "mixed blood" without specifying "the qualities that distinguish them from other citizens" – namely, whether they were black, mulatto, or quadroon (those regarded as having one quarter black ancestry). "Arrêt de Règlement du Conseil du Port-au-Prince," September 24, 1761, LC, 4:412; Garrigus, *Before Haiti*, 164.

THE "FREEDOM TAX"

In light of long-standing concerns over the commercialization of (private) manumission, the campaign to regulate freedom may have led inexorably toward taxation as a remedy. In the 1760s, conflicts between colonists and administrators broke out over the legitimacy and amount of the so-called *droits de Liberté* (freedom duties), a form of taxation that, as noted earlier, first came into use in Saint-Domingue sometime in the late 1730s or early 1740s. (The *droits de Liberté* hearkened back much further to the lex Manlia of 357 B.C., which imposed a duty of 5 percent of the slave's value upon manumission in Rome.) In 1761, the intendant of Saint-Domingue ordered that all taxes imposed upon the manumission of "mulattos and other persons of mixed blood" be reported to the controller of the navy. The revenues at issue – eight hundred livres per freed person – were to be considered as forming part of the "funds of the colony."[55] Thus, by the 1760s, the fungibility of freedom had become a function both of official colonial policy and the underground manumission economy.

The taxation of mulatto manumissions, it turns out, was one item on the agenda of an extended general protest against colonial fiscal policies and practices in 1764. A bit of background about the fiscal status of Saint-Domingue within the French empire helps to illuminate this controversy. The colony's two Conseils Supérieurs were responsible for assessing and collecting all taxes in Saint-Domingue, but the actual orders to impose new taxes came from the governor and intendant. Unlike the other French Caribbean colonies, Saint-Domingue enjoyed a specially protected fiscal status. Because the colony had been founded at great cost on "private" initiative rather than by royal agents, Saint-Domingue had been accorded a "complete freedom from taxation," in the words of the 1703 royal instructions to the governor.[56] The result was not the tax-free regime that those instructions would suggest, but rather a fiscal tradition that called for royal consultation with the Conseils Supérieurs whenever any taxes (new or customary) became necessary.[57]

---

[55] "Ordonnance de l'Intendant," October 3, 1761, LC, 4:417. It is unclear whether freedom taxes were imposed on the manumission of blacks as well, and what the status of such taxes would have been. Given that mulattos were the primary beneficiaries of manumission to begin with, the administrators may simply have reasoned that it was not worthwhile to collect taxes from the owners of black slaves.

[56] Quoted in Fieldhouse, *The Colonial Empires*, 40.

[57] Ibid., 41.

In 1764, the two high courts were asked to impose a total of four million livres in new and additional taxes in order to support the costs of colonial administration.[58] In a public statement of opposition to these prospective burdens, the colonists railed against the practice of taxing mulatto manumissions, which they blamed on royal ordinances and the colonial administrators rather than on the Conseils (which were simply the conduits for assessing and collecting taxes).[59] Specifically, the colonists' remonstrance invoked the 1713 and 1736 royal ordinances and the Code Noir's policy of confiscating (mulatto) children born of the "concubinage" of masters with their slaves. This reference to article 9 of the Code Noir was, in effect, a frank acknowledgment that manumission in Saint-Domingue was driven by the prevalence of sexual relations between masters and their slave concubines. (No effort was made, here or elsewhere in the archival records concerning manumission, to distinguish between consensual and coerced encounters.) Since the passage of the 1736 legislation, whether for purposes of punishing such concubinage or raising funds for "pious works," the governor and intendant during the 1740s (de Larnage and Maillart) had proposed taxing the required ratification of mulatto manumissions in the amount of "a certain sum" for the funding of the colonial *hôpitaux* (a kind of religious establishment for the care of the sick and needy).

The colonists' statement in opposition denounced these earlier eighteenth-century exactions as unfair, arbitrary, and unpredictable – all the more so once the revenues from the "freedom tax" (which amounted to 18,700 livres annually) began entering straight into the royal coffers rather than going to the benefit of the local hospitals.[60] Recalling the specially protected fiscal position of Saint-Domingue within the French state, the protest declared the "odious" freedom tax to have "no legal basis." But the *droits de Liberté* suffered from an even more important vice.

If one can, if one must punish libertinage, because it is dangerous and criminal, one must spare the fruit of this libertinage, because it is innocent. It is forbidden to sell freedom to the slaves or to give it to them conditionally. Will the king practice for his own part that which he prohibits for his subjects?[61]

---

[58] "Procès Verbal de l'imposition de quatre Millions faite par l'Assemblée des deux Conseils Supérieurs de la Colonie," January 30 to March 12, 1764, LC, 4:658–706.

[59] There is a brief discussion of this controversy in Fieldhouse, *The Colonial Empires*, 41.

[60] "Procès Verbal de l'imposition de quatre Millions," Jan. 30 to March 12, 1764, LC, 4:670. A *procès-verbal* is essentially an authorized statement.

[61] Ibid., 681.

The libertinage of certain masters, in other words, was a blatantly insufficient reason to hold hostage the freedom of the colony's mulatto population. This rhetoric plainly amounted to indicting the royal taxation of manumissions for complicity with the same commercialization of freedom that had first prompted administrators to scale back article 55 of the Code Noir in 1711.

The remonstrance contained two additional features worth noting. First, it indicated that even if the colonists' preferred solution – namely, the complete suppression of the freedom tax – was unrealistic, it was "indispensable" to limit the tax to mulatto manumissions only. Second, the *procès-verbal* called on the king to prohibit all testamentary manumissions because of the incentive they provided slaves to kill their owners in hopes of receiving liberty earlier than would otherwise be the case: "How many well-doing colonists [are] sacrificed to the impatient desire to hasten a freedom promised after [their] death!"[62]

In producing at least part of its intended effect, the planters' protest again highlighted the basic conflict between manumission and the claims of social order in the slave society of Saint-Domingue. In October 1764, the new administration of governor Charles d'Estaing reduced the freedom tax from eight hundred to three hundred livres. In doing so, the administrators announced their motive of increasing the size of the free population of Saint-Domingue while also preventing the increase from getting out of hand: "[W]e have aimed to realize both the great end of increasing the free citizens of this colony, and at the same time to prevent that increase from becoming abusive."[63] This formulation, evoking as it did Montesquieu's discussion of the dilemmas of manumission under the Roman Republic, rendered explicit the tension between *favor libertatis* (the principle of favoring freedom) and the need to contain the size of

---

[62] Ibid. I have not seen any evidence that this actually happened.

[63] "Ordonnance des Administrateurs," October 10, 1764, LC, 4:798–799. The tax was suppressed altogether by the royal ordinance on the civil government of Saint-Domingue of February 1, 1766 (LC, 5:18–19), but only temporarily. By 1775 the governor and intendant were once again authorized either to charge or dispense with freedom taxes, as the officials saw fit in particular cases. The 1764 *procès-verbal* did not mention any gender differential in the tax, and it is not clear whether Saint-Domingue followed the practice in Martinique, where the tax was gender specific. Between 1745 and 1766, planters in Martinique paid one thousand livres for male manumissions and six hundred for female manumissions. After 1766, male freedom taxes throughout the French Caribbean were set at one thousand livres and female taxes at two thousand livres where the female slaves in question were less than forty years of age. Debien, *Les esclaves aux Antilles françaises*, 374. See also Lucien Peytraud, *L'esclavage aux Antilles françaises avant 1789, d'après des documents inédits des Archives coloniales* (Paris: Hachette, 1897), 413.

the free colored population. Further, it sought to remind colonists of the destabilizing potential of an overly large community of freed persons. By force of circumstance, the debate over the freedom tax, like other efforts to regulate manumission, unfolded in relation to a preemptive strategy that viewed the free colored community as a harbinger of black unrest, if not revolt.

From the point of view of the *gens de couleur* themselves, it was the permeability of the line between slavery and freedom that caused concern. To judge from the language of the 1764 ordinance, many free persons of color faced considerable difficulties in being able to provide valid documentation of their freedom. The 1764 legislation reflected these difficulties with its assurance that "all those who pretend to have obtained their freedom" will receive the formal "act of freedom" upon presentation of the "necessary certificates" from their (former) masters, as well as a receipt for payment of the three-hundred-livre tax to the treasurer of the colony.[64] In addition to such formal proof of free status, the administrators noted that they would provide free people of color with the "distinctive prerogatives and marks that seem useful to us for ensuring that these persons not be confused with slaves from now on."[65]

Prior and subsequent records clarify that colonial administrators understood the problem of "confusion" in two senses. First, in the sense described here, free persons of color faced the possibility of being held in slavery in violation of their actual status. In the absence of a rigorously enforced documentation system, however, colonial administrators were no less concerned about the possibilities available to slaves to pass as free. The "distinctive prerogatives and marks" that were granted to free persons of color could be just as useful for purposes of policing the second of these concerns as they were for purposes of preventing the first. The Conseil d'État in Versailles demonstrated as much with its decision of July 21, 1767. In a rare exercise of its final jurisdiction over the colonial high courts, the Conseil provided that all blacks who had been imprisoned on suspicion of running away (*marronage*) and who were unable to prove their freedom in accordance with the 1713 ordinance were to be sold as abandoned slaves.[66]

---

[64] "Ordonnance des Administrateurs," October 10, 1764, LC, 4:798.

[65] Ibid., 799.

[66] "Arrêt du Conseil d'État," July 21, 1767, LC, 5:93–94. This decision was confirmed by a royal ordinance of November 18, 1767 (LC, 5:141). The Conseil d'État was acting to quash a 1764 administrative ordinance that tried to replace the policy of selling arrested fugitive slaves at the king's profit with a policy of forcing them to labor in the chain gangs

REENSLAVEMENT, RACE, AND REFORM

It is not coincidental that the mid-1760s witnessed such rising concern over the "confusion" caused by manumission and the porosity of the line between slavery and freedom. The heavy French losses in North America stemming from the Seven Years' War, formalized in 1763 with the Peace of Paris, were rife with implications for the French Caribbean territories, especially for Saint-Domingue. As metropolitan administrators sought to restructure and reform the French empire along more military lines in the years after 1763, they looked with skepticism on the loyalty of the leading white colonists of Saint-Domingue. The colonists sought at once to counter these concerns and to vindicate their own interests in the process of imperial reform by joining with colonial administrators in the adoption of an increasingly patriotic, pro-metropolitan orientation. As John Garrigus has argued, the patriot agenda of these years took the form of a turn to biological racism, which had the effect of subjecting free people of color to a much wider and more pronounced set of disabilities than they had ever previously encountered. According to Garrigus, the legal fashioning of a new "white" political community not only helped bridge the gap between colony and metropole, but it also mollified the resentment of *petits blancs* toward the wealthier white and free colored residents of Saint-Domingue.[67]

Predictably, in this context, the putative risks of manumission were increasingly cast in dire racial terms after the Seven Years' War, and free people of color were correspondingly assertive in protecting their status. If anxiety over the "confusion" caused by manumission was one reflection of this postwar turn to racism, another was the more extreme phenomenon of reenslavement. The possibility of an actual return to slavery hung ominously over the heads of those fortunate enough to escape from bondage in Saint-Domingue. Not coincidentally, the question of whether and under what conditions freed persons could be reenslaved raised some of the same issues of jurisdiction and sovereignty that manumission brought to the fore.

A fascinating and probably unrepresentative example of the reenslavement cases involved a free woman of color and resident of Le Cap named

established in different parts of the colony. The nature of the proof needed to establish a slave's freedom depended on whether the manumission took place before or after 1738.

[67] Garrigus, *Before Haiti*, 8, 109–170. Contrary to Garrigus, Guillaume Aubert traces the emergence of a racialism that emphasized ancestry over social and political rank to well before the Seven Years' War. Aubert, "'The Blood of France.'"

Marion.[68] In 1765, the governor and intendant of the colony, Estaing and Magon, presided over a special trial for Marion that upheld her manumission against the wishes of a master who wanted her reenslaved for "ingratitude," pursuant to article 58 of the Code Noir. The defendant was a tailor named Arnaud Bruère ("dit Villeneuve"), a resident of Cap Français. As plaintiff, Marion had filed the initial suit with a *sénéchal* of Le Cap six years before, in 1759, one year after her manumission in reward for "good and agreeable services"[69] had been ratified and confirmed. The procedural background reveals the many obstacles placed in the way of free persons of color (and perhaps especially free women of color) who tried to use the colonial court system to defend their rights against white colonists. Marion's determination to have her case fully heard in spite of those obstacles paid off, for she ultimately succeeded in carrying her appeal directly to the governor and intendant: another measure of the unusual and highly sensitive nature of the proceedings.[70]

In 1762, Villeneuve had joined the case in opposition to the ratification of Marion's freedom, which he insisted had been issued in a "surprise to the religion of our predecessors."[71] His argument before the governor and intendant in 1765 was, quite simply, that Marion had violated article 58 of the Code Noir by failing to demonstrate sufficient "gratitude" to him. Under article 58, all freed persons were to show "a singular respect towards their former masters, their widows, and their children; so that the injury a [freed person] may do to them is punished more seriously than if it had been done to another person."[72]

At the same time, the article went on to specify, this duty of gratitude did not sanction any other "burdens, services, or beneficiary claims" that a former master might find it in his arbitrariness to impose. As one example of Marion's ingratitude, Villeneuve argued that she had refused to remain in his household for a period of fifteen days after the ratification of her freedom.

In response, Marion asserted that Villeneuve's only real grievance was her determination to enjoy the privileges of her freedom. "The state of

---

[68] Marion's full name is unavailable.

[69] "Extrait de l'instance jugée au tribunal du Général et de l'Intendant," August 6, 1765, ANOM, CSD, F/3/272, fol. 833.

[70] "Jugement de Mrs. les Général & Intendant," August 6, 1765, ANOM, CSD, F/3/272, fols. 829–30.

[71] This is a somewhat ambiguous phrase apparently intended to signify that the ratification did not accord with judicial precedent.

[72] Code Noir, art. 58 (1685).

freedom that a [female] slave acquires as a result of manumission," she argued, "may be impaired after the fact only by circumstances capable of affecting public policy [*la politique*] and government."[73] Just as colonial administrators had invoked a broader "public" interest to justify their restrictions on manumission, Marion's approach appealed to the idea that there were distinct limits to the domestic sovereignty of masters, whether in respect of manumission or reenslavement. Any attempt to exceed those limits implicated concerns that went beyond the interests of particular plantations, masters, or slaves. Marion conceded that she owed a lifelong duty of respect to Villeneuve, but she insisted that this duty did not authorize him to demand her services as a slave after he had himself decided to free her. Estaing and Magon rejected Villeneuve's case on the grounds that he had failed to demonstrate "any proof" of Marion's ingratitude.[74]

This case was only one of several to involve the phenomenon of reenslavement in the eighteenth century. Other cases held in favor of reenslavement as a way of punishing what colonial authorities regarded as the most serious crimes a free person of color could commit.[75] In terms of manumission policy generally, however, Marion's case was all too typical in that it symbolized the renewed determination of the monarchy and its colonial administrative agents to protect and advance the interests of "policy and government" that Marion identified as central to her own case. In 1766, as part of a general ordinance reorganizing the "civil government" of Saint-Domingue in the aftermath of the Seven Years' War, the king provided that permissions for manumission were to be granted conjointly by the governor and intendant.[76] This was not so much a change in the legal requirements for manumission, as the 1736 ordinance had required the permission of both officials. Rather, it appears to have

---

[73] "Extrait de l'instance," August 6, 1765, fols. 833–834. These are not the direct words of Marion but rather a summary of her remarks as that summary appears in the "Extrait de l'instance." I have interpolated the adjective "female" here to reflect the use of the expression "une esclave" in this passage.

[74] Ibid.

[75] "Ordonnance du Roi," June 10, 1705, LC, 2:36–37 (providing that free persons of color who help slaves run away will be reenslaved); "Arrêt du Conseil de Léogane," January 14, 1744, ANOM, CSD, F/3/271, fol. 166 (reenslaving a free woman of color who beat her female slave to death); "Arrêt du Conseil du Port-au-Prince," May 10, 1764, ANOM, CSD, F/3/272, fol. 565 (reenslaving a *gen de couleur* for killing another black; the act was defined as a homicide in the case title provided by Moreau de Saint-Méry, although not necessarily in the opinion itself).

[76] "Ordonnance du Roi," February 1, 1766, LC, 5:18–19.

been a move to prevent possible conflicts of opinion between the two administrators (or, in what amounted to the same thing, efforts to bypass the potential refusal of one and to curry favor with the other).

Even for those free persons of color who, like Marion, managed to avert the fate of reenslavement or were careful enough to carry around at all times the documents needed to ward off "confusion," life on the other side of slavery rarely amounted to the rosy condition promised in article 59 of the Code Noir. Far from the state of complete legal equality with persons "born free" that was enshrined in that article, the experience of freedom for most if not all free persons of color in the 1760s and 1770s could never be totally severed from the conditions and legacies of slavery. The capacity of manumission to draw a sharp line between slavery and freedom was limited partly by the influence of Roman legal precedents (as in the duty of "gratitude" owed by freed persons to their patrons under article 58). Yet the most important and pervasive reason why manumission was never allowed to achieve its full force in Saint-Domingue was the obvious one of racism.

This was not just any form of racism, but a particular understanding whereby slavery was held to leave a permanent stamp on all blacks and their descendants, regardless of whether they had been born free or enslaved. Such a view approximated the "one drop rule" of the American antebellum South, although it was never applied in truly systematic fashion in Saint-Domingue, even after the Seven Years' War.[77] The clearest expression of the new attitude was a ministerial directive dated January 7, 1767, that touched on the comparative status of manumitted persons of Indian and African descent in Saint-Domingue. "His Majesty has always admitted, and he intends that his High Courts admit as well, an essential difference between Indians and Negroes," the directive stated. Unlike Indians, who were born free and could be assimilated (however incongruously) to the category of "Subjects of the King originating from Europe," blacks had been brought to the colonies strictly for purposes of enslavement. That "first stain" "extends to all of their descendants, and … cannot be erased by the gift of freedom."[78] This concept of race as

---

[77] See Garrigus, *Before Haiti*, 3, 7.

[78] The original wording for "the gift of freedom" is "le don de la liberté." Minister to the Administrators, January 7, 1767, LC, 5:80 ("containing a decision on three points relative to the black and Indian races"). This document has many other interesting things to say about perceptions of Indians and persons of Indian descent in colonial Saint-Domingue, but I use it here only to underline the point about the perceived "stain" of slavery.

irrevocable stain conflicted with the monarchy's original guarantee, in the Code Noir, of full legal equality to manumitted slave. The thrust of the ministerial directive, by contrast, was that continued racial subordination was justified, not by race per se, but rather slavery – thus evoking the legacy of colonial history *since* the time of the Code Noir as a rationale for departing from that code. Slavery was capable of closing the perceived loophole that had been opened up by the availability of manumission under the royal slave legislation.

The new racism of the post–Seven Years' War period coincided with a move by the colonial high courts to assert jurisdiction over manumission. In 1767, the Conseil of Port-au-Prince issued a new set of regulations more elaborate than anything the previous administrative ordinances had devised. Acknowledging violations of the 1738 and 1766 ordinances, the Conseil required that before manumission could take effect, a master would have to "publish" the requisite permission of the administrators before three consecutive audiences of the local court in whose jurisdiction he resided.[79] The primary rationale was to permit creditors of the master an opportunity to assert their interests in connection with the sale of valuable slaves.[80] The next month, the Conseil of Cap Français followed with an almost identical *arrêt* of its own.[81]

In response, the Conseil d'État used its appellate authority to quash the decision of the Cap Français high court as contrary to the 1766 ordinance on civil government and as a violation of the general principle that only the king could modify the terms of his ordinances (in this case, the 1736 royal ordinance on manumission). Three years later, the parallel decision by the Port-au-Prince tribunal was quashed on essentially the same grounds: "[E]verything touching on manumissions belongs exclusively to the [jurisdiction of] the governor and intendant of the islands."[82]

The king was evidently more concerned with colonial judicial overreaching than with the substance of the quashed decisions. For on the same day in July 1768 that it threw out the decision of the Conseil in Le

---

[79] "Arrêt du Conseil du Port-au-Prince," December 29, 1767, LC, 5:149.
[80] Garrigus, *Before Haiti*, 86.
[81] "Arrêt du Conseil du Cap," January 28, 1768, LC, 5:153.
[82] "Arrêt du Conseil d'État," May 16, 1771, ANOM, CSD, F/3/273, fol. 437. It is curious that the decision of the Port-au-Prince Conseil was allowed to stand for three and a half years whereas the same decision by the northern Conseil was not. The gap may reflect simple unevenness and inefficiency in the appellate process, or it may have reflected the delicacy of the question of manumission.

Cap, the monarchy reentered the fray with its own attempt to seal the porous boundary between slavery and freedom. Three aspects of the new ordinance are of particular significance here. First, the law underlined the "very uncertain" and insecure status of freed slaves formerly in the ownership of planters indebted to creditors back in France. Enough of these creditors were taking steps to make good on their loans by nullifying the manumission of and seizing their debtors' human property to prompt the intervention of the monarchy. Second, the ordinance singled out the "numerous slaves" who claimed to be free simply on the basis of permits issued by their masters – the system of the Code Noir, still alive and well after eighty-three years. Finally, the new measure criticized the behavior of masters and their inheritors who "use ... against their slaves the vices stemming from their manumission, and return them to slavery after having allowed them to enjoy the advantages of freedom for several years."[83] The monarchy thus demonstrated that it was capable of recognizing the manipulation involved in supposing that free people of color had become "corrupted" by the combination of their mixed-race background and life without slavery.

The 1768 ordinance reflected the competing interests at stake in the debate over how to reform manumission. By the 1760s, these included the commercial interests of creditors in addition to the efforts of colonial administrators to prevent slaves from passing as free. Most remarkably, the law incorporated the protests of free persons of color who faced legal or extralegal reenslavement in violation of their protected status under the Code Noir – an indication of the growing political and economic power of free people of color in the face of growing racism. Few documents better illustrate the regulatory "predicament" (*embarras*, to use Montesquieu's term) of manumission in this slave society, for it was clearly impossible, in the long run, to satisfy all of these conflicting agendas.

The intractable nature of the predicament was borne out by the essential similarities between the monarchy's dictates and the recent colonial judicial measures they had just superseded. Indeed, the 1768 royal ordinance seems to have simply taken the substance of the Conseil's *arrêts* and dressed them up in a form more compatible with the monarchy's view of its own sovereign prerogatives. Predictably, the royal ordinance called for the renewed enforcement of the 1736 and 1766 ordinances. It then went on to provide for a new fine of three hundred livres for any

[83] "Ordonnance du Roi," July 10, 1768, LC, 5:190–191.

master who failed to observe the threefold publication requirement that had been proposed in the Conseil's decision.[84]

The Conseils Supérieurs of Le Cap and Port-au-Prince appear to have taken the message from the monarchy, at least to judge from the absence of any subsequent royal disallowances of colonial decisions on the subject of manumission. Problems remained, however, at the level of the practical implementation of the royal ordinances. One such problem involved yet another variation on the theme of "confusion" that had preoccupied judicial and administrative commentary about colonial manumission law since the early eighteenth century. To the preexisting confusion of free persons of color with slaves (and of slaves trying to pass as free) was added a form of ambiguity that cut across the dividing line of race.

In mid-1773, the administrators issued a regulation complaining that manumitted slaves were assuming their former master's last names, with deleterious consequences for the orderly disposition of property in the colony and, more broadly, for the color line itself:

The usurped name of a white race can place in doubt the state of persons, throw confusion into the order of inheritances, and ultimately destroy the insurmountable barrier between the whites and the *gens de couleur* that public opinion has put in place and that the Government in its wisdom maintains.[85]

The "insurmountable barrier" of skin color, according to this regulation, was a product, not of law, but social custom, or "public opinion." To guard the integrity of that barrier, it was necessary to prevent the "usurpation" of names supposedly belonging to the "white race." To this end, the regulation required masters henceforth to provide freed slaves with "African" names and to use only those names on manumission acts. In addition, priests, notaries, clerks, and other officials were all prohibited from issuing or acknowledging the legitimacy of any documents on which "Negroes and persons of color" – whether born free or manumitted – inscribed as their own (or asked to have so inscribed) the last names of their masters or "putative fathers." Colonial legal officials and clerics were further required to advise the royal attorney whenever any

[84] Ibid. It is interesting, in light of the possible connections between colonial manumission policy and the "police des noirs" in the metropole discussed in note 45 of this chapter, that one year after the events just described, the minister issued a directive to the administrators calling on them to close a loophole exploited by colonists who either brought free persons of color to France or freed their slaves before doing so. Minister to the Administrators, October 3, 1769, ANOM, CSD, F/3/273, fols. 341–342.

[85] "Règlement des Administrateurs," June 24 and July 16, 1773, LC, 5:449.

nonwhite persons attempted to enter into contracts. Before they could do so, free people of color would be required to present their baptismal certificates or acts of freedom.[86]

A complex pattern of behavior was at work here, involving elements of both attribution and appropriation. On the one hand, by banning masters or colonists holding "public" offices from *attributing* "white" names to slaves, the regulation revealed a degree of collaboration between whites and free persons of color in confounding the barriers of race in Saint-Domingue. The reference to the putative fathers of *gens de couleur* highlights the blood ties that united (white) fathers, black or mulatto slave mothers, and their mixed-race children in the act of manumission. In naming their own sons and daughters after themselves, white colonists bestowed a form of social prestige that could mitigate the discrimination to which free blacks and mulattos were subject. On the other hand, the use of the adjective "putative" indicates that, in some cases, whites sought to deny their blood ties to their mulatto children. Considered from this perspective, the sharing of names between white fathers and mulatto children was regarded as a sign of dishonor that could serve to stigmatize and discredit the former in the eyes of colonial society. Denying parentage was the most direct way of warding off this stigma, but it often failed to work. Increasingly toward the end of the eighteenth century, controversies over the supposed "stain" of having fathered a mulatto or other nonwhite child were the subject of quite contentious and sensitive litigation.[87] For their part, free persons of color could and did try to capitalize on the racial dividends paid by a "white" or "European" name. As the 1773 regulation suggests, there were ways of asserting title to an unwilling master's name with the cooperation of members of low-level colonial officialdom.[88]

---

[86] Ibid., 449–450.

[87] A good example is the case of a white militia officer named Chapuiset, accused in the 1770s of having "mixed blood." See Garrigus, *Before Haiti*, 164–165. By the eve of the Revolution, an elaborate and oft-remarked pseudo-biological classification scheme had been developed by Moreau de Saint-Méry to account for all of the various degrees of "racial mixing" that had developed in the colony. The further down the generations one traced these relationships, the greater the number of "racial types" Moreau was able to identify. Moreau was able to count and label 128 such types (256 by some accounts, depending on how far down the generational lines one goes). See Moreau de Saint-Méry, *Description topographique*, 1:86–89; Garrigus, *Before Haiti*, 156–159.

[88] After the regulation was promulgated, some free people of color responded by inverting their former names: Thus Jean Décopin became Jean Pain Cordé, for example. *Gens de couleur* also had recourse to such remedies as hyphenation, the adoption of African names, and borrowing of names from other members of one's family network. See John

THE CASE OF MARIE-VICTOIRE

The showdown over naming practices attested not only to elite white anxiety about racial confusion and the breakdown of hierarchy, but also to the legal savvy and pragmatism of free blacks and people of color, who were discovering new paths around the impediments colonial administrators set in their path. The running eighteenth-century tug-of-war between administrators and planters over the legitimacy of "unconfirmed" manumissions had given rise to a host of unanticipated battles over passing, reenslavement, naming, and related phenomena. In taking on these battles, freed persons demonstrated their determination to seize control of their fates in a world that lay beyond, but never far from, slavery. As they fought to preserve and consolidate their free status, *affranchis* and *gens de couleur libres* proved that no legal cards were off the table, and they invoked the authority of the law – particularly the banal but immensely valuable powers of the notariat – against whites with increasing confidence in the 1760s and 1770s.[89] Indeed, as Dominique Rogers has argued (contrary to Garrigus), this confidence may well reflect the increasing integration of free people of color into elite colonial society during the late ancien régime, particularly in the urban centers of Cap Français and Port-au-Prince, notwithstanding the racial legislation enacted in the aftermath of the Seven Years' War period. Whatever the reality may have been, it is clear that, far from being inert targets of administrative risk management, freed persons moved in a world structured by their own evolving perceptions of risk, and they actively managed the risks to their freedom that they daily faced.[90]

If this entailed defending the sovereignty and prerogatives of current or former masters in the face of administrative opposition, freed persons were entirely willing to oblige (provided, of course, that the master was disposed in favor rather than against the freedom of his slave). However, it was also possible for the competing interests at stake in manumission to align in more contradictory and less predictable ways. This was partly because slaves who received their freedom as a result of a master's last will and testament, pursuant to article 55 of the Code Noir, often had to

D. Garrigus, "'Sons of the Same Father': Gender, Race, and Citizenship in French Saint-Domingue, 1760–1792," in *Visions and Revisions of Eighteenth-Century France*, ed. Christine Adams, Jack R. Censer, and Lisa Jane Graham (University Park: Pennsylvania State University Press, 1997), 149 n.35.

[89] See Rogers, "On the Road to Citizenship," 67; Garrigus, *Before Haiti*, 88–95.

[90] Rogers, "On the Road to Citizenship," 76.

fend off the contrary claims of both creditors and inheritors. The possibility of a more contradictory outcome arose, too, because colonial governance involved multiple jurisdictional levels that did not always line up in the same way.

The obstacle course created by these dynamics, as well as the perseverance of free people of color in seeking to overcome them, are illustrated by an extraordinary 1775 case featuring a mulatto woman and her child.[91] The case began with the last will and testament of a planter in Saint-Domingue and went on to receive a hearing at the highest level of royal administrative and judicial authority in France. Philippe Morisseau, a resident of the colony's Artibonite valley, left behind a will that provided for the manumission of six of his slaves, all of them mulattos. At his death in 1770 or 1771 (the exact date is unclear), all six apparently left the plantation, allegedly "without the permission" of the inheritor, who was the deceased planter's brother, sieur Morisseau d'Ester (hereafter referred to simply as Morisseau). Morisseau brought suit against the (former) slaves before the governor and intendant of the colony, claiming that the six were required by law to obtain his consent to the manumission as the inheritor and current owner of his brother's property. In light of this "certain principle" of colonial law (as the case report described it), Morisseau asserted his right to demand that the fugitive slave police, known as the *maréchaussée*, seek out and arrest the departed slaves. The governor and intendant ruled in his favor by an ordinance dated February 15, 1771. At the same time, the ordinance "exhorted" Morisseau to grant the freedom that his deceased brother evidently intended to confer upon the six mulattos if they proceeded "by their conduct to merit" the enforcement of the will.[92]

According to the case report, the six mulattos began to "defy and desert" him. The report singled out a mulatto woman (Marie-Victoire) as the principal culprit of the six, responsible for delivering "the most insolent addresses" to Morisseau and his wife. The aggrieved inheritor merely wished "to make them feel their ingratitude and to make them see that their fate depended on him." The reference to ingratitude confirms that Morisseau and the administrators were relying at least in part upon the "respect" provision enshrined in article 58 of the Code Noir. Upon publication of the ordinance, four of the six mulattos returned to the plantation and submitted themselves to Morisseau's authority, in

---

[91] A brief account can also be found in Peabody, "Négresse, Mulâtresse, Citoyenne," 62–63.
[92] "Arrêt du Conseil d'État," December 22, 1775, LC, 5:653–654.

recognition of which the inheritor proceeded to "solicit ... and obtain from the [governor and intendant] the ratification of their freedom." Only Marie-Victoire and her daughter, named Marie-Rosalie-Florimonde Cocosby, "remained in a state of revolt." They were duly chased down by the fugitive slave militia, and the mother was "placed in bars" for a few days. Both were then brought back to the plantation to be "left in freedom." Marie-Victoire went on to escape with her daughter a second time, was again returned, and then proceeded to escape yet a third time. Unlike the previous two, this last flight was keyed to a specific political event: the departure of the colony's governor and intendant, Pierre Gédéon de Nolivos and Alexandre-Jacques de Bongars. According to the case report, Marie-Victoire had hoped "to profit from [their] absence" in attempting her third escape.[93] Assuming that this characterization of her motives was indeed accurate, it reveals that at least some slaves and freed persons were attuned to the implications that changes in colonial administration might have on their lives. Rotations in the colonial leadership may well have been seen as giving rise to temporary power vacuums in Saint-Domingue.

At this point in the chain of events, an unnamed notary found a way of bringing Marie-Victoire's situation to the attention of the colony's incoming governor and intendant, Louis-Florent de Vallière and Jean-François Vincent de Montarcher. In response to the notary's pleadings on her behalf, Morisseau submitted a number of letters to the new administrators, making his case that he had a "right" to Marie-Victoire until such time as she had acted to "merit" her freedom, and that there were "dangers" in favoring the "public revolt of a slave against her master." It could hardly have been incidental to Morisseau's sense of his putative "rights" as an owner of slaves that the "rebel" in question was a woman. And the reference to the "dangers" that would ensue from an administrative intervention on Marie-Victoire's behalf served to invoke the dogma that only respect for the absolute domestic sovereignty of masters could prevent the colonial social order from unraveling. Yet the "intrigues" of the notary (as the case report characterized his role in the matter) apparently rendered this argument powerless, as the new governor and intendant proceeded to issue an ordinance declaring Marie-Victoire and her daughter free by birth. Morisseau and his wife were expressly prohibited from attempting to press any further legal claims to the mulatto woman and her child.[94]

[93] Ibid., 654.
[94] Ibid., 654–655.

Not surprisingly, Morisseau was not content with such a resolution, and he proceeded to appeal the case all the way to the Conseil d'État in Paris.[95] Even assuming he had spoken truthfully in declaring his willingness in the end to free Marie-Victoire on the basis of merit, considerations of honor and Morisseau's sense of prerogative led him to pursue the matter to this final stage of the legal process. Morisseau argued in his appeal that the intervention of Vallière and Montarcher had the consequence of tending "to withdraw slaves from the authority of their masters." This was a direct echo of the rhetoric of domestic sovereignty that Morisseau had used in his plea to the administrators of Saint-Domingue. Whether out of deference to such claims or alarm over the anonymous notary's efforts on Marie-Victoire's behalf, the Conseil d'État was more favorably disposed to Morisseau's side of the argument than the successors to Nolivos and Bongars had been. On December 22, 1775, the high court issued its own ordinance striking down the declaration of the new colonial administrators and declaring that Nolivos and Bongars had gotten everything right from the beginning. "Masters are not alone capable of giving freedom to their slaves," held the Conseil d'État. Rather, "good order" required that colonial administrators "evaluate the reasons for this benefit, and ensure that it is not granted with indiscretion." Vallière and Montarcher lacked the authority to override the 1713 and 1736 royal ordinances requiring administrative approval of manumissions.[96] Like earlier controversies involving metropolitan disallowance of colonial decisions,[97] Marie-Victoire's case implicated the sacrosanct principle that only the king or his administrative proxy, the Conseil d'État, could revise or undo what royal authority had mandated.

In addition to this traditional absolutist concern about the monarch's indivisible sovereignty, there was another, more complicated and arguably even contradictory dynamic at work here. In order to make his case, Morisseau had appealed to the principle that it was dangerous for anyone (regardless of social and political ranking in the colony) to do anything that tended to encourage the "withdrawal" of slaves from the authority of their masters. In order to support Morisseau in his appeal against the

---

[95] It is the report of this council that made its way into Moreau de Saint-Méry's collection of *Loix et constitutions*.

[96] "Arrêt du Conseil d'État," December 22, 1775, LC, 5:655.

[97] "Arrêt du Conseil d'État," May 16, 1771 (quashing an *arrêt* of the Port-au-Prince Conseil on grounds that only the governor and intendant have authority over manumissions and only the king can change his 1736 ordinance), ANOM, CSD, F/3/273, fol. 437.

new administrators, on the other hand, the Conseil d'État invoked an argument that cut in the opposite direction: Masters were "not alone capable" of committing the very act – manumission – that had caused all of this "trouble" in the first place. This argument had been rendered necessary because of Marie-Victoire's repeated efforts to defy the 1771 administrative order that she receive the consent of the inheritor before her freedom could be considered "complete."[98]

The case of Morisseau and Marie-Victoire thereby exposed a tension in the law and politics of manumission in Saint-Domingue. This tension was a function not only of the confusion, instability, and ambiguities that manumission created in a social order based on slavery, but also of the multiple and sometimes conflicting levels of administrative authority that were responsible for policing that social order. Hence it was entirely possible, within the context of the very same case, for one level of colonial administrative authority to use the argument from "order" in favor of a master's putative rights over a slave or freed person, and for another level of authority to use the same argument to subvert or deny that master's rights. Two different but related understandings of how social stability in a slave colony could best be achieved were simultaneously available as sources of legal argument. One of these arguments favored the master's view of his sovereign prerogatives and the other opposed it, but depending on the precise circumstances and the modalities of slave inheritance, the two arguments could be combined in unpredictable ways. At one stage of the case, Morisseau (and the departing colonial administrators, Nolivos and Bongars) made an argument that emphasized the external limits on a slaveholder's authority – namely, the legal insufficiency of Philippe Morisseau's testamentary manumission. At another stage, in collaboration with the Conseil d'État, Morisseau made a different argument that emphasized the sanctity and domesticity of the master's authority over his slaves. In the matter of Marie-Victoire, it is possible to see that domestic and colonial administrative sovereignty were not necessarily or always opposed in practice.

Even when not so opposed, however, the arguments about manumission continued to reflect an undercurrent of anxiety about the instability of the plantation regime, which all too often was identified with the anomalous place of free people of color. Marie-Victoire's case, one of a handful from the colonial period that made their way to the Conseil d'État, was in part a function of a rare constellation of circumstances

---

[98] "Arrêt du Conseil d'État," December 22, 1775, LC, 5:655.

involving a change in the administrative leadership of Saint-Domingue.[99] Her claims gave rise to legal arguments that were atypical in the degree of their plasticity. However, Marie-Victoire's experience was far from exceptional for having illustrated the highly politicized nature of manumission as both a symbol of risk and an instrument of risk management in the heart of the French Atlantic empire.

There is one final twist in Marie-Victoire's story to be told, albeit one difficult to pin down with certainty. In its holding, the Conseil d'État faulted the new administrators not only for trying to "reform" a preexisting royal ordinance, but also for asserting that Marie-Victoire and her daughter had gained their liberty *as a right of birth* rather than as a result of Philippe Morisseau's last will and testament.[100] To support this claim, which could only have originated with Marie-Victoire herself, Vallière and Montarcher had relied on two documents. The first was Marie-Victoire's baptismal act, which indicated the status of her mother as "free." This act was signed by both "François and Philippe Morisseau, father and godfather." The record is not entirely clear, but it appears from this reference that Morisseau's full name may have been François Morisseau d'Ester, and that he was not only the plaintiff in the case but also Marie-Victoire's biological father (as well as the brother of Marie-Victoire's godfather, Philippe, by whose will Marie-Victoire had first claimed her freedom).[101]

Regardless of the plaintiff's actual relation to Marie-Victoire, the Conseil d'État rejected the evidence concerning Marie-Victoire's mother on the grounds that "these enunciations are without consequence in the baptismal extracts, which are not the acts by which one frees slaves."[102] That statement confirms that the Conseil d'État was searching for an argument with which to defeat Marie-Victoire's claim to be free in accordance with article 13 of the Code Noir, whereby the status of the mother determined the status of the child.[103] Whether the administrators or Marie-Victoire

---

[99] For another example from the post-1775 period, see "Arrêt du Conseil d'État," January 4, 1779, LC, 5:850 (revoking the freedom granted to a slave by the governor of the Spanish side of Hispaniola).

[100] "Arrêt du Conseil d'État," December 22, 1775, LC, 5:655.

[101] It is also possible that the case report has mistakenly inverted the names of François and Philippe or the terms "father" and "godfather" here, which would make the deceased Philippe the father of Marie-Victoire. Alternatively, it is conceivable that François was simply a relation of the plaintiff (and of Philippe) who was not involved in the litigation over Marie-Victoire's status.

[102] "Arrêt du Conseil d'État," December 22, 1775, LC, 5:655.

[103] Code Noir, art. 13 (1685).

could have offered *any* evidence that would have satisfied the metropolitan tribunal on this score is unclear. Even the second document invoked by Vallière and Montarcher – the ratification of the manumission of Marie-Victoire's mother – proved inadequate for the task. In the opinion of the Conseil d'État, Marie-Victoire had been held in slavery during the life of the person who had freed her mother, which meant that Marie-Victoire could not have been born free. Possession counted more than paper in proving personal status. On the basis of all of these reasons, the Conseil nullified the ordinance of the new administrators as "incompetently rendered."[104] Marie-Victoire's story ended where it had begun: in slavery.

THE MILITARIZATION OF MANUMISSION

At about the same time that the Conseil d'État announced its convoluted rationale for the reenslavement of Marie-Victoire, colonial administrators took a decisive step toward reformulating the relationship between manumission and social order in Saint-Domingue. Two principal developments characterized the new regulatory regime. First, the overall number of manumissions seems to have declined – dramatically so after 1784. Before the tide of manumissions was fully reversed, however, administrators gravitated toward the view that manumission could be made to serve as well as subvert colonial strategic goals, and they opened a new path to freedom for slaves willing to serve those goals. Manumission became the handmaiden of colonial militarization.

In September 1775, the colonial governor, Victor-Thérèse Charpentier d'Ennery, issued a directive on the question of the "disorderly [state] of manumissions" ("libertés mal en ordre"). In this document, Ennery ordered his subordinates to undertake a thorough inquiry into the manumission of all persons claiming to be free by virtue of the "simple will of their masters." The directive did not go so far as to provide that all such manumissions were to be irrevocably nullified, but rather instructed that male and female mulattos and female blacks (note the omission of male blacks) be required to serve in the segregated *gens de couleur* units of the colonial military and militia. In exchange for an unspecified period of service in these units, which were responsible for chasing and capturing fugitive slaves, the blacks and mulattos in question would receive their freedom free of charge.[105]

---

[104] "Arrêt du Conseil d'État," December 22, 1775, LC, 5:656.
[105] "Lettre du Gouvernement," September 12, 1775, ANOM, CSD, F/3/273, fols. 1005–1006.

The realization that manumission could be made to strengthen slave society was not invented out of whole cloth in the 1770s. As early as 1709, the administrators of Saint-Domingue attempted to provide slaves with incentives to serve in the colonial militias, including manumission as a reward for "distinguished actions."[106] Moreover, the use of military service as a kind of substitute levy on manumission hearkened back to the old taxation system first put in place in the 1740s.[107] Yet the pressures toward colonial militarization in the aftermath of the Seven Years' War period were undoubtedly the driving force behind the new manumission regime. During the 1760s, the administrators began turning to the military-service incentive to advance a variety of different purposes. It could be used to help in the ongoing campaign to capture and reduce the runaway slave population of Saint-Domingue or to ease planter complaints about the manumission tax regime, an especially ripe bone of contention for slaveholders, as the 1764 grievances over colonial taxation illustrated. Finally, provided that it was carefully and faithfully implemented, the military-service requirement could be used to tackle the problem of the uncertain status of some blacks and *gens de couleur* arising from ambiguities in the boundary between slavery and freedom.

The practice of using free people of color to patrol for maroon slaves in the colony's forested mountain regions dated back to at least the 1730s, when administrators took steps to recruit *gens de couleur* as a substitute for the scarce supply of poor whites willing to serve in such a capacity.[108] By the 1760s, it was typical for free people of color to serve as militia commanding officers, a role that provided a source of social respect and financial success within the *gens de couleur* community, particularly in the northern province.[109] In the southern and western provinces, by contrast, time spent in the militia units was generally seen as a distraction from more pressing commercial activities.[110] Nonetheless, even in the

[106] "Ordonnance des Administrateurs," September 9, 1709, LC, 2:167–168.

[107] "Lettre des Administrateurs au Procureur-Général du Port-au-Prince," September 8, 1773, ANOM, CSD, F/3/273, fols. 759–760 (concerning the establishment of a "caisse des libertés," or freedom fund, for purposes of "public utility").

[108] Garrigus, *Before Haiti*, 103. In 1739, the Cap Français Council established a new *maréchaussée* to address growing concern about the "neglect" of "public safety" in the colony. "Arrêt en règlement du Conseil du Cap," August 7, 1739, LC, 3:568.

[109] King, *Blue Coat or Powdered Wig*, xiii.

[110] Garrigus, *Before Haiti*, 214–215, 224–225; John D. Garrigus, "Saint-Domingue's Free People of Color and the Tools of Revolution," in Geggus and Fiering, *The World of the Haitian Revolution*, 56–57.

south, free people of color could and did seek to use militia service as a means of showing their civic virtue and dedication to colonial security.

By the 1760s, responsibility for hunting down maroon slaves was shifted away from the free colored militia units – which were then desperately needed to address the external military threats brought into focus by the Seven Years' War – and toward the *maréchaussée* (or fugitive slave police).[111] First created in 1721, the fugitive slave police had traditionally overlapped in functional terms with the militias but was organizationally distinct from them. Moreover, service in the *maréchaussée* brigades was less than to be desired, not surprisingly given the brutal nature of the work it entailed. Per the Code Noir, two-time recidivist maroons were punished by having their hamstrings cut, and three-time recidivists were subject to the death penalty.[112] In theory, these punishments were to be administered by the colonial executioners rather than the archers of the fugitive slave police. As a practical matter, however, maroons were often killed in the actual course of being chased down.[113] Free people of color were not shy about complaining of these burdens, especially given that white officers were invariably in command where the *maréchaussée* was concerned.[114] The heightened security needs of the Seven Years' War period led administrators to expand the fugitive slave police brigades, which continued to be staffed by *gens de couleur*. It is not surprising to learn that colonial administrators betrayed more than a little anxiety about the wisdom of entrusting people of color with a responsibility so fundamental to colonial security.[115] The administration of the fugitive slave police, like manumission itself, was inflected by both real and perceived anxieties about an incipient breakdown in social order.[116]

---

[111] Garrigus, *Before Haiti*, 97.

[112] Code Noir, art. 38 (1685).

[113] "Règlement du Conseil de Léogane," January 17, 1739, LC, 5:555 (providing that the *maréchaussée* archers were to be paid 100 livres for the head of each maroon slave captured on the Spanish side of Hispaniola, and 60 livres for those caught in the mountains on the French side); "Lettre des Administrateurs au Ministre," November 10, 1767 (concerning fugitive slaves), ANOM, CSD, F/394, fol. 89.

[114] Garrigus, *Before Haiti*, 103–104.

[115] Ibid., 104.

[116] Notwithstanding these racialist fears, as Stewart King explains, free people of color generally regarded fugitive slave policing as a matter of defending elite creole society from a common enemy. Stewart R. King, "The Maréchaussée of Saint-Domingue: Balancing the Ancien Regime and Modernity," *Journal of Colonialism and Colonial History* 5, no. 2 (Fall 2004).

After the Seven Years' War ended, a movement to protest the imposition of military rule in Saint-Domingue united whites and free people of color against local administrators. This movement culminated in 1769, when free colored planters and whites in the southern and western provinces mounted an armed revolt against the new governor, the Prince de Rohan-Montbazon, who had arrived in the colony in 1766. Quickly suppressed, the revolt against colonial ministerial "despotism" – which had echoes of contemporaneous parliamentary struggles against royal authority in France itself – represented a final moment of interracial unity in elite creole society. As Garrigus has argued, the alliances of 1769 were soon superseded by an increasingly rigid separation between white and free colored political elites and the elimination of opportunities for *gens de couleur* to serve in leadership roles in the free colored militias.[117] The pacification of the antimilitia movement left Governor Rohan-Montbazon free to implement his detested 1769 reforms, which entailed mandatory military service along with the reservation of all commissioned ranks for white men. In addition, the new regime ushered in a de facto merger of the militias with the fugitive slave-hunting brigades, as the colony's administrators were now free to supplement *maréchaussée* forces with militiamen.[118]

The preoccupation with *marronage* that helped fuel these political contests of the 1760s was itself rooted in the same concern about the dangers of unofficial manumission that spawned earlier legislation on the status of free people of color. In a 1767 letter to the naval minister explaining how they intended to handle the problem of *marronage*, Rohan-Montbazon and the intendant (Bongars) wrote that "slaves can never become free except by means of a manumission conforming to the law." "Freedom is never acquired by prescription," they declared, because "color is here a status (*titre*) of the slave."[119] A doctrine of property law with origins in Roman usage, prescription was the means by which one acquired property after a long and uninterrupted possession.[120] It is nothing short of remarkable to read that colonial administrators interpreted the actions and aspirations of fugitive slaves through the lens of this very technical Roman legal doctrine, and one wonders whether any fugitive

---

[117] Garrigus, *Before Haiti*, 108, 131, 138–139.
[118] Ibid., 131, 204, 210.
[119] "Lettre des Administrateurs au Ministre," November 10, 1767, ANOM, CSD, F/394, fol. 89.
[120] In the seventeenth and eighteenth centuries, French lawyers could find exegeses of the doctrine of prescription in the widely used civilian treatises of Domat and Pothier, among other authors.

slaves may actually have sought to press a claim to freedom before the colonial courts based on such an analysis. Regardless, the association between illegal manumission and *marronage* manifested in the administrators' letter helps account for the arc of manumission policy in Saint-Domingue against the backdrop of colonial militarization.

By the mid-1770s, a new understanding of manumission as a source of colonial strategic opportunity had taken root. On October 23, 1775, the administrators issued an ordinance concerning the collection of manumission taxes that addressed the "doubtful state" of "various blacks and *gens de couleur*, who enjoy a sort of freedom, more of fact than of law, [and which] has seemed to us too important to fix [with certainty], not to determine the degree of validity of their titles and possessions."[121] The notion of a "sort of freedom, more of fact than of law," is a telling description of the "twilight zone" of ambiguity that administrators felt they had to eliminate to stabilize the political and social order of the colony. To this end, the ordinance set forth various ways for masters to manumit their slaves free of charge in exchange for the military- or militia-service option. One provision enabled masters to liberate their slaves by enlisting them as drummers in the Port-au-Prince and Cap Français regiments or the artillery companies. Eight years of consecutive service with "fidelity and precision" would culminate in a tax-free manumission.[122] A second provision authorized manumission in exchange for ten consecutive years of similarly exemplary service behind the free people of color who manned the fugitive slave police.[123] The 1775 ordinance also called yet again for renewed enforcement of prior regulations on manumission.

Of course, technically one remained a slave during the years of service required under the 1775 ordinance. The effect of such service, however, was to associate oneself with the free people of color who had traditionally manned the militias and *maréchaussée*. The practical significance of that association was heightened after 1779, when a venerable *gens de couleur* unit known as the Chasseurs Volontaires embarked from Cap Français for the Georgia coast to participate in former governor Charles

---

[121] "Ordonnance des Administrateurs," October 23, 1775, LC, 5:610. The measure refers to article 11 of a May 22, 1775, royal ordinance as authorizing the colonial administrators to tax the confirmations of freed slaves. But we know from various earlier documents, including the 1773 letter cited above, that this was not the first time the administrators were authorized to collect such a tax.

[122] "Ordonnance des Administrateurs," October 23, 1775, LC, 5:610 (Art. XI).

[123] Id. (Art. XII). The *maréchaussée* service requirement was reduced to six years in 1789. Garrigus, *Before Haiti*, 201.

d'Estaing's expedition in support of the American revolutionary forces besieged by the British at Savannah.[124]

Even after the victorious Savannah experience, most free people of color, and especially those who owned plantations or were otherwise commercially active in the southern province, continued to find in militia and *maréchaussée* service more penury than privilege.[125] Nonetheless, the new approach to manumission announced in 1775 established an important precedent and set the slave society of Saint-Domingue on a path toward the militarization of freedom from which it would never fully retreat, as would become clear with the advent of the revolutionary years.[126] Even as colonial administrators were seeking to restrict, if not close off altogether, the underground and informal passageways to freedom carved out by slaves in the decades since the Code Noir, military service was a door through which aspiring freed persons could thenceforth walk. It was a door opened partly by perceptions of the ever-present risk that maroon communities posed to the plantation world, and partly by a newly sharpened administrative awareness of the utilitarian value of manumission.

THE END(S) OF MANUMISSION

Manumission itself did not necessarily expand during the late colonial years. Indeed, it should not be forgotten that the 1775 ordinance, although authorizing military emancipations, was in essence an effort to stem the growth of the free black population. Although that population

---

[124] Garrigus, *Before Haiti*, 206–210; Gérard Laurent, "Les Volontaires de St. Domingue," *Conjonction* 131 (Nov. 1976): 39–57.

[125] Garrigus, *Before Haiti*, 213–215.

[126] David Geggus notes that, as a result of the enlistment of slaves in the colonial *maréchaussée*, armed blacks were an increasing presence in Saint-Domingue and other French Caribbean colonies. He expresses skepticism, however, that the *maréchaussée* set an important precedent for the use of slave soldiers to combat the Saint-Domingue slave revolt during the 1790s. David Geggus, "The Arming of Slaves in the Haitian Revolution," in Brown and Morgan, *Arming Slaves*, 211. Geggus underestimates the revolutionary-era significance of the colonial tendencies toward the militarization of manumission and the arming of slaves and freed persons, a question I revisit in greater detail in Chapter 6. As Laurent Dubois writes in a contribution to the same volume on the arming of slaves, "service in the [French Caribbean] republican army was in many ways the continuation of pre-revolutionary service in militias and the *maréchaussée*." Laurent Dubois, "Citizen Soldiers: Emancipation and Military Service in the Revolutionary French Caribbean," in Brown and Morgan, *Arming Slaves*, 235.

continued to grow as a result of natural reproduction, the most recent scholarship suggests that manumission levels in Saint-Domingue were probably decreasing overall after 1775 and that they continued to do so for the remainder of the Old Regime.[127]

Nor was militarization the only dynamic affecting manumission policy during the last two decades of the colonial period. In the southern province, free persons of color resorted to marriage on a widespread basis as a way of avoiding payment of the freedom tax.[128] In so doing, they, like white planters before them, were engaging in another kind of appeal to the original policies and principles of the Code Noir. Article 9 of the Code Noir provided that slave women held in concubinage would become "free and legitimate" by means of marriage to the free men who kept them.[129]

Other questions about manumission first raised prior to 1775 remained open as well, such as whether a slave could establish freedom simply on the basis of a baptismal act or other legal document. Perhaps in response to the air of ambiguity that hovered over this issue, the Conseil Supérieur of Le Cap issued a decision concerning "the police of slaves" in 1777 that required manumitted mulattos and blacks to register their freedom with the court clerks. *Gens de couleur* who were born free, for their part, were required to register the freedom of their mothers (in a reinstatement of the requirements of an earlier regulation first issued in 1758).[130]

---

[127] Geggus, "Saint-Domingue on the Eve of the Haitian Revolution," 198.

[128] Garrigus, *Before Haiti*, 198–200.

[129] Code Noir (1685), art. 9.

[130] "Arrêt du Conseil du Cap," October 15, 1777, ANOM, CSD, F/3/274, fols. 333–34. See Peabody, "*There Are No Slaves in France*," 7, 111–119. Once again, it is interesting to note a coincidence in the timing of metropolitan and colonial "freedom" legislation. In August 1777, the monarchy adopted legislation prohibiting the entry of all "blacks, mulattoes, and other people of color" into the metropole. This was in response to the ineffectiveness of earlier legislation in forcing masters to follow the prescribed formalities and restrictions of the 1716 and 1738 royal ordinances, as well as in response to the increase (both real and perceived) in the slave and free colored population of metropolitan France following the Seven Years' War. There is no scholarly consensus as to the actual number of free persons of color residing in France at this time. Sue Peabody suggests that no more than four to five thousand (and possibly far fewer) free blacks and mulattos were present in the metropole at any one point during the eighteenth century. Peabody, "*There Are No Slaves in France*," 4. The most recent and authoritative treatment of this subject is Pierre H. Boulle, *Race et esclavage dans la France de l'Ancien Régime* (Paris: Perrin, 2007), but see also Johnson, "The Reinvention of Slavery in France."

In spite of this "freedom registration" policy, the two high courts of Saint-Domingue continued to issue divergent opinions as to what constituted valid proof of manumission. In November 1777, the Council of Le Cap nullified the freedom granted to a mulatto woman and her daughter by the Spanish government. The holding undoubtedly stemmed from the French colonial government's desire to put an end to the efforts of slaves to seek their freedom by crossing the border to the Spanish side of the island. However, the decision went on to set a number of requirements that applied to manumissions generally. Clergy were prohibited from designating the freedom of the children of *gens de couleur* in baptismal and marriage documents absent proof of validity.[131] A few months later, however, the Conseil of Port-au-Prince issued a much less formalistic decision that was far more favorable to the defense of freedom claims. In the absence of a baptismal act, the court held, certificates demonstrating that an *affranchi* was born of a manumitted mother and had been baptized as free would suffice. Numerous Roman law provisions were cited in support of the court's opinion, and it seems likely that the magistrates relied in particular on the doctrine of *favor libertatis*.[132]

The difficulties of administering manumission in light of the multiple and overlapping layers of colonial legal authority – including what administrators regarded as the ever-nettlesome mediating role played by notaries – persisted into the 1780s. Two examples are worth noting. In 1780, the Cap Français Council held that a manumission would take effect only as of the day the government granted its permission – as clear a statement as could be imagined that sovereignty over this subject matter lay exclusively in the hands of the governor and intendant.[133] In April 1784, the Conseil of Port-au-Prince, for its part, prohibited a notary from exercising his functions for one month to punish him for having designated some *gens de couleur* as free without mentioning the acts "constitutive" of their manumission, in violation of a recent royal regulation.[134]

All of these measures were but preludes to the monarchy's climactic effort, in the waning years of the Old Regime, to stamp out once and for

---

[131] "Arrêt du Conseil du Cap," November 25, 1777, LC, 5:802–803.

[132] "Arrêt du Conseil du Port-au-Prince," February 23, 1778, ANOM, CSD, F/3/274, fol. 414. On the principle of *favor libertatis*, see Watson, *Roman Slave Law*, 12.

[133] "Arrêt du Conseil Supérieur du Cap," January 21, 1780, ANOM, CSD, F/3/275, fol. 5.

[134] The regulations invoked in this *arrêt* were dated January 9, 1778; these were probably (though not necessarily) a response to the November 25, 1777 decision of the Conseil of Le Cap discussed above.

all the risks associated with "illegal" manumission. The move came as part of a vigorously contested reform of plantation-management practices that focused on the role of the managers and agents (*économes* and *procureurs*) appointed by absentee planters. In royal ordinances dated December 1784 and December 1785, which are discussed more fully in the next chapter, the monarchy sought to reduce the discretionary powers of plantation managers in a range of areas first regulated by the Code Noir, most notably corporal punishment and alimentary provisions. The legislation also sought to realize the aims of colonial administrators who had been seeking for decades to contain the growth of the free black population. The new measures did so by cutting back on the ability of managers and agents to petition the intendant for the freedom of slaves they deemed most worthy of the privilege.[135]

The colonists greeted the 1784 and 1785 legislation with near universal contempt. Despite skepticism about whether the reforms were likely to achieve their intended goals where the abuse of slaves was concerned,[136] it is relatively clear that the new measures had a significant impact on manumission practices. In the final four or five years of the Old Regime, the level of manumissions declined from a total of 739 in 1785 to the parsimonious number of 256 in 1789.[137] By the end of the Old Regime, manumission itself had come, for all intents and purposes, to an end.[138]

What remained was a profoundly influential legacy that would mark the course of the Haitian Revolution in more ways than one. At the level of political and legal theory, the colonial experience with manumission revealed that enfranchisement was not simply the negation of a master's property rights over his slaves, but rather a continued exercise of those rights: the "last stage" in the government of slavery. Manumission, for masters and colonial administrators alike, entailed something more than just the "end" of slavery: There is no other way to explain why it proved to be such a recurring source of legal conflict in the Old Regime.[139]

---

[135] Debien, *Les esclaves aux Antilles françaises*, 389.

[136] More than one commentator in 1785 described the 1784 reforms as futile for lack of any effective enforcement mechanism. See Debbasch, "Au coeur du 'gouvernement des esclaves'," 43–45.

[137] Geggus, "Saint-Domingue on the Eve of the Haitian Revolution," 10.

[138] In 1789, the departing governor of the colony, the Marquis du Chilleau, instructed his interim replacement to consent to the manumission of "blacks or persons of color" who had served only six rather than ten years in the fugitive slave police. Debien, *L'esclavage aux Antilles*, 390. The proposal was denounced as dangerous by local authorities. Geggus, "The Arming of Slaves in the Haitian Revolution," 211.

[139] Cf. Patterson, "Three Notes of Freedom," 20.

At the level of lived experience, the jousting over manumission consistently betrayed racial anxieties that a growing free colored population would "corrupt" the colony's mores and alter the local balance of power. In their often fragile pursuit of personal liberty, free people of color learned to navigate the ins and outs of the colonial legal system: an important way station on the road to political activism. In this effort, they may well have been supported by officials in the Naval Ministry's Colonial Bureau and by the judges of the colonial high courts. Beginning in the early 1780s, ministry officials directed an end to new forms of discriminatory legislation targeting free people of color, and instructed colonial administrators to consult with the Conseils Supérieurs in seeking to tamper the prejudicial effect of existing legislation. Indeed, in 1782, the high court judges successfully persuaded the ministry to recall Intendant Alexandre Lebrasseur on the grounds that his campaign to enact ordinances prohibiting free people of color from working as goldsmiths conflicted with articles 57 and 59 of the Code Noir. The ministry's newfound sense of egalitarianism was informed by the realization, long in the making, that discriminatory laws weakened "the strongest barrier against any rebellion of the enslaved" (in the words of one administrator).[140]

Finally, as that comment suggests, the history of manumission law in Saint-Domingue discloses how colonial administrators arrived – in fits and starts – at an essentially pragmatic or prudential vision of enfranchisement, whereby manumission could be co-opted to serve the political end of military recruitment and contain the risks of slave resistance. In short, toward the latter part of the colonial period but still well before the advent of the revolutionary crisis, manumission had become not simply a source of risk but also a locus of potential return. The exact nature of that return would depend, at least in part, on how administrators and slaveholders decided to treat the vastly larger population of enslaved persons who would never know the opportunity of legal freedom under the Old Regime.

---

[140] Rogers, "On the Road to Citizenship," 70.

3

Reconciling Humanity and Public Policy

Well before the Revolution, the edicts of Louis XVI frequently spoke of natural law and the rights of man.

> – Alexis de Tocqueville, *The Old Regime*
> *and the French Revolution* (1856)[1]

The transformations wrought by the Seven Years' War in Saint-Domingue were decisive not only for manumission policy, but also for an area more conventionally associated with colonial administration in the tropics: plantation management and the treatment of slaves. The 1760s and 1770s witnessed a rising groundswell of attention to the theme of the "arbitrary" or "private" authority of slave masters in Saint-Domingue. The problem of the renegade or "barbarous" planter transcended the specific concerns and agendas of administrators, judges, and pamphleteers. Indeed, it became a preoccupation even for planters themselves, including the very ones whose conduct was most at issue. The "domestic sphere" of slavery in Saint-Domingue provided a coherent focal point around which a variety of different interests converged, occasionally to defend the absolutism of that sphere from within, but more often to criticize it from the outside.

As in the context of manumission, the legal and political debate over the "arbitrary" and "despotic" slave master proceeded from colonial "first principles" but very quickly devolved into a clash over consequences. Competing claims of sovereignty – on the one hand, royal authority as expressed in the Code Noir, and on the other, slaveholder

---

[1] Tocqueville, *The Ancien Régime and the French Revolution*, 134.

notions of natural or domestic right – gave form to the debate. Yet what animated these abstract claims and made them genuinely salient was their perceived ability to forecast and help manage the hazards generated by plantation governance and master-slave relations. Where both manumission and the abuse of slaves were concerned, administrators believed they were on solid precautionary ground in seeking to limit the asserted prerogatives of the plantation complex. In the case of manumission, that strategic reasoning reflected fears that an overly populous and "licentious" free colored community would "corrupt" and subvert the racial and political hierarchies on which slave society was based – unless the path to freedom could be channeled instead, through military service, toward the containment of slave resistance. In the context of concerns about the arbitrary nature of plantation management, a different but not unrelated concern was at work: the belief that a small number of especially depraved and tyrannical colonists would jeopardize the viability of an entire colonial system by multiplying the incentives for a slave revolution. Montesquieu's analysis of the "dangers" and "abuses" of slavery crystallized this problem for a colonial audience by questioning, in effect, whether a slave had any incentive to tolerate the abuses of plantation life if that life was worse than the consequences of its overthrow.

Thus framed, the risk of the renegade planter was especially cogent because it entailed that nothing less than the survival of colonial slavery was perceived to be at stake. The ethics of managing such a threat were both prudential and existential. Colonial administrators, magistrates, and commentators were not shy to invoke the overall stability of Saint-Domingue as a justification for their insistence on establishing and maintaining the rule of law. In defending the prerogatives of royal authority in Saint-Domingue, however, they frequently mixed strategic language with moral and humanitarian rhetoric. Beginning well before but then maturing with particular emphasis in the 1770s and 1780s, a powerful alliance was formed between the case for stability and the denunciation of a slave regime that tolerated planter brutality.

This strand of rhetoric, which steadfastly defended the institution of slavery but vigorously criticized those planters who were held to threaten its continued viability, has received relatively little attention in the scholarship on the origins of the antislavery movement.[2] In 1971, Michèle Duchet published a pathbreaking study showing that, beginning

---

[2] Yvan Debbasch distinguishes usefully between antislavery and the critique of the slaveholding system, arguing that the two have often been confused. He suggests furthermore that the critique of the slaveholding system developed with special force in France during the 1770s and 1780s. Debbasch, "Au coeur du 'gouvernement des esclaves,'" 36, 40.

in the 1760s, colonial administrators throughout the greater French Caribbean began to insist on the need to rein in the cruelties of masters in order to prevent the spread of *marronage*. In Duchet's view, a fear of *marronage*, dating back to the Jamaican experience of the 1730s and 1740s, impelled French administrative efforts to recast colonial slavery along more benevolent lines. She neatly documented the links between this administrative reform campaign and the ambiguous convergence of appeals to "humanity" and "interest" in late-eighteenth-century French antislavery ideology.[3] However, Duchet's analysis was also limited by a somewhat narrow focus on *marronage* as well as a relative lack of attention to legal processes and to the unfolding of events over time in specific locales (most notably Saint-Domingue).[4] Moreover, Duchet's vaguely neo-Marxist thesis that reformist antislavery ideology served to advance the capitalist interests of a "metropolitan bourgeoisie" has not stood the test of time.[5]

Duchet was entirely correct, however, to note the ambiguous character of the administrative campaign to reform French colonial slavery after the Seven Years' War.[6] The difficulty of disaggregating our modern, compartmentalized notions of the wellsprings of human behavior and human rights in eighteenth-century discussions of slavery's excesses is an unavoidable aspect of the problem to be addressed. For the humanitarian sensibility that emerged out of the critique of renegade planters in late colonial Saint-Domingue was characterized above all by its ambiguity with respect to the dichotomy of strategy and benevolence. This ambiguity pervaded the sense of existential danger that administrators and other observers believed hovered over colonial society in the post–Seven Years' War period. The radical abuse of slaves imperiled, as it were, both the body and soul of colonialism – but without any conviction that salvation

---

[3] Duchet, *Anthropologie et histoire*, 145–177. As Duchet puts it, humanity and interest were "but one and the same thing" in these writings, part of the same "principle of government" (152).

[4] On *marronage* as the "sociological basis" of the "theme of revolt" in French antislavery ideology, see ibid., 145. On Saint-Domingue, see ibid., 158–160.

[5] On the alignment between the antislavery reform campaign and the metropolitan bourgeoisie's financial interests in the colonies, see ibid., 146 n.47, 150, 160. Duchet posits that, with the end of the monopoly granted to the Compagnie des Indes in 1769 and the rise of independent colonial trading companies, the French bourgeoisie began to accumulate growing stakes in the stability of Atlantic commerce. Ibid., 146 n.47. For critiques of the Marxist or social interpretation of the Old Regime and the French Revolution, see Alfred Cobban, *The Social Interpretation of the French Revolution* (Cambridge, UK: Cambridge University Press, 1964); and François Furet, *Interpreting the French Revolution*, trans. Elborg Forster (Cambridge, UK: Cambridge University Press, 1981), 81–131.

[6] Duchet, *Anthropologie et histoire*, 136.

of the soul is what finally mattered in the end. This was an entirely secular anxiety, but its existential nature invoked the dreaded possibility of life after slavery. The awareness of that possibility generated whatever hope colonial administrators could muster for a reform of the status quo: a reform that would salvage the plantation experiment from the damage wrought by its most refractory participants. In short, the renegade planter posed a classic collective-action problem for colonial society.

Historicizing the ambiguous political ethics of this critique of slavery's extremes is a complicated matter. Expediency and the rule of law were clearly not the only elements in the administrators' move to set limits on recalcitrant planters. For the very notion of a "barbarous" or "unjust" master, of course, implied the existence of other masters who were supposedly *not* barbarous and *not* unjust. By singling out the renegade planters, in other words, it was possible to cast a favorable light on the larger number of planters who were described in various documents as moderate, "humane," "benevolent," and "legitimate."[7] Accordingly, one must mind the gap between prudential or even moral opposition to the cruelties of slavery on the one hand, and ideas that can properly be described as embracing abolitionist sentiment on the other. Similarly, the commonwealth ethics of slavery in Saint-Domingue implicated the cardinal distinction between preservationist critics of the plantation regime – those who aimed to maintain the system and plug its leakages – and more radical critics who aimed either to weaken or to do away with the system altogether. With very few exceptions, the former rather than the latter category is at issue here. The figure of the refractory planter reflected the preemptive dynamics of colonial administration in a slave society believed to teeter on the edge of disaster.

The administrators' efforts to justify a pragmatic agenda in the language of humanitarianism may therefore appear, to the contemporary eye, disingenuous and unconvincing. Yet consequences matter as well as

---

[7] Hendrik Hartog suggests that the North American slave codes served as mechanisms for the legitimation of "moderate," law-abiding slaveholders vis-à-vis their (more) abusive brethren. Hartog, *Man and Wife in America*, 166. On Southern U.S. antebellum law governing the abuse and homicide of slaves by masters, see Thomas D. Morris, *Southern Slavery and the Law, 1619–1860* (Chapel Hill: University of North Carolina Press, 1996), 161–208; Mark Tushnet, *Slave Law in the American South: State v. Mann in History and Literature* (2003); and Walter Johnson, "Inconsistency, Contradiction, and Complete Confusion: The Everyday Life of the Law of Slavery," *Law and Social Inquiry* 22 (1997): 405, 415. Johnson writes: "Over the course of the 19th century, crimes of wanton murder and indiscriminate violence against slaves by slaveholders were increasingly punished in Southern courts, though legal action remained rare and the emergent legal standard – 'moderate force' – elastic."

intentions: Unintended meanings may stray from and sometimes even outstrip an author's purpose in making a particular statement.[8] The cases and controversies discussed in this chapter amounted to more than just an ideological smokescreen for the defense of colonial slavery and the legitimation of the "mainstream" or "civilized" planter.[9] Nor is the campaign to save colonialism from certain colonists best understood as an expression of an underlying capitalist economic dynamic, whereby the stakes of putative middle-class shareholders in the profits of colonial trading companies translated into pressure for better living conditions for slaves in the French Caribbean, as Duchet argued.[10] Rather, we must turn to the development of patterns in colonial legal culture, which pitted the "domestic" sovereignty of planters against the "public" authority of administrators in a specific history of recurring controversies about the risks to which slave societies were prone.[11] In Saint-Domingue, perhaps more than anywhere else in the Atlantic world, the conflict between the claims of stability and the pursuit of unchecked mastery over the slave most often and most clearly came to a head.

Come to a head these conflicts did, in 1784 and 1785, when the monarchy took the most decisive steps of any eighteenth-century sovereign in the Atlantic world to manage the risks of refractory planter conduct. The

---

[8] See the observations of Quentin Skinner in *Meaning and Context: Quentin Skinner and his Critics*, ed. James Tully (Princeton, NJ: Princeton University Press, 1988), 55, 271–272. Insisting on the importance of recovering authorial intentions, Skinner nonetheless acknowledges that "any text of any complexity will always contain far more meaning ... than even the most vigilant and imaginative author could possibly have intended to put into it" (272).

[9] Anthony Pagden notes Condorcet's and Diderot's critique of those in the eighteenth century who called for stricter enforcement of laws intended to protect slaves from the violence of their masters. In Diderot's view, these calls merely "added hypocrisy to barbarism." Quoted in Anthony Pagden, *Lords of All the World: Ideologies of Empire in Spain, Britain, and France, c. 1500 – c. 1800* (New Haven, CT: Yale University Press, 1995), 171.

[10] To be clear, Duchet did not claim that capitalist pressures in fact resulted in better living conditions for slaves in the French Atlantic colonies.

[11] On this theme, see Debbasch, "Au coeur du 'gouvernement des esclaves.'" Debbasch argues insightfully that although many scholars have pointed out the extent to which colonial administrators were simply unable to govern the master-slave relationship in any meaningful way, few scholars have sought to understand and conceptualize the underlying reasons for that state of affairs. Historians have taken for granted that "domestic sovereignty" is the "natural modality of power" in a slave society, and they have therefore considered it unworthy of critical examination (31). Emphasizing the colonists' fear of poisoning at the hands of their slaves, Debbasch's article analyzes the theory and practice of domestic sovereignty in the eighteenth-century French Caribbean, beginning with the Code Noir (which, he argues, essentially ratified the preexisting practice of leaving matters up to the domestic will of the planters) and ending with writings of the late 1780s that equated slavery with despotism.

1784 and 1785 measures crystallized the stakes and codified the terms of colonial anxiety about the internal dynamics of plantation governance, heightening awareness in Saint-Domingue of the possibility of life after slavery. Moreover, the ambiguous ethics of the precautionary critique of slavery did not expire with the end of the Old Regime. The connection between order and morality, the stabilizing function that humanitarian rhetoric both expressed and disguised – these were distinctive character-istics not only of the colonial commentary that appeared in the 1770s and 1780s, but also of revolutionary-era efforts to grapple with the devel-opment of slave resistance into outright rebellion. Colonial administra-tive prognostications about the dangers of permitting outlaw planters to run amok echoed unmistakably in the subsequent emergence of more steadfast abolitionist and egalitarian ideologies and programs during the revolutionary period. These continuities bridged the gap between the Old Regime and the Haitian Revolution.

"THE TRUE INTEREST OF THE MASTERS"

The strategic ethics of slavery in Saint-Domingue took shape against the backdrop of a powerful idea with roots going back to the ancient world. As discussed in Chapter 1, the belief that the master-slave relationship was autonomous and self-regulating – beyond the reach of law alto-gether – had its sources in the Roman law doctrine of *patria potestas*. In the realm of the household, fathers and husbands reigned supreme. This tradition found a natural habitat in the sugar and coffee plantations of Saint-Domingue, where renegade planters fell back on it during the late colonial period as a defense against accusations that their conduct as masters had crossed legal or moral bounds. One of the themes of the cri-tique of planter sovereignty run amok during the 1770s and 1780s was the idea that slaves could and ought to be governed by the "civil law" rather than by the "law of the master" or – in what one critic labeled as the same thing – the "law of the family."[12] The civil law was shorthand for the Code Noir and its implementing rules and regulations, most nota-bly provisions for the nourishment, clothing, and medical care of slaves (articles 22–27 of the Code) and limitations on the prerogative of mas-ters to inflict torture and punishment (articles 42–43). The function of the civil law was not simply to vindicate the absolute sovereignty of the

---

[12] Michel René Hilliard d'Auberteuil, *Considérations sur l'état présent de la colonie de Saint-Domingue: ouvrage politique et législative* (Paris: Grange, 1776), 1:143.

monarchy but, more practically, to serve as a counterpoint to the ancient tendency of masters to press at the boundaries of their domestic authority over others.

In other words, the task of the civil law was to perform the delicate balancing act that Montesquieu argued was necessary in any slave society that aimed to endure. Montesquieu's vision of the tension between the "abuses" and "dangers" of slave society suggested that the refractory master suffered from a self-destructive cognitive deficiency: an inability to see beyond the needs of the present moment. In the French Caribbean, Montesquieu's ideas served as a foil for polemicists and a frame of reference for events that usually unfolded quite independently of the concerns of metropolitan legal theorists and political commentators. Nonetheless, the governance of slavery in Saint-Domingue all too often reflected an unmistakable tension between colonial administrative and judicial ideas about the "true" or long-term interests of the planters on the one hand, and a planter culture that looked inward rather than outward for its understanding of self-interest and legitimacy on the other.

From the very start, implied concepts of sovereignty lay at or near the surface of this jousting over planter brutality, just as they had informed the to-and-fro over manumission policy. The desire of the monarchy and its judicial representatives in the Caribbean to restrain the ability of masters to torture and abuse their slaves shaped the agenda of the framers of the Code Noir. In the world of the Code Noir, the most serious forms of corporal punishment and discipline – torture, mutilation, and capital punishment – were the prerogative of the monarch rather than of his subjects: The colonies inherited and then cast in racial terms the metropolitan distinction between *haute* and *basse justice*.[13] This was so even

---

[13] Chesnais, introduction to Chesnais, *Le Code Noir*, 11. See also Bloch, *La société féodale*, 502–508. In the early modern French tradition, the distinction between public and domestic authority was also expressed in notion of "household" or "family" governance or jurisdiction. See Bodin, *Six Bookes of a Commonweale*, 32 (discussing the law of slavery as part of the "government of Households"). For the common law variation on this theme, see Adam Smith, *Lectures on Jurisprudence*, ed. R. L. Meek et al. (Oxford, UK: Oxford University Press, 1978), 175 (discussing "the relations which may subsist within a family," including the master-servant relation); Robert J. Steinfeld, *The Invention of Free Labor: The Employment Relation in English and American Law and Culture, 1350–1870* (Chapel Hill: University of North Carolina Press, 1991), 55–60 (discussing the early modern English labor relationship as a form of "household" jurisdiction, which entailed the jurisdiction of the master as head of the household over wives, children, and servants); Carole Shammas, "Anglo-American Household Governance in Comparative Perspective," *The William and Mary Quarterly* 52, no.1 (1995): 104

though the overall thrust of the Code Noir was to leave most aspects of plantation governance and the master-slave relationship in the hands of the planters themselves.[14]

After the Code Noir's promulgation in 1685, the monarchy and the colonial courts made repeated attempts to enforce this theoretical division of punitive labor between public and private authority. Although it must be used with care, the distinction is not anachronistically applied in this context. A royal ordinance of December 30, 1712, prohibited masters "by their private authority" from torturing slaves on the grounds that such abuses provoked slave desertion and caused "a great disorder in the said islands."[15] In 1727, the minister of the navy advised the administrators of Saint-Domingue that they were to take action against colonists who "license themselves to cause by their own authority the death of their slaves."[16] In 1741, the minister wrote again to complain of a planter who punished his slave by means of "cruelties that cannot be tolerated." It was necessary, said the minister, to interpose "the authority of the king" in response to such brazen violations of the Code Noir.[17]

The use of phrases such as "private authority" and "the authority of the king" speaks to a perspective distinct from that of purely or even primarily humanitarian concern. In part, the monarchy's effort to enforce the Code Noir reflected its belief that a struggle over sovereignty was at stake. In the conduct of that struggle, the welfare of the slave population of Saint-Domingue was a means to various ends. The monarchy's interest in seeing its dictates respected outweighed whatever benefits there were to be gained from deferring completely to the arbitrary will of the masters. If the 1741 decision was not essentially humanitarian in nature, however, neither was it the product of an abstract or theoretical political calculus. A broader pattern of preemptive administrative practice was at work, one that equated deterrence of radical abuse with the long-term interests of the planters themselves and of the colonial project as a whole.

("During the first two and a half centuries of Anglo-American settlement, the household constituted the primary unit of governance for the vast majority of the inhabitants – married women, minors, servants, and slaves.").

[14] Debbasch, "Au coeur du 'gouvernement des esclaves,'" 33–34.
[15] "Ordonnance du Roi," December 30, 1712, LC, 2:337.
[16] Minister to the Administrators, September 30, 1727, LC, 3:221.
[17] Minister to the Administrators, July 25, 1741, LC, 3:674.

In February 1762, the naval minister, Etienne-François de Choiseul de Stainville, issued a set of instructions to the colonial high courts, asking them to produce guidelines for a commission to investigate the welfare and treatment of slaves. The third of Choiseul's instructions called for an inquiry into

the means of reconciling the authority of masters over slaves, so necessary to maintain, with that which is required by humanity, sound government [*la saine politique*], and the true interest of the masters, for the nourishment, clothing, care in sickness, and punishment of the slaves.[18]

The wording of this instruction highlights in concise terms the connection between strategic and moral claims – between an ideology of order and a self-described humanitarianism – that would feature in French colonial writings of the post–Seven Years' War period. Although acknowledging that even the monarchy and the colonial administrators had an interest in supporting "the [necessary] authority of masters over slaves," Choiseul pointed to the need to "reconcile" this authority with the countervailing imperative to enforce or even enhance Code Noir provisions for the welfare of slaves. Not only the concerns of "humanity" but also those of "sound government and the true interest of the masters" called for protecting the slave from the arbitrary rules of domestic government.

It is both impossible and misguided to seek to determine whether humanitarian concerns counted more or less than prudential or political goals in the naval minister's worldview. The point is that Choiseul's instructions did not regard these differing motivations as incompatible or even in tension with one another. Whatever importance Choiseul placed on humanitarian imperatives, those imperatives could always be placed alongside the tactics of "sound government" and a farsighted understanding of self-interest. Conversely, the strategic dimension of royal slave law could always seek legitimacy in the language of "humanity."

The equation of moderate, humane treatment of slaves with the "true interest of the masters" reflected the mundane reality that the monarchy was no less interested in the maintenance of colonial society than were the colonists. That shared interest could be served by conceding some of the playing field to the planters and their "necessary" sphere

[18] "Instructions demandées aux Conseils Supérieurs des Colonies," February 3 and 15, 1762, LC, 4:444.

of authority, so as to avoid the implication of any gratuitous conflicts between royal and planter sovereignty. Yet to accomplish this goal, the naval minister had effectively to place himself – and, by extension, the colonial judiciary – in the position of determining the actual needs of the planters. Some higher authority was needed to tell the planters that their perceived short-term interest in asserting an "absolute" right to domestic governance was incompatible with their long-term interest in stability. In one sense, this was simply another way of expressing the existence of a conflict between two forms of sovereignty: that is, a royal or colonial administrative sovereignty that had responsibility for the whole and a planter sovereignty that catered to the interests of the individual parts. However, the strategy of distinguishing between the merely apparent and the truly authentic interests of the colonists had the advantage for the administrators of bypassing an open conflict between metropolitan and colonial circles. By defining a broader sphere of interests that could encompass the concerns of both administrators and planters, it might be possible to avoid deciding whether Montesquieu was in fact correct that the "absolute" nature of the master-slave relationship inevitably sowed the seeds of its own demise.

Colonial administrators at all levels had their own unacknowledged reasons for postponing such a day of reckoning. With each new case to involve the abusive treatment of slaves, the more eager were administrators and magistrates to avoid an all-out conflict over the extent of their sovereignty. Enforcement of the Code Noir against renegade masters provided occasions to ostracize those planters who most egregiously mistreated their slaves. Still, in pursuing these cases, colonial administrators and judges were also indirectly testifying to the limits of their own power and to the corresponding prerogatives of planters. There was thus something of a risk in trying to hold too many masters accountable before the law. Every acknowledgment of a Code Noir violation also implied a corresponding enforcement failure, a flaw in the blueprint by which the French monarchy purported to impose its authority across the widening breach that separated it from its colonies.

"PRUDENT GOVERNMENT"

Absent a systematic breakdown of colonial authority, who really bore the risks of failing to enforce the Code Noir? It might seem that this cost was greater the higher up the ladder of authority one went. The monarchy's ability to assert control in Saint-Domingue depended on the maintenance of a reliable and consistent administration of justice. The naval minister, as the royal official ultimately responsible for carrying out the king's will in the colonies, was also closely implicated in the treatment of slaves in Saint-Domingue. And, as Choiseul's instructions clarify, the governor and intendant of the colony were feeling considerable pressure by the 1760s to put a stop to the excesses and brutalities of refractory planters.

Yet all of these officials, from the king to his deputies in the Caribbean, were removed to one degree or another from the ground level of judicial administration in Saint-Domingue. None was personally responsible for policing the treatment of slaves on individual plantations, or for ensuring that the Code Noir was properly applied in litigation bearing on that treatment. These burdens fell above all to the officers of the court system: the *conseillers* (judges), *procureurs* (prosecutors), and *huissiers* (clerks) of the high courts, and the magistrates of the local courts of first instance (*sénéchaux*). The documents they left behind provide invaluable glimpses of the kinds of discipline slaves regularly incurred, how they sought to respond, and how the judicial personnel of the colony made legal and political sense of those responses. With different levels of judicial authority in Saint-Domingue came different ideas about how to assess and manage the risks created by the abusive handling of slaves. A pair of interrelated cases from the early 1770s involving the torture, overworking, and neglect of slaves by planters demonstrates the range of approaches that could be applied to the task of enforcing the Code Noir on the ground.

On June 4, 1771, the officers of the *sénéchaussée* of Le Cap drew up a *mémoire* (a written account or statement of a case) concerning a group of ten slaves who had come forward with a "denunciation of atrocious deeds committed against them by their masters." Owned by a man named Dessources, the slaves had arrived at least one month before as "fugitives" at the residence of the *sénéchal* of Le Cap, in the company of the concierge of the court.[19] Because *marronage* was a crime regularly prosecuted under the Code Noir, the slaves were careful to point

---

[19] "Mémoire des officiers de la Sénéchaussée du Cap au Conseil du Cap," June 4, 1771, ANOM, F/3/90, fol. 149. The *mémoire* uses the phrase "*mai dernier*" ("last May"), leaving unclear whether May 1770 or May 1771 is meant. I am assuming from the urgency and immediacy of their *mémoire* that the *officiers* were motivated to write in response to a very recent happening. Yet it is possible that they were writing about events that happened roughly a year before. The *officiers* do refer to an October 1770 decision of the Conseil Supérieur of Le Cap, about which more later, that is dated "last October" and can only mean October 1770.

out that they "were only fugitives for purposes of throwing themselves into the hands of justice in order to avoid perishing one after the other." The slaves reported that Dessources, after torturing one slave with the use of fire and forcing him to deliver a "confession," had charged the entire work force of the plantation with the crime of "macandalisme" (poisoning) and the burning of a commander named Jauncton.[20] As punishment for these alleged offenses, Dessources proceeded to burn the feet and legs of one male (Cézar) and two female slaves (Fanchette and Jaunette) before burying them all alive. Dessources had also burned the feet and legs of an unnamed pregnant slave and subsequently placed her in a *cachot* (or cell of solitary confinement), as a result of which she eventually died.[21]

The day after the slaves arrived in Le Cap to report these events, another slave, named Pantin, came in search of the same magistrates to declare that he "was placing himself in the hands of justice so that he could be punished if he was guilty and protected if he was innocent." Pantin reported that in the past few years his former master, a woman, had burned between eight and ten slaves, and that the new master of this plantation showed every sign of continuing the policy. The judge ordered Pantin and the group of slaves who had arrived before him to be held in the town prisons pending an investigation.

The magistrates of the *sénéchaussée* interrupted their narrative at this point to note that the Code Noir and judicial precedent prior to October 1770 were clear about how the case should be handled. Article 42 of the Code provided that planters found guilty of torturing or mutilating their slaves faced criminal prosecution and the confiscation of the slaves.[22] A range of cases decided earlier in the eighteenth century confirmed, according to the magistrates' *mémoire*, that the royal prosecutor could and ought to press charges against the masters at issue. However, all of that had changed when, on October 2, 1770, the Conseil Supérieur of Cap Français rendered a decision in the case of a Mr. and Mrs. Cassarouy,

---

[20] François Macandal, a Muslim, Arabic-speaking slave from "Guinea," was burned at the stake in January 1758 on charges of poisoning whites and of spreading knowledge about the use of poison to other slaves in the colony. His name became associated with a specific crime – "Macandalisme" – and was invoked by the courts and by colonists throughout the rest of the colonial period in Saint-Domingue as a symbol of the dangers of slave crime. See Fick, *The Making of Haiti*, 59–73; Pierre Pluchon, *Vaudou, sorciers, empoisonneurs: De Saint-Domingue à Haïti* (Paris: Éditions Karthala, 1987), 165 ff. I take up this subject in further detail in Chapter 4.

[21] "Mémoire des officiers de la Sénéchaussée," June 4, 1771, fol. 149.

[22] Code Noir, art. 42 (1685).

a decision that resulted in "the greatest perplexity" for the royal prosecutor and judge responsible for trying the cases of Cézar, Fanchette, Jaunette, and Pantin.[23]

The Cassarouy case involved a group of slaves who had run away from their plantation after being repeatedly overworked and deprived of food rations. Cassarouy and his wife had inherited the plantation under somewhat controversial conditions, so their titles to the land and to the slaves who worked it were not as solid as they could otherwise have been. This did not stop Cassarouy from having the slaves arrested by the fugitive slave militia, brought to Le Cap, scorched with burning hot wax on their hands, arms, and backs, and then thrown into prison. A few days later, the slaves were brought back to the plantation. A pair of them subsequently escaped again and, as authorized by article 26 of the Code Noir, took out complaints against Cassarouy before the royal prosecutor, who proceeded to launch an investigation.[24] Two sets of charges were brought. The first involved a challenge to the legality of the Cassarouys' title to the plantation and its slave community. The second stemmed from the complaints of the slaves who had suffered mutilation at the hands of Cassarouy. Because their wounds served as evidence for the prosecution, these slaves were ordered removed from the plantation and placed in prison. Upon arriving at the plantation to carry out this order, the clerks of the court and their police escorts found a female slave "suspended in the air by her arms."[25] She was taken down and brought back to Le Cap in the company of the tortured slaves. Despite all of this direct, compelling evidence, the Conseil Supérieur refused to admit any of the charges against Cassarouy, nullified the complaints and remonstrances filed against him, and ordered that all of the slaves who had been removed from the plantation be returned.[26]

---

[23] "Mémoire des officiers de la Sénéchaussée," June 4, 1771, fols. 149–150. The authors of this *mémoire* are indicated at the end as "Estève, St. Martin, and Créton."

[24] "Slaves who are not fed, clothed, and maintained by their masters as we have ordained may give information thereof to the attorney general of the Conseil Supérieur, and may put the written exposition of their wrongs into his hands; upon which information, and even *ex officio*, should the information come from elsewhere, the attorney general shall prosecute said masters without charging any costs to the complainants. It is our will that this regulation be observed in all accusations for crimes or barbarous and inhuman treatment brought by slaves against their masters." Code Noir, art. 26 (1685). For this article of the Code Noir I have borrowed freely from the translation provided in Charles Gayarré, *History of Louisiana: The French Domination*, 4th ed. (New Orleans, F. F. Hansell & Bro., 1903), 1:533–534.

[25] It is unclear whether she had been suspended from a tree or some other elevated position.

[26] "Mémoire des officiers de la Sénéchaussée," June 4, 1771, fols. 151–152.

The proper interpretation to be given this precedent emerged as a key issue in the Dessources investigation. In their *mémoire*, the *sénéchaussée* officers found that, all appearances to the contrary notwithstanding, the high court had ruled in the Cassarouy case on substantive rather than procedural grounds. The "natural and literal" meaning of the holding was "precisely that neither the royal prosecutor nor the judge has the right to monitor the severity of the discipline [*police*] that masters exercise over their slaves, even when bodily mutilation is involved." The judgment in favor of Cassarouy had served to nullify the proceedings against him "as far back as the remonstrant's complaint." Such a result necessarily entailed that "the nullities pronounced by the decision stem not from the proceedings but rather from the matter of the case [*la chose*] in itself."[27] The Cassarouy holding, in other words, was as an unambiguous endorsement for the principle of absolute domestic sovereignty.

That, at least, was the interpretation to which the officers prosecuting Dessources seemed bound. Yet it was not a conclusion at which they lightly arrived. To the contrary, it seems that the *sénéchaussée* officers were looking for every bit of wriggle room possible to escape from having to apply the stark logic behind Cassarouy's acquittal to Dessources. At some stage, the officers must have brought their reservations to the attention of their superiors, for upon hearing of those concerns, the presiding magistrate responded that the Code Noir authorized the royal prosecutor to bring charges against a master only if his neighbors took steps to denounce him. This assertion, the officers replied, was plainly incorrect: Article 26 of the Code explicitly authorized slaves to bring their own complaints and said nothing about the need for a neighbor's denunciation. It was true that, before a prosecution could commence, information about a master's conduct had to "come from elsewhere" than the slave whose grievance had brought that conduct to light. The Code also provided, however, for the prosecution of masters found guilty of mutilating or killing their slaves without the need for third-party evidence or indeed for any information other than a slave's complaint.[28]

These objections notwithstanding, the judgment of the high court in Cap Français was unambiguous: In cases of this nature, prosecutors and judges "were wrong to involve themselves in the discipline or rather

---

[27] Ibid., fol. 152. Underlining in the original.
[28] Ibid., fols. 152–153. The officers were here referencing articles 42 and 43. Even in disagreement, the officers may have conceded a bit too much with this argument, as article 26 required third-party evidence only in the event that the royal prosecutor was proceeding "by right of office," without the benefit of information provided by a mistreated slave.

in the excess of discipline exercised by these masters." In disposing of the Cassarouy case, the Conseil Supérieur evidently aimed to establish a "model of behavior with respect to actual masters and owners" – an allusion to the Cassarouys' disputed title to their plantation and slaves. In the view of the *sénéchaussée* officers, all of this flew in the face of the policies embodied in the Code Noir. The monarchy had "wanted, intended, enjoined and ordered" its judicial representatives in the colonies to take action against masters who "mutilated, inflicted barbarities upon, or killed their slaves." It was simply not possible that "the sovereign tribunal, natural protector of the laws it is charged with executing, could have wanted to do away with this right of action, which resides immediately in the officers of the jurisdictions."[29]

Yet that appeared to be the brunt of the matter. Cassarouy's absolution had made clear that the enforcement scheme envisioned by the Code Noir had fallen into abeyance and lost its grip on the colony's judicial system. There was a logical explanation for that development, according to the officers charged with deciding on Dessources's fate. The "colonial regime, and the system of inspection with which the officers of justice are charged by [the Code Noir]" had become "gentler" in practice. It was "unheard of" in any jurisdiction, and particularly in the jurisdiction of Le Cap, for an officer of the court system to enter "the interior of the plantations" to verify whether slaves were receiving adequate nourishment and clothing or whether they were being whipped more than the twenty-five times permitted by the law.

The regime of the colony has changed in proportion as the colonists have become civilized and as the plantations have internalized a regulated system of government that conforms to the manner in which slaves should be managed; this is what has led ever so imperceptibly to that relaxation of the right of inspection ordained by the laws.[30]

A system of "internalized government" could be tolerated in the colony so long as it conducted itself according to the rule of the Code Noir. Yet what was responsible for leading the masters as domestic sovereigns to moderate and "civilize" the manner in which they treated their slaves? The *mémoire* singled out a decline in the use of poison by slaves against both their masters and fellow slaves as the essential reason for the change. Although the officers did not specify a precise time period, the height

---

[29] "Mémoire des officiers de la Sénéchaussée," June 4, 1771, fol. 154.
[30] Ibid., fol. 155.

of the "poison scare" in Saint-Domingue came during the 1750s (with Macandal's activities) and 1760s.[31] During that period, "it was considered necessary (and with good reason) to leave the tormented masters" considerable authority to commit acts "of an excessive severity relative to the times but necessary in the circumstances."[32]

The nature of the risk at issue no longer justified such leeway, according to the officers. The courts of justice were not required to continue closing their eyes to the commission of acts that could only be regarded as "inhuman." The officers acknowledged that the use of poison by slaves had been a real problem for the colonists, but they also noted that many masters had used this pretext as a justification for intensifying their "natural ferocity" toward their slaves and for taking vengeance on some of them for unrelated reasons. As a result, many slaves had been either falsely accused of poisoning their fellow slaves or else left to die of hunger on the more poorly cultivated plantations. While the judicial system held its silence, the "small planters" of the colony began making a habit of "the most horrible excesses."[33] However, the flexibility granted planters during this period reflected a temporary emergency arrangement rather than a statement that the "municipal law" could be done away with altogether.[34] The Cassarouy case had posed a test of whether the Code Noir would continue to lie in a state of desuetude or serve as the basis for a newly revitalized system of colonial governance.[35]

In criticizing the Conseil Supérieur's decision, the *sénéchaussée* officers echoed both Montesquieu's analysis of slavery and Choiseul's 1762 instructions calling on the same tribunal to check the "private authority" of planters in the name of "sound government." The Romans' absolute right of life and death over their slaves, even if it was still embraced by certain peoples in the present day,[36] was nonetheless offensive to "religion, humanity, and our manners." The ancient doctrine of *patria potestas* was incompatible with "the public policy [*la politique*] that

---

[31] Yvan Debbasch makes much of the significance of this "reign of poison" in his article, although he emphasizes its political consequences for the post-1770 period. Debbasch, "Au coeur du 'gouvernement des esclaves,'" 38. See Chapter 4 for further discussion of the role of poison in the terror-torture nexus of Saint-Domingue.

[32] "Mémoire des officiers de la Sénéchaussée," June 4, 1771, fol. 155.

[33] It is unclear whether the officers were distinguishing between or equating two types of slaveholders: those whose lands were poorly cultivated and "small planters."

[34] "Mémoire des officiers de la Sénéchaussée," June 4, 1771, fol. 156.

[35] Ibid.

[36] This may have been an allusion to the treatment of slaves in the British, Spanish, and other sugar colonies of the New World.

must serve as the basis of the colony's regime." Once made sufficiently aware that the "barbarities exercised against them" would go unpunished, the slaves would inevitably decide to take matters into their own hands.[37] The only way to avoid that fate was to enforce a "municipal law tempered in its use."[38]

Here too, as in Choiseul's instructions, the aspiration to control the risks of planter brutality involved a mix of precautionary and moral rationales with no clear distinction between the two. In stopping the "barbarities of the masters," the colonial courts would serve to "tranquillize" the slave population and prevent its most traumatized members from delivering themselves to the "last desperation" – a somewhat oblique phrase that could have alluded either to slave suicides (sufficiently numerous to become a source of official concern)[39] or to the possibility of an organized slave rebellion. Yet the need to deter such "desperation" was one of several dictates that included "religion, humanity, our morays, our precise and declared laws [*loix positives*], and, finally, the most prudent government [*politique*] of the colony." All of these, the *sénéchaussée* officers declared, "require placing limits on the tolerance shown towards masters who abuse their authority over and property in human slaves [*les hommes esclaves*]."[40]

The *sénéchaussée* officers concluded, somewhat boldly, by calling on the Conseil Supérieur to "reassure" them of the grounds of the Cassarouy decision. In particular, the officers wanted to know that the decision was not intended to "deprive them of [their] right to exercise vigilance over and to prosecute" the kinds of "delicts" at issue. To be sure, the *sénéchaux* would use "discretion" in exercising a power the "limits" of which they fully recognized.[41] In so reassuring the high court, the officers acknowledged that the dangers of planter brutality had to be balanced against the countervailing hazard of emboldening slave insubordination. Although it was essential to enforce the protections of the Code Noir, it was also important to preserve the necessary integrity of the domestic sphere.

---

[37] "Mémoire des officiers de la Sénéchaussée," June 4, 1771, fol. 156.
[38] Ibid., fol. 157. See also Pluchon, *Vaudou, sorciers, empoisonneurs*, 197–199.
[39] See, for example, "Arrêt du Conseil du Cap Français," September 7, 1722, LC 3:23 (concerning an escaped slave who killed herself before her trial for *marronage* could take place); and "Arrêt du Conseil du Cap Français," May 8, 1733, LC 3:359 (concerning a slave who committed suicide in the course of a criminal trial). In both of these cases, the issue was whether the master was entitled to compensation from the colonial treasury for the death of his slave. See also Fick, *The Making of Haiti*, 46–48.
[40] "Mémoire des officiers de la Sénéchaussée," June 4, 1771, fol. 158.
[41] Ibid.

We do not know whether the Conseil Supérieur responded to the officers' request for what was, in effect, an advisory opinion on the prosecution of Dessources (if not a petition to overrule the Cassarouy decision). Whatever formal or informal feedback may have issued, the Dessources case was resolved in a manner that seemed to reflect both the Cassarouy precedent and the officers' own views about the need to exercise their "right of vigilance." One week after the officers wrote their *mémoire* on June 4, 1771, the *sénéchal* responsible for adjudicating the slaves' complaints handed down his ruling. The decision mandated that the slaves, then being held in the town prison, be returned to the plantation from whence they had "escaped." However, the judge also went on to insist that, even though Dessources was entitled to the renewed possession of his property, it could only be on condition that he "justify" the death or sale of any of the slaves returned to him.[42] The judge seems to have anticipated that Dessources, in an effort to take revenge on his slaves for having accused him before the public authorities, would seek either to sell them away from their family and friends or to murder them. This requirement of justification was perhaps a small measure of vindication for the cause of prudential government, even if it afforded little reassurance to the group of ten slaves facing imminent return to a master whose authority they had so boldly challenged.

"ORDER" AND "HUMANITY"

By invoking the requirements of "religion" and "humanity" alongside those of "prudent government," the magistrates in the Dessources case echoed Choiseul's 1762 instructions to the colonial courts to crack down on recalcitrant planters in the name of both "humanity" and "sound government." Such language might be thought of as an instance of what the contemporary economist and philosopher Amartya Sen labels "plural grounding," that is, "using a number of different lines of condemnation, without seeking an agreement on their relative merits."[43] Without coming close to questioning the justice of slavery per se, the

---

[42] "Ordonnance du Juge du Cap qui ordonne la remise de plusieurs esclaves à leur maître," June 10, 1771, ANOM, F/3/90, fol. 159. This ordinance appears right after the officers' *mémoire* in the same bound volume of documents.

[43] Sen, *The Idea of Justice*, 2. Sen is here commenting on the complexities in a much more thoroughgoing criticism of injustice, namely Edmund Burke's great speech in the British Parliament in support of the impeachment of William Hastings, the governor of the British East India Company.

officers nonetheless gave voice to what would become an increasingly prevalent form of criticism of certain segments of and tendencies in the French planter community.

There is indeed some evidence that Choiseul's instructions were having at least some of their intended effect. On several occasions, both before and after the Cassarouy case, the two high courts took action against masters for offenses involving the mutilation and abusive treatment of slaves. In 1764, the Port-au-Prince tribunal ordered a particularly "violent" master to sell his slave to a new owner.[44] In 1774, the Conseil Supérieur in Le Cap – the same court that had ruled in Cassarouy's favor three years prior – ordered a colonist to render an account every six months of the condition of one of his slaves. In a somewhat euphemistic style, the decision mandated that the slave at issue not "be exposed" to any "unjust" or "unfounded" mistreatment.[45] A few years later, the same Conseil required a master accused of castrating his slave to present the victim to the royal prosecutor, presumably for the purpose of preparing evidence to use against the master. The record does not indicate whether the master in that case received any punishment.[46]

These scattered rulings, of course, represented only a small subset of the total universe of behaviors involving the mutilation and physical abuse of slaves. Most such cases never made it to the attention of the royal prosecutor, despite the formal availability of a complaint procedure enshrined in article 26 of the Code Noir. Of the cases that did find their way into court, there is little evidence that masters ever received any punishment more severe than a fine or (as in the rare instances previously cited) the forced sale of their slaves. The complaints that proceeded to investigation and trial are useful primarily as evidence of broader patterns of torture and abuse in Saint-Domingue.

Those cases are also significant for two other closely related reasons, however. First, they reveal something of the risks that slaves, in certain rare instances, were willing to take in responding to the everyday violence inflicted on them. Whereas article 26 of the Code Noir licensed the bringing of complaints against refractory planters, article 38 of the Code defined slave flight from the plantation as a crime of its own: *marronage*.[47]

---

[44] "Arrêt du Conseil du Port-au-Prince," November 16, 1764, ANOM, CSD, F/3/272, fol. 673.

[45] "Arrêt du Conseil du Cap," December 13, 1774, ANOM, CSD, F/3/273, fol. 895. The passive voice here may have reflected the power of plantation managers and the phenomenon of absentee ownership more than anything else.

[46] "Arrêt du Conseil du Cap," May 17, 1779, ANOM, CSD, F/3/274, fol. 783.

[47] Code Noir, art. 38 (1685).

The contradictions embodied in the Code Noir placed slaves who sought to claim its protections in the ambiguous position of having to violate the rule of law in seeking to enforce that rule. For at least some slaves, that double bind was the necessary and acceptable cost of seeking to rein in the excesses of their masters. Its necessity stemmed from the absence of royal prosecutors from the world of the plantations, which by definition were at a remove from the urban and village nerve centers of the judicial system. The intertwined cases of Cassarouy and Dessources are especially revealing in this regard. In submitting themselves to the *sénéchal* of Le Cap for judicial protection from Dessources, as we have seen, the ten slaves evidently found it necessary to justify their flight from the plantation. They had become "fugitives" only to avoid being killed by their master.[48] For these slaves and for others, the risk of being apprehended for *marronage* paled in comparison to the risk of retaliation incurred by daring to accuse one's master or plantation commander before the authorities.

Second, the article 26 cases indicate that colonial administrators and jurists interpreted the behavior of masters and slaves alike through a prism that conflated humanitarian concerns with the rule of law. From the point of view of the colonial administration, the use of torture and mutilation by masters and the resulting efforts by slaves to run away from the plantations were two sides of the same coin – and both were equally threatening to the cause of maintaining social stability. Whatever was useful in containing the risk of slave resistance in general and *marronage* in particular (the most significant and effective form of slave resistance) was also praiseworthy from the standpoint of "humanity" and "religion."[49] As the monarchy stated in its instructions to Jean-Etienne-Bernard de Clugny, intendant of Saint-Domingue from 1760 to 1764, it was important to ensure that masters "treat their slaves with humanity, and provide them with food and clothing in accordance with the ordinances. This is the surest method of preventing *marronage*."[50] The task of the administrators and judiciary was to break the perceived vicious circle of crimes (torture and mutilation) and "countercrimes" (*marronage*) by stemming it at its source: the rule of domestic sovereignty.

[48] "Mémoire des officiers de la Sénéchaussée," June 4, 1771, fol. 149.

[49] On *marronage* and the theme of slave revolt in eighteenth-century French colonial thought, see Duchet, *Anthropologie et histoire*, 139–152.

[50] Quoted in ibid., 151. These instructions were issued in 1760.

Both of these dynamics – the efforts by slaves to manage the risks of plantation life and the close administrative ties between considerations of order and humanity – are illustrated by the 1775 deposition of a slave named Thomas, taken by the *sénéchal* of Le Cap. Slave depositions are among the rarest of eighteenth-century colonial legal records: Only a handful exist for the entire colonial period. The Code Noir prohibited slaves from serving as "arbiters, experts, or witnesses" in civil or criminal court cases. Slaves could be deposed or interrogated, but their testimony could be used in court only as "supplementary" statements to help judges "clarify their understanding of things," not to "infer any presumptions, conjectures, or dispositive proofs."[51] A royal ordinance promulgated in 1738 somewhat eased these restrictions by admitting a slave's testimony into evidence if there were no white witnesses and if the slave was an essential witness.[52] Together with the Code Noir provision on the "supplementary" use of slave testimony, the 1738 rule acquired a special significance during the perceived mid-century "reign of poison" by slaves. Yet even under the new regime, a slave could not testify against his own master.[53] It remained almost unheard of for a judicial officer or royal prosecutor to rely on a slave's testimony for purposes of advancing a case against a white colonist, particularly if that colonist was also a person of some social standing.[54]

Thomas lived on a plantation in the northern plains of Saint-Domingue owned by a woman named de l'Isle Adam.[55] A creole (or American-born) slave who also served as commander of the plantation, Thomas escaped a year and a half before the deposition was taken. He returned to the plantation a few weeks before the investigation of the case was opened.

---

[51] Code Noir, art. 30 (1685).

[52] Fick, *Making of Haiti*, 283 n.108.

[53] Ibid.

[54] More typical in this respect is the March 1788 case of a planter named Maguero who had mutilated several of his slaves but could not be indicted because slave depositions, which were the only available evidence against him, were unacceptable in the courts of law. Hence it was necessary for the colonial administrators to take action against him independently of the court system. In their *lettre commune* about this case the administrators wrote, "The judicial system having unfortunately had no hold over this guilty person, it has seemed to us necessary to proceed against him by means of an administrative proceeding." The letter acknowledged the "inconveniences" of removing the owner from his plantation, but also noted that this was far from the only such case involving abusive treatment of slaves. There were other "even more serious" cases that posed the same evidentiary problems. "Lettre commune des Administrateurs sur les Barbaries commises par le Sr. Maguero envers les Nègres de son Habitation," March 25, 1788, ANOM CGSD, C/9A/160, fols. 78–79. Chapter 4 considers this case in further detail.

[55] As is characteristic of colonial records, Thomas's last name is not provided.

At the time the investigation began, Thomas was being kept in the royal prison in Le Cap by virtue of the French equivalent of a writ of *habeas corpus*. Asked by the *sénéchal* of Le Cap to explain the reason for his *marronage*, Thomas explained that he had been threatened by the *procureur* (agent) of the plantation, M. Chapuzet. Chapuzet had promised to kill Thomas in retaliation for causing the death of a mule kept on the plantation. Indeed, Thomas testified, Chapuzet had a prior record of murdering slaves he claimed were responsible for causing the death of animals on the plantation. Asked how Chapuzet carried out these crimes, Thomas replied that Chapuzet placed them in a solitary confinement cell on what seems to have been a neighboring or nearby plantation. Some of the slaves died as a result of unbearable conditions in the cell, and others as a result of being buried alive by Chapuzet.[56]

These reports of travesty notwithstanding, the *sénéchal's* questions were clearly geared toward eliciting information about the *marronage* of Thomas as much as they were designed to ascertain the criminal conduct of Chapuzet. For example, the *sénéchal* asked Thomas whether other slaves had taken flight from the plantation as a result of Chapuzet's punishments. Thomas replied that "several" others had resorted to *marronage*, but that he had personally encountered only one in the area where he had taken refuge. Queried whether he himself had been responsible for "inciting" these other fugitive slaves to leave the plantation, Thomas responded no. Alluding to (without explicitly citing) the language of article 38 of the Code Noir, the magistrate further asked Thomas whether he knew of the potential penalties for *marronage*. Thomas responded that he was unaware of these provisions, but that he had taken flight for fear of being killed in the manner of his father, another victim of Chapuzet. According to Thomas, his father had met with Chapuzet's wrath after killing a slave to whom he (Thomas's father) had been married. Thomas concluded his deposition by affirming that his responses had been sincere and truthful.[57]

It is a measure of the irony and ambiguity of Thomas's deposition that it created a basis for the magistrate to indict *either* Chapuzet for serial slave murder or Thomas for *marronage*. Because the deposition of a slave could be used only as a means of "clarifying" a judge's understanding of the facts and not as the basis for establishing the guilt or innocence of a

---

[56] "Interrogation d'un nègre de l'habitation de la Dame de l'Isle Adam," January 25, 1775, ANOM, F/3/90, fols. 160–161.
[57] Ibid., fols. 161–162.

party, the *sénéchal* was free to dispose of the case as he wished. How (or even whether) this case was actually resolved is unclear. Yet Thomas's deposition exemplifies the tendency of colonial judges to identify even the worst abuses of planter sovereignty and the prevalence of *marronage* as reciprocal and coordinate phenomena in Saint-Domingue. When magistrates and administrators singled out planter brutality as the *cause* of *marronage*, they did so as much out of a concern for overall social order as out of any sense that the abuses in question were intolerable from a moral or religious point of view.

The belief that abusive treatment imperiled the social order was not limited to the colonial officiate of judges, clerks, royal prosecutors, and administrators. Nor were slaves alone in calling the risks and tragedies that shadowed their daily existence to the attention of the authorities, whether by means of *marronage* or other forms of social protest. Occasionally, white colonists acting as "private" citizens took steps to bring the most notorious violations of the Code Noir to light. One such case involved a resident named Courrejolles who hailed from Limonade, a town in the northern department not far from Cap Français. Courrejolles took matters into his own hands by writing a letter to the royal prosecutor in Le Cap about the "revolting cruelties" inflicted on two slaves (a woman and child) and one free person of color. All three had been found by Courrejolles on a plantation in Limonade owned by a M. de la Chapelle.[58] The free person was a child identified as a *quarteronne* (the daughter of a white father and a mulatto mother). In this case, the child also happened to be the daughter of one of the masters at issue in Courrejolles' complaint. Courrejolles reported that the culpable masters had cut the tongue and torn out several teeth of the slave woman and burned the slave child with red-hot irons. The free child, for her part, had fled from the plantation in order to avoid the "perpetual cruelties" of her father.[59]

Insisting that "such cruel treatment should not rest unpunished," Courrejolles urged that all three of the victims be placed "under the protection of justice." He requested that the royal prosecutor bring the three

---

[58] This may have been a plantation belonging to the Fournier de la Chapelle family, which inherited six sugar plantations in the Limonade area upon Fournier's death in 1714. See the online index of names transposed by the website *Généalogie et Histoire de la Caraïbe* from the Maurel/Taillemite edition of Moreau de Saint-Mery's *Description topographique*, at http://www.ghcaraibe.org/livres/ouvdiv/stmery/stmery-E.html (last viewed Sept. 6, 2009).

[59] "Ordonnance du juge du Cap touchant des cruautés exercées contre des Esclaves et une libre," February 15, 1781, ANOM, F/3/90, fol. 189.

to Le Cap where they could be kept in prison pending further investigation. Courrejolles observed that the two slaves and the free child "will tell you the name of their masters," implying that more than one master was involved and that Courrejolles himself was either unable or unwilling to disclose their names.[60] "I believe that the interests of good order and of humanity in particular argue for placing a curb on the rage of a violent person [*un furieux*]," Courrejolles concluded.[61]

It was no accident that Courrejolles used the term humanity as if it were a subset or variant of the category of "good order." For Courrejolles, the ethics and injustice of slavery were a branch of the discipline of prudential government, a handmaiden rather than an alternative to the strategic administration of colonial life. Even a colonist acting in his private capacity, someone with no official responsibility for investigating reports of planter brutality or bringing the guilty parties to justice, could share the feeling that order and humanity converged in demanding a remedy for the excesses of refractory planters. Without arriving at the conclusion that slavery itself was unjust or needed to be abolished, Courrejolles nonetheless implicated the tendency of slavery, as it existed in Saint-Domingue, to veer toward the most extreme forms of human conduct.

The report for this case does not indicate the decision taken by the *sénéchal* of Le Cap. However, the title of the ordinance implies that some form of punishment was given to those responsible for the crimes alleged by Courrejolles.[62] Courrejolles' suspicion that more than one master had committed the abuses in this particular case was called into question by a note that Moreau de Saint-Méry likely appended to the end of the document. "The perpetrator of all these atrocities," the note reads, "was Mr. Jouammicault, a resident of Le Cap. It is difficult to conceive of how such black deeds [*noirceurs*] could go unpunished."[63]

---

[60] This is an exact translation of the passage in question. Courrejolles writes, "Ces malheureuses vous diront le nom de leurs maîtres." The grammatically correct expression, of course, would have been "les noms de leurs maîtres." Yet it is also possible that Courrejolles was simply unsure of how many masters were involved here.

[61] "Ordonnance du juge du Cap," February 15, 1781, fol. 190. The original reads, "Je crois qu'il est du bon ordre et particulièrement du bien de l'humanité."

[62] The title of this ordinance is consistent with that of similar ordinances assessing a fine on or confiscating the slave of a master found guilty of mutilating or torturing his slave.

[63] "Ordonnance du juge du Cap," February 15, 1781, fol. 190. My conclusion that Moreau authored this note is consistent with Moreau's practice of annotating cases and judicial decisions on which he reported in his "Code de Saint-Domingue" (CSD) collection.

THE LATE COLONIAL DEBATE OVER PLANTER BRUTALITY

In time, the proliferation of cases involving planter brutality generated a stream of commentary about the risks that unconstrained domestic authority posed to the stability of the colonial project as a whole. The core of this debate, which unfolded between 1776 and 1789, did not typically encompass condemnations of the legitimacy of slavery per se. At its outer edges, however, the controversy over the phenomenon of radical abuse generated a small number of proposals for the wholesale reform or even abolition of slavery. These proposals highlight the sense of urgency that attended the discussion of refractory planter conduct in Saint-Domingue – a discussion that was dominated by less far-reaching but still sharp criticisms of the domestic sphere as well as more apologetic materials that affirmatively defended the prerogatives of renegade planters. Together, these polemics reveal the anxieties and strategies of administrators and colonists as they maneuvered, by turns cooperatively and antagonistically, to draw an increasingly tenuous line between acceptable and unacceptable methods of plantation government.

Although this debate reached its apogee in late colonial Saint-Domingue, it extended to other areas of the French Caribbean as well. Indeed, one of the earliest (if not the very first) proposals for abolition in the French empire emanated from French Guiana, on the northeast coast of South America, adjacent to the Dutch colony of Surinam. In 1768, the Baron de Bessner, a military officer, proposed to make "free cultivators" of the children of slaves and all slaves under the age of ten then living on the Mont Joly plantation in Cayenne, the capital of French Guiana.[64] A colonial variation of serfdom, Bessner's plan would have obliged the plantation workers to continue laboring for their masters "as in the past"

---

[64] "Plan proposé pour opérer successivement la Suppression de l'esclavage dans l'habitation du Mont Joly à Cayenne," 1768, ANOM, F/3/90, fol. 141. Bessner was a military officer from Alsace who had been assigned to undertake an investigation in French Guiana in the aftermath of the Seven Years' War. After arriving in Guiana in 1765 and finding his role reduced to a purely military one, he tried unsuccessfully to start up a new colonization company with a plan to cultivate an area near Cayenne, the colony's capital. Bessner was named governor of French Guiana in 1781 and died there in 1785. For more on his career and proposal for gradual emancipation, see Pierre-Victor Malouet, *Mémoires de Malouet, publiés par son petit-fils le Baron Malouet*, 2nd ed. (Paris: E. Plon et cie, 1874), 1:74–93, 386–389; Duchet, *Anthropologie et histoire*, 154–157; and Tarrade, "De l'apogée économique," 301.

until the age of twenty-five. At that time they would receive a piece of land of predetermined size, which they would be allowed to keep and transmit to their descendants in exchange for working five days a week on the plantations of their former masters. The children of this first generation of nominally "free cultivators" would also serve in the plantation labor force until attaining the age of twenty, when they would receive full "civil liberty" from the government.[65]

Bessner's definition of "civil liberty" made clear that a concern with the consequences of planter brutality and the ideology of domestic sovereignty informed his proposal for gradual emancipation. Civil liberty, wrote Bessner, entailed the "prerogative ... to see oneself freed of the arbitrary authority of private persons, and to be subject only to the laws and regulations of the public administration [*police*]." In the very next sentence, the proposal prohibited masters from mistreating their slaves and from "rendering justice themselves."[66]

Bessner was thus no starry-eyed idealist. A future governor of French Guiana, he was sufficiently moved by the dangers of continued planter abuse to extend his 1768 plan for gradual emancipation on the Mont Joly plantation to the colony as a whole in 1774.[67] "The relation that subsists today between master and slave," he wrote then, "leads to the mutual corruption of each other."[68] In the 1770s, Bessner was also deeply involved on the colony's behalf in negotiations with the maroon communities who sought refuge in the interior regions of Guiana.[69] In short, Bessner's career was a paradigmatic embodiment of the prudential morality of slavery in action. He went further than others in his advocacy of gradual emancipation, but he was also not an isolated figure in the colonial milieu. To the contrary, he belonged to the colonial political establishment. Indeed, Bessner's proposal for gradual emancipation went so far as to be discussed in 1779 by the Naval Ministry's committee on colonial legislation.[70] The proposal never made it it out of that committee. But the connection that Bessner's project drew between the "arbitrary authority of private persons" and the abuse of slaves would figure repeatedly in the debates of the 1770s and 1780s concerning Saint-Domingue.

[65] "Plan proposé pour opérer successivement la Suppression de l'esclavage," 1768, fol. 141.
[66] Ibid.
[67] Duchet, *Anthropologie et histoire*, 154.
[68] Quoted in ibid., 155.
[69] Ibid., 155.
[70] Tarrade, "L'administration coloniale en France à la fin de l'Ancien Regime," 113. Tarrade's source for this assertion is Bessner's contemporary and collaborator Pierre-Victor Malouet, about whom more later.

One of the most powerful voices for these positions was Michel René Hilliard d'Auberteuil, who published a major two-volume polemic entitled *Considérations sur l'état présent de la colonie française de Saint-Domingue* in 1776 and 1777. Born in France and educated as a lawyer there, Hilliard d'Auberteuil moved to Saint-Domingue to ply his trade as a colonial *avocat*.[71] His sometimes vituperative attacks on the royal bureaucracy and his passionate defense of colonial autonomy earned him a prominent place in the creole legal community of Saint-Domingue. The *Considérations* was suppressed in both France and the colonies soon after its publication by a 1777 *arrêt* of the Conseil d'Etat.[72] As Gene Ogle has shown, however, censorship did little to stop the book from inciting great controversy in Saint-Domingue, and indeed the Naval Ministry took various steps to facilitate Hilliard d'Auberteuil's authorial aspirations, including by covering the debts he incurred in the course of publishing the book.[73] Hilliard d'Auberteuil evidently hoped that the work's appearance would support his bid for a position in the colonial judiciary – a campaign he began mounting upon returning to France in 1775 to find a printer for his book.[74]

Hilliard d'Auberteuil's work illuminates several important strands of thought in the colonial Enlightenment, such as the movement to reform colonial law in light of local custom and the ideology of white supremacy.[75] For present purposes, however, Hilliard d'Auberteuil's views on the treatment of slaves in Saint-Domingue are of greatest interest. In a critical passage of the section on slavery in volume 1 of the *Considérations*, Hilliard d'Auberteuil argued that planters ought to treat their slaves humanely, not primarily for moral reasons, but rather for the practical purpose of extracting the maximum amount of labor. From

---

[71] Frostin, *Les révoltes blanches*, 21. On Hilliard d'Auberteuil's career and thought, see Gene E. Ogle, "'The Eternal Power of Reason' and 'The Superiority of Whites': Hilliard d'Auberteuil's Colonial Enlightenment," *French Colonial History* 3 (2003): 35–50; Lewis, *Main Currents in Caribbean Thought*, 129–136; Garrigus, *Before Haiti*, 160–161; and Lewis Leary, introduction to *Miss McCrea: A Novel of the American Revolution*, by Michel René Hilliard d'Auberteuil, trans. Eric LaGuardia (Gainesville, FL: Scholars' Fascimiles and Reprints, 1958), 6–11.

[72] "Arrêt du Conseil d'État," December 17, 1777, LC, 5:805–06; Debien, *Les colons de Saint-Domingue et la Révolution*, 157 n.19

[73] Ogle, "'The Eternal Power of Reason' and 'The Superiority of Whites,'" 39.

[74] Ibid., 37, 39.

[75] On the first of these themes, see Ghachem, "Montesquieu in the Caribbean"; on the second, see Ogle, "'The Eternal Power of Reason' and 'The Superiority of Whites,'" 40–44; and Garrigus, *Before Haiti*, 160–161.

this economic perspective, the best policy was to "gradually accustom" the slaves to an "exact and invariable discipline," one that would compare favorably to the treatment accorded the peasants of France.[76] The utilitarian character of this analysis reinforces Ogle's thesis that Hilliard d'Auberteuil's thought participated in a broader discourse of utility that linked the colonial Enlightenment to imperial reform projects.[77]

At the same time, however, Hilliard d'Auberteuil was responding to a very specific line of argument in a debate over planter brutality that both predated and would outlive the *Considérations*. The strategic imperative of humane treatment stood in opposition to the dogmatic claims of renegade planters and their apologists, those who argued that "slaves were incapable of being contained by the civil laws because they form no part of society, and that they can only be subjected to a law of the family, which is to say, the law of the master." To embrace this position was "to confound all idea of justice," Hilliard d'Auberteuil retorted. "[I]t is necessary to subject this colony's slaves to a civil law, which cannot be altered, rather than to the law of the master, which is nothing other than his will." Subordinating the slave to the exclusive law of the master – to give the master, in effect, "a right of life and death" over the slave – "is repugnant to all principles; the master would be at once the offended party, the accuser, and the judge!"[78]

These strictures against the unchecked rule of domestic law, invoking as they did the despotic connotations of the Roman law doctrine of *patria potestas*, translated an early modern tradition of writing about slavery into more polemical and local terms. In a line of thought that links Bodin, Montesquieu, and Adam Smith, as we have seen, the master-slave relation was both absorbed into and helped constitute the Roman law paradigm of domestic or household governance. Indeed, Hilliard d'Auberteuil essentially plagiarized Montesquieu's definition of slavery as an absolute right of control over the life and death of the slave, right down to the detail about the dangers of letting masters install themselves as the arbiters of "justice" in their own right. The circulation of Montesquieu's ideas about slavery extended deep into the eighteenth-century Atlantic world.[79]

Nonetheless, in contrast to Montesquieu, Hilliard d'Auberteuil was careful not to expose himself to the charge of questioning slavery *tout*

---

[76] Hilliard d'Auberteuil, *Considérations*, 1:133–134.
[77] Ogle, "'The Eternal Power of Reason' and 'The Superiority of Whites,'" 37, 40, 44–47.
[78] Hilliard d'Auberteuil, *Considérations*, 143.
[79] See generally Ghachem, "Montesquieu in the Caribbean."

court as incompatible with the laws of nature. To the contrary, as already noted, his condemnation of planter brutality and arbitrariness was explicitly motivated by the desire to sustain and improve the efficiency of the plantation system rather than to undermine or transform it. (Indeed, this utilitarian impulse itself represented, for Hilliard d'Auberteuil, a kind of "justice.") After denouncing the contempt that the more egregious planters showed for the "civil law," Hilliard d'Auberteuil's analysis took a somewhat less combative turn. Although acknowledging the injustice of laws that prevented blacks from defending themselves against the violence of white subjects, he went on to say that it would be "dangerous" to adopt policies that were "too favorable to the slaves."[80] The ideal model of behavior could be found in the approach of those colonists who combined "vigilance with gentleness."[81] This may have been partly a concession to Hilliard d'Auberteuil's concern, as an aspiring magistrate, not to appear overly critical of the planter community in Saint-Domingue. In the same spirit, Hilliard d'Auberteuil sought to distinguish his position from that of the philosophes, who had unfairly blamed the colonists for having to live with an institution that, although sinful, was purportedly not of their own making. "Do the philosophes have a right to reproach us for an evil that we have found already in place?" Slavery was an "inhuman policy," Hilliard d'Auberteuil conceded, but it was also "advantageous" to the colonists. Provided the slaves were treated with humanity, it was unnecessary to decide whether the holding of property in human beings was a "legitimate" undertaking.[82]

These disclaimers and qualifications did not entirely shield Hilliard d'Auberteuil from suspicions that he was a closet abolitionist, at least to judge from the response four years later by his arch-critic Paul-Ulric Dubuisson. Dubuisson had worked as a postal inspector in Saint-Domingue before returning to the metropole in 1778 to begin a career that would make him one of the most influential French pamphleteers on colonial affairs in the 1780s.[83] The crux of the dispute between Hilliard d'Auberteuil and Dubuisson was the relative balance to be struck between those colonists who embodied a "moderate" and "humane" style of slave ownership versus those who visited brutality on their slaves. In

[80] Hilliard d'Auberteuil, *Considérations*, 145.
[81] Ibid., 146.
[82] Ibid., 131–132 ("I will hardly detain myself to examine whether this property is legitimate; it is at least profitable").
[83] *Dictionnaire de Biographie Française*, ed. Roman d'Amat and R. Limouzin-Lamothe (Paris: Librairie Letouzey et Ané, 1966), 65:1114.

Dubuisson's view, Hilliard d'Auberteuil had gotten the proportions and dimensions of the problem at hand completely wrong.

Published in 1780, Dubuisson's *Nouvelles considérations* – the title was an obvious echo of Hilliard d'Auberteuil's – portrayed itself as an effort to recalibrate the balance. "After having known the colonist and his political existence [*existence politique*] in the midst of his slaves," Dubuisson wrote, he would "blush" before "slandering" the planters of Saint-Domingue with the label of "tyrants." Contrary to rumor, there were only a "few" examples of such planters in the colony, and their conduct was sufficiently "rare" to be contained by the "hatred of their neighbors and compatriots." There was, in other words, a workable solution to the collective-action problem posed by (the exceedingly rare instances of) planter brutality. Concern for reputation and honor could be channeled into a means of community or self-policing. The constraints of social ostracism would serve as the first and most effective barrier to the "furors" of extremist planters. As if to justify these excesses, Dubuisson went on to explain that that "[n]egroes are not naturally industrious." Indeed, African society was supposedly characterized by an "inordinate leisureliness."[84]

Despite their rhetorical differences, it is difficult to know whether the argument between Hilliard d'Auberteuil and Dubuisson was an example of disagreement masking consensus. Dubuisson was clearly more of a reactionary and an apologist than his counterpart. On the other hand, both men at least claimed to believe in the principle that slaves ought to be treated humanely and that renegade planters deserved to be censured, if not outlawed altogether. Both shared a belief that the plantation system was worthy of perpetuation and that threats to its existence should be pursued with vigilance. The very project of debating the relative balance between "moderate" and "extreme" planters in Saint-Domingue implied an accord that plantation slavery itself was beyond reproach. Both authors were, in this sense, apologists for the status quo.

Within the broad parameters of self-interest, however, there was room for a wide range of views. In the end, the debate between Hilliard d'Auberteuil and Dubuisson does not seem an entirely illusory one. As the jostling over the Cassarouy precedent and the deposition of Thomas suggest, there were important and concrete administrative stakes in the decision of whether to apprehend or immunize planters who transgressed

---

[84] Paul-Ulric Dubuisson, *Nouvelles considérations sur Saint-Domingue, en réponse à celles de M. H. D.* (Paris: Cellot & Jombert, 1780), 1:72.

the Code Noir. Above all, none of the participants in the late colonial debate over planter brutality seemed capable of obscuring or denying the ever-present prospect of slave revolt. For some, the task of imagining life without slavery, unwelcome though that prospect might be, was central to the process of analyzing and managing the hazards entailed by the worst excesses of plantation governance.

THE PROSPECT OF REVOLT

By the 1770s, a number of influential voices in the colonial arena had begun to sound the note of planter brutality leading inevitably, if unintentionally, to slave revolt. Perhaps the most well-known example is the Abbé Raynal's *Histoire philosophique et politique des Deux Indes*, published in numerous editions in the 1770s and 1780s. Raynal's work, written collaboratively with Diderot and with significant input from officials in the Naval Ministry, famously conjured up the image of a black Spartacus rising to liberate the slaves of the New World from their sufferings at the hands of ruthless masters. Raynal had drawn on the earlier vision of a writer named Louis Sebastien Mercier, who published in 1771 a futuristic account titled *L'an 2440*, which featured (among other novelties) the imposing image of a black figure on a pedestal inscribed with the words "To the Avenger of the New World."[85]

The writings of Raynal and Mercier have been extensively analyzed elsewhere, and their significance to the French Enlightenment cannot be discounted.[86] From the viewpoint of Saint-Domingue and colonial

---

[85] See Dubois, *Avengers of the New World*, 57; Geggus, "Saint-Domingue on the Eve of the Haitian Revolution," 3–4; Marcel Dorigny, "Le mouvement abolitionniste français face à l'insurrection de Saint-Domingue ou la fin du mythe de l'abolition graduelle," in *L'insurrection des esclaves de Saint-Domingue (22–23 août 1791)*, ed. Laënnec Hurbon (Paris: Éditions Karthala, 2000), 97–101; and Benot, *La révolution française et la fin des colonies*, 22–29. Among other editions of Mercier and Raynal that could be cited, see Guillaume Thomas Raynal, *Histoire philosophique et politique des établissements et du commerce des Européens dans les Deux Indes* (Geneva, 1780); and Louis Sebastien Mercier, *L'an deux mille cent quarante: Rêve s'il en fut jamais* (1770; reprint, Paris: F. Adel, 1977).

[86] On the discussion of slavery in Raynal's *Histoire* (which was drafted by the resolute antislavery critic Jean de Pechmeja), see especially Duchet, *Anthropologie et histoire*, 170–177. Robin Blackburn observes that a concern for "stability" was an important part of Raynal's critical approach to slavery. "The Abbé Raynal saw himself as an exponent of France's true colonial interests. He claimed that slaves were treated better in the French than in the British colonies but he was nevertheless concerned that huge aggregations of plantation slaves endangered the colonial order." Blackburn, *The Overthrow of Colonial*

administrative history, however, a far more important exemplar of the tendency to envision revolt as a likely consequence of slavery's excesses was Pierre-Victor Malouet. A naval commissioner and administrator in Saint-Domingue from 1765 to 1769, Malouet was subsequently appointed administrator (*ordonnateur*) of French Guiana, where he became a sometime collaborator of Bessner. From his base in Cayenne, the capital of Guiana, Malouet authored the anonymous 1776 manuscript entitled "Du traitement et de l'emploi des nègres" ("On the treatment and usage of negroes").[87]

Like Bessner, Malouet was the antithesis of the abstract philosophical critic of slavery. He was deeply invested in the colonial project, as reflected not only in his official titles but also in the plantation that he owned through his wife in Saint-Domingue.[88] His stance on slavery, which evolved over time, was shot through with the studied ambivalence of one who partook of both the colonial administrative and planter cultures. In his 1776 manuscript on the treatment of slaves, however, Malouet played very much the part of the apologist for Cassarouy, Dessources, and company, opening his analysis with an expression of alarm at the spread of abolitionist proposals and rumors that the government was preparing to act on those proposals.[89] (In retrospect, it appears that the

Slavery, 170. On Mercier's utopian imagination, see Robert Darnton, *The Forbidden Best-Sellers of Pre-Revolutionary France* (New York: W.W. Norton, 1995), 115–136.

[87] Naval Minister Antoine Raymond de Sartines appointed Malouet to this position. Malouet, *Mémoires de Malouet*, 1:51–73. For more on Malouet's role in the projects to reform French colonial slavery, see Michèle Duchet, "Malouet et le problème de l'esclavage," in *Malouet, 1740–1814: actes du colloque des 30 novembre et 1er décembre 1989*, ed. Jean Ehrard and Michel Morineau (Riom: La Revue d'Auvergne, for the Association riomoise du bicentenaire de la Révolution française and the Société des amis du Centre de recherches révolutionnaires et romantiques, 1990), 63–70; Gaston Raphanaud, *Le baron Malouet, ses idées, son oeuvre, 1740–1814* (Paris: A. Michalon, 1907); and Jean Tarrade, "L'esclavage est-il réformable? Les projets des administrateurs coloniaux à la fin de l'Ancien Régime," in Dorigny, *Les abolitions de l'esclavage*, 133–141.

[88] Tarrade, "L'esclavage est-il réformable?" 138.

[89] Pierre-Victor Malouet, "Du traitement et de l'emploi des Nègres dans les colonies," 1776, ANOM, F/3/90, fol. 165. (I have modernized Malouet's spelling of the term "traitement," which appears as "traitemens" in his manuscript.) Some idea of Malouet's frame of reference can be garnered from the following comments in a letter by Naval Minister Sartines written in March 1776: "Misintended persons have spread [a rumor] ... in the various ports of the Kingdom that the government was planning to grant freedom to the negroes." Letter from Antoine Raymond Gualbert Gabriel de Sartine, Naval Minister, to the Chambers of Commerce, March 25, 1776, Archives de la Chambre de Commerce de Marseille, H 44, fol. 20. This letter was a circular sent to the chambers of commerce of

rumors were not entirely unfounded, given that Malouet would publicly reveal in 1779 that the Naval Ministry's committee on colonial legislation had given at least formal consideration to Bessner's proposal for gradual emancipation.)

The heart of Malouet's *mémoire* consisted of a summation of the key claims of antislavery critics of the colonial regime, followed by responses written in Malouet's own voice. Not surprisingly, one of these claims invoked the familiar specter of the inhumane master. "[I]t is unjust and barbarous to arrogate to yourselves the right to beat, mutilate, and cause the death of slave[s]," Malouet intoned in the voice of the outraged opponent of planter absolutism. "This is what makes slavery odious and impossible to justify."[90]

Maloeut's response evoked an equally familiar set of motifs: the Roman law doctrine of *patria potestas* and the force of social pressure. The same "powerful motives" that united a father to his wife and children governed a master's treatment of his slave, wrote Malouet. "The father of a family, harsh and severe in his home, makes his wife and children unhappy; [but] would that give you reason to sunder the bonds of domestic authority? No, one would impose a curb on him [instead]."[91] Just as Dubuisson would insist four years later in his *Nouvelles considérations*, Malouet expressed confidence that "laws, opinion, example, scorn and esteem, welfare, remorse, [and] personal interest" would all work in the direction of limiting the arbitrary will of the planters. In contrast to Hilliard d'Auberteuil, Malouet found little reason to worry that the moderation of the vast majority of the slaveholding community was at risk. The infractions of renegade planters were "rare and isolated" acts of barbarism "that cause horror in America as in France." In short, there was no reason to impugn the entire planter community as a fraternity of "ogres."[92]

Malouet did not entirely overlook the difficulties that lax enforcement of the Code Noir created for his position. He observed that the colonial administration would penalize "excesses when they are known" – thereby

---

Bordeaux, La Rochelle, Nantes, St. Malo, Le Havre, Rouen, Marseille, and Dunkerque. Allegations were made at the time that Turgot's administration was giving serious consideration to these proposals. See Tarrade, "Les colonies et les principes de 1789," 16 n. 13.

[90] Malouet, "Du traitement," 1779, fol. 170.
[91] Ibid.
[92] Ibid.

conceding, in effect, that the double bind imposed on slaves who dared to report incidents of abuse pursuant to the Code Noir would prevent those cases from ever coming to light in the first place. Yet the intent of the Code Noir, at least, was clear enough, according to Malouet. "[T]he Legislator, in permitting the slave trade, did not intend to send men to the butcher. [Instead] he regulated their treatment and punishment." Coercion and physical discipline were necessary elements of that treatment because slaves, like peasants and schoolchildren, would never "apply themselves to their task" without the "fear of punishment."[93] Malouet echoed one of Montesquieu's principal explanations for the origins of slavery in *The Spirit of the Laws*: "There are countries where the heat weakens the body, and so impairs one's courage, that men are only brought to carry out onerous duties by the fear of punishment."[94]

There is some evidence that Malouet himself did not fully embrace the harsh position he had staked out in this anonymous and unpublished manuscript. One year later, in 1777, he wrote an ambiguously worded letter from Cap Français to two acquaintances concerning the circumstances under which he had composed the 1776 document. Malouet recalled that he had presented his manuscript to the king and his royal council in response to a period of "crisis" involving a "deviation of principles of more than one sort." This language is too euphemistic to be certain what Malouet had in mind by such a "crisis." However, a reference to metropolitan "economists," who had obtained a copy of the *mémoire* and threatened to denounce it publicly, suggests that Malouet may have been alluding at least in part to the appearance of abolitionist proposals and antislavery writings in France. In this context, Malouet's letter continued, "it was highly advisable for me to remain unknown."[95]

At the same time, the "deviation of principles" to which Malouet mysteriously referred was "of more than one sort." This language betrayed a further layer of complexity in Malouet's position, one that placed him unmistakably in the prudential tradition and drew him far closer to the physiocratic critics of slavery than he was willing to publicly allow at the

---

[93] Ibid.
[94] Montesquieu, *The Spirit of the Laws*, 251. I have modified the translation of this passage.
[95] Pierre-Victor Malouet to Narre [spelling unclear] and Renaut, September [month unclear] 28, 1777, ANOM, F/3/90, fol. 178. By "economists," Malouet was evidently referring to physiocrat critics of colonial slavery. Malouet divulged that Mirabeau, one of the most prominent members of the physiocrat movement, had commented on his manuscript.

time. Indeed, Malouet confessed to his correspondents that, even under cover of anonymity, he had "put off for another occasion a demonstration of the means necessary for reconciling humanity and public policy in this area." In the characteristic voice of the colonial administrator concerned with the long-term stability of empire, Malouet emphasized that colonists owed "duties" to their slaves. "It is in the interest [both] of the government and of private persons," he wrote, to ensure that these responsibilities were fulfilled with greater energy than they had previously been:

If we don't alleviate the condition of the slave, if we don't inculcate in him that portion of morals and of religion of which he is susceptible, if domestic despotism and its excesses are not suppressed, if we don't place a restraint on the licentious manners that result, our colonies will undergo the same revolutions as those that have befallen [Dutch] Surinam.[96]

With his reference to the "domestic despotism" of the masters, Malouet had suddenly crossed the line all the way over to Hilliard d'Auberteuil's position in the *Considérations*. Even more striking was the explicit connection Malouet drew between the prevalence of planter brutality and the threat of a slave revolt. (In 1763, a major slave revolt took place in the Dutch colony of Surinam, adjacent to French Guiana on the northeastern coast of South America.)

The administrative relationship between "humanity" and social order (or "public policy") would emerge as the central problem in Malouet's thought. Here and elsewhere, that theme led him to sound the alarm of a tight causal chain that ran from radical abuse to the prospect of a slave rebellion. According to Malouet, there were only two ways to sever that link: Expose slaves to the principles of religion, or refocus the "eye of the administration" on planter "deviations." The combination of religious indoctrination and a vigorous regime of plantation surveillance had worked in Surinam, wrote Malouet, who, to a degree unusual among his contemporaries, made it his business to travel to and study the non-French (particularly Dutch) slave colonies in the greater Caribbean.[97] Wherever administrators had come to understand the "necessity of a strict regulation (*police*) of the masters," *marronage* had disappeared as a phenomenon.[98] The message was clear: It was well past time for the

---

[96] Ibid., fols. 178–179.
[97] Ibid. On Malouet's studies of the greater Caribbean, see Tarrade, "L'esclavage est-il réformable?" 138.
[98] Malouet to Narre and Renaut, September [?] 28, 1777, fol. 179.

monarchy to reform the outdated Code Noir, then close to a century old, and put something more effective and imposing in its place.

"THE KING WISHES TO BE OBEYED"

In the waning years of the Old Regime, the inability of existing enforcement mechanisms to contain the threat of planter brutality continued to manifest itself. In 1782, the Conseil Supérieur in Port-au-Prince heard argument in the case of a female slave and her children who had been abused and mistreated by their master. The mother sought to have herself and her children's tutor (a person appointed to look after the slaves' interests and take legal actions on their behalf) petition for the minors' freedom as a way of sparing them from further exposure to their master. When the master's widow sued to reclaim the slaves, the court held that the slaves were limited to remonstrating before the royal prosecutor pursuant to article 26 of the Code Noir.[99] A few months later, the same court issued a general ruling "permitting" slaves to present formal grievances against their masters before the prosecutor, again in accordance with the text of the Code Noir.[100]

These and earlier rulings testify to the powerful obstacles, legal and practical, that remained in the way of slaves who sought to avail themselves of the cover of law in Saint-Domingue. On December 3, 1784, almost exactly a century after Louis XIV promulgated the Code Noir, the monarchy finally took decisive steps to overhaul the edict. A confluence of factors made action possible at this time: the efforts of military officers and administrators in Saint-Domingue to convince officials in the Colonial Bureau of the Naval Ministry of the urgent need for reform of the status quo; predictions of an impending crisis in the colony prompted by isolated reports of small-scale uprisings on the plantations; and a climate of opinion (both colonial and metropolitan) that had begun to swing decisively against the most notorious of the planters.[101] The rising

99 "Arrêt du Conseil du Port-au-Prince," July or August 1782, LC, 6:266–267. The court's holding referred to both versions of the Code Noir, 1685 and 1724. The record does not reveal whether the mother and her children tried to pursue this remedy, and if so, whether their effort was successful.

100 "Arrêt du Conseil du Port-au-Prince," October 17, 1782, ANOM, CSD, F/3/275, fol. 713.

101 Debien, *Les colons de Saint-Domingue et la Révolution*, 30–32. As evidence of the "impending crisis" mentality, Debien cites a 1785 letter between Stanislas Foäche, a commercial deputy in Le Havre, and his correspondent in Saint-Domingue, Morange. Robin Blackburn hints at a possible quid pro quo linking the monarchy's 1784 decision to relax the *Exclusif* (the system of laws restricting colonial trade) with the strengthening

influence of antislavery sentiment notwithstanding, it would be too much to say that the demands of abolitionists forced the hands of Louis XVI and the French naval minister, Charles-Eugène de la Croix de Castries.[102] Rather, the 1784 ordinance represented the culmination of the same prudential anxiety about planter brutality and its potential to incite a slave revolution that had characterized the thinking of administrators and judges in Saint-Domingue for decades.

At the same time, the monarchy's new strategy for minimizing the hazards of uncontrolled domestic sovereignty introduced an element that had figured only implicitly in the earlier case law and commentaries. As a result of an unusually high rate of absentee plantation ownership relative to other New World slave colonies, disciplinary authority over the slaves of Saint-Domingue tended to devolve to overseers and agents on the colonial ground.[103] As colonial administrators saw the issue, the

---

of controls over the plantation regime. Blackburn, *The Overthrow of Colonial Slavery,* 165. The two sets of reforms were close enough in time to make this linkage a possibility. However, the 1784 commercial reforms were also intimately tied to the outcome of the American Revolutionary War, whereas it is difficult to see what connection (if any) may have existed between that outcome and the plantation reforms.

[102] For the claim that the 1784 ordinance was issued "at the demand of the abolitionists," see Philippe Haudrère, "Code Noir," in *Dictionnaire de l'ancien régime,* ed. Lucien Bély (Paris: Presses Universitaires de France, 1996), 274. Citing no evidence for this proposition, Haudrère seems to have confused the reaction to the new law with the actual circumstances behind its promulgation. It is true that the Abbé Raynal had included proposals to increase the authority of colonial administrators over the planters in the 1781 edition of his *Histoire philosophique et politique des deux Indes.* Blackburn notes that Raynal "was on good terms with senior officials of the Colonial Bureau and for a time in receipt of a subsidy from this quarter." However, Blackburn also goes on to observe that the 1784 reforms fell "well short" of Raynal's proposals. Blackburn, *The Overthrow of Colonial* Slavery, 170. This did nothing to prevent the planters from suspecting that the hand of "philanthropy" was behind the 1784 regulations, of course.

[103] There are no reliable figures for the rate of planter absenteeism relative to Saint-Domingue in the eighteenth century. Robin Blackburn has suggested that French Caribbean absenteeism was "a little less extensive" than its British counterpart. In 1770, he estimates, about one-third of Jamaica's sugar estates (representing 40% of the colony's total sugar output) was owned by absentee planters. Blackburn, *The Making of New World Slavery,* 406, 441. Carolyn Fick estimates that by the latter decades of the eighteenth century, more than 50% of Saint-Domingue planters resided permanently in France. Fick, *The Making of Haiti,* 16. Darrell Meadows has found that roughly 20% of claimants for public assistance from the French government during and after the Haitian Revolution came under the heading of absentee planters. R. Darrell Meadows, "Social Networks and Transatlantic Migration: Saint-Domingue Refugees during the French and Haitian Revolutions" (Working Paper No. 01–19, International Seminar on the History of the Atlantic World, 1500–1825, Harvard University, Cambridge, MA), 10–11, 14. His analysis of this question is complicated, however, by the need to distinguish between "absentees" and "true refugees" during the revolutionary period.

pervasiveness of radical abuse on the plantations stemmed from the overseers' and agents' lack of a long-term, proprietary stake in the slaves over whom they lorded. With *de jure* owners of slaves safely ensconced faraway in the metropole, few if any barriers hindered the reign of overseers and agents as the de facto masters of slave society. The philosophy that animated the new measure involved, in part, a direct appeal to the long-term self-interest of proprietary stakeholders in the colonial enterprise as a way of restoring balance to the tumultuous world of the plantations.

Reflecting the special place of Saint-Domingue in the French empire and its image as a hotbed of colonial risk, the 1784 ordinance opened with a statement of the king's awareness of the "abuses that have been introduced into the management of plantations located in Saint-Domingue." The new law banned agents from accepting assignments to more than two plantations at a time. It also required both managers and agents to keep a careful register of the births and deaths of all slaves on their plantations, as well as to record "accidents and events of any nature ... relative to the administration [of the plantation]." Once every month, that register was to be sent to the plantation's legal owner in France.[104] The evident purpose of these bookkeeping measures was to hold overseers and agents accountable for acts of brutality resulting in the deaths of slaves. Along this same line, the ordinance prohibited "all owners, agents, and overseers from treating their slaves inhumanely, by giving them more than fifty lashes of the whip, by beating them with a stick, by mutilating them, or finally by causing them to die in different ways."[105]

The ineffective enforcement mechanisms that had previously inhibited application of the Code Noir were augmented by procedures for the "revocation" of renegade overseers and agents.[106] Less dramatically, slave owners or their representatives (as well as "displaced managers") were permitted to demand a legal audit or accounting of the management of their plantations. Independent "commissioners" appointed for this task would "verify with the greatest care" that slaves received adequate supplies of food and medical treatment. The commissioners would also interview the slave force of a plantation for evidence of "excessive

---

[104] "Ordonnance du Roi," December 3, 1784, LC, 6:656–657.
[105] The ordinance also granted each slave a portion of land to tend his or her gardens. Ibid., 657.
[106] Ibid., 660.

punishments, mutilation or murders, nocturnal labor ... contraventions of the relief measures prescribed for pregnant negroes," and other violations of royal slave law.

The punitive measures that accompanied these new substantive policies were, by and large, unprecedented. The governor and intendant were authorized to prosecute overseers who violated any of the provisions of the new ordinance.[107] Owners, agents, or overseers found guilty of excessive corporal punishment would be declared "incapable of possessing slaves" and deported to France. Those found guilty of mutilating slaves would be branded with "notices of infamy." Finally, and most dramatically, persons responsible for causing "of their own authority" the death of a slave were made subject to capital punishment, a policy that was, quite simply, unheard of in the context of existing practices.[108] Only a handful of documents from the eighteenth century ordered punishment of any sort for whites who mistreated or killed their slaves.[109] To the best of my knowledge, there is no evidence that any white (poor or rich) was ever sentenced to capital punishment for causing the death of a slave or free person of color.[110]

However, the most ambitious aspect of the new ordinance was its introduction of a system for the "ongoing regulation" of the plantations ("police courante des habitations"). The governor and intendant were granted exclusive responsibility for this surveillance regime and were directed to include within their jurisdiction, among other things,

---

[107] Ibid., 662.

[108] Ibid., 665.

[109] "Arrêt du Conseil du Petit Goâve," January 3, 1724, ANOM, F/3/90, fols. 123–125 (convicting a master of burning the feet and legs of a female slave who died from the wounds; the punishment included a fine and three months' imprisonment); "Arrêt du Conseil de Léogane," September 2, 1726, ANOM, F/3/90, f. 187 (condemning a slave driver to three years of galley labor for killing a slave "in a fit of anger"); "Arrêt du Conseil du Port-au-Prince," March 11, 1780, ANOM, F/3/90, f. 51 (condemning a colonist to be whipped, marked, and sent to the galleys in perpetuity for having "coldly and unnecessarily" slit the throats of two fugitive slaves arrested by him); and the 1788 Maguero case mentioned earlier in this chapter. As early as August 28, 1673, whites in the French islands were freed of any liability for killing fugitive slaves: "Ordonnance du Gouverneur-Général des Isles," August 28, 1673, LC, 1:268–269. The March 11, 1780 case was a rare exception to that general rule.

[110] In his 1998 article on the Code Noir, Jean-Louis Harouel refers to an October 15, 1786, ordinance that mandated capital punishment for any master who caused the death of his slave. This is probably an indication that the identical provision in the 1784–1785 regulations was disregarded entirely by the colonists. Jean-Louis Harouel, "Le Code Noir," in *Abolition de l'Esclavage: Mythes et réalités créoles* (Paris: Comité des Fêtes du Vᵉ Arrondissement, avec le concours du Centre culturel du Panthéon, 1998), 27.

the "reclamations of slaves unjustly mistreated."[111] The administrators were to decide on punishments for owners and slaves alike, provided that these disciplinary actions did not interfere with legal proceedings unfolding in the court system. At the same time, the colony's tribunals were directed to refrain from asserting jurisdiction over conduct that implicated the new system of "ongoing police" as defined by the 1784 ordinance.[112]

Such a systematic overhaul of the norms governing plantation management triggered a predictable uproar in Saint-Domingue. At an institutional level, the planter opposition was reflected in the prolonged delay of the Conseil Supérieur in Cap Français in registering the new ordinance. During the spring and early summer of 1785, the tribunal issued a string of remonstrances and insisted that the administrators personally attend the court's sessions devoted to debating the new law. This combination of traditional and unconventional assertions of independence elicited an angry letter of denunciation from the Marquis de Castries in November. The Cap Français high court, said the naval minister, had "fundamentally attacked the constitutive principle behind the establishment of the Conseils Supérieurs of the colonies, which permits neither suspensions, nor delays in registering the ordinances or orders emanating" either from the king or his administrators in Saint-Domingue. The court's "vehement criticism and excessive declamations" were responsible for inducing a "fermentation" in the colony "capable of producing the very disorders that you pretend you want to prevent."[113] Such allegations, bordering on charges of judicial treason, did not stop the tribunal in Le Cap from withholding its imprimatur until May 11, 1786 – more than a year and a half after the ordinance was first promulgated.[114] (By contrast, the Port-au-Prince court had conceded by April 6, 1785.[115])

---

[111] "Ordonnance du Roi," December 3, 1784, LC, 6:666. Also included in the governor's and intendant's jurisdiction were the nocturnal entry of whites and free persons of color on the plantations and the harboring of fugitive slaves.

[112] Ibid., 667.

[113] Minister to the Magistrates of the Conseil of Cap Français, November 15, 1785, LC, 6:893–894.

[114] LC, 6:667.

[115] The relative docility of the Conseil Supérieur of Port-au-Prince surely had something to do with memories of its earlier confrontations with royal authority. In 1769, the judges of the Port-au-Prince tribunal had been arrested and jailed for their role in fomenting opposition to the drafting of white colonists into the militia units. In the years following, the administrators had kept a close eye out for any further signs of "sedition" from these judges, whose conduct at the time stood in marked contrast to the more "loyalist" policies of the court in Cap Français. Frostin, *Les révoltes blanches*, 342–348. For the edict

The protests of the Conseil Supérieur in Cap Français induced the monarchy to modify significant aspects of the 1784 ordinance almost exactly one year after it was initially promulgated. Bluntly worded, the December 1785 amendments made no secret of the Naval Ministry's awareness that judicial opposition to the original measures reflected a broad swath of militant planter opinion in Saint-Domingue. The colonial court's remonstrances, began the new ordinance, "find their source in large measure in the personal discontents of those whose vicious management made [the 1784 regulations] necessary."[116] Among other concessions, the amendments provided an opportunity to appeal the findings of the independent commissioners responsible for investigating violations of plantation-management practices. In addition, the section of the 1784 regulations concerning "crimes and punishments" was revised to emphasize the duties of "respect and obedience" that all slaves owed to the agents and overseers of plantations as well as to their masters. Within the limits of the Code Noir, agents and overseers were "enjoined" to punish slaves in cases of "insubordination, neglect, relaxation of discipline, and disobedience." Finally, and perhaps most tellingly, the 1785 ordinance specified that the new rules were to be applied on a prospective basis only, effectively pardoning all crimes committed against slaves for which legal proceedings had not yet commenced.[117]

In a letter to the colonial administrators accompanying these amendments, Naval Minister Castries pointedly expressed his confidence that the new legislation "will be received with pleasure in the colony; you will find in it some changes or developments that allow no further pretext for false interpretations." Before proceeding to secure judicial registration of the new ordinance, however, the administrators were first directed to demand from the intransigent Cap Français tribunal its endorsement of the initial 1784 regulations. "The king wishes to be obeyed," wrote the minister, before threatening to recall any uncooperative colonial magistrates to the metropole to "render an account of their conduct."[118]

reestablishing the Port-au-Prince Conseil, see "Édit de Création du Conseil Supérieur du Port-au-Prince," April 1769, LC, 5:241–243.

[116] "Ordonnance du Roi," December 23, 1785, LC, 6:918–919.

[117] Ibid., 927–928. The exact expression here read: "Sa Majesté ... impose silence à ses Procureurs-Généraux sur les délits qui auroient pu commis envers les Esclaves par les Propriétaires ou leurs fondés de pouvoirs, avant l'enregistrement et publication du présent Règlement" (928).

[118] Minister to the Administrators, December 23, 1785, LC, 6:929. The question of returning judges on the Conseil of Le Cap to France was taken up in further detail on the same

This unprecedented threat may have been partly a face-saving measure designed to soften the reality that the monarchy had blinked first. The confrontation of 1784 to 1786 was, at least in part, a matter of safeguarding institutional terrain in the name of absolutist principles. As discussed previously, the northern high court had issued its own warnings in the decades before 1784 about the dangers of allowing masters to run roughshod over their slaves, if not necessarily with the same frequency as the court in Port-au-Prince. At the same time, the constitutional impasse between the monarchy and the Conseil Supérieur in Le Cap reflected a divergence of views about how best to contain the twin threats of planter brutality and slave resistance. The Naval Ministry clearly considered successful implementation of the 1784 regulations (as amended) to be vital to the continued stability of the Crown's wealthiest overseas possession. In this sense, the colonial reforms evoke – and can be seen in part as an extension of – the measures that Louis XVI pursued in the late 1770s and the 1780s to meliorate the condition of peasants and laborers in metropolitan France.[119]

"THE OVERTHROW OF THE COLONY"

It is possible, if doubtful, that planter brutality actually declined in Saint-Domingue in the aftermath of the 1784 and 1785 reforms. David Geggus points tentatively to a general diminution in the incidence of atrocities in the late colonial period, a trend that contemporaries observed as early as 1770.[120] The contrary proposition might just as easily be defended. Whatever the truth may have been, the colonists continued to protest the

---

day by way of a separate letter from the minister to the administrators, December 23, 1785, LC, 6:930.

[119] These measures include the abolition of personal labor services (*mainmorte*) in France in 1779, discussed briefly in Chapter 5. Tocqueville's influential analysis of the monarchy's "belated" drive to reform under the Old Regime can be found in Book 3, Chapter 5 of *The Ancien Régime and the French Revolution*, 160–165. Entitled "How Attempts to Relieve the People Stirred Them to Revolt," that chapter must nonetheless be read against the grain before its insights can be applied to events in the colonial arena. On the implications of the 1784–1785 plantation-management reforms for the subsequent course of events in Saint-Domingue, see Chapters 4 and 6 of the present study. A good discussion of Tocqueville's paradoxical and slippery insight that "the most dangerous time for a bad government is usually when it begins to reform" can be found in Jon Elster's introduction to Tocqueville, *The Ancien Régime and the French Revolution*, xxi–xxiii (quotation at 157).

[120] Geggus, "Saint-Domingue on the Eve of the Haitian Revolution," 10.

imposition of the new regulations until the time of the French Revolution, when the legitimacy of slavery itself was openly questioned.[121] Those protests notwithstanding, any legislative attempt to cut back significantly on the discretion inherent in plantation management was bound to have at best a marginal impact on the daily treatment and welfare of slaves in Saint-Domingue.[122]

Few observers of the colonial scene were as attuned to this reality as Malouet, whose 1776 *mémoire* had so polemically defended masters against the charge of pervasive abuse. While insisting in that manuscript that "powerful motives" of self-interest and public opinion would constrain planters from mistreating their slaves in the first place, Malouet also argued that enforcement of the Code Noir could deter the worst offenders.[123] Some two decades after taking this position, Malouet changed his tune dramatically. In 1785, and perhaps partly in connection with the controversy over the new plantation-management regulations then unfolding, Malouet published a book entitled *Essai sur l'Administration de Saint-Domingue*. The book appeared under the name of the famous antislavery advocate the Abbé Raynal, which alone should suffice to indicate the extent of the shift in Malouet's thinking in the years since 1776.[124] Malouet had long since returned from Guiana to France to take up the position of superintendent of the navy in Toulon. He nonetheless retained a colonial fortune owing to his plantation interests in Saint-Domingue, where he had witnessed the political conflagrations of the late 1760s as an administrator.[125]

In the book's pivotal section on slavery, Malouet began, not unlike Hilliard d'Auberteuil, by painting a picture of master-slave relations

---

[121] Debbasch, "Au coeur du 'gouvernement des esclaves,'" 46.

[122] See Harouel, "Le Code Noir," 27; and Carl L. Lokke, *France and the Colonial Question: A Study of Contemporary French Opinion, 1763–1801* (New York: Columbia University Press, 1932), 68–69.

[123] Malouet, "Du traitement," 1776, fol. 170.

[124] For the view that Malouet was the likely author of the *Essai*, see Anatole Feugère, *Un précurseur de la Révolution: L'Abbé Raynal (1713–1796)* (Angoulême: Imprimerie ouvrière, 1922; reprint, Geneva: Slatkine Reprints, 1970), 364 n. 20. For the (not incompatible) argument that the *Essai* was compiled from passages of Raynal's *Histoire philosophique et politique des deux Indes*, see the entry on Raynal in the *Biographie universelle, ancienne et moderne* (Paris: Michaud, 1811–28), 37:182. Michèle Duchet notes simply that the *Essai* was "inspired" by Malouet. Duchet, *Anthropologie et histoire*, 135. Malouet and Raynal had been friends since well before the latter's return to France from exile in 1785.

[125] Duchet, *Anthropologie et histoire*, 157. Duchet notes an analogous shift in Malouet's thinking about Bessner's proposal for gradual emancipation.

characterized by fear, loathing, and violence. Slaves were left to get by on the most inadequate and rudimentary of provisions, and thus forced to devote time to the cultivation of foodstuffs that should have been used for rest. At all other times, the slave was made to cater entirely to the whims of his master, who could inflict punishments at will without worrying about the possibility that an "impotent" system of law would prosecute him. From this state of affairs resulted "desperation, vengeance, poisonings, [and] fires. Such are the relations between master and slave."[126]

In such a situation, it no longer made sense to think of Saint-Domingue in traditional absolutist terms, as an overseas French territory subject to the sovereign rule of royal administrators representing a distant monarch. Instead, Malouet declared, "[t]here are … two governments in Saint-Domingue, the principles of which are different: that of public authority, and that of domestic authority." The consequences of this dichotomy were profound, Malouet insisted, and took the form of a set of legal dualisms: "two bodies of law, two administrations, two forms of justice." Previous commentators had simply failed adequately to grasp this underlying reality: "I don't believe that people have insisted enough on this distinction and on its effects relative to [colonial] administration."[127] Even if everything else went as planned, Malouet observed, a failure to appreciate the intractability of this problem of dual sovereignty would allow it to "disturb the public order." "[W]e do not adequately perceive that this disturbance might, in the long run, anticipate the overthrow [*renversement*] of the colony," he wrote.[128]

Here was the sharpest formulation yet of the precautionary politics of plantation administration that had shaped colonial slave law in Saint-Domingue since the early eighteenth century. The controversies of 1784 and 1785 help explain why Malouet believed such an explicit diagnosis of the situation was necessary. Indeed, Malouet may well have intended to fortify the monarchy's will to resist the fervent protests against the new plantation reforms emanating from Saint-Domingue. Alleviating the climate of fear and violence that characterized master-slave relations was,

---

[126] Guillaume-Thomas-François Raynal, abbé [Pierre-Victor Malouet], *Essai sur l'administration de Saint-Domingue* (n.p.: n.p., 1785), 13–14.

[127] Ibid., 14.

[128] Ibid. Significantly, this passage about the "two governments" of Saint-Domingue and the prospect of a slave revolt was absent from the abridged version of the *Essai* published in Port-au-Prince in 1790.

in any case, a paramount strategic imperative. At stake was nothing less than the ability of colonial administrators to prevent the "overthrow" of public order in Saint-Domingue.

Even as he advanced this quintessentially strategic argument, Malouet also grounded his position in an appeal to justice and humanity. The 1685 Code Noir dated to a time when "experience was lacking," he explained. "What it prescribes for tempering the rigors of slavery, [and] for containing the injustice and cruelty of masters has never been enforced."[129] No longer could administrators or colonists shy away from embracing a policy of "containment" on the grounds that it was futile, dangerous, or worse. The colony and its stability had, in effect, become hostage to a "small number" of renegade planters responsible for the lion's share of the problem. "The deplorable victims of their barbarism" shared common cause with the "honest and useful colonist" in seeing to the enforcement of the Code Noir.[130] Prudence and justice alike counseled the same approach to the problem of dual sovereignties that had emerged with the initial development of slave plantations in the Caribbean, and had matured into a public policy dilemma of the first order four years before the outbreak of the French Revolution.

We do not know whether Malouet believed that the 1784 and 1785 reforms answered the call of his *Essai*. He would not have been surprised to see the new regulations condemned by the planters and then left to stagnate by the wayside. Yet the likely failure ever to enforce that legislation in the way its framers had intended was only part of the story. Malouet's analysis tapped into a long-standing, fundamental anxiety on the part of colonial administrators and planters. That anxiety found expression in an administrative language of long-term self-interest inflected by Enlightenment notions of morality and benevolence. The sincerity of the prudential argument can hardly be doubted. What Malouet in his heart of hearts really thought about the institution of slavery, by contrast, is simply off limits to the historian. Malouet was not an abolitionist, and his criticisms of planter brutality, closely connected as they were to the preservation of a moderate slave society, did not amount to opposition to the principle of human bondage. In isolating for critical analysis the extreme forms of behavior toward which slavery tended in Saint-Domingue, however, Malouet had taken the momentous step of

---

[129] Ibid.
[130] Ibid., 15.

envisioning for his readers the possibility of colonial life after slavery. That reformist, strategic vision of a world without slavery, at least as familiarly constituted, would prove to be a critical way station on the road to more radical understandings of the disadvantages and injustices of chattel bondage.

4

Stop the Course of these Cruelties

How many secret evils the eye of the courts is incapable of penetrating!
– Governor and intendant of Saint-Domingue
to the French naval minister (1788)[1]

In the spring and summer of 1788, a master was prosecuted for the torture of two female slaves who lived on a coffee plantation near Plaisance, in the northern province of Saint-Domingue. The exceptional nature of the case was immediately obvious to the participants who lived through it. The colony's governor and intendant, deeply vested in the outcome of the affair, described it as a "unique opportunity to arrest, by means of a single example, the course of so many cruelties."[2] In 1788, the most recent victims of this long eighteenth-century history of cruelties included two slaves known only as Zabeth and Marie-Rose, who were ostensibly tortured because they were suspected of having administered poison to their master and fellow slaves. This chapter tells the story of the prosecution of the master who tortured them, Nicolas Lejeune.[3]

---

[1] Letter from François Barbé de Marbois, intendant, and Alexandre de Vincent de Mazarade, governor, to César-Henri de la Luzerne, naval minister, Aug. 29, 1788, ANOM, F/3/90, fol. 258.

[2] Ibid., fol. 266.

[3] The most extensive treatment of the Lejeune affair is Jacques Thibau, *Le temps de Saint-Domingue: L'esclavage et la Révolution française* (Paris: J.-C. Lattès, 1989), 17–93 passim, an account embellished with various novelistic details that do not seem solidly grounded in the sources. Extended extracts from the F/3/90 manuscripts relating to the case are reproduced in Antoine Gisler, *L'esclavage aux Antilles françaises (XVIIᵉ-XIXᵉ siècle)*, rev. ed (Paris: Éditions Karthala, 1981), 117–127. Brief accounts can also be found in Fick, *The Making of Haiti*, 37–38; idem, "L'Affaire LeJeune," in *Dictionnaire historique de la*

The violence of slavery took many forms in Saint-Domingue. However, one form was particularly central to the colony's history, its political culture, and its fate: torture, or the use of coercive means by public or quasi-public actors to induce cooperation or a confession from a criminal suspect. This is not because torture was somehow "worse" than or radically different from the many other forms of violence by which slaves were made to suffer in Saint-Domingue. Indeed, this chapter seeks in part to demonstrate that "torture" in colonial Haiti was not always seen as the legally specialized and distinctive form of state-sanctioned violence that features in the historiography of criminal procedure. Rather, torture was identified as part of a continuum of practices that included cognate forms of brutality. Torture nonetheless occupied a prominent place in the set of techniques by which masters sought to discipline and terrorize their slaves, and this prominence undoubtedly derives in good measure from torture's close relationship to law and the methods of legal inquiry.

To understand torture in Saint-Domingue is to grasp its situation in the larger strategic project of the Code Noir, as implemented and understood over the course of the eighteenth century by administrators and jurists, by planters, and also by slaves. For the explosive implications of torture were an inescapable aspect of the commonwealth ethics of slavery. The Lejeune prosecution crystallized the various elements of the terror-torture nexus that shaped the political imagination of colonial administrators and planters on the eve of the French and Haitian Revolutions: the fear of slaves as "domestic enemies," the notion that slavery's abuses threatened the stability of Bodin's "well-ordered commonwealth," and the determination of slaves to register their resistance in the form of law even when that resistance was believed to harbor only violence.

In 1788, the slaves on Lejeune's plantation (at least) were finally able to register their resistance to this cycle of violence in the form of law. That

Révolution haïtienne, ed. Claude Moïse (Montreal: Les Éditions du CIDIHCA, 2003), 29–30; Pluchon, *Vaudou, sorciers, empoisonneurs*, 199–202; James, *The Black Jacobins*, 22–24; Pierre de Vaissière, *Saint-Domingue: La société et la vie créole sous l'ancien régime* (1629–1789) (Paris: Perrin et Cie, 1909), 186–188; Dubois, *Avengers of the New World*, 56; and Colin [Joan] Dayan, *Haiti, History, and the Gods* (Berkeley: University of California Press, 1995), 215–218. See also *Le petit juge et le maître cruel ou la question de l'esclavage à Saint-Domingue à la veille de la Révolution* (France Inter radio broadcast, March 2, 2008, rebroadcast July 6, 2008). I have not been able to access a copy of this program.

they did so is owed in part to a seeming anomaly of legal history: the prohibition of torture incorporated into the 1685 Code Noir. As is well known, the legal systems of all of the major continental European states regularly resorted to torture as an official part of the inquisitorial system until the end of the ancien régime.[4] At one level, the Code Noir was entirely consistent with this state of affairs, because it prohibited the use of torture by masters vis-à-vis their slaves, not the use of torture by the colonial courts. There was at least some judicial torture of slaves during the colonial period in Saint-Domingue, although it is difficult to tell just how much, given the periodic destruction of slave criminal-trial records during the eighteenth century.[5] Yet the very definition of torture as a technique of official investigative procedure means that although individual acts of torture outside the judicial system were presumably also illegal on the continent, the phenomenon of extrajudicial torture posed far less of a challenge to sovereignty and stability in France (if indeed it posed any such challenges there at all) than it did in the colonies. The anomaly cannot be resolved simply by writing the use of torture on the colonial

---

[4] John H. Langbein, *Torture and the Law of Proof: Europe and England in the Ancien Régime*, new ed. (Chicago, IL: University of Chicago Press, 2006), 3. Moreover, although torture never systematically established itself as an element of English criminal procedure, it played a role in England and other common law jurisdictions as well. Ibid., 73. See also John H. Langbein, "The Legal History of Torture," in *Torture: A Collection*, ed. Sanford Levinson (New York: Oxford University Press, 2004), 99–100 (noting that although the system of judicial torture was never institutionalized in English law, English courts experimented with using torture to investigate crime during the Tudor-Stuart period).

[5] Criminal procedure in late-seventeenth- and eighteenth-century France was governed by a 1670 royal ordinance that provided for the use of judicial torture (*"questions et tortures"*) in the trial courts. See *Ordonnance criminelle*, tit. 19 (1670). This ordinance also applied to Saint-Domingue, albeit with complaints on the part of commentators and the colony's high courts that certain provisions were incompatible with local conditions and that trial judges were neglecting to conform their practices to the letter of the law. See Ordonnance Criminelle, August 1670, LC, 1:198 (noting the colonial high courts' adoption of the 1670 ordinance, "several provisions of which cannot suit the American islands"); Arrêt du Conseil du Port-au-Prince, June 17, 1779, ANOM, F/3/274, fol. 810 (calling for adherence to the 1670 ordinance). The colonial high courts sought to require trial judges to "interrogate" slave defendants within the first twenty-four hours of their imprisonment, in conformity with the 1670 ordinance, but such interrogation did not involve coercive methods. See Arrêt du Conseil du Port-au-Prince, Mar. 7, 1777, ANOM, CSD, F/3/274, fols. 257–258. The appellate court records preserved in Moreau de Saint-Méry's collection give no indication one way or the other of the extent of the use of judicial torture of slaves. For further discussion, see pp. 179–180.

plantations out of the definition of torture: For the Code Noir, which is indisputably a legal and official document even in the conventional sense, used the technical term "torture" to describe the torture of slaves by their masters, as did the participants in the Lejeune prosecution. The French colonial prohibition of torture thus stands as a curious puzzle in the history of Western law, one that has yet to be solved in the disconnected literatures on the laws of torture and slavery.[6]

   This should not be entirely surprising, for in all of the eighteenth-century agitation over torture that preceded and accompanied its initial abolition in revolutionary and Napoleonic Europe, the torture of slaves overseas seems to have played no discernible role.[7] Despite torture's apparent origins in ancient Greek and Roman law as a practice targeted initially at slaves, the modern scholarship on the law of torture takes as its object of study an institution conventionally defined without reference to the dynamics at play in torture's Atlantic colonial theatre.[8] This demarcation of the subject points to a limitation inherent in the historiography of torture, which emphasizes its strictly procedural or evidentiary role as an instrument of "state actors" engaged in the investigation of crime.[9]

---

[6] On the legal historiography of torture, see the sources cited in note 9; and Langbein, "The Legal History of Torture."

[7] The closest connection I have seen drawn in this respect is Lynn Hunt, *Inventing Human Rights: A History* (New York: W.W. Norton, 2007), 105–106, discussing Jacques-Pierre Brissot de Warville's career in the 1780s, first as a critic of torture, and then as founder (in 1788) of the French antislavery Society of the Friends of the Blacks. However, Hunt suggests only a general association – not a direct connection – between these two aspects of the future revolutionary's pre-1789 activism. Judicial torture was abolished in two stages in eighteenth-century France. The so-called *question préparatoire* – torture for purposes of securing a suspect's confession – was abolished by royal decree in 1780. The *question préalable* – torture of a convict just prior to execution for purposes of securing the names of accomplices or information about other crimes – was provisionally abolished by the monarchy on May 1, 1788, then definitively by the National Assembly on October 8, 1789. Ibid., 76, 240 n.4. I have seen no indications that the abolition measures of either 1780 or 1788 were invoked in connection with the Lejeune prosecution, which preceded the 1788 abolition by roughly one month.

[8] See, for example, Michel Foucault, *Discipline and Punish: The Birth of the Prison*, trans. Alan Sheridan (New York: Vintage Books, 1979), 39 (noting that torture "is of ancient origin: it goes back at least as far as the Inquisition … and probably to the torture of slaves"); and A. Lawrence Lowell, "The Judicial Use of Torture, Part I," *Harvard Law Review* 11, no. 4 (1897): 220.

[9] See Edward Peters, *Torture*, exp. ed. (Philadelphia: University of Pennsylvania Press, 1996), 4 ("Torture began as a legal practice and has always had as its essence its public character, whether as an incident in judicial procedure or as a practice of state officials outside the judiciary proper."); Lisa Silverman, *Tortured Subjects: Pain, Truth, and the Body in Early Modern France* (Chicago, IL: University of Chicago Press, 2001), x

The essence of torture, in this literature, lies in its functional relationship to the law of evidence.[10] Given that the legal systems of Saint-Domingue and other New World slave societies generally barred the use of slave testimony, a prohibition of torture seems superficially amenable to a functionalist explanation. In principle, there is no need to procure through the use of torture evidence that has no legally recognized status. However, as we saw in Chapter 3, the exclusion of slave testimony in the French colonial courts – never complete to begin with – was relaxed early in the eighteenth century. So the judicial torture of slaves could thereafter be thought to have a renewed rationale as a means of extracting confessions.[11] In any case, the Code Noir itself had no bearing on judicial torture per se. A functional rationale for the prohibition on the torture of slaves might have some purchase if in fact the Code Noir had been meaningfully capable of deterring masters from torturing their slaves. Yet both common sense and the archival evidence tell us that, absent actual enforcement on the ground of Saint-Domingue, the Code Noir itself neither did nor could play such a role.

This does not mean, however, that the French colonial ban on torture (and kindred provisions of the Code Noir) should be seen as quaint relics or purely phantom efforts to regulate the conduct of masters as well as slaves. According to what is probably the dominant line of interpretation, the antitorture provisions were so rarely enforced that they can only be

("When I speak about torture, I am speaking about the legal practice of torture that permitted the infliction of pain by officers of the state on the bodies of suspects in capital cases"); James Q. Whitman, *Harsh Justice: Criminal Punishment and the Widening Divide between America and Europe* (New York: Oxford University Press, 2003), 20 (torture is "best understood in its technical sense, as harsh treatment intended to coerce persons to cooperate or confess"); Langbein, *Torture and the Law of Proof*, 3 (distinguishing between punishment and torture and defining the latter as "the use of physical coercion by officers of the state in order to gather evidence for judicial proceedings"). The focus on judicial torture per se seems unduly narrow, as Peters has acknowledged in the preface to the new edition of his work. See Peters, *Torture*, viii. It is no coincidence that all four of the works cited here, with the partial exception of Whitman's book, overlook the colonial law of antitorture and thus are unable to account for the legal politics of torture in the context of Atlantic slavery.

[10] Indeed, in the most influential account, by Langbein, this functionalism is what accounts for the eventual demise and abolition of torture. According to Langbein, the Roman canon law of proof – which required that defendants in capital cases be convicted on the strength either of a confession or the testimony of two witnesses – began to dissolve in Europe in the seventeenth century. In its place, there developed a more free-ranging judicial examination of the evidence, of the kind we associate today with the inquisitorial style of criminal procedure, thereby rendering torture obsolete. See Langbein, *Torture and the Law of Proof*, 11–12.

[11] See p. 141.

seen as ideological figments that served to disguise the true purpose of the law of slavery, which was to legitimate the sovereignty of masters over slaves.[12] There is some truth to this claim. Indeed, one can hardly avoid looking at Old Regime colonial law with at least some degree of skepticism, given that many nations have continued, well after the late-eighteenth-century abolition of torture and even into our own day, to use torture as an instrument of law enforcement, despite contrary international and domestic legal commitments.[13] The story of torture in modern Western legal history is one of continuities as well as rupture; and an important chapter of that story involves the subjection of slaves and their descendants in the Atlantic world to practices that can be described, with greater or lesser precision, as torture.

As with other areas of the law of slavery, however, the assumption of a straightforward relationship between torture and colonial administration, or between colonial administration and the demands of planters, can be misleading. The prosecution of torture raised profound issues of individual standing and sovereign immunity in the legal order of Saint-Domingue.[14] The Lejeune affair sheds a rare light on the genealogy of and relationship between these tightly linked concepts as they crystallized in the distant but nonetheless recognizably modern forms of slave standing to sue and planter immunity from prosecution. The heavy weight of racism and social hierarchy in the French Caribbean had an enormous impact on the contemporaneous understanding of these legal forms. Yet ideas about the legitimacy of slave resistance through law and the domestic sovereignty of planters were also filtered through a prudential prism of risk and revolution, which recast those ideas in complicated and surprising ways.

Central to both sides of the argument over Lejeune's fate was the question of what it would mean for the colony as a whole to allow slaves to press claims against their masters in court for violations of the Code Noir. For Lejeune and his sympathizers, permitting such prosecutions would embolden the slaves of Saint-Domingue to resist the demands of

---

[12] See the sources cited at p. 12, n.30.

[13] See Peters, *Torture*, 103–187; Oona A. Hathaway, "The Promise and Limits of the International Law of Torture," in Levinson, *Torture*, 201–204.

[14] Cf. Sanford Levinson, "Slavery and the Phenomenology of Torture," *Social Research* 74 (2007): 150 (2007) ("[T]he most fundamental legal and moral issues raised by slavery and torture are astonishingly similar. Both ultimately raise issues of 'sovereignty' – that is, the possession of absolute unconstrained power – and, therefore, the challenge to 'sovereignty' that is implicit in any liberal notion of limited government.").

plantation labor and to regard their masters not as absolute authorities but rather as subjects of a higher law. Once the dam of planter immunity and sovereignty was broken, the argument went, there would be no way to prevent charges of torture and other forms of brutality from flooding the legal system.[15] Legitimated in their efforts at resistance by the judiciary and administrative authorities, the slaves would then turn to extralegal forms of "insubordination" on a wide scale, culminating in a slave revolution. The only way to prevent this outcome was to leave the planters with an unrestrained hand over their slaves.

On the other side, the governor and intendant of the colony argued that the real danger lay in *preventing* the claims of slaves against their masters from being heard by the court system. If the slaves were not persuaded of the public authorities' ability to deter planters from inflicting physical abuse on their slaves, slaves would have even less incentive to cooperate with the existing order than they already had. They would therefore turn to their own form of justice, a private system of retribution that both paralleled and aimed to eliminate their masters' reliance on domestic punishment. The result would be the same as the one predicted by the argument of Lejeune and his fellow planters: a slave revolution. To prevent that from happening, only a public and "exemplary" punishment of Lejeune would suffice.

Diametrically opposed in one sense, these contrasting arguments were perfectly symmetrical in another. By 1788, the fear of a generalized slave revolt, present in one form or another since the second decade of the eighteenth century, had become such a widespread point of reference that it could be used to powerful effect both by the planters who mobilized around Lejeune and by the administrators who pressed for his conviction and punishment.[16]

---

[15] On the relationship between torture and punishment in the Code Noir, see pp. 180–181.

[16] For the earlier eighteenth-century background, discussed in chapters one and three, see Ordonnance des Administrateurs, March 27, 1721, LC, 2:726 (concerning slaves deserting to and being welcomed on the Spanish side of the island, thereby risking "a general revolt, and consequently the total ruin of the residents of Le Cap, and even … the complete loss of the colony because of a bad example"); Arrêt du Conseil du Port-au-Prince, July 21, 1768, ANOM, CSD, F/3/273, fols. 250–54 (concerning a *procureur* suspended from his functions for six months because he refused to follow up on the prosecution of several blacks; the suspended *procureur* was accused of saying that the "persecution" of slaves might lead them to revolt, and of having failed to arrest a group of blacks claiming that "the time of the whites is finished"); Letter from Pierre-Victor Malouet to Narre [spelling unclear] and Renaut, Sept. [month unclear] 28, 1777, ANOM, F/3/90, fol. 179; and Raynal [Malouet], *Essai sur l'administration de Saint-Domingue*, 14.

The Lejeune prosecution culminates the eighteenth-century tug-of-war over planter brutality discussed in Chapter 3 of this book – the cases and controversies from the period of the 1760s to the 1780s in which the torture of slaves by their actual and putative masters figured repeatedly. Yet the Lejeune case also points forward in time, suggesting the pragmatic, administrative wellsprings of certain key streams of antislavery thought and, ultimately, abolitionist practice.[17] More than just a *cause célèbre* in its time, the story stands as a microhistorical archive of that quintessentially juristic, administrative spirit so characteristic of the colonial Enlightenment, with its ambiguous convergence of prudential and humanitarian currents. If this worldview sought to appeal to the interests of masters, it was not by trying to appease the plantation owner's pursuit of short-term profits at any expense (even though the planter and legal elites overlapped considerably in Saint-Domingue as elsewhere in the Atlantic world). Rather, it was by evoking a vision of colonial stability that unfolded in the longer stream of time. The power of this broader temporal vision – its ability to discipline the conduct of masters and their representatives – seemed to derive not primarily from traditional absolutist claims of authority or the call of benevolence, but from its incorporation of a futuristic scenario of "catastrophic" slave revolt. In 1788, the materialization of that scenario still lay in the future, but it was beginning to require less imagination than ever before.

THE COLONIAL PROHIBITION OF TORTURE

Even as they terrorized the slaves who far outnumbered them, the planters of eighteenth-century Saint-Domingue felt terrorized *by* their slaves, and specifically by their suspected use of poison to kill blacks and whites, slaves and free persons alike. As a technique of intimidation and resistance, poison was characterized, above all, by its invisibility. Indeed, the hidden nature of poison was the very source of its power to sow fear in the minds of masters and overseers, which it most certainly did (to judge from the 1770 and 1771 cases of Dessources and Cassarouy).[18] As the

---

[17] Christopher Brown's distinction between antislavery thought, abolitionist programs of reform, and the actual achievement of abolition and emancipation is (again) particularly useful in this context. Brown, *Moral Capital*, 17–18.

[18] See Chapter 3.

colonial administrators would note in one of their interventions into the Lejeune case, poison was a method of "secret vengeance."[19] A practice of ancient pedigree that was also strikingly modern and disciplinary in its consequences, poison effected violence without resort to conventional methods. Its operation on the body required no overt physical invasion, rendering its effect on the psyche all the more powerful.[20]

The true dimensions of this reputed reign of terror are probably forever lost to history. What we can say is that, in Saint-Domingue, that reign was associated at its origins with a Muslim, Arabic-speaking slave from West Africa named Macandal.[21] After eluding capture for many years, Macandal was burned at the stake in 1758 on charges of poisoning whites and spreading knowledge about the use of poison to other slaves in the colony. His name became associated with a specific crime – "Macandalisme" – and was invoked by the colonial courts and by colonists throughout the rest of the colonial period in Saint-Domingue as a symbol of the dangers of slave resistance.[22]

Macandalisme united in one name the twin planter fears of poisoning and slave *marronage* (or fugitive slavery). Slaves who fled their plantations were punished the first time by having their ears cut off and a shoulder marked with the *fleur de lis*, the second time by having their hamstrings cut (and the other shoulder marked), and the third time by death.[23] *Marronage* spawned a vigorous culture of slave resistance in Saint-Domingue, and no maroon was more famous in the eighteenth

---

[19] Letter from François Barbé de Marbois, intendant, and Alexandre de Vincent de Mazarade, governor, to the members of the Cap Français Chamber of Agriculture, April 17, 1788, ANOM, F/3/90, fol. 208.

[20] Because it could be placed in food or drink and then left to await consumption, poison had the additional terrifying aspect of being at least partly self-administered. Although poison played a role of special importance in the Caribbean colonies, it was feared by planters throughout the Americas. See James, *The Black Jacobins*, 16–17; and Eugene Genovese, *Roll, Jordan, Roll: The World the Slaves Made* (New York: Vintage, 1976), 616. For a study of the trial of slaves for poisoning in early-nineteenth-century Martinique, see John Savage, "Between Colonial Fact and French Law: Slave Poisoners and the Provostial Court in Restoration-Era Martinique," *French Historical Studies* 29, no. 4 (2006): 565–594.

[21] Pluchon locates the first official reference to poison as a crime punishable by death in Saint-Domingue in a June 1723 decision of the high court of Le Cap. Pluchon, *Vaudou, sorciers, empoisonneurs*, 152.

[22] See Fick, *The Making of Haiti*, 59–73; Pluchon, *Vaudou, sorciers, empoisonneurs*, 165 ff.

[23] Code Noir, art. 38 (1685). Enforcement of these provisions depended heavily on the fugitive slave police, in which free people of color played a leading role. See Chapter 2.

century than Macandal, who organized bands of fellow fugitives from his base in the mountains to carry out attacks on plantations throughout the northern province of the colony. Slaves identified the culture of maroon resistance with autonomy and release from the rigors of the plantation; masters associated it with brigandage and guerilla-style terrorism.[24] It was largely in connection with the dreaded specter of Macandalisme that torture was deployed so pervasively in Saint-Domingue during the second half of the eighteenth century.[25]

The legacies of Macandalisme would appear and reappear throughout the Lejeune affair. In another respect, however, the case was virtually unprecedented in the annals of Saint-Domingue. For this was one of the very few instances (if not the only one) in which slaves were successful in using the criminal-justice system to press charges against their master. The prosecution unquestionably came as a complete surprise to Nicolas Lejeune, whose father had bequeathed to him a coffee plantation earlier in the 1780s, located in the northern province near Plaisance, some twenty miles southwest of the commercial capital of Cap Français. The Lejeune plantation had been the scene of several previous incidents involving the torture of slaves on suspicion of having administered poison to their master and fellow slaves. None of these previous infractions of the Code Noir had ever resulted in the actual investigation or prosecution of either the elder Lejeune or his son, a situation typical of broader patterns in the colony.

Lejeune's slaves were able to pursue their claims in 1788 because of that mix of very old and quite recent law discussed in Chapter 3: the 1685 Code Noir and the plantation-management ordinances promulgated almost exactly one century later. Article 26 of the Code allowed slaves to bring a complaint to the royal prosecutor in cases of malnourishment, lack of clothing, or improper "maintenance," and mandated the prosecution of masters for the "barbarous and inhumane treatment" of their slaves.[26] Article 42 punished masters who tortured or mutilated their slaves by confiscation of the injured slave and prosecution of the master (although it permitted masters to chain or whip those of their slaves

---

[24] On Macandalisme and maroon resistance in Saint-Domingue, see Fick, *Making of Haiti*, 59–73.
[25] Debbasch, "Au coeur du 'gouvernement des esclaves'," 31–54 (emphasizing the relationship between poisoning and torture); Pluchon, *Vaudou, sorciers, empoisonneurs*, 196–197.
[26] Code Noir, art. 26 (1685).

who, in the Code's term, "deserved" such punishment).[27] Finally, article 43 commanded the king's colonial officers to prosecute masters or overseers who killed slaves "under their power or under their direction" and to "punish the murder according to the atrocity of the circumstances." Yet it also permitted the royal officers to "absolve" such masters where appropriate, without the need to obtain a royal pardon.[28]

Whereas these provisions of the Code Noir were largely directed toward masters, the 1784–1785 reforms, recognizing that steadily growing absentee-ownership rates left the discipline of slaves in the hands of their owner's agents in Saint-Domingue, had specifically targeted plantation managers and overseers. For these individuals, the newly imposed threat of revocation and/or prosecution in cases of abuse was substantially softened in the aftermath of the planter outcry against the 1784 ordinance.[29] The significance of that ordinance for the Lejeune affair derived as much from memories of the political conflict it triggered – still ripe in the spring and summer of 1788 – as from the actual text of the controverted measures. Partly in response to northern obstreperousness in the face of the plantation-management reforms, the intendant of Saint-Domingue, François Barbé de Marbois, had suspended the Conseil Supérieur of Cap Français in January 1787 and essentially merged it with its more docile counterpart in Port-au-Prince, where the colony's administrative seat was located.[30] The reactions of Lejeune and his neighbors to

[27] Ibid., art. 42 ("Only masters shall be permitted, when they believe their slaves so deserve, to chain them and beat them with canes or rope. *We forbid masters from applying torture to their slaves* or from inflicting any kind of mutilation, on pain of confiscation of the slaves and special prosecution of the masters.") (emphasis added). See also Ordonnance du Roi, Dec. 30, 1712, LC, 2:337. The heading for this 1712 ordinance in Moreau de Saint-Méry's compilation is worth quoting in full: "Ordinance of the King that prohibits all of his subjects in the American islands from applying torture [*la Question*] to their slaves by their private authority, under whatever pretext." The ordinance described the king's distress at being informed that planters in the French Caribbean colonies were using torture in violation of the Code Noir and "with unheard cruelty, even among the most barbarous nations, such that [their] slaves were unable for long periods to render any service." Meanwhile, other slaves, "intimidated by the example," were led to desert the plantations for fear of being subjected to "such inhumanity," all of which caused "great disorder" in the colonies. The ordinance established a fine of five hundred livres per violation and called on slaves who were suspected of committing crimes to be prosecuted by the court system. Ibid.

[28] Code Noir, art. 43 (1685).

[29] See Chapter 3.

[30] Debien, *Les colons de Saint-Domingue et la Révolution*, 53-54; Blackburn, *Overthrow of Colonial Slavery*, 166. The suspension lasted until June 1787. The court in Le Cap was replaced by an elected Chamber of Agriculture that served as the northern colonists'

the 1788 prosecution make clear that they interpreted the case through the lens of this institutional history and the broader pattern of "administrative despotism" that it symbolized for them.[31]

Torture clearly represented a bone of special contention between planters and administrators in late colonial Saint-Domingue. Yet what explains the original decision to ban its use by planters? The sources behind the drafting of the Code Noir suggest a general concern with breaking the vicious cycle of slave "crimes" and planter retaliation that administrators and jurists perceived in the French Caribbean world of the mid- to late seventeenth century.[32] Beyond this, the article 42 prohibition appears to reflect not only the old feudal distinction between *haute* (high) and *basse* (low) justice, but also the principle that "in criminal matters the establishment of truth was the absolute right and the exclusive power of the sovereign and his judges."[33]

From another point of view, the Code Noir ban on torture might be viewed as a form of exception to the widespread seventeenth-century reliance on delegated corporate authority. Many New World slave colonies, Saint-Domingue included, were originally administered as royally chartered trading companies, exercising authority delegated to them by European monarchies. Moreover, it may be that, in this institutional setting, individual planters were similarly seen as possessing certain default powers and privileges that would have otherwise accrued (on the other side of the Atlantic) to the monarchy. Saint-Domingue's corporate phase had ended more than ten years before the Code Noir, in 1674, when the colony was directly absorbed into the royal domain. Even after 1685, however, the individual plantations exercised quasi-public powers delegated by the imperial administration, such as the enforcement of police regulations and court sentences relative to slaves.[34] Against this backdrop,

---

only representative institution until the convocation of the Estates General (announced in May 1788 and set for May 1789).

[31] For the colonists' grievances against "administrative despotism," see Tarrade, "Les colonies et les principes de 1789," 11–13; and Geggus, "Saint-Domingue on the Eve of Revolution," 13.

[32] See Chapter 1.

[33] On the medieval law background, see Robert Chesnais, introduction to *Le Code Noir*, ed. Robert Chesnais (Paris: L'esprit frappeur, 1998), 11. On the monarchy's inquisitorial monopoly, see Foucault, *Discipline and Punish*, 35. Foucault is here discussing Old Regime French criminal procedure, including the use of judicial torture, but his point also (and somewhat paradoxically) illuminates the ethos of the Code Noir's ban on the torture of slaves by masters.

[34] See Ogle, "Policing Saint Domingue," 111. I thank Errol Meidinger for his thoughts on this subject.

the administration of colonial criminal justice does not lend itself to any clear public-private distinction of the kind familiar to modern law. On the other hand, the public-private dichotomy is not entirely anachronistic even in the world of the Code Noir. By 1712, at the latest, it was recognized that masters who engaged in the torture of their slaves were acting in a "private" (and illegal) capacity.[35]

Article 42 does not mean that slaves were exempted from the use of judicial torture (*la question*) in Saint-Domingue.[36] An early draft of the Code Noir implies that torture could lawfully be administered to slaves in the colonial courts.[37] Slave criminal-trial records were periodically destroyed during the colonial period, making it difficult to tell just how often *la question* may have been used in prosecutions of slaves. The surviving eighteenth-century appellate records gathered in Moreau de Saint-Méry's voluminous collection give no clear indication one way or the other.[38] Pierre Pluchon has written of a 1755 case from Martinique in which a master used torture to elicit an initial confession from a slave whom he suspected of poisoning a fellow slave. At trial, the defendant retracted his confession as having been made under duress, leading the judge to apply two rounds of *la question* before obtaining the desired admission.[39] Macandal himself, according to a contemporary account, was subjected to a form of judicial torture known as the "*question préalable*," in the course of which he is said to have confessed the names of a "prodigious" number of coconspirators, who were themselves arrested and questioned under torture. That same account attributed the apprehension of Macandal to the threatened used of torture against a female slave (herself suspected of using poison) in December 1757.[40] It

---

[35] See note 27, and Chapter 3.

[36] I thank Kenworthey Bilz and Andrew Koppelman for their questions on this point.

[37] "Projet de règlement de Mrs. de Blenac et Patoulet sur les Esclaves des Isles de l'Amérique," May 20, 1682, ANOM, F/3/90, fol. 5.

[38] Cases involving the death penalty were subject to mandatory appeal to the Conseils Supérieurs. Ogle, "Policing Saint Domingue," 340. Poisoning was a capital offense, and it therefore seems significant that no appellate decisions reference the torture of slaves by trial courts. Ogle's thesis alludes to the role of torture in Old Regime French criminal procedure but does not cite any specific instances of the judicial torture of slaves in eighteenth-century Saint-Domingue. On the periodic destruction of slave criminal trial records pursuant to royal order during the first half of the eighteenth century, see ibid., 92, 308; and Pluchon, *Vaudou, sorciers, empoisonneurs*, 152.

[39] Pluchon, *Vaudou, sorciers, empoisonneurs*, 159–161. In a 1712 letter to the naval minister, the intendant of the Windward Islands, Vaucresson, used the term *la question* to describe the "private" torture of slaves by masters. Ibid., 207.

[40] *Relation d'une conspiration tramée par les nègres dans l'îsle de S. Domingue* (N.p.: n.p., 1758), 3–4, 6–7. See also Pluchon, *Vaudou, sorciers, empoisonneurs*, 170–176, 238.

seems likely that judicial torture was applied to slaves at other times in Saint-Domingue.[41]

At the same time, however, such cases cannot have been very common, not only because of the limits on the use of slave testimony in court (which will be discussed later), but also given the reality that masters and their representatives rarely found it necessary or proper to avail themselves of the royal tribunals when dealing with slaves accused of poison. In these and other situations, slaves were effectively tried and convicted on the plantation, often with the illegal use of private torture.[42] When slaves were brought to trial, it seems they were typically condemned on the basis of mere rumor and the master's word, rather than on the basis of slave evidence.[43]

At the end of the day, the Code Noir prohibition on torture seems at least partly inconsistent with the definition of torture as a presumptive monopoly of the state. That inconsistency looms even larger in light of a second axiom in the historiography of criminal law that sharply distinguishes the practice of torture from the administration of painful punishments.[44] The Code Noir, by contrast, links torture (in article 42) to such clearly punitive practices as mutilation, whipping, and chaining.[45] In so doing, the Code Noir evokes the anthropological analysis of Michel Foucault, who argued that torture in Old Regime Europe "functioned in that strange economy in which the ritual that produced the truth went side by side with the ritual that imposed the punishment." In this

---

[41] In the aftermath of the August 1791 slave revolt, slaves believed to have participated in the uprising were tortured on the wheel by officials in Cap Français, for what seem to have been punitive as much as investigative reasons. See Dubois, *Avengers of the New World*, 96.

[42] Pluchon, *Vaudou, sorciers, empoisonneurs*, 196–197.

[43] Ibid., 162. The difficulty of proving poison cases against slaves prompted a number of extraordinary suggestions for the reform of colonial criminal justice during the eighteenth century. In 1726, the Conseil Supérieur of Martinique proposed a kind of itinerant, emergency form of justice, whereby magistrates would travel immediately to a plantation upon being informed of a poisoning incident. A rapid, on-site criminal trial and sentencing would ensue. In 1749, the administrators of the Windward Islands began requiring autopsies of suspected poison victims, in an apparent effort to introduce some scientific rigor into an otherwise arbitrary system of proof. In 1763, the intendant of Saint-Domingue proposed to the naval minister that suspected poisoners be deported to France in light of the difficulty of adducing adequate evidence to convict them. Despite such attempted reforms, rumors and presumptions continued to dominate the accusation and conviction of slaves in poison cases, which were disposed of by masters and their agents at the "private" level of the plantation. Ibid., 153–154, 196.

[44] See Langbein, *Torture and the Law of Proof*, 3; and the other sources cited in note 9.

[45] See note 27.

interpretation, "the regulated pain involved in judicial torture was a means both of punishment and of investigation."[46] Although directed at masters rather than magistrates, article 42 of the Code Noir suggests an understanding of torture as comparable to or continuous with the exercise of punishment and the deliberate infliction of suffering.

This understanding reflected the specific circumstances of the slave society that the Code Noir was designed to regulate but may not have been purely local in nature either. There appears to be a broader etymological dimension to the association between torture and punishment. In the mid-fifteenth century, the French word "torture" signified "a serious penalty, a corporal punishment that could result in death."[47] By the late sixteenth century, the term had taken on its modern sense of "intense physical suffering inflicted in order to extract confessions."[48] This linguistic shift, however, did not preclude subsequent connotations of intolerable physical suffering, as reflected first in a 1631 usage and then reappearing in the mid-seventeenth century.[49] Thus, a broader and perhaps more popular meaning of torture both predates and postdates the technical definition of the term. As an historical matter, the jurisprudential effort to segregate these technical and popular meanings has not prevented them from cross-fertilizing each other, even within the domain of law itself.

In any case, for those who found themselves on the receiving end of these practices and understandings, whether in France or its overseas territories, torture was no mere semantic exercise. As we will see, whatever the exact relationship between colonial torture and metropolitan (judicial) torture may have been, it is hard to view the use of torture in the Lejeune affair as anything other than a particularly brutal and volatile mix of punitive and investigative practices operating in that twilight space of sovereignty that was the slave plantation. Yet the implications of colonial torture were even more complicated and far-reaching than this image suggests.

THE DEPOSITION OF THE SLAVES

The criminalization of torture was not the only precondition of Lejeune's prosecution. Another was the willingness of Lejeune's slaves to bring

---

[46] Foucault, *Discipline and Punish*, 42.
[47] *Dictionnaire historique de la langue française*, ed. Alain Rey (Paris: Le Robert, 1998), 3:3857.
[48] Ibid.
[49] Ibid.

charges against their master. In order to do so, they had to be allowed to present their version of the facts to a judicial officer, and their account in turn had to be recognized by a court of law. Because slaves were barred under the Code Noir from serving as witnesses in civil and criminal matters alike, and judges could not use a slave's deposition to draw inferences or to establish proof of guilt, the logistical aspect of this dilemma was no mere detail.[50] As the 1775 case of the slave Thomas reminds us, slave depositions could be used, at most, only to assist judges in clarifying the circumstances of a matter.[51] Even after 1738, when the testimony of an essential slave witness was made admissible into evidence absent any white witnesses, a slave could not testify against his own master.[52] Moreover, the 1784–1785 regulations permitting a slave to denounce the abuses of a master, overseer, or plantation manager did nothing to change the preexisting evidentiary restrictions of the Code Noir. On another day, in another area of the colony, a case such as the one brought against Lejeune might well have gone unnoticed, as nearly every such case did. Just as plausibly, the case might not have been allowed to proceed all the way to a trial and appeal.

We can get some sense of the fragility and contingency of the slaves' success in pressing charges from the account of an analogous case that came to a head in Saint-Domingue just as the Lejeune prosecution was getting off the ground. On March 25, 1788, the colony's intendant (Marbois) and governor (Alexandre de Vincent de Mazarade) reported to Naval Minister César-Henri de la Luzerne on the "barbarities committed by" a planter named Maguero against the slaves of his plantation.[53] The report was based on the letter of a commander named Coutard, who was

---

[50] Code Noir, art. 30 (1685). Article 31, for its part, prohibited slaves from becoming parties to civil or criminal matters. Only a master could represent the slave's interest in civil matters. Similarly, only the master could pursue criminal remedies to compensate for "outrages and excesses" committed against his slaves. Ibid., art. 31.

[51] See Chapter 3.

[52] Fick, *Making of Haiti*, 283 n.108. Cf. Thomas Jefferson, "Notes on the State of Virginia," in *Thomas Jefferson: Writings*, ed. Merrill Peterson (New York: Library of America, 1984), 268 ("With the Romans, the regular method of taking the evidence of their slaves was under torture. Here it has been thought better never to resort to their evidence."). As Langbein has demonstrated, torture was necessary to continental criminal procedure because the Roman canon law of proof required either a confession or two witnesses in cases involving blood sanctions (that is, execution or mutilation). Langbein, *Torture and the Law of Proof*, 12. As explained earlier, however, the law of evidence alone seems unable to account for the status of torture in the Atlantic colonial context.

[53] La Luzerne had himself served as governor of Saint-Domingue from April 1786 until November 1787, when Vincent was named to succeed him.

present in Port-au-Prince to receive the news while the administrators were away on a trip to Gonaïves, a town on the western coast roughly sixty miles north of the capital. Coutard reported that "the tribunals were finding it impossible to take cognizance of this case, because the law rejects the depositions of slaves and there was no other available proof." When the administrators returned to Port-au-Prince, they summoned Maguero and his slaves to present their respective accounts of the incident. In the course of this interrogation Maguero confessed to wounding one of his male slaves with a gunshot and mutilating a female slave. The administrators allowed other charges made against Maguero – including the suggestion that the number of slaves on his plantation had somehow "diminished" over time from twenty-five to three – to go unexplored.[54]

"The courts of justice having unfortunately no hold over this guilty person," Vincent and Marbois wrote, "it has seemed to us necessary to deal severely with him by way of an administrative proceeding." Maguero was ordered deported to France on the next available passage, where he would undergo "several months of detention" and be barred from ever returning to the colony. The administrators acknowledged the "inconveniences" of removing a slaveholder from his plantation, in consideration of which they appointed the royal prosecutor to make arrangements for the supervision of Maguero's property. They then concluded their letter by emphasizing that Maguero's crime was "not the only one of this nature. There have been crimes committed on other plantations that are even more serious." These other cases, however, lacked the "clarity" of proof afforded by a planter's own confession. Vincent and Marbois promised to take steps to "stop the course of these cruelties" by making an "example" of their punishment, as in the case of the deportation meted out to Maguero. Yet the underlying problem of the court system's rejection of slave testimony remained.[55]

Whether the administrators had in mind the Lejeune case with their reference to other crimes yet "more serious" than those committed by Maguero is unclear. Vincent and Marbois wrote their first letter commenting on Lejeune's prosecution four days after reporting on the Maguero case. Yet there would have been no shortage of other incidents on which to base this claim about the severity and extent of planter brutality in

---

[54] Letter from François Barbé de Marbois, intendant, and Alexandre de Vincent de Mazarade, governor, to César-Henri de la Luzerne, naval minister, March 25, 1788, ANOM, CGSD, C/9A/160, fols. 78–79.

[55] Ibid., fol. 79.

Saint-Domingue. Far more than the question of severity, what distinguished the Lejeune case from its counterparts was the decision of the court of first instance (*sénéchaussée*) to order and accept the deposition of Lejeune's slaves. This decision not only prevented the case from joining the vast number of incidents that were never reported in the first place, but also kept the determination of Lejeune's fate out of the discretionary jurisdiction of the administrators, a fact that had a considerable impact on the ultimate resolution of the affair.

By the time Vincent and Marbois first learned of what had transpired on Lejeune's plantation, in fact, the judicial process was already well under way. On March 13, 1788, a magistrate (*sénéchal*) named Buffon[56] and the royal prosecutor of Cap Français, Jean-Baptiste Suarez d'Almeida, wrote a letter to the administrators reporting that fourteen slaves had arrived at the town prison from Plaisance the previous Sunday evening to ask for "the protection of the judicial system" from the "cruelties of their master's son." The slaves charged that on two separate occasions Nicolas Lejeune had used a torch to burn his slaves. The first of these incidents came the year before and involved two slaves, one female and one male. The second incident had occurred only the previous Friday when Lejeune used a torch to burn the legs of two female slaves, Zabeth and Marie-Rose.[57] Since that time, he had kept the two women locked up in a cell. The fourteen slaves reported that "the fear of undergoing similar treatment, with which they had been threatened, forced them to flee" the plantation.[58] In this instance, as in a mere handful of other eighteenth-century cases that led to the prosecution of masters under articles 26 and 42 of the Code Noir, a group of slaves who took the risk of trying to establish that their master had violated the Code Noir's prohibition on torture could only succeed in doing so by violating another provision of the same code.

For this particular group of slaves, however, the initial risk paid off. The *sénéchal* Buffon agreed to pursue the complaint by means of a special investigation that would seek to establish the dimensions of the alleged

---

[56] Buffon's full name is not revealed in the standard biographical references.

[57] Relying on Thibau, Joan Dayan's account of the case notes that Marie-Rose was a slave from the Congo and Zabeth an Ibo from the Niger Delta. Dayan, *Haiti, History, and the Gods*, 321 n.73. I have no reason to question this information but have not seen it confirmed in the primary sources, and Thibau's narrative makes somewhat imaginative use of secondary background literature on the slave trade in seeking to reconstruct the African background of both women.

[58] Letter from Buffon, sénéchal, and Jean-Baptiste Suarez d'Almeida, royal prosecutor, to François Barbé de Marbois, intendant, and Alexandre de Vincent de Mazarade, governor, March 13, 1788, ANOM, F/3/90, fol. 200.

crime "with the least amount of scandal possible."[59] This was the first indication of an official nature that the prosecution of Lejeune would require treading on highly sensitive territory. Buffon entrusted his junior colleague on the *sénéchaussée*, Couët de Montarand (a former assistant magistrate), with the task of traveling to the Lejeune plantation and taking the depositions of all those involved in the incident.[60] Montarand arrived at the plantation to discover Zabeth and Marie-Rose locked up in a *cachot* (cell of solitary confinement) with burns to their feet, legs, and thighs. Asked to provide his version of the events, Lejeune declared that he suspected the two slaves of having used poison to murder another female slave, Julie, who had died suddenly in her sleep. Lejeune further stated that an autopsy of Julie undertaken by his "surgeon" had revealed the presence of undigested food in her intestines and "stains" in other parts. Lejeune also alleged that he himself had survived an attempt at poisoning by Zabeth and Marie-Rose, in proof of which he offered a container of powder to the clerk who accompanied Montarand on his investigation.[61] We learn from subsequent accounts of the case that Zabeth and Marie-Rose would eventually die of the wounds they had received from Lejeune, only a matter of days after they were found locked up in the *cachot*.[62] Before their deaths, however, both were able to testify that it was only the physical torment they experienced that had forced them to confess to anything Lejeune wanted them to admit. In confirmation of this claim, an analysis of the powder Lejeune had submitted by a doctor and surgeon appointed by Montarand had revealed evidence of nothing more than common smoking tobacco interspersed with five bits of rat stool. "That is ... the exact account of this scene of atrocity, of which

[59] Ibid.

[60] Montarand had served as an assistant magistrate (*conseiller assesseur*) of the *sénéchaussée* until 1787, when he was promoted by Marbois and La Luzerne to the office of *conseiller* (*sénéchal*). Charles Edmond Regnault de Beaucaron, *Souvenirs de famille; voyages, agriculture, précédés d'une Causerie sur le passé* (Paris: Plon-Nourrit et cie, 1912), 98, 101–102. It seems likely, but is not certain, that this is Jean-Baptiste Louis-Augustin Couët de Montarand, who owned four coffee plantations and two houses in Cap Français, and eventually served as a judge on the Conseil Supérieur of Le Cap. See *Généalogie et Histoire de la Caraïbe* 30 (Sept. 1999): 399 http://www.ghcaraibe.org/bul/ghco30/po399. html (last viewed May 7, 2010). A detailed account of the Montarand family assets in Saint-Domingue is given in Regnault de Beaucaron, *Souvenirs de famille*, 97.

[61] Letter from Buffon and Almeida to Marbois and Vincent, March 13, 1788, fol. 200.

[62] Letter from François Barbé de Marbois, Intendant, and Alexandre de Vincent de Mazarade, Governor, to the *Commandants* and *officiers d'administration*, March 27, 1788, ANOM, F/3/90, fol. 198; Letter from Vincent and Marbois to La Luzerne, Aug. 29, 1788, fol. 263.

unfortunately there are only too many examples," Buffon and Almeida concluded.[63]

However, there was more to this initial report by the two judicial officers than a factual account of the case as they had come to understand it from Montarand's investigation. The two incidents of torture of which Nicolas Lejeune stood accused were not the first such instances on this particular plantation. "Similar cruelties" had been inflicted by the senior Lejeune in 1781 and 1782, for which he had been reprimanded by the government "without a scandal" (*sans éclat*).[64] Moreover, Lejeune père's nephew (Nicolas Lejeune's cousin) had followed the "same principles" in applying discipline to his slaves, as a result of which he eventually became the "victim of [their] vengeance, or of [their] desperation." (The slaves judged responsible for killing the senior Lejeune's nephew were all subsequently executed on the wheel.) Nicolas Lejeune's atrocities were therefore only the latest installment in a long-standing pattern of events. In all three cases, Buffon and Almeida implied, the perpetrators had rationalized the use of torture as a response to the suspected use of poison by slaves.[65]

Despite this history of brutality, there were countervailing considerations. Perhaps the most revealing passage in the March 13 report came near its end, where the *sénéchal* and royal prosecutor warned the administrators of the risks associated with any serious effort to bring Nicolas Lejeune to justice:

[Y]ou are aware of the danger that such an affair, if allowed to explode, could pose to the regime of the colonies. It is greatly to be feared that the negroes would confuse the right of complaint with insubordination, which would become difficult to put down if they believed themselves to be backed up by the laws.[66]

This argument about the "danger" of lending too much publicity to the case and of encouraging the slaves to treat their "right of complaint" as a license for "insubordination" would become the keystone of Lejeune's defense. It is therefore all the more significant that it was first articulated by the officials responsible for bringing the case to light. Having acknowledged the danger that might result from their interventions,

---

[63] Letter from Buffon and Almeida to Marbois and Vincent, March 13, 1788, fol. 200.
[64] The implication here is that the administrators or their subordinates, rather than the colonial judicial system, had been responsible for taking action against Lejeune in these earlier cases.
[65] Letter from Buffon and Almeida to Marbois and Vincent, March 13, 1788, fols. 200–201.
[66] Ibid., fol. 201.

Buffon and Almeida then ended their report with an ambiguous promise to continue the prosecution until and unless they receive orders from the colonial governor and intendant to stop.[67] Whether this was an invitation to Vincent and Marbois to take the matter out of the lower court's hands or a mere question of formality and deference, it was clear that the *sénéchal* and prosecutor were not accustomed to dealing with complaints of the sort they now found themselves in charge of adjudicating.

"THE FEELING OF ABSOLUTE POWER"

Over the next two weeks, calls to end the prosecution of Lejeune were sounded in other, more predictable corners of the colony. The first came on March 23, in the form of a letter to Vincent and Marbois from Lejeune's fellow planters in the district of Plaisance. They urged the administrators to dissolve the proceedings on the grounds that "already, the plantations adjacent to Lejeune's are murmuring, and it is possible that this event will become the signal of a general revolt." No credibility could be given to the claims of a slave community that was guilty not only of the attempted assassination of Lejeune's manager ten years before and the successful assassination of his nephew, but also of no fewer than ten attempted uprisings. Moreover, the planters asserted, the "execrable Mme. Rose" had administered fatal doses of poison to twenty victims "of her own color" in previous years, and had even tried to do the same to her master. Stopping the prosecution of Lejeune was the only way to "assure public tranquility and the common good."[68]

The reference to the "execrable Mme. Rose" points to an inescapable undercurrent of gendered anxiety that informed planter reactions to the case, beginning with Nicolas Lejeune's use of torture in retaliation for the perceived crimes of Zabeth and Marie-Rose. A putative association between the subtle, noninvasive violence of poison and the sinister machinations of women slaves – possibly overlaid with similarly gendered stereotypes of vodou as a magical, pagan practice akin to sorcery – seems to have pervaded much of the affair.[69] Indeed, Nicolas's torture of Zabeth and Marie-Rose might even be compared to some of the witchcraft trials

---

[67] Ibid.

[68] Letter from Residents of the *quartier* of Plaisance to François Barbé de Marbois, intendant, and Alexandre de Vincent de Mazarade, governor, March 23, 1788, ANOM, F/3/90, fol. 197.

[69] On the colonists' association of poison with sorcery and vodou, see Pluchon, *Vaudou, sorciers, empoisonneurs*, 169–172; and Bell, *Toussaint Louverture*, 68.

of the sixteenth and seventeenth centuries.[70] However far that analogy may extend, the nexus between poison and torture in late-eighteenth-century Saint-Domingue was powerfully reinforced by the distinctive anxieties that feminized resistance to slavery evoked in the French colony. Further, it seems equally likely that Nicolas Lejeune's indignation at having to defend himself from the likes of Buffon and Almeida was heightened by the thought that his prosecution stemmed from an (alleged) act of female-slave insubordination in its most quintessential and dangerous form.

Whatever its deeper psychosocial sources, Nicolas Lejeune's reaction to the affair reflected a quite deliberate elevation of the stakes. A week later, he came forth with a defense of his own that echoed his fellow planters' allusion to the possibility of a slave revolution if steps were not taken to halt the prosecution. Of all the unfortunate things that could happen to a colonist, he wrote the administrators on March 27, "the most terrible and the most dangerous to public tranquility" is the "humiliating necessity" of having to defend oneself against one's own slaves. It was only "the spirit of rebellion and, even more, the fear of being declared accomplices to all the crimes committed on [a] plantation" that had turned his slaves "into the accusers." Rather than complain, the slaves ought to realize that nothing prevented them from being "incomparably happier" than the peasants of France, who were responsible for supporting entire families on the basis of little more than a cottage and the fruit of their labors.[71]

In support of his claim that there was now a real and pressing danger of an outright slave revolt, Lejeune enlisted the support of the colony's favorite philosophe and legal theorist, Montesquieu. In a controversial and ambiguous passage of *The Spirit of the Laws*, Montesquieu had written that only the "fear of punishment" could inspire the slave to carry out "onerous duties" in lands where extreme heat enervated both the body and the will.[72] Lejeune took this formulation and gave it an even

---

[70] On the use of torture against witches in early modern England and Scotland, see Hunt, *Inventing Human Rights*, 77. Thanks to Susan Slymovics for suggesting this line of comparison.

[71] Statement (*mémoire*) of Nicolas Lejeune to François Barbé de Marbois, intendant, and Alexandre de Vincent de Mazarade, governor, March 27, 1788, ANOM, F/3/90, fols. 202–203 bis. A *mémoire* has the sense of a party's statement of a legal case. A *mémoire judiciaire* is what we would call a legal brief. This statement was signed by Nicolas's father, Lejeune père, "in the absence of his son." Ibid., fol 205.

[72] Montesquieu, *Spirit of the Laws*, 251. I have modified the translation of this passage to more accurately reflect the original.

more Machiavellian twist, arguing that if one destroyed that "salutary fear of punishment" that induced slaves to show obedience toward their masters, what hope of security would three or four whites have in the midst of one or two hundred whose willingness to rebel had been sanctioned by the colonial legal system? No real distinction could be made, he added, between the conduct of his slaves and the slave population of Saint-Domingue generally, because a revolt on one plantation would spark revolts on all the others. For that reason, Lejeune wrote, "my cause in this case becomes the cause of every colonist: It must interest all men reduced to living among beings in whom one can assume the existence of neither character (*moeurs*) nor moral principles."[73] The assumption of the Code Noir, and of colonial administrators and judges more generally, that the planter community could be safely and legitimately divided into "responsible" and "irresponsible" factions was no more valid than the idea that one group of slaves could be distinguished from another.

The accused planter's debt to Montesquieu was more than implicit. Lejeune went on to cite "the celebrated author of *The Spirit of the Laws*" for the principle that in all countries where slavery was founded on the use of force and violence, it could only be maintained by "the same means." It was not the "fear ... of the law that prevents the negro from stabbing his master," but rather "the feeling of absolute power that [the master] exercises over [his slave's] person." Remove this restraint, Lejeune remarked, and the slave would dare anything to improve his condition. Not surprisingly, the decision of the lower court to go ahead with the prosecution was portrayed in just that light, as a victory for the subversive principle that the master-slave relationship was one of relative rather than absolute domination. "What a triumph for my negroes; and what a revolution it has effected in the spirit of these men accustomed to servitude! This is new for them."[74]

Had Lejeune been interested in exploring the full range of Montesquieu's observations about slavery, he might have come across the philosophe's argument that men will accustom themselves to anything, including slavery, "provided that the master is not harsher than the servitude."[75] As it

---

[73] Statement of Nicolas Lejeune to Vincent and Marbois, March 27, 1788, fol. 204.

[74] Ibid., fols. 204–205. Lejeune's argument about the need for absolute power over the slave can be compared to the famous 1830 opinion of the North Carolina Supreme Court in *State v. Mann*, 2 Devereux (13 N.C.) 263 (1830). On *State v. Mann*, which held that masters could not be prosecuted for assaults on their slaves, see Tushnet, *Slave Law in the American South*.

[75] Montesquieu, *Spirit of the Laws*, 502.

was, Lejeune was far more preoccupied with what he described as the heavy costs of leniency. Some of the most distinguished residents of the colony, he wrote, had paid with their lives for exercising "complacency" toward their slaves. For Lejeune, this price was best measured in the "incredible number" of slaves who, between 1769 and 1771, had been executed on charges of having murdered their masters.[76]

A FUGITIVE FROM JUSTICE

Sometime between March 13, when Buffon and Almeida sent their initial report to Vincent and Marbois, and March 27, when the two administrators made their initial intervention in the affair, two important events transpired: The *sénéchaussée* of Cap Français issued a warrant for the arrest of Nicolas Lejeune, and Lejeune became a fugitive from justice.[77] Whether he was the first white planter in the colony's history to attain this status is not clear, but this development was certainly a tremendous anomaly against the long eighteenth-century backdrop of planter preoccupation with the problem of fugitive slaves (*marrons*).[78] Over the next few weeks, the fact of Lejeune's escape would transform his case into a colonial *cause célèbre*, with the administrators and the fugitive's fellow planters lined up on opposite sides of the debate over whether the "public interest" militated for or against his arrest and conviction.

By March 18, although still pending before the trial court in Cap Français, the case had been brought to the attention of Guillaume-Pierre-François de la Mardelle, the royal prosecutor attached to the

---

[76] Statement of Nicolas Lejeune to Vincent and Marbois, March 27, 1788, fol. 205. A marginal note at the end of Lejeune's statement reads: "In 1754, at the time of Mr. le Courtin, it was a veritable slaughterhouse [*boucherie*]. From morning til evening executions were carried out." Ibid. It is not entirely clear that Lejeune himself inserted this final note; it is possible that the remark was added by one of the administrators who received the *mémoire*, but there is nothing in the text itself to suggest that the addition was not by Lejeune. "Mr. Le Courtin" was probably Sebastien Jacques Courtin, who served during the period of the Macandal affair in various positions including royal prosecutor before the high court in Cap Français, notary general, and sénéchal (trial judge). The investigation and trial of Macandal and his accomplices were presided over by Courtin as judge. Pluchon, *Vaudou, sorciers, empoisonneurs*, 174–175, 208.

[77] Letter from Vincent and Marbois to the *Commandants* and *officiers d'administration*, March 27, 1788, fol. 198.

[78] In a 1774 case involving a white plantation manager accused of ordering a slave to assault a white peddler in the marketplace of Petite Rivière, the plantation manager failed to appear for a second round of questioning when required by the trial judge. As Ogle writes, the plantation manager "had taken what was often a quite effective route to avoid the law's rigor in Old Regime France and its colonies – he ran away." Ogle, "Policing Saint Domingue," 331.

(now-merged) Conseil Supérieur of Saint-Domingue in Port-au-Prince. In a remarkable letter that he addressed directly to Montarand, de la Mardelle urged the magistrate to stick to his guns in the face of planter opposition. "Principles of humanity" and "raison d'état" together argued in favor of protecting the "population of Africa [which] diminishes appreciably each day.... [I]t is necessary to support, defend, and encourage that of Saint-Domingue, otherwise in fifty years the sugar colonies will be only imaginary entities for the European powers who have them." As for the suggestion "constantly put forward" that slave insubordination would ensue from the prosecution of Lejeune, de la Mardelle concluded, the only real risk of revolt stemmed from "extreme injustice and barbarism."[79]

In this same spirit, on March 27, Vincent and Marbois issued a directive to the commanders and administrative officers in all three provinces of the colony. By this time, Lejeune stood accused not merely of torture but also of murder, as Zabeth and Marie-Rose had both died of their wounds in the days after the initial investigation of the case was conducted. The administrators insisted that Lejeune was undoubtedly "guilty of this atrocity": His flight from Plaisance and from the "just punishments with which he was threatened" merely served to confirm that culpability. The directive ordered the commanders and administrative officers to make every effort to arrest Lejeune at the earliest moment, including taking steps to prevent him from escaping abroad via one of the ports of Saint-Domingue. At stake was a combination of strategic and humanitarian interests that the colony could not afford to ignore: "The peace of the colony depends upon the exemplary punishment of crimes of this nature; humanity begs it, and all of the planters, with only a very few exceptions, eagerly wish that a curb be placed on all these barbarities."[80] The planters of Plaisance having made known their opposition to Lejeune's prosecution in their letter of March 23, it is not difficult to imagine what Vincent and Marbois meant by the phrase "very few exceptions." It is far less clear on what basis the administrators purported to have the support of the near totality of the colony's planters, but this assertion nonetheless

---

[79] This March 18, 1788, letter is reproduced in full in Regnault de Beaucaron, *Souvenirs de famille*, 99–100, where de la Mardelle is incorrectly identified as La Luzerne's successor as governor-general of Saint-Domingue. On de la Mardelle's career in Saint-Domingue, see Jean-André Tournerie, "Un projet d'école royale des colonies en Touraine au XVIIIᵉ siècle," *Annales de Bretagne et des pays de l'Ouest* 99, no.1 (1992): 33–60.

[80] Letter from Vincent and Marbois to the *Commandants* and *officiers d'administration*, March 27, 1788, fol. 198.

makes sense as an effort to counter Lejeune's argument that his cause was also "the cause of every colonist."[81]

By way of supplementing their March 27 directive, Vincent and Marbois wrote that same day to the officers of the *sénéchaussée* of Le Cap, asking them to exercise "the most particular care" to prevent Lejeune's escape from the colony. "We would greatly regret to see a crime this big remain unpunished," they noted with a hint of resignation at the unlikelihood of actually bringing the infamous planter to trial. The administrators also enjoined the lower court magistrates to treat Lejeune's surgeon, Magre, as a codefendant in the case and to arrange for his arrest. It was Magre and not Lejeune, the administrators alleged, who had actually used the pinewood torch to burn Zabeth and Marie-Rose. Magre's role in the affair was therefore "doubly criminal," because it would have been his responsibility before anyone else's either to "moderate the violence of [his] master" or to come to the aid of "the objects of [Lejeune's] fury."[82]

The administration's determination not to allow Lejeune's escape to stand in the way of his prosecution seems to have registered with those in the slaveholding community who sympathized with Lejeune. Among the voices raised in defense of the fugitive planter was that of the recently created Chamber of Agriculture of Cap Français, the successor institution to the Conseil Supérieur, which had been suppressed and merged with the high court in Port-au-Prince in early 1787. Although endowed with fewer prerogatives than its predecessor, the Chamber of Agriculture was nonetheless encouraged to act as a conduit for the grievances of planters in the northern province of the colony. On April 4, the chamber's secretary, a Cap Français attorney by the name of Pierre-Joseph de Laborie, submitted a petition to Vincent and Marbois emphasizing "the dangers the colony would face from giving publicity to the punishments inflicted on masters who might have misused their authority over their slaves in committing acts of barbarism."[83] Unlike Lejeune's own brief, which denied the possibility that a master could misuse an authority that by definition was absolute, the chamber's petition acknowledged that Lejeune had violated the Code Noir in committing an "act of barbarism." Yet despite the

---

[81] Statement of Nicolas Lejeune to Vincent and Marbois, March 27, 1788, fol. 204.

[82] Letter from François Barbé de Marbois, intendant, and Alexandre de Vincent de Mazarade, governor, to the *officiers* of the *Sénéchaussée* of Cap Français, March 27, 1788, ANOM, F/3/90, fol. 207.

[83] Letter from Pierre-Joseph de Laborie, Secretary of the Cap Français Chamber of Agriculture, to François Barbé de Marbois, Intendant, and Alexandre de Vincent de Mazarade, Governor, April 4, 1788, ANOM, F/3/90, fol. 199.

protection accorded slaves by the laws of Saint-Domingue, and despite the chamber's disavowal of any intention to ignore the "severity" of those laws, the reality was that a public sanctioning of Lejeune would do more to undermine than stabilize the plantation regime. The only risk-free solution was to expel Lejeune from the colony.[84]

A similar line of reasoning featured in another petition signed six days later by seventy or so residents of the northern department.[85] Far be it from them to "justify the cruelties" that Lejeune inflicted on his slaves, the colonists wrote to Vincent and Marbois; "we cherish the sentiments of humanity that dictated your rigorous orders" of March 27. However, the planters also asked for the administrators' "help" and "prudence" in a matter on which depended

the peace, good order, [and] even the possession of a colony precious to the State. Our fortunes, your life [*vie*], ours, the existence of ten thousand families in France all depend on the subordination of the slaves, and on the results of their labor. Humanity may be revolted by the rules that ancient and modern policies have adopted; [but these] conventions have been made and slaves exist![86]

That Lejeune was not being prosecuted for following the "conventions" of either "ancient" Roman or "modern" French slave law did not trouble the authors of this petition. His conviction would also be an indictment of the institution of slavery itself, which the colonists had merely inherited from an earlier age. Furthermore, the administrators themselves – many of whom acquired plantations during their tenure in Saint-Domingue, although they were barred by royal decree from doing so[87] – had a quite personal stake in the immunity of Lejeune from all further prosecution, as the reference to "your life" tried to suggest.

Thus even though it was important for reasons of humanity and justice to prevent "cruel men from giving themselves over to violent outbursts," it was no less important to avoid the "humiliation" of the colony's "privileged sorts" for reasons of "sound government" (*la saine politique*). Lejeune's *mémoire* had identified the experience of humiliation in the eyes of his own slaves as the most damaging aspect of the proceedings.[88] In this April 10 petition, that experience was characterized

[84] Ibid.
[85] The number of signatories is given in Gisler, *L'esclavage aux Antilles françaises*, 118–119.
[86] Letter from residents of the northern part to François Barbé de Marbois, intendant, and Alexandre de Vincent de Mazarade, governor, April 10, 1788, ANOM, F/3/90, fol. 209.
[87] Blackburn, *The Making of New World Slavery*, 298.
[88] Letter from residents of the northern part to Vincent and Marbois, April 10, 1788, fol. 209.

as one Lejeune would share with his fellow planters. "Sound public policy" – a phrase that had appeared in a number of earlier eighteenth-century legislative and judicial efforts to counteract planter brutality in Saint-Domingue[89] – was here invoked not in tandem with but rather in opposition to the counsels of "humanity and justice." For the northern residents, the choice between the two presented a set of clear alternatives, one that the administrators could resolve by transferring the case to their special jurisdiction: "You owe it to the good of the State [and] to the preservation of this Colony to use your private authority to pass sentence on him." If the judicial system were allowed to proceed with the case and hand down an "authentic judgment," that would only legitimate Lejeune's "rebellious" work force. Every slave would then feel justified in "insubordination" and would refuse to accept any more discipline. All orders to labor in the coffee and sugar fields would be "a vexation, all punishment a crime." Sooner rather than later the colonists would find that "we are all lost; all is overturned and we touch on a coming revolution in the colony, a revolution the horrors of which we leave you to contemplate."[90] To judge from this kind of rhetoric, the Chamber of Agriculture's April 4 petition would appear to have struck at least some planters of the northern department as overly passive and insufficiently alarmist.

Realizing they had a dilemma on their hands, Vincent and Marbois took the highly unusual step of responding directly to the concerns of the northern planters, in the form of a letter dated April 17 and addressed to the Chamber of Agriculture. (There is no evidence of a separate response to the "private" April 10 letter, but that may be because the administrators felt it more appropriate to channel their comments through an officially sanctioned institution. In any event, the letter reads as a response to both petitions.) There seemed to be a consensus for the idea that masters must be prevented from committing "barbarities of the sort that are being prosecuted at this moment" by the *sénéchaussée* of Le Cap, Vincent and Marbois noted. However, the administration and the chamber differed as to the nature of the punishment to be imposed, a disagreement that centered on the question of whether that punishment ought to be made public or kept secret. The northern planters were justified in expressing

---

[89] See Chapter 3.
[90] Letter from residents of the northern part to Vincent and Marbois, April 10, 1788, fol. 209.

concern about their personal safety and the security of the colony as a whole, but they were mistaken about the real threat to their self-interest. The danger emanated not from the likes of Buffon and Almeida, but rather from Lejeune himself. "No planter [*habitant*] would feel secure in his home if the negroes were not assured of the protection of the tribunals." Absent any sense of the rule of law, the slaves would give themselves over to "acts of retribution," ignoring that both the Code Noir and the colonial administration tended to their welfare. "They would avail themselves of a way of justice that they believe society refuses them, and we know how many means domestic enemies can use to carry out their acts of secret vengeance."[91]

The reference to methods of "secret vengeance" can hardly have missed its mark, given the pervasive anxiety among planters about the use of poison by slaves, an anxiety present since the late 1750s and of which Lejeune was merely the latest example.[92] Whether or not they intended it as such, the administrators' invocation of the risks of poison was precisely the inverse of Lejeune's in his March 27 *mémoire*. Lejeune had argued that the crime of poisoning had always eluded the eye of the judicial system and thereby demonstrated the necessity of leaving unlimited disciplinary power in the hands of the master. In their April 17 response to the Chamber of Agriculture, the administrators stood this assumption on its head with the argument that unrestrained plantation justice was the very reason slaves felt it necessary to use poisoning in the first place. By relying on the court system to prosecute planters such as Lejeune, the colonists might one day no longer have to run the risk of this undetectable method of retaliation. The "peace of the colony" required that whites be punished no less publicly for their crimes than slaves. If any uncertainty existed about the propriety of this policy, the administrators concluded, the monarchy's plantation-management regulations of December 1785 sufficed to remove all doubts.[93]

[91] Letter from Marbois and Vincent to the Chamber of Agriculture, April 17, 1788, fol. 208.

[92] For more on the relationship between the "epidemic of poisoning" and the rule of law in Saint-Domingue, see Debbasch, "Au coeur du 'gouvernement des esclaves'," 38.

[93] Letter from Vincent and Marbois to the Chamber of Agriculture, April 17, 1788, fol. 208. The final line of the manuscript is partly illegible here, but it can be established that Vincent and Marbois were referring to one of the articles in Title 11 of the December 23, 1785, royal ordinance. On the threat that planter brutality posed to colonial stability, see also the March 18, 1788, letter from de la Mardelle to Couët de Montarand, in Regnault de Beaucaron, *Souvenirs de famille*, 99–100.

PATERNAL INTERVENTION

More than a month passed before the next major development in the case. On May 21, 1788, with his son still at large and in contempt of the law, Lejeune père intervened in the proceedings with a petition to the *sénéchaussée* of Cap Français, which urged the court to dismiss all charges against Nicolas Lejeune and instead prosecute Montarand, the magistrate who had been dispatched to Plaisance back in early March to investigate the allegations of Nicolas's fourteen slaves.[94] Montarand's depositions of Zabeth, Marie-Rose, and other slaves had led to the issuance of a warrant for Nicolas's arrest, and Lejeune père believed the taking of those depositions to have been itself a criminal act.[95]

The petition of Lejeune père is a rambling diatribe, embittered and paranoid even by the standards of eighteenth-century Saint-Domingue. Nonetheless, two overarching themes are apparent throughout. The first was the need to safeguard the planter's familial and racial honor.[96] "Here is a father defending the honor of his own blood," Lejeune père wrote.[97] Charging that Nicolas's slaves had gathered together beforehand to orchestrate their story, Lejeune père insisted that no colonist could consider his "honor" to be secure if he was at the mercy of his slaves' testimony.[98] Lejeune père's petition to intervene, then, just like Nicolas's claim that his cause "was the cause of every colonist," was put forth as an act of public service no less than of self-interest. It was the principle of honor that united these two causes.[99]

Second, Lejeune père argued that the prosecution of a master for torture necessarily entailed the risk of a slave revolution, and that the only

---

[94] Minutes of the Clerk of the *Sénéchaussée* of Cap Français, May 21, 1788, ANOM, F/3/90, fol. 250. The technical term for such a petition was a *requête d'intervention*, so named because it constituted a request on the part of a third party to be received judicially on behalf of an absent plaintiff or defendant. At the end of his petition Lejeune père cited a criminal law treatise by the jurist Daniel Jousse for the proposition that a parent or other close relative of a defendant held in contempt of the law had a right to be received judicially on the defendant's behalf. The treatise is probably Daniel Jousse, *Traité de la justice criminelle de France: où l'on examine tout ce qui concerne les crimes & les peines en général & en particulier* (Paris: Debure Père, 1771).

[95] Lejeune père's first name is not given in any of the sources, primary or secondary, bearing on this case.

[96] This theme will be particularly familiar to students of the American antebellum law of slavery. See Tushnet, *Slave Law in the American South*, 50–52.

[97] Minutes of the Clerk of the *Sénéchaussée*, May 21, 1788, fol. 234.

[98] Ibid., fol. 244.

[99] On the racialization of honor in Saint-Domingue, see Ogle, "Policing Saint Domingue."

way to avert this prospect was to endorse a rule of private plantation law unconstrained by outside authority. Lejeune père thus essentially reprised his son's thesis that masters should be given discretion to use torture against their slaves in light of the systematic failure of the legal system to deter the crime of poisoning. In Lejeune père's view, the trial of Nicolas was the result of a uniquely sinister plot formed "in the very shadow of the laws." If the court were to allow even one of these cases to succeed, it would open the door to a thousand other similar conspiracies. An outbreak of "individual revolts" would pave the way for a "general revolt on the part of our slaves [and then for] the disastrous revolution that [those little revolts] will have brought about."[100] Here again was the image of the slippery slope that Nicolas and the colonial administrators had used to opposite effect in their earlier interventions. According to this logic, the only way to prevent the colony from slipping down the slope of revolution was effectively to disregard any sharp distinctions between "public" and "domestic" justice.

The heart of the petition was an extended disquisition elaborating on the relationship between the use of poison by slaves and the necessity of "private justice." The impunity with which slaves were able to administer poison underlined a fundamental reality of the colonial legal system: "There are truths no laws can suppress," truths different from "those that are recognized as such by the courts." Somewhat ironically, this argument could also have been applied to the phenomenon of planter brutality: If poison remained beyond the purview of the court system, so too did planter violations of the Code Noir provision prohibiting the use of torture. In fact, these two "truths" were intimately linked to each other, as the administrators' April 17 letter to the Chamber of Agriculture had argued. In Lejeune père's view, however, the conclusion to be drawn from these "truths" was simple:

One must indeed permit private persons to render justice themselves, at least when the crimes are such as to become easily contagious, and when [those crimes] can lead to the ruin, overthrow, and destruction of an entire class of the society at the heart of which they are committed. For such is [the crime of] poison on the part of the slaves.[101]

Invoking a well-worn creole theme of "local knowledge," Lejeune père argued that in Europe it was simply not essential to discover and punish

---

[100] Minutes of the Clerk of the *Sénéchaussée*, May 21, 1788, fol. 213.
[101] Ibid., fol. 217 (emphasis in the original).

the "hidden and tenebrous" crime of poisoning. In the metropole, poisoning was not "the ordinary crime of one class against another class of men." In Saint-Domingue, on the other hand, whoever was not a master was a slave, according to Lejeune père, and there were many more of the latter than of the former. Moreover, the two "classes" were necessarily enemies of each other. In such a state of war, the slave class could be contained only by means of "despotism," which is to say by means of "a power that [was], so to speak, absolute."[102] Like his son's, the father's portrait of the power dynamics at work in this slave society reflected an unmistakable (but incomplete) borrowing from Montesquieu.

The primary restraint on the legitimate absolutism of the master class, in Lejeune père's view, was the 1685 Code Noir, in particular articles 26 and 42 (banning the practice of torture and mutilation and authorizing prosecution of masters who engaged in those practices).[103] In order to demonstrate the nefariousness of these provisions, however, he was forced to argue that planters had frequent resort to torture and mutilation as disciplinary tools, but that they should not be punished for so doing. This concession Lejeune père was more than willing to make. The problem was not that such violations of the Code Noir were deeply rooted in plantation culture, he argued, but rather that they could only be suppressed by means of the "the greatest inconveniences." The Code Noir – "the law that prohibits masters from <u>torturing</u> their slaves"[104] – had been promulgated at a time when the colonists were still "ferocious," having barely begun to leave behind their origins as "barbaric" pirates and buccaneers. Moreover, there had been many fewer slaves in 1685 than there were now; the prohibition on torture might have made sense as a way of preventing the strongest from oppressing the weakest in an earlier time, but now the scale had tipped in the opposite direction.[105] It was the masters who needed protection from their slaves.

More than simply unwarranted, the antitorture provisions of the Code Noir were also unnecessary given the master's self-interest in the welfare of his slaves, argued Lejeune père. Since the time of the Code Noir's promulgation, "the enlightenment [*les lumières*] that has penetrated even as far as this colony has civilized minds and demonstrated above all the

---

[102] Ibid.

[103] Lejeune père does not identify the two provisions by article number, but it is clear from his discussion that he is referencing articles 26 and 42.

[104] Minutes of the Clerk of the *Sénéchaussée*, May 21, 1788, fol. 219 (emphasis in the original).

[105] Ibid.

accord of humanity with the interest of property." Once strangers to an insignificant slave population, whites had become "so familiar to the slaves" as to no longer require any constraints on their actions other than a concern for the value of one's property and the dictates of humanity. It stood to reason, then, that articles 26 and 42 were rarely, if ever, enforced in the colony, despite a history of brazenly repeated acts of torture and mutilation. Paradoxically and incoherently, Lejeune père also argued that the antitorture laws signaled to slaves who poisoned their masters that the king's men would protect them from the physical retaliation of their overlords. Nonetheless, Lejeune père insisted that the Code Noir, an "antique law" that "seems to have been made for another colony," had simply "fallen into desuetude."[106] By implication, what made his son's prosecution so objectionable and arbitrary was precisely the defunct nature of the Code's prohibition on torture.

All of these points contributed to a portrait of slave society as a place of incipient anarchy, ready to be overturned at the tip of a magistrate's hat. For any law that impinged on "a system of domestic justice enclosed within rightful limits" brought with it the prospect of slave insubordination.[107] The slaves who gave testimony against Nicolas, argued Lejeune père, were guilty of manipulating the December 1785 royal ordinance – a law that had caused "a lot of noise among the slaves." Although it had served to mollify planter opposition to the reforms passed the previous year, even the modified ordinance was a means by which slaves could "vex" their masters at will. The prosecution of Nicolas proved that his slaves were aware they could use royal legislation and the colonial legal system to stir up trouble on the plantation. The quashed prosecution of the planter Cassarouy in 1770, a year "remarkable" for the "revolution" it witnessed in the "character of our slaves," was said to confirm the same point. By deciding, on appeal, to nullify the proceedings against the defendant in that case, the high court in Le Cap had left no room for a similar "uprising" of slaves against their masters until the post-1785 period.[108] Two prosecutions in almost twenty years sufficed, in this view, to establish that slaves could threaten the racial hierarchy of Saint-Domingue merely by availing themselves of the colony's legal system.

Lejeune père conceded that his son had used "a bit of violence," but only to get to the bottom of a secret that threatened the safety of his plantation.

---

[106] Ibid., fols. 219–220.
[107] Ibid., fol. 220.
[108] Ibid., fols. 222–225. On the Cassarouy case, see Chapter 3.

Nicolas's crime was therefore attenuated by necessity. By contrast, the plantation on which Zabeth and Marie-Rose labored had always been one of the most "villainous" in the entire colony. The Lejeune slaves had simply failed to "learn" the lesson taught them earlier in the decade, after they had been punished on suspicion of repeatedly using poison against fellow slaves, their master, and his animals.[109] It was also significant for Lejeune père that Julie, the slave whom Nicolas had accused Zabeth and Marie-Rose of poisoning, was "one of the most beautiful negresses of the plantation." Moreover, notwithstanding the testimony of Pierre Darius, the plantation cook, that Nicolas had used torture on them, Marie-Rose and Zabeth could not have had the "freedom of mind" to make up a "lie" while a flaming pinewood torch was being pressed to their skin.[110]

It remained only for Lejeune père to condemn a character even more "villainous" than the slaves themselves: the investigating magistrate who had taken the initial depositions. Lejeune père accused Montarand of a range of evidentiary and procedural violations in his handling of the case, from failing to ask a single question of either Zabeth or Marie-Rose, to dispensing with the need to seal the container in which the alleged poison was stored. Most seriously of all, upon discovering Marie-Rose and Zabeth on the Lejeune plantation, Montarand had failed to release them from the stone cell to which they were confined, thereby depriving them of urgently needed medical care. Montarand's delayed decision to transport the two women to a different plantation in conditions of rain and cold, Lejeune père charged, was responsible for their eventual demise (Marie-Rose on March 12, Zabeth on March 14): "One can truthfully state that Couët [de Montarand] himself is the murderer of these two negresses."[111] Lejeune père concluded by demanding that Montarand be tried for the murder of Marie-Rose and Zabeth, the charges against Nicolas be dismissed, and the testimony of the fourteen slaves be rejected and condemned as seditious, calumnious, and a threat to the security of the colony.[112]

Although clearly rooted in a kind of desperation, these demands at least had the virtue of being consistent with the rest of the elder Lejeune's

---

[109] Ibid., fols. 213–215.

[110] Ibid., fols. 222–223, 226.

[111] Ibid., fols. 227–234. Before accusing Montarand of the murder of Zabeth and Marie-Rose, Lejeune père sought to minimize the extent of their burns. Zabeth and Marie-Rose, he wrote, had attributed these burns to Nicolas and Magre "because their master was accusing them of being Macandals." Ibid., fol. 230.

[112] Ibid., fol. 250.

reasoning, and they must not have sounded as preposterous to contemporary ears as they seem to ours. Montarand himself certainly took the accusations in all seriousness. Three days later (May 24), he replied with a formal declaration maintaining that Lejeune père's petition provided no evidence of a "design" to "get rid of" (*perdre*) Nicolas, and further failed to establish any of the grounds required by law for the recusal of an investigating magistrate.[113] Ever the dutiful civil servant, Montarand protested that he had fulfilled "in my soul and conscience" the commission charged to him by the lower court of Cap Français.[114] Nonetheless, the lower court judges, after a long series of delays, returned a decision nullifying Montarand's findings of fact (*procès-verbaux*) and dismissing all charges against Nicolas and Magre.[115] We cannot say for certain that Lejeune père's intervention was the pivotal factor, but the holding conformed to his most important demands.

APPELLATE INTRIGUE

Were it not for the efforts of the royal prosecutor in Cap Français, Almeida, the Lejeune affair might have ended then and there with the lower court's dismissal. Aware that he enjoyed the support of Vincent and Marbois, however, Almeida succeeded in securing an appeal to the Conseil Supérieur in Port-au-Prince (known since January 1787 as the Conseil Supérieur de Saint-Domingue), a move that stirred outrage among the colony's planters.[116]

By right of their respective offices, Vincent and Marbois both held seats on the Conseil Supérieur, which added yet another layer of political controversy to this final stage of the proceedings. For it was clear to all involved, and especially to Lejeune père, that the two administrators had already arrived at an understanding of Nicolas's culpability and of the need for a public punishment. On June 26, with the appellate decision still pending, Lejeune père wrote again to Vincent and Marbois, imploring the two administrators to abstain from participating in the hearing

---

[113] Montarand alludes to the "grounds for recusal [that are] authorized by the ordinance." Ibid., fol. 251. It is unclear whether this refers to the December 1785 plantation-management ordinance or to another law.

[114] Ibid., fol. 251.

[115] Letter from Vincent and Marbois to La Luzerne, Aug. 29, 1788, fol. 265; James, *The Black Jacobins*, 23.

[116] James, *The Black Jacobins*, 23; Moreau de Saint-Méry, *Description topographique*, 1:103.

of the case, and to discontinue their practice of referring to Nicolas in their official correspondence as "guilty" rather than merely "accused."[117] "[N]o consideration will stop me when it is a question of defending a good as precious as" the life and honor of his son and family, Lejeune père exclaimed, not even the fear of "displeasing" the king's highest representatives in the colony.[118]

At some point between this June 26 letter and August 29, when Vincent and Marbois submitted a report to Naval Minister La Luzerne summarizing the entire history of the case, the prosecution of Nicolas Lejeune came to a head.[119] In recognition of the special sensitivity and importance of the case, Marbois had appointed the senior member (*doyen*) of the Conseil Supérieur in Port-au-Prince to serve as the *rapporteur* (judge-advocate) in the appellate trial.[120] On the day of the hearing, however, the *doyen* decided not to show up at the courthouse. C. L. R. James suggests that the *doyen*'s nonappearance was prompted by a concern that he would be unable to find enough votes to convict Nicolas.[121] If so motivated, the strategy proved especially counterproductive: By what appears to have been a single vote, the court proceeded to absolve Nicolas once again of all charges. Thus ended the long and hotly contested trial of a case unlike any the colony had ever witnessed.

It is difficult to know exactly what happened at the appellate stage of the case to produce this result. As best we can tell, the decision was a dramatically close one: A rare opportunity to affirm the antitorture provisions of the Code Noir had indeed slipped away. On a fourteen-judge court, eight votes were necessary to convict Nicolas, and either seven or eight had made known their sympathy for the prosecution's position in advance of the hearing. One of these belonged to Marbois – who presided over the proceedings as intendant – and another to Vincent. Assuming

[117] Letter from Lejeune père to François Barbé de Marbois, intendant, and Alexandre de Vincent de Mazarade, governor, June 26, 1788, ANOM, F/3/90, fol. 255. The precise phrase Lejeune père uses here is "l'accusé coupable." In their March 27, 1788, directive to the commanders and administrative officers of the colony, Vincent and Marbois had described Nicolas as "guilty of this atrocity." Letter from Vincent and Marbois to the *Commandants* and *officiers d'administration*, March 27, 1788, fol. 198. See also Letter from Vincent and Marbois to the *officiers* of the *Sénéchaussée* of Cap Français, March 27, 1788, fol. 207 (describing Nicolas as "not the only guilty one").

[118] Letter from Lejeune père to Vincent and Marbois, June 26, 1788, fol. 256.

[119] The August 29 report is the principal source for our understanding of the Lejeune affair. Most of the documents cited previously were included in an appendix sent to Naval Minister La Luzerne.

[120] Letter from Vincent and Marbois to La Luzerne, Aug. 29, 1788, fol. 264.

[121] James, *The Black Jacobins*, 23.

that six of the remaining judges voted for acquittal, therefore, the administrators' two votes would have sufficed to convict. However, after considering Lejeune père's objections, the Conseil decided to require Marbois to abstain, thereby allowing the decision to go in Nicolas's favor.[122]

As Vincent and Marbois later argued to the naval minister, this result could only be explained as the result of a concerted effort at public intimidation of the judiciary that pervaded the entire litigation. Appending and referencing the various letters and petitions from the planters of Plaisance and the northern department in their report to La Luzerne, the administrators sought in part to demonstrate just how many colonists had a perceived investment in seeing Nicolas Lejeune avoid a conviction.[123] This orchestrated opposition accounted, first of all, for the failure of the local authorities to arrange for his capture following the taking of the slaves' deposition. The administrators professed "profound sorrow" at having to then stand by and watch their own subordinates frustrate "the efforts of justice and of the administration." The hostile "agitation" in Cap Français on the eve of the trial, which culminated in the *sénéchaussée*'s decision to nullify Montarand's findings of fact, made it further "obvious that the public had intimidated the judges."[124] In short, as a result of a failure of judicial backbone, the only punishment this "murderer of four slaves" received consisted of an order to "produce" the rest of his surviving slaves upon request and "other provisions no less frivolous in a matter involving human life."[125] The end result, although a clear corruption of legal justice from one point of view, was perfectly consistent with the Code Noir, which authorized the king's colonial officers, where appropriate, to "absolve" masters found guilty of murdering their slaves without the need for a royal pardon.[126]

In their final summation to the naval minister, the administrators endeavored to impress upon the metropole the depths of the administrative dilemma in which the colony now found itself. The gaping holes

---

[122] Letter from Vincent and Marbois to La Luzerne, Aug. 29, 1788, fols. 264–265. The report was somewhat ambiguous on the headcount issue, indicating that seven to eight judges were "favorable" but without specifying the position to which they were sympathetic. I have imputed that Vincent and Marbois meant "favorable to the prosecution's case" based on a subsequent passage referring to the likelihood that the intendant would have been the eighth and decisive vote in favor of Nicolas's conviction.

[123] Ibid., fol. 264. The administrators' voluminous attachments and point-by-point refutation of Lejeune père's protestations suggest that a further appeal to the Conseil d'État in Versailles, or perhaps even a post-appellate ministerial fix, might still have been within reach.

[124] Ibid., fol. 265.

[125] Ibid., fol. 266.

[126] Code Noir, art. 43 (1685).

in colonial law enforcement, in effect, created a void that could only be filled by the ancient state of war between masters and slaves. Treating whites dramatically differently from blacks when it came to the punishment of crime was not a reliable formula for achieving stability in Saint-Domingue, the administrators argued. In fact, it tended to produce just the opposite effect: "[I]t does not seem that the judicial system has at any time reprimanded the inhumanity of the masters, and this erroneous policy that leads to punishing blacks severely [while] pardoning whites for everything they do has not produced the anticipated effect."[127] The slaves simply continued with their "insubordination" and the masters "with their cruelties." It was for this reason that Lejeune père, no longer feeling himself safe on his own plantation, had decided to abandon it to his son in the first place; and Nicolas's pathological mismanagement ended up reproducing the same cycle of violence and retribution that the authors of the Code Noir had sought to foreclose back in 1685.[128]

None of Lejeune père's conspiratorial ramblings and denunciations could alter this reality, said the administrators, and the evidentiary basis for the case was unimpeachable in any event. The deposition of the fourteen slaves was entirely consistent with their initial declaration before the *sénéchal* in the Cap Français prison; and it was no accident that the seven witnesses who testified in Nicolas's favor were all white.[129] The evidence provided by Nicolas's cook, Darius, also confirmed the allegations of the fourteen slaves, who could not have coordinated their story with his while imprisoned far away from the location of the Lejeune plantation in Plaisance. Moreover, the elder Lejeune had neglected to mention that Julie – the slave alleged to have been poisoned – had fallen ill two months before her death due to complications arising from childbirth.[130]

For his offense in manifesting "zeal for humanity," meanwhile, the hapless Montarand had been punished with a humiliating injunction.[131] The investigating magistrate had earned this dishonor not because of mishandled evidence or irregular interrogations, wrote Vincent and Marbois, but rather because of his "humanity and zeal."[132] The campaign to discredit and vilify Montarand, the "first officer of justice who

[127] Letter from Vincent and Marbois to La Luzerne, Aug. 29, 1788, fol. 258.
[128] Ibid.
[129] Ibid., fols. 261–262.
[130] Ibid., fols. 262–263.
[131] Ibid., fol. 266.
[132] Ibid., fols. 261–262.

dared to raise his voice in favor of the negroes" in order to protest "one of the greatest outrages done to humanity," was yet another example of the role of public intimidation in the proceedings. The "vehemence" and "vigor of the attack" directed against him were clearly intended "to discourage … all those who might be tempted in the future to lend their hand to this unfortunate class."[133]

The failure to lend such a hand spoke to the inherent limits of judicial institutions in slave societies (although perhaps not only in such societies). "How many secret evils the eye of the courts is incapable of penetrating!" Vincent and Marbois exclaimed. Each new case that "publicly demonstrate[d]" the "impotence" of the colonial administration and legal system made it increasingly harder to set any effective limits on the autonomy of the planters and on their potential for causing unintended social upheavals. The Lejeune scandal involved not just any form of administrative "impotence," however, but a particularly insidious kind that resulted from the "courts join[ing] forces with barbarous colonists in the oppression of [their] unfortunate [slaves]." For a century, such oppression had been allowed to go unpunished. Finally, after so many atrocities that the judiciary was unable to reach, an ideal case for conviction had presented itself. Yet "the judicial system chooses to let slip this unique opportunity to arrest, by means of a single example, the course of so many cruelties."[134]

We do not know how the naval minister may have reacted to this report, but its casting of moral issues in a prudential framework both reflected and appealed to the complex motives of an imperial administration deeply concerned with the reform of slavery. Vincent and Marbois did not shy away from speaking directly to the "considerations of humanity" that figured in the case, and to what they regarded as La Luzerne's own concerns in this regard. "You are privy to all the misfortune of [the slaves'] condition, whatever pains are taken to hide a part of it from the administrators," they respectfully (if self-servingly) noted. "And we know how much you would like to be able to ease the wretchedness of this class of men."[135] At the same time, the pragmatic consequences of the Lejeune case were unavoidable. From this perspective, judicial integrity and courage were intimately linked to the colony's security. If they were to sustain the rule of law within the political constraints of a plantation

---

[133] Ibid., fols. 264–265.
[134] Ibid., fol. 266.
[135] Ibid.

society, judges required incentives and assurances. The outcome of the Lejeune affair, however, made it highly improbable that other magistrates would follow Montarand's precedent and risk public defamation to carry out investigations of planters and their agents. Terrorized slaves would be left with "no other resource than vengeance and no other feeling than desperation." And whereas the prospect of "general revolts strike[s] us as little to be feared," the report continued, individual revolts must be averted "in order to prevent [the need for] punishments."[136]

This fusion of moral and precautionary considerations itself had a very practical and immediate purpose: to persuade the naval minister "not to let the transgressions of Lejeune go entirely unpunished."[137] Vincent and Marbois requested that the king declare Nicolas incapable of owning slaves in the future and order him deported to France if the fugitive planter ever dared to reappear on his father's plantation. By giving "publicity" to such orders, the damage caused by Nicolas's acquittal might still be undone.[138]

If Vincent and Marbois believed that all hope for the colony was not yet lost, it was in part because their critique of the Lejeune dynasty served also to defend the nonrefractory planter population. The majority of colonists adhered to a "moderate regime" on their plantations, claimed the administrators, and by 1788 the "rigors of slavery" had become less pronounced than they were twenty years ago. Yet there remained "entire areas [of the colony] where the old barbarism still exists in all of its force."[139]

DEATH AND SURVIVAL

How best to make sense of this ambiguous opposition between "barbarism" and "moderation" is a complicated matter. That it had a distinctly apologetic, preservationist thrust seems indisputable.[140] We can acknowledge this thrust and nonetheless recognize that the administrators' report also

---

[136] Ibid., fol. 267.

[137] Ibid.

[138] Ibid.

[139] Ibid., fols. 267–268.

[140] This apologetic thrust is well captured in the November 1790 observation of Nicolas Robert, marquis de Cocherel, a white deputy from Saint-Domingue to the National Assembly. Seeking to justify a constitution for Saint-Domingue based on local customs, Cocherel argued that the planters could be counted on to take benevolent care of the slaves for reasons of "humanity, interest, and the law." Quoted in Florence Gauthier, *L'aristocratie de l'épiderme: Le combat de la Société des Citoyens de Couleur 1789–1791* (Paris: CNRS Éditions, 2007), 51.

encompassed a robustly critical dimension, perhaps even an element of emancipatory potential. The better part of wisdom may simply be to hold both characteristics in tension, while not losing sight of the human stories that underlay the ideological dimensions of slavery.

Zabeth and Marie-Rose did not live to see the undoing of barbarism in Saint-Domingue, but the investigating magistrate who so passionately took up their cause survived. His professional reputation apparently more or less intact, Montarand was eventually named to a judgeship on the Conseil Supérieur of Cap Français (which was reconstituted in early 1790 after a four-year period of desuetude). These good fortunes did not last long, however. During the Terror of 1793–1794, Montarand was denounced as a counterrevolutionary and targeted for the guillotine. He remained at his post as *conseiller* of the high court in Cap Français until that city was burned to the ground in June 1793.[141] Montarand then managed to escape on an American naval ship bound for New York, where he married a fellow refugee by the name of Jeanne-Louise Marguerite Joséphine Désirée Jauvin. After Napoleon restored de facto slavery in Saint-Domingue in 1802, Montarand returned to the colony, only to have to leave again in 1803, when war broke out between Napoleon's army and the black forces led by Jean-Jacques Dessalines. Montarand fled first for Cuba, on a ship that he shared with none other than one "M. Lejeune."[142] If the same Lejeune who had tormented Zabeth and Marie-Rose some fifteen years before, the coincidence suggests that Vincent and Marbois were not successful in their entreaty to La Luzerne to salvage something from the wreckage of Montarand's quest.

After a period in Cuba, Montarand departed for Santo Domingo, on the Spanish side of Hispaniola (then controlled by France). In 1809, he was captured by combined British-Spanish forces allied against France, and taken to Jamaica. His colonial fortune lost, in 1811 Montarand managed to make his way back to his ancestral home in Orléans, France, the capital of the Loire valley and the point at which sugar from Saint-Domingue was transported overland to Paris and elsewhere.[143] A royalist,

---

[141] Regnault de Beaucaron, *Souvenirs de famille*, 107. For the events of June 1793, see chapter 5.

[142] See Charles Edmond Regnault de Beaucaron, *Souvenirs anecdotiques et historiques d'anciennes familles champenoises et bourguignonnes* (Paris: Plon-Nourrit et cie, 1906), 254, 323–324; idem, *Souvenirs de famille*, 106–144; *Généalogie et Histoire de la Caraïbe* 30 (Sept. 1991): 399 http://www.ghcaraibe.org/bul/ghc030/p0399.html (last viewed May 7, 2010). Thanks to Rebecca Scott for putting me on this trail and for the information regarding Lejeune's possible presence on Montarand's ship to Cuba.

[143] On the role of Orléans in the colonial sugar trade, see Dubois, "An Atlantic Revolution," 660.

he was named a chevalier of the Legion of Honor by King Louis XVIII in 1814 and refused to take the oath to Napoleon during the Hundred Days. Montarand went on to serve as a judge on the Court of Appeals of Paris and then as attorney general (*procureur général*) in Orléans. On February 22, 1816, on the occasion of his installation as attorney general, Montarand delivered an address that, in the words of one contemporaneous observer, "deserves to be placed alongside those of the celebrated men who honor the French magistracy." In that speech, Montarand intoned that "the death of the warrior who perishes on the field of honor is no more glorious than that of the magistrate who dies in the defense of the laws." Montarand died in Orléans on October 16, 1824.[144]

Montarand's dedication to the rule of law notwithstanding, the Lejeune affair seems to support what many scholars have long argued, namely, that the Atlantic slave societies were committed to "a space of sovereignty beyond law."[145] That space was, of course, the plantation, ruled over by a most unruly sovereign who was not quite "public" in the modern sense, but not nearly a "private" subject either, at least insofar as he was capable of inflicting a form of violence over slaves that was recognized at the time as torture.[146]

That planters were deemed capable of torture per se suggests that we must look beyond the narrow province of the courts and of judicial torture if we are to understand how torture worked in the wider Atlantic world, and particularly in the domains of plantation slavery. The story of colonial slave law suggests the limits of a functional, evidentiary, or instrumental approach to torture: the emphasis on torture as a strictly investigative and "official" technique for the securing of confessions or cooperation, an understanding that pervades the legal scholarship on this subject. That approach tends to downplay the performative and ritualistic aspects of torture, whether as a means of inflicting humiliation upon the body of the suspect or enacting the sovereignty of the

---

[144] Regnault de Beaucaron, *Souvenirs anecdotiques et historiques*, 323–324; idem, *Souvenirs de famille*, 145–162; *Généalogie et Histoire de la Caraïbe* 30 (Sept. 1991): 399 http://www.ghcaraibe.org/bul/ghc030/p0399.html (last viewed May 7, 2010).

[145] Paul Kahn, *Sacred Violence: Torture, Terror, and Sovereignty* (Ann Arbor: University of Michigan Press, 2008), 2.

[146] I do not mean to suggest that torture is the only context in which colonial planters can be understood as "sovereigns." In the American South and elsewhere, as Genovese demonstrated, slave law "came to accept an implicit duality: a recognition of the rights of the state over individuals, slave or free, and a recognition of the rights of the slaveholders over their slaves." Genovese, *Roll, Jordan, Roll*, 45–46.

torturer.[147] Above all, however, the theatre of Atlantic colonial slavery reveals torture's character as a process rather than a status or institution – a process that, once set in motion, seems to partake inevitably of punitive dynamics and to generate meanings transcending the definitional assertion that torture involves the state's investigation of crime.[148]

At the same time, the notion of "sovereignty beyond law," which informs a good deal of the literature on the Code Noir, tells only part of the story.[149] It is only the beginning, not the end, of what we can learn from the Lejeune prosecution and the law of slavery more generally. The salience of that space of extralegal sovereignty is not fully realized unless the domestic sovereignty of the plantation is situated in relation to – and thus in tension with – the sovereignty of the imperial administration. Although colonial slavery was genuinely committed to "a political practice of violence beyond the reach of the law,"[150] the consequences of that commitment were neither foreordained nor always intended.

Put differently, the law of slavery, understood as a set of strategic techniques for mediating the anxious world of masters and their captive "domestic enemies," was far more generative than the "extralegal sovereignty" thesis (and the scholarship that shares its orientation) suggests. For the consequences of colonial torture and violence were shaped by the very limits of slave law themselves. The Lejeune case reveals a nearly

---

[147] See Joshua Cole, "Intimate Acts and Unspeakable Relations: Remembering Torture and the War for Algerian Independence," in *Memory, Empire, and Postcolonialism: Legacies of French Colonialism*, ed. Alec G. Hargreaves (Lanham, MD: Lexington Books, 2005), 125–137; and Foucault, *Discipline and Punish*, 32–69.

[148] These issues of meaning and definition remain alive (and contested) today. The United Nations Convention Against Torture (UNCAT), which came into force on June 26, 1987, defines "torture" broadly so as to include the infliction of "punishment" by way of severe pain or suffering. "Convention Against Torture and Other Cruel, Inhuman or Degrading Treatment or Punishment," June 26, 1987, art. 1, *United Nations Treaty Series* 1465: 85 http://www.hrweb.org/legal/cat.html (last viewed May 11, 2010). The UNCAT also subjects states to liability for acts of "cruel, inhuman, or other degrading treatment or punishment" when committed by private persons with the acquiescence of government officials. Ibid., art. 16. See also *Hudson v. McMillian*, 503 U.S. 1, 18 (1992) (Thomas, J. dissenting) (arguing that the Eighth Amendment was traditionally thought to ban only "torturous punishments meted out by statutes or sentencing judges").

[149] See, *inter alia*, the sources cited at p. 12, n.30. For a useful review of the scholarship on the limits of law as well as a cogent critique of the notion that law's limits are merely empirical or normative in nature, see Austin Sarat, Lawrence Douglas, and Martha Merrill Umphrey, "At the Limits of Law: An Introduction," in *The Limits of Law*, ed. Austin Sarat, Lawrence Douglas, and Martha Merrill Umphrey (Stanford, CA: Stanford University Press, 2005), 1–11.

[150] Kahn, *Sacred Violence*, 4.

paradoxical portrait of the Code Noir – the basic law of slavery in the French colonies, often violated and rarely enforced – as an important source of human rights law and ideology.[151] It was, after all, the anti-torture provisions of articles 26 and 42 of the Code Noir, as refracted through the 1784–1785 royal ordinances, that initially authorized the prosecution of Lejeune. (The article 43 requirement that masters who kill their slaves be prosecuted also applied once the torture of Zabeth and Marie-Rose was found to have resulted in their deaths.) In this context, the law of slavery was interpreted to signify the role of the king, not as oppressor-in-chief, but as protector of all persons residing within the royal dominion, including slaves.

This is not to say that the slave enjoyed the status of royal subject in any technical or even vernacular sense under Old Regime law.[152] Yet it does suggest that the Code Noir may have been not only "stretched and frayed, but also reconstituted and reinvigorated by contact with its own limiting condition."[153] And it goes some way toward explaining why the protective mandate of the Code Noir turns out to have been such a pronounced feature of the political culture of the slave insurgency that dominated the course of events in Haiti as of late 1791. As we will see in the final chapter of this book, however, the generic category of "royalism" does not adequately capture the distinctive concepts and attitudes that informed the approaches of the principal insurgent leaders and their followers. The Lejeune affair helps to unpack some of the constituent elements of this culture, in which the complex legal relationship between slavery and torture (and other forms of the physical abuse of slaves) seems to have played a prominent role.

---

[151] Cf. Sala-Molins, *Le Code Noir*, viii. Whatever else may be said of Sala-Molins's interpretation, the Code Noir did not legitimate the torture of slaves by their masters.

[152] The Code Noir seems (albeit by implication) to distinguish fairly clearly between subjects and slaves in article 5 (forbidding Protestants from interfering with the exercise of Catholicism in the colonies), and articles 57 and 59 (on manumission) refer to the status of freed persons as equal to that of "natural subjects" of the French king, which confirms the slave/subject distinction. Code Noir, arts. 5, 57, and 59 (1685). Peter Sahlins finds a category of absolutist legal citizenship at work under the Old Regime that was distinct from royal "subjecthood" as well as from the national citizenship model eventually inaugurated by the French Revolution. On Sahlins's reading of the early modern jurists, although a slave could not be a subject, the defining characteristic of the citizen was that he was not a foreigner. Peter Sahlins, *Unnaturally French: Foreign Citizens in the Old Regime and After* (Ithaca, NY: Cornell University Press, 2004), x–xi, 4, 19–23.

[153] Sarat, Douglas, and Umphrey, "At the Limits of Law," 2.

5

Less Just than a Despot?

Will the National Assembly be less just than a despot?
– Julien Raimond, *Observations sur l'origine et le progrès du préjugé des colons blancs contres les hommes de couleur* (1791)[1]

The recurring controversies over a rule of "private" justice in eighteenth-century Saint-Domingue were hardly abstractions or figments of the imagination. The claim of the slave proprietor to be a kind of sovereign ruler was made (and often taken) in all seriousness. Slavery as a form of property ownership both mimics and challenges Jean Bodin's canonical theory of sovereignty, with its insistence that "the main point of sovereign majesty and absolute power consists of giving the law to subjects in general without their consent."[2] The colonial-era debates over manumission and planter brutality, which culminated in a sense with the Lejeune affair in 1788, gave shape and content to the idea of sovereignty in Saint-Domingue. These debates were ripe with consequences for the lives of individual slaves, freed persons, and masters, and they provide the backdrop against which the Haitian Revolution unfolded.

The law of slavery did not end with the beginning of the Haitian Revolution, but rather lived on for many years afterward, infiltrating

---

[1] Julien Raimond, *Observations sur l'origine et le progrès du préjugé des colons blancs contre les hommes de couleur* (Paris: Belin, 1791), 28 (also quoted in Dubois, *Avengers of the New World*, 60).
[2] Bodin, *On Sovereignty*, 33.

the ideology and rhetoric of the Revolution's proponents and enemies alike. The story of this infiltration is relatively foreign to our notions of law and of the Haitian Revolution itself. Consider, for example, this statement by the constitutional theorist Paul Kahn: "The politics of revolution ... remain outside of law." In Kahn's view, revolution has much in common with such practices as torture and slavery: All three are, in a sense, "political practice[s] of violence beyond the reach of the law."[3] They are the epitome of anti-law: efforts to govern human affairs through what is now sometimes referred to as the "state of exception," wherein law lies dormant while political violence works out the terms of a New Regime.[4]

Given this conjunction of phenomena, it is understandable that the Haitian Revolution itself has often been regarded as having very little, if anything, to do with law. Indeed, the stereotype of revolutionary politics as a process of "extralegal" violence, although not unique to the Haitian case, seems particularly steadfast and ingrained where Haiti's Revolution is concerned. In David Geggus's words, "[t]he emblematic event of the [Haitian] revolution was a slave uprising, not a declaration of independence or a constitution."[5] Yet it is not obvious that the Boston Tea Party and the storming of the Bastille (or the Terror) are less emblematic of the American and French Revolutions. More to the point, revolutionary emblems are not givens of history; their creation is not an objective or neutral process detached from the comparative politics of the eighteenth-century Atlantic world and its legacies. The strength of the extralegal interpretation, as compared to our understanding of the other late-eighteenth-century Atlantic revolutions (particularly the French Revolution), undoubtedly owes much to the pervasively racial context

[3] Kahn, *Sacred Violence*, 4, 127.
[4] The key contemporary thinker along these lines is Giorgio Agamben, building on the controversial work of Carl Schmitt. See Giorgio Agamben, *State of Exception*, trans. Kevin Attell (Chicago, IL: University of Chicago Press, 2005).
[5] David Geggus, "Print Culture and the Haitian Revolution: The Written and the Spoken Word," in *Liberty! Égalité! Independencia: Print Culture, Enlightenment, and Revolution in the Americas, 1776–1838* (Worcester, MA: American Antiquarian Society, 2007), 79. Geggus goes on to qualify his contrast between the Haitian and the other Atlantic revolutions. Yet he does so only to the extent of saying that the "internal" conflicts among white colonists over political autonomy and commercial freedom in the early years of the Saint-Domingue Revolution, from 1789–1793, also reflected the influence of the print culture of Enlightenment Europe. Ibid., 80. This qualification does not go nearly far enough, for reasons explained later.

of the Haitian Revolution.⁶ To many observers at the time – and to many since – the overthrow of color privilege and colonial slavery could not have proceeded without resort to extralegal violence. Depending on the point of view of the observer and the specific acts at issue, this use of violence was either gratuitous and vengeful or necessary and justified, or perhaps both.⁷

If the politics of understanding the role of violence in the Haitian Revolution remain complex, the role of violence per se in the Revolution is undeniable. Much of the Revolution unfolded in the form of armed conflict of a formal or informal nature. The contest between France, Britain, and Spain for control over the territory of Hispaniola during the 1790s was, in many ways, a resumption of battles left unfinished at the conclusion of the Seven Years' War, when the Caribbean territories of European monarchs seemed to change hands like so many cards in a deck. And the last two to three years of the Revolution, which saw Napoleon's massive expedition and culminated in the proclamation of Haitian independence at the beginning of 1804, are now typically treated as belonging quintessentially to the field of military history.⁸

We can acknowledge these realities without going so far as to conclude, in the manner of Simon Schama's rendering of the French Revolution, that "violence *was* the revolution itself."⁹ Left out of this image of the Revolution as a phenomenon that unfolded "outside of law" is precisely the rootedness of revolutionary change in the patterns of colonial legal culture and the forms of law. Two canonical examples drawn from

---

⁶ Cf. Bruce H. Mann, "Revolutionary Justice: Law and Society in the American Revolution" (inaugural lecture as holder of the Carl F. Schipper, Jr. Professorship of Law, Harvard Law School, May 13, 2009) http://www.law.harvard.edu/news/spotlight/faculty-research/lectures.html (last viewed May 10, 2010), arguing that "[e]ven in the middle of war and occupation, Americans tried to give legal legitimacy to their actions"; and Miranda Spieler, "The Legal Structure of Colonial Rule during the French Revolution," *William and Mary Quarterly* 66, no. 2 (Apr. 2009): 365–408.

⁷ On the politics of representing the violence of the Haitian Revolution, see Laurent Dubois, "Avenging America"; and Ghachem, "The Colonial Terror."

⁸ See, for example, the remarks of the Haitian historian Vertus Saint-Louis, in Pierre Richard Cajuste, "Un livre d'histoire, un livre actuel: Une interview avec le professeur Vertus Saint-Louis," *Haïti en Marche*, May 3, 2006. The military history of the final years of the Haitian Revolution is covered in Claude B. Auguste and Marcel B. Auguste, *L'Expédition Leclerc, 1801–1803* (Port-au-Prince: Henri Deschamps, 1985).

⁹ Simon Schama, *Citizens: A Chronicle of the French Revolution* (New York: Knopf, 1989), xv. The novelist (and historian) Madison Smartt Bell has been influential in putting forward a similar view of the Haitian Revolution, particularly in the first volume of his fictional trilogy: *All Souls' Rising* (New York: Pantheon, 1995).

the early Revolution will suffice to suggest the contours of this point. The National Assembly's April 4, 1792, decision to grant full political rights to free people of color in Saint-Domingue fulfilled the Code Noir's promise of equal "rights, privileges, and immunities" for freed persons – albeit applied on a far wider scale than Louis XIV could ever have anticipated.[10] The emancipation of all slaves in the French colonies, by decree of the National Convention dated February 4, 1794, followed a series of provisional emancipations proclaimed in Saint-Domingue in the previous months by the French civil commissioners (and jurists) Léger-Félicité Sonthonax and Étienne de Polverel. By granting citizenship and not just liberty to the freed slaves, this first abolition of slavery in Saint-Domingue (Napoleon's reactionary colonial policies would eventually necessitate a second) also hearkened back to the egalitarian promise contained in the colony's original slave charter. For their role in ushering in these changes, Sonthonax and Polverel were accused of treason and tried before a special commission of the National Convention – a legal process that unfolded over the course of many months and gave rise to some of the most important sources for the study of the Haitian Revolution.[11]

The forms and rituals of law gave shape and content to the Revolution. Yet it was not just the actions (and reactions) of successive French revolutionary governments that lent the Haitian Revolution its legal character. Some of the central strategic moves by the leaders of the Revolution were cast as pronouncements of law. The most well known is perhaps Toussaint Louverture's 1801 Constitution, which Napoleon interpreted as a quasi-declaration of independence and greeted with the sending of a massive expeditionary force across the Atlantic. This bold assertion of authority was preceded by an October 1800 enactment by which Louverture essentially militarized what remained of plantation labor in the colony.[12] The 1804 Declaration of Independence by Jean-Jacques Dessalines, which paid unspoken deference to the precedent of America's

---

[10] Code Noir, art. 59 (1685).

[11] See Yves Benot, "Le procès Sonthonax ou les 'débats entre les accusateurs et les accusés dans l'affaire des colonies' (an III)," in *Léger-Félicité Sonthonax: La première abolition de l'esclavage: La Révolution française et la Révolution de Saint-Domingue*, ed. Marcel Dorigny (Paris: Société française d'histoire d'outre-mer, 1997), 55–63. The trial proceedings were published in eleven volumes in 1795: Commission des Colonies, *Débats entre les accusateurs et les accusés dans l'affaire des colonies*, 11 vols. (Paris: Imprimerie Nationale, 1795).

[12] See Vertus Saint-Louis, "Régime militaire et Règlements de culture en 1801," *Chemins critiques* 3, nos. 1–2 (Dec. 1993): 207–212.

1776 declaration while rejecting its style and content, is a third example of the translation of revolutionary change into the terms of legal
authority.[13]

That many of these pronouncements were largely instrumental measures designed to contain the threat (and reality) of disorder, revolt,
and violence does not make them any less legal in nature, or any less
fundamental to the course of the Revolution. To the contrary, the legal
and strategic characters of the Haitian Revolution go hand in hand,
reinforcing one another even as they pointed to the inescapable role
of political practices that fell outside of law's empire. The law of the
Haitian Revolution consisted not simply in the plethora of legal pronouncements by which various revolutionary actors sought to advance
their agendas and counteract those of their opponents. The nature of
revolutionary change was also shaped in part by the very limits of colonial law: the century-long effort, during the colonial period, to constrain both manumission and planter brutality under the regime of the
Code Noir. That this effort was largely unsuccessful does not negate
the impact of the colonial law of slavery on the revolutionary period.
Rather, the dynamics of colonial-era efforts to control the outer boundaries of the master-slave relationship remained at the center of the revolutionary agenda. The regulation of manumission and the radical abuse
of slaves took on new and sometimes surprising forms after 1789, but
these forms retained something of the distinctive flavor of their Old
Regime precursors.

The legal hallmarks of the revolutionary period showcase the relationship between the Old Regime and the Haitian Revolution, revealing
unmistakable traces of the prudential spirit of the colonial law of slavery.
Much of what we think of as the Haitian Revolution's contribution to the
law of human rights and democracy was the product of a search for stability during the revolutionary period. The great emancipatory moments
of the Haitian Revolution are striking exceptions to the general rule that
legal change takes place at a measured, evolutionary, and deliberate pace.
Yet even those moments betrayed the influence of a long prior colonial
history, and despite their transformative ambitions, it would be a long

---

[13] Cf. David Armitage, "The Declaration of Independence and International Law," *The
William and Mary Quarterly* 59, no. 1 (Jan. 2001): 42 (characterizing the American
Declaration as an intervention in the late-eighteenth-century discourse of the law of
nations); idem, *The Declaration of Independence: A Global History* (Cambridge, MA:
Harvard University Press, 2007), 114–117 (contrasting the American and Haitian decla-
rations of independence and arguing that the former had little influence on the latter).

time before the changes they purported to enact would actually take hold in Haiti. The Code Noir's promise of a unitary and undifferentiated class of freed persons remained an unfulfilled one well after the Haitian Revolution proper had ended in 1804.

The last two chapters of this book set forth an interpretation of the Haitian Revolution as a strategic implementation of human rights that was marked through and through by the traces of Old Regime law. It is important to emphasize the limits of this endeavor. I do not purport to provide anything even remotely resembling a continuous or complete narrative account of the Revolution. Many events, themes, and personalities of the period from 1789 to 1804 are touched on here only in passing, or not at all. I make direct use of various pamphlets as well as key legal documents from the revolutionary era. However, of necessity, this chapter also relies on the growing body of Haitian revolutionary scholarship, to which the reader is referred for more detailed information about particular problems. Within these constraints, my objective is to provide an interpretive account of three critical turning points of the Revolution that have in common two features. First, these are all moments at which the force of law was brought to bear on the course of events. Second, in their different ways, they each illustrate the point that some of the central transformations of the revolutionary period involved the working out of the legacies of the Old Regime.

These moments are the granting of full political rights to free blacks and people of color by the National Assembly, beginning in 1790 and culminating in April 1792; the negotiations between the French civil commissioners and the leaders of the slave insurgency in the north (Jean-François Papillon and Georges Biassou) between late 1791 and mid-1792; and the abolition of slavery in 1793–1794. This chapter addresses the first of these phases. The next and final chapter of the book looks primarily at the last two. The book's conclusion briefly takes up a fourth such moment: Toussaint Louverture's enactment of a constitution for Saint-Domingue in the summer of 1801, which simultaneously confirmed the first abolition of slavery and codified Louverture's quest to militarize the colony's plantation-labor regime.

At each of these stages of the Revolution, political and legal change were fundamentally driven by a search for stability – a quest to realize Bodin's "well-ordered commonwealth" in the face of actual (rather than imagined) revolt on the part of the colony's free people of color and slaves. The strategic use of an emerging law of human rights to cut off the prospect of further instability in Saint-Domingue reflected the reality of the disruptions that free people of color and slaves had caused to the status quo through their acts of resistance and insurgency. Those disruptions were themselves cast in the form of adherence to a colonial legal script, the Code Noir. Casting reactionary white planters and colonial administrators as the true radicals, free people of color selectively invoked those provisions of absolutist law that seemed most favorable to their demands for a new and more egalitarian regime. Moreover, although the evidence is far scanter on this point, the leaders of the slave insurgency in the northern province seem to have followed a similar tactic, at least for a time.

The emancipatory tactics of French revolutionary administrators, for their part, also reflected a belief that the colony was not so removed from the prior situation of stable plantation labor to rule out a return to something approaching the status quo ante. Betraying signs of this awareness, the administrators' understanding of "emancipation" drew self-consciously on the framework built up by the colonial law of slavery in seeking to institutionalize the new freedoms. Indeed, the work of imagining a new scheme of colonial administration into being began in 1788 and 1789 – that is, before the outbreak of revolt in France or Saint-Domingue – with proposals for the eradication of the most abusive planter practices and for the replacement of slavery by a regime of serfdom.

Scholars have long recognized the pragmatic, instrumental nature of the revolutionary legal enactments, particularly the abolitions of racial discrimination in April 1792 and of slavery in 1793–1794.[14] Indeed, a self-consciousness about the strategic value of institutionalizing equality and liberty in Saint-Domingue dates back to the very acts in question. The April 1792 decree ending racial discrimination against free people of color was itself presented as a reaction to the slave revolt that commenced in August 1791.[15] And Sonthonax's emancipation proclamation of August 29, 1793, made no bones about the fact that it was intended to restore "order and tranquility" in Saint-Domingue.[16] The threat that British and Spanish military intervention presented to French sovereignty over the colony was transparently a factor in the decision making of Polverel and Sonthonax, for whom abolition represented the promise of an infusion of military manpower from among the newly freed.

[14] See, for example, "Aux origines de l'abolition de l'esclavage: Proclamations de Polverel et de Sonthonax, 1793–1794," *Revue d'histoire des colonies* 36 (1st trimester, 1949): 26, and 36 (3rd and 4th trimesters, 1949): 356 n. 2; Dubois, *Avengers of the New World*, 130; and Popkin, *You Are All Free*, 1, 15.

[15] *Loi relative aux colonies, & aux moyens d'y appaiser les troubles* (Paris: L'Imprimerie Royale, 1792).

[16] Léger-Félicité Sonthonax, "Proclamation relative à l'émancipation générale dans la province du Nord, Aug. 29, 1793," in "Aux origines de l'abolition de l'esclavage," 36 (3rd and 4th trimesters, 1949): 348.

Yet to emphasize the tactical incentives for enfranchisement and emancipation in Saint-Domingue does not seem to do justice to the particular forms of instrumentalism that underlay the human rights landmarks
of the early revolutionary years. The decisions of 1790–1794 were not
simply pragmatic inventions of the moment. They were also extensions
of long-standing patterns in the colonial law of slavery, whereby manumission and the discipline of slaves were regulated so as to forestall
the specter of instability. Moreover, in their revolutionary permutations,
these prudential patterns were not confined to the strategies of metropolitan administrators reacting to the unfolding unrest in Saint-Domingue.
The precautionary dynamics of colonial law also figured significantly in
Biassou's and Jean-François' early negotiations with the civil commissioners for a negotiated end to the insurgency, and in Toussaint Louverture's
pivotal contribution to the constitutional order of revolutionary Saint-
Domingue.

The 1801 Constitution, sandwiched as it was between draconian measures militarizing the plantation-labor system, embodied Louverture's own
vision of the "well-ordered commonwealth" – a concept that Louverture
himself invoked.[17] Louverture's effort to create a stable social order underwritten by a broad popular adherence to the rule of law in Saint-Domingue
is best understood not simply as a form of authoritarianism *avant la lettre*,
nor as an immediate response to the challenge of resisting Napoleon's
restorationist designs on the colony. Rather, the 1801 Constitution and its
accompanying regulations also reflected the Haitian revolutionary leader's
own anxiety about disorder and resistance in a society no longer slave but
not yet entirely free. His solution to that dilemma – to guarantee liberty
for the former slaves by imposing harsh requirements in the way of plantation labor – differed significantly in its motives and objectives from the
solutions put forth by his predecessors.[18] However, Louverture's policies
were recognizably descended from the efforts of the late colonial and early
revolutionary years to close the loopholes of the Code Noir by controlling the more radical implications of manumission and the discipline of
slaves. In this way, Louverture's contributions to the law of the Haitian
Revolution continued in a long line of interactions between administrators, planters, free people of color, and slaves that unsettled and ultimately
transformed the world of the Code Noir.

[17] See Toussaint Louverture, Proclamation, November 1801, in Moïse, *Le projet national
de Toussaint Louverture*, 150, also cited in Dubois, *Avengers of the New World*, 248.
[18] Cf. Saint-Louis, "Régime militaire et Règlements de culture en 1801."

THE CODE NOIR AS BRIDGE

The emerging human rights law of the early revolutionary period drew, above all, on two texts separated in time by more than a century: the 1685 Code Noir and the 1789 Declaration of the Rights of Man and the Citizen. These two documents were clearly odd bedfellows. The Code Noir was the last of the great Colbertian ordinances enacted by the Bourbon monarch Louis XIV. It was the culminating product of the legal infrastructure of early modern absolutism, heavily influenced by seventeenth-century French Caribbean precedents: a document designed to shape and control the growth of a burgeoning slave society.[19] The Declaration of the Rights of Man, by contrast, was designed to play out on the stage of revolution. It gathered under one umbrella a set of Enlightenment maxims intended to accompany and frame a new constitutional charter for the French state. Where the Code Noir provided for the execution of slaves who had escaped three times from their plantations, the Declaration announced that "men are born and remain free and equal in rights" and that these "natural and imprescriptible" rights include "liberty" and "resistance to oppression."[20] As a matter of surface appearances, at least, from the standpoint of 1789, the Code Noir pointed distinctly backward in time, and the Declaration of the Rights of Man unequivocally forward.

The coexistence of these two documents in early Haitian revolutionary political culture is not the complete paradox that it appears to be, however. For one thing, the Declaration drew on notions of sovereignty, right, and duty that bore heavy traces of the influence of Old Regime political culture.[21] Moreover, the Declaration was designed to be fully compatible with a functioning monarchy. Issued in the context of ongoing deliberations within the National Assembly over the terms of a new constitution for France, the Declaration was finalized and approved on August 26,

[19] On the relationship between Roman and Caribbean influences on the Code Noir, see the debate played out in the sources referenced in Chapter 1, notes 136 and 137.
[20] Declaration of the Rights of Man and the Citizen, arts. 1 and 2 (1789).
[21] See generally Dale Van Kley, ed., *The French Idea of Freedom: The Old Regime and the Declaration of Rights of 1789* (Stanford, CA: Stanford University Press, 1994), especially the essays by Keith Baker and David Bien therein. See also Keith M. Baker, "Sovereignty," in *A Critical Dictionary of the French Revolution*, ed. François Furet and Mona Ozouf, trans. Arthur Goldhammer (Cambridge, MA: Harvard University Press, 1989), 844–858. For a critique of this line of interpretation, see Isser Woloch, "On the Latent Illiberalism of the French Revolution," *American Historical Review* 95, no. 5 (1990): 1452–1470; and Hunt, "Forgetting and Remembering," 1125–1128.

1789, and then ratified, under pressure, by Louis XVI on October 5. The Declaration was issued as a separate document only because the National Assembly was, at that time, still very far from being able to promulgate the new charter it had sworn to deliver the French nation with the Tennis Court Oath of June 20, 1789. The break with monarchy was still very much in the future when the revolutionaries announced the "Rights of Man."

Finally, the Declaration proclaimed certain libertarian values that could be used to counter the emancipatory implications of its opening articles. Thus the Declaration included "property" among its list of "natural and imprescriptible rights." Moreover, it stated, in keeping with Bodin's theory of sovereignty, that "no one may be deprived of [property] except when public necessity, certified by law, obviously requires it, and on the condition of a just compensation in advance."[22] These offsetting principles had a special (and largely) unintended significance in the colonial context, but they were also ripe with implications for all manner of property relations in the metropole. In all of these respects, the Declaration of the Rights of Man can be seen as an interim bridge between the Old Regime and the French Revolution.

Similarly, although perhaps to an even greater degree, the Code Noir can be seen as a bridge between the colonial Old Regime and the Haitian Revolution. From this point of view, the Code Noir had certain inherent advantages over the Declaration as a framework for legal reform and political mobilization in the early revolutionary years. The Code had been in force (if not always enforced) for more than a century. And it offered something that the Declaration, by its very nature, could not: a relatively detailed guide to how to organize a society based on slave labor. Put differently, the Code Noir filled in the gaps left by the abstract principles of the Declaration: It provided a roadmap for how to get from point A to point B during a period when the only other directly relevant legal authority consisted of a handful of vague and seemingly contradictory decrees of the National Assembly bearing on the legal status of freed persons.

---

[22] Declaration of the Rights of Man and the Citizen, arts. 2 and 17 (1789). Bodin put it as follows in the *Six livres de la république*: "If the prince ... does not have the power to overstep the bounds of natural law, which has been established by God ... he will also not be able to take another's property without just and reasonable cause." Bodin, *On Sovereignty*, 39. The equivalent page reference for the Knolles/McRae translation used in Chapter 1 is Bodin, *The Six Bookes of a Commonweale*, 109.

That "point B" ultimately involved something radically different from the old systems of coercive chattel labor and racial hierarchy is an aspect of hindsight knowledge that we ought, for the moment, to put aside. For in seeking to understand the emancipatory achievements of the early Haitian Revolution, it is essential to account for the waning but still significant role of the Code Noir in the unfolding of a revolutionary process whose outcome was not clear to the actors involved. This was abundantly true of the period from 1789 to the August 1791 slave revolt. Yet the Code Noir remained significant even after the 1791 uprising on the northern plains of Saint-Domingue. That event was initially perceived in different ways by different observers. However, the available evidence suggests that, to its leaders, the revolt represented an uprising of limited scope and with limited objectives – to wit, the melioration of the plantation-labor regimen – rather than an absolute attack on the institution of plantation slavery.[23] Throughout this period, the Code Noir was in part a symbol of all that the Haitian revolutionaries sought to put behind them. At its under-enforced boundaries, nonetheless, it was also a precursor of a different style of empire, one that did not necessarily involve the abolition of plantation slavery, but rather its reform and reorganization under more humane and progressive principles.

Daily life under the regime of the Code Noir did not stop after the storming of the Bastille in Paris or the burning of fields on the Plaine du Nord. The plantations continued to churn out refined sugar, slaves kept running away, masters continued to manumit their interracial descendants, and administrators remained fully engaged with the responsibility of figuring out how to keep the entire system running. At the same time, however, administrators, free people of color, and slaves alike began using the Code Noir to articulate their visions of a way out of the violent and oppressive stalemate that plantation slavery and racial discrimination had created. The Code was radicalized in the course of these imaginings. Appropriated ever more forcefully and widely for

[23] See the letters of Jean-François and Georges Biassou to Sonthonax and Polverel, December 12 and 21, 1791, reprinted in Laurent Dubois and John D. Garrigus, *Slave Revolution in the Caribbean, 1789–1804: A Brief History with Documents* (Boston, MA: Bedford/St. Martin's, 2006), 99–102; and the July 1792 letter of Jean-François, Biassou, and Belair reprinted in Nathalie Piquionne, "Lettre de Jean-François, Biassou et Belair, juillet 1792," *Chemins critiques*, 3 (1997): 206–220. Questions have been raised about the authenticity of the July 1792 letter. See also Popkin, *You Are All Free*, 17; and Bell, *Toussaint Louverture*, 32–33, 36.

strategic purposes, the Code Noir was eventually superseded by other legal formations that spoke more directly to the challenges at hand. Yet the paths that led to these new formations traveled inescapably through the wreckage of the old.

Two paths would prove to be of particular significance to the egalitarian and antislavery achievements of the Haitian Revolution. First, under the leadership of Julien Raimond, free people of color began with increasing assertiveness to invoke the Code Noir's guarantee of equal rights to freed persons. In so doing, they used what was left of the moral authority of the Old Regime to shame the French National Assembly into living up to its revolutionary ideals.[24] This inversion of moral scales was supported by a pragmatic agenda that dated back to the 1770s: The argument for fully enfranchising free people of color during the early years of the revolution relied, in part, on their critical strategic role in policing the colony's fugitive slave population.

Second, in the aftermath of the 1791 revolt, the very limited evidence at our disposal suggests that some of the insurgents in the northern province, claiming allegiance to the authority of Louis XVI, may have tried to reappropriate the authority of the Code Noir so as to denounce their former masters' violations of its protective provisions.[25] This tactical and ironic use of Louis XIV's 1685 edict (if that is what it was) appealed to a vision of emancipation based on principles of legality and justice rather than the spirit of vengeance implied by the image of slaves as "domestic enemies." Here, as with the free coloreds' campaign for equality, there was both continuity and change in the work of envisioning a new colonial order. Using the authority of the Code Noir to demand redress for the abuses of masters was rare under the Old Regime, but not unprecedented. The administrators' pragmatic concern to forestall the unintended consequences of torture had always depended on a kind of unspoken collaboration with the willingness of certain slaves to denounce their owners and overseers. Yet claiming the mantle of the Code Noir in the aftermath of the August 1791 revolt involved speaking from a position of altogether different authority. The insurgents who spoke from that new position of

---

[24] See Gauthier, *L'aristocratie de l'épiderme*. On honor as a source of human rights, see Kwame Anthony Appiah, *The Honor Code: How Moral Revolutions Happen* (New York: W.W. Norton, 2010).

[25] Letters of Jean-François and Biassou to the Civil Commissioners, Dec. 12 and 21, 1791, in Dubois and Garrigus, *Slave Revolution in the Caribbean*; Bell, *Toussaint Louverture*, 84–85.

power were well aware that the "offers" of freedom extended them by Sonthonax and Polverel were means of accommodation to the changing political and military landscape.

Even before it became part of a more radical quest by freed persons and slaves, the unfulfilled promise of the Code had also begun to take on more subversive connotations as part of a continuing conversation within elite administrative reform circles about how to avert a colonial catastrophe. The best illustration of this convergence of administrative anxieties with the antislavery agenda circa 1789 is Pierre-Victor Malouet, that longtime student of French Caribbean slavery who had served as an administrator in Saint-Domingue in the 1760s and in French Guiana in the 1770s.[26] Through his wife, who held title to property in Saint-Domingue, Malouet was a plantation owner himself. In 1776, as we saw in Chapter 3, he penned an anonymous manuscript "On the treatment and usage of negroes" that defended the planter community from charges of engaging in the widespread abuse of slaves. Instead, wrote Malouet, the vast majority of slaveholders were moderate figures whose sense of self-interest and paternal concern for their domestic "families" would suffice to prevent excesses in the treatment of slaves. One year later, in 1777, Malouet seemed to retract this position in his private correspondence, asserting that it was necessary to soften the discipline of slaves in order to avert the fate that had befallen Dutch Surinam, site of a 1763 slave revolt. In the 1780s, Malouet's position evolved yet further. His 1785 *Essai sur l'Administration de Saint-Domingue*, with its denunciation of the despotism of the planters' "domestic sphere," captured the essence of the commonwealth ethics of slavery.[27]

By the eve of the French Revolution, Malouet had become an important, if somewhat shadowy, member of the club of elite administrators (current and former) who had begun to conceive of alternatives to traditional chattel slavery in the French colonies.[28] Their thinking reveals volumes about the path along which the strategic critique of slavery was traveling at the moment it was transformed by the French Revolution and

---

[26] Christopher Brown's distinction between antislavery thought (the "development of ideas and values hostile to slavery and the slave trade"), abolitionism (the "crystallization of programs to reform or transform imperial and colonial policy"), and the actual achievement of abolition and emancipation remains pertinent to the early Haitian Revolution but becomes radically compressed in that context. Brown, *Moral Capital*, 17–18.

[27] See Chapter 3.

[28] Tarrade, "L'esclavage est-il réformable?" 133–141.

the initiatives of freed persons and slaves in Saint-Domingue. Although these administrators were confirmed advocates of the reform of plantation slavery, they remained, for the most part, manifestly hostile to the more radical elements of the abolitionist program. The agenda of gradual emancipation, identified with the Society of the Friends of the Blacks, was not part of Malouet's vision. Malouet nonetheless perceived in the gradualist movement a serious, if profoundly misguided, source of competition in what was still a relatively small world of prominent intellectuals and politicians genuinely concerned with the need for colonial reform.

What links the earlier Malouet to the Malouet of 1788–1789 – and beyond him to French colonial administrators of the early Haitian Revolution – is an urgent conviction that the systematic abuse of slaves by refractory planters was inconsistent with the survival of the plantation economy. In its place, Malouet proposed a neofeudal system of manorial surveillance: serfdom instead of slavery. He announced the new turn in his thinking in a 1788 pamphlet entitled *Mémoire sur l'esclavage des nègres*.

The *Mémoire* was a riposte to Condorcet's *Réflexions sur l'esclavage des nègres*, first published pseudonymously in 1781 and then under Condorcet's own name in 1788. In his *Réflexions*, the senior Enlightenment statesman had denounced the laws of slavery as contrary to "the laws of natural morality." The power and riches of an entire nation were as nothing, Condorcet wrote, compared to the "the right of a single man" to be free from servitude. Only this principle distinguished a well-regulated society from a "horde of thieves."[29] Representative of a certain strand of Enlightenment antislavery thought, Condorcet's absolutist position did not exclude the possibility of arguing along more pragmatic lines as well. Slavery is "just as opposed to the interests of trade as it is to those of justice," he wrote. In order to end slavery, it was necessary to enlist the support of the political classes: those for whom "the voice of justice is foreign and who see themselves as statesmen … [who] look at injustice with cold blood" and permit it to endure.[30]

---

[29] Marie Jean Antoine Nicolas de Caritat, marquis de Condorcet, *Réflexions sur l'esclavage des nègres* (Neuchâtel, Switzerland: La Société Typographique, 1781), 13, 18.

[30] Ibid., 19. Consistent with this pragmatism, Condorcet's 1781 emancipation scheme envisioned replacing slavery with other systems of work discipline and guarantees of continued plantation labor. See Blackburn, "Epilogue," in Geggus and Fiering, *The World of the Haitian Revolution*, 395. For a discussion of the development of Condorcet's antislavery views and abolitionist project, see Laurent Dubois, *A Colony of Citizens: Revolution and Slave Emancipation in the French Caribbean, 1787–1804* (Chapel Hill: University of North Carolina Press, for the Omohundro Institute of Early American History and Culture, 2004), 177–182.

Condorcet's willingness to entertain tactical as well as principled objections to slavery was not coterminous with the precautionary critique of slavery associated with colonial policy-making circles, however. The essence of the latter approach was its focus on the mistreatment of slaves, construed in terms of an administrative ambition to close the loopholes of the Code Noir. Malouet's answer to Condorcet perfectly illustrates this difference. Like Condorcet, Malouet was entirely capable of arguing on different levels. "Slavery is and will always be a violation of natural law," he insisted. Man is born free in the state of nature. However, "as a result of the Order established or tolerated by Providence, this liberty undergoes strange revolutions!" he exclaimed.[31] According to Malouet, the abolition of slavery was an "impossible task": The "causes that render it necessary" go back to the discovery of America and inhere in the very "civil, moral, and political state of France, England, and several other nations of Europe."[32] Abolishing the slave trade in lieu of dismantling plantation slavery was an illusory alternative, for the two were inseparable from each other.[33] The task of responsible legislators, therefore, was to limit the more nefarious aspects of this necessary institution, by "softening and attenuating" the "evils and abuses" whose source could not be entirely eliminated.[34]

Malouet suggested in passing, without adducing any evidence, that the primary perpetrators of the abusive treatment of slaves were "freed persons, artisans, and small proprietors."[35] He thereby implicitly exculpated the *grands blancs* proprietors and their agents from liability for the excesses of plantation discipline. The problem of planter brutality, he nonetheless believed, continued to pose a profound general challenge to the regime of the Code Noir, incapable as that regime was of punishing and deterring behavior that occurred at such a distance from the colonial courts.[36] "The Government has never endeavored to regulate, with sufficient care, the treatment of slaves." In an apparent reference to articles 42 and 43 of the Code Noir – permitting the shackling and whipping of slaves but authorizing the prosecution of masters who tortured, mutilated, or murdered their slaves – Malouet observed that

---

[31] Pierre-Victor Malouet, *Mémoire sur l'esclavage des nègres* (Neuchâtel, Switzerland: n.p., 1788), 21.
[32] Ibid., 9.
[33] Ibid., 11.
[34] Ibid., 6.
[35] Ibid.
[36] Ibid., 7.

"several vicious and incomplete provisions" had confirmed the Code's own obsolescence. Even "honest" white colonists – those who recognized the "abuses of the colonial regime" – reverted to the traditional dogma that no "mediating power" could be allowed to come between the master and the slave if the right of private property was to have any meaning.[37]

The upshot of Malouet's argument was that a new legal regime had become necessary, one that would "reduce and modify servitude, as much as possible, while maintaining it."[38] Malouet came forth with that new system of law in 1789, by way of a draft law that was a throwback to the feudal ages. Lingering insecurities about the sensitive nature of his agenda in light of a rapidly shifting metropolitan political climate may have caused Malouet to refrain from publishing his proposal, although his 1788 *Mémoire* indicates that he submitted the draft to the naval minister for consideration.[39] The very title suggests the anomalous connotations of the project: "Proposed Law on the treatment and Police of Negro Serfs in the Colonies." It was the intent of "our predecessor Kings," Malouet announced, to "limit the authority of masters." The "impotence" of administrators in seeking to enforce these limits left slaves with no other recourse but "their own system of justice" – a generic but unmistakable allusion to methods of resistance probably meant to encompass everything from poison and *marronage* to outright revolt.[40] Rather than permit zealous opponents of slavery to exploit this violent stalemate, Malouet argued, the colonists ought to realize that their own self-interest required a law that would prevent them from abusing "the right they have acquired to the work and obedience of their Negroes."[41]

Without intending to disturb the foundations of that right, the new regime would set firm boundaries on the absolutist pretensions of the colonial elites. And it would go by a different name. The very first article

---

[37] Ibid., 15–16.
[38] Ibid., 12.
[39] Ibid., 63. The proposal exists only in manuscript form today and is conserved in the French Colonial Archives in Aix-en-Provence.
[40] Pierre-Victor Malouet, "Projet de loy sur le traitement et la Police des Negres Serfs dans les Colonnies," ANOM, F/3/90, fol. 276. Of course, a willingness to resist does not entail that slaves lacked their own ideas about crime and punishment. On practices of criminal justice developed by Caribbean slaves themselves on the plantations, see Natalie Zemon Davis, "Judges, Masters, Diviners: Slaves' Experience of Criminal Justice in Colonial Suriname," *Law and History Review* 29, no. 4 (Nov. 2011): 925–984.
[41] Malouet, "Projet de loy," fol. 276.

declared that "with respect to Negroes presently residing in or transported in the future to our Colonies, we abolish the label 'Slaves' as
representing an unlimited form of dependence." Instead, such persons
were to be known henceforth as "serfs."[42] Extending the feudal analogy, Malouet further prescribed that each plantation consisting of sixty
or more serf families would be reconstituted as a "fief," with the owner
exercising the "first level" of authority over his charges. A "domestic tribunal" was to be established in each colonial parish, with responsibility
for the "inspection and police" of the plantations and power to enforce
the "respective duties of Masters toward their Serfs and of Serfs toward
their Masters."[43] The serfs would be required to work for the profit of
their feudal lords, but masters could no longer pretend to exercise an
"unlimited authority" over their subjects, whether in respect of punishments, overtime work, or inadequate food and maintenance. Slaves chosen by the domestic tribunals from among each of the fiefs would have
the authority to bring the "legitimate" complaints of their fellow serfs to
the judiciary's attention.[44]

In some ways, this was old wine in a new bottle, an intriguing but not
necessarily persuasive reformulation of selected provisions of the Code
Noir and the 1784 plantation-management ordinance. Certainly it was
not anything that can be fairly described as a proposal for the "abolition" of slavery per se, as Malouet himself correctly insisted. Yet a kind
of slavery was in fact outlawed by this quirky design, if only by virtue of
the proposal's resuscitation of a seemingly very distant legal regime. The
replacement of "slavery" with "serfs" and "fiefs" was partly symbolic,
but also partly substantive. The master's authority over the slave, implicitly restricted under the regime of the Code Noir, was here reduced as a
matter of explicit principle. Further, the double bind facing slaves who
dared to flee their plantations to bring a judicial complaint against their
master was eliminated.

Seen in hindsight, Malouet's reversion to a feudal recipe for the reform
of slavery in 1789 strikes a puzzling, perhaps even bizarre note. Placed
in its historical context, however, the proposal seems less anomalous.
The comparison of peasants with slaves had been a persistent theme of

---

[42] Ibid. As Rebecca Scott has pointed out to me, this strategy would later surface in other
   parts of the nineteenth-century Caribbean world, including Jamaica (where the term
   "apprentices" was used) and Cuba (where slaves were reclassified as "*patrocinados*" in
   the 1880s).
[43] Ibid., fol. 277.
[44] Ibid., fol. 278.

proslavery rhetoric in the late colonial period, which included Malouet's own earlier contributions to the analogy.[45] Moreover, the legal status of serfdom was in fact a live issue during the waning decades of the Old Regime. Louis XVI had abolished the feudal institution of *mainmorte* – a term used to describe the legal attachment of serfs to their lord's estate, as well as the lord's right to inherit his serfs' property upon their death – on royal lands by edict in August 1779. The king then invited the lords of the realm to do the same of their own initiative, which most declined to do.[46] (The final abolition of serfdom would await the night of August 4, 1789, when what remained of the feudal order under the French monarchy was abolished in the space of a few hours.)

Malouet's scheme was, of course, never put into place. Yet its backward-looking framework should not be allowed to overshadow the proposal's more modern and even prescient aspects. How to attach laborers to their plantations without embracing a system of chattel slavery; how to assure stability in a plantation economy after the phasing out of an outmoded social order; what kind of legal and judicial system would fill in the gaps left behind after the formal demise of the regime of the Code Noir: these were some of the most persistent and vexing issues that French colonial and Haitian revolutionary administrators would confront in the years to come, from Sonthonax and Polverel to Toussaint Louverture and even beyond. As a prognosis of the social conflicts that these and other revolutionary abolitionists would address on the ground of Saint-Domingue in the 1790s, Malouet's quixotic 1789 manuscript was not very far from the mark, and some of its provisions were effectively implemented, after the fact, in the evolving policies of Sonthonax, Polverel, and Louverture. As Malouet wrote in his 1788 *Mémoire*, the emancipation of the slaves was indeed out of the question, but only "until we can reconstruct, on new foundations, a portion of the social edifice."[47]

The consequences of the radical abuse of slaves proved to be a consistent thread in these administrative visions of a new foundation for Saint-Domingue. This legal issue – a systemic regulatory weakness in

---

[45] Malouet, *Mémoire sur l'esclavage des nègres*, 3; ibid., "Du traitement et de l'emploi des Nègres dans les colonies," 1776, ANOM, F/3/90, fol. 170. See also Malick Ghachem, "The Colonial Vendée," in Geggus and Fiering, *The World of the Haitian Revolution*, 157–159.

[46] See Jean Bart, "Esclavage et servage tardif," in Dorigny, *Les abolitions de l'esclavage*, 29. The relationship between the abolitions of serfdom and slavery in France is a topic deserving of further research.

[47] Malouet, *Mémoire sur l'esclavage des nègres*, 13.

the regime of the Code Noir – motivated ever more radical visions of administrative reform just as the Old Regime gave way to the French Revolution. Although the specific terms of Malouet's proposal were largely idiosyncratic to him, the underlying concerns it expressed were more widely shared, even by those willing to go much further in the direction of emancipation.

In 1785, for example, Daniel Lescallier was named *commissaire général de la marine* and administrator of Malouet's old terrain, French Guiana, where Lescallier remained until 1788. Along with his fellow administrator, the Baron de Bessner,[48] Lescallier had received secret instructions from Naval Minister Castries in 1785 to emancipate all of the monarchy's slaves in Guiana, along with directions to encourage the planters to free their own slaves. Echoing the process that Louis XVI had used to abolish *mainmorte* in 1779, these instructions were inspired more immediately by a pioneering (and ill-fated) experiment conducted by the Marquis de Lafayette in Guiana itself.[49] In 1785, Lafayette purchased two plantations in the South American colony and appointed an engineer named Henri de Richeprey to develop them. Lafayette directed Richeprey to ensure the religious instruction of the plantation laborers, pay them a regular salary, and govern them according to the same laws that applied to white colonists. Corporal punishment was prohibited. In 1789, Lafayette formally manumitted all of his Guianese slaves. Yet his two properties were sequestered after Lafayette was imprisoned while attempting to escape France for America during the Terror.[50]

At least some of Lafayette's fellow plantation owners in Guiana seem to have followed the general's example (by applying something similar to the Richeprey regime, if not necessarily by formally emancipating their slaves).[51] Yet Castries's instructions to Lescallier were never implemented. This was not on account of local resistance: As of the late 1780s, the monarchy continued to subsidize the importation of slaves to Guiana.[52] Whatever Castries's intentions with respect to the royal slaves may have

---

[48] See Chapter 3.

[49] The text of the instructions is reprinted in "Aux origines de l'abolition," 36 (1st trimester, 1949): 33–34.

[50] Étienne Taillemite, "La Fayette et l'abolition de l'esclavage," in *L'esclave et les plantations: De l'établissement de la servitude à son abolition: Un hommage à Pierre Pluchon,* ed. Philippe Hrodĕj (Rennes: Presses Universitaires de Rennes, 2008), 231–233.

[51] Ibid., 231.

[52] Ciro Flamarion Cardoso, *La Guyane française: 1715–1817: Aspects économiques et sociaux: contribution à l'étude des sociétés esclavagistes d'Amérique* (Petit Bourg, Guadeloupe: Ibis Rouge Éditions, 1999), 329, 334–335. I thank Miranda Spieler for guidance on this matter.

been, therefore, the metropolitan administration did not seriously contemplate a general emancipation in Guiana at this time. Nonetheless, in
1789, Lescallier went on to propose just this: the abolition of the slave
trade and the gradual abolition of slavery. In his *Réflexions sur le sort des
Noirs dans nos colonies*, published that year, Lescallier argued that the
best-maintained and most profitable plantations were those in which the
slaves were treated in the least arbitrary way.[53]

Similarly, a deputy to the National Assembly named Jean-Louis
Viefville des Essars, from Vermandois, prepared a proposal for abolition
in 1789 whose revealing title is worth quoting in full: *Discours et Projet
de Loi pour l'affranchissement des Nègres, ou l'Adoucissement de leur
Régime, et Réponse aux Objections des colons* ("Speech and Proposed
Law in favor of the emancipation of the Negroes, or the Softening of
their Regime, and Response to the colonists' Objections"). The proposal
reads in part:

The Code Noir is and remains abolished and suppressed, from this day forward,
as inhumane and barbarous; plantation foremen, masters, and slave drivers are
prohibited from arbitrarily and out of their own authority punishing or causing
to be punished, striking or causing to be struck any slaves, for whatever reason or
pretext; and all persons are [prohibited] from arrogating to themselves the right
to inflict any sort of punishment on slaves, who are placed from this moment
forward under the protection of the law.[54]

The essence of slavery, on this reading, was the abuse of the master's physical control over his slave. Abolishing planter brutality was tantamount
to abolishing the institution of slavery. In Viefville des Essars's view, the
Code Noir could no longer sustain the new order to come. However, his
very focus on the question of treatment suggested a vision not altogether
dissimilar to Malouet's: The Code Noir would be gone, but the quest for
a more humane and lawlike regime of black plantation labor commenced
by Louis XIV would remain.

What served as a rationale for reconfiguring slavery along feudal lines
in one administrator's hands became a justification for open (if gradual)
abolition in the proposals of Lescallier, Viefville des Essars, and others.

---

53 See Tarrade, "L'esclavage est-il réformable?" 140–141.
54 Jean-Louis Viefville des Essars, *Discours et Projet de Loi pour l'affranchiseement des
Nègres, ou l'Adoucissement de leur Régime, et Réponse aux Objections des colons* (Paris:
L'Imprimerie Nationale, [1789]), 21. Although not dated, the proposal is included among
a series of other pamphlets all published in 1789 and included in the John Carter Brown
Library's "Mélanges sur l'Amérique" collection, vol. 4, no. 7.

The distinctions matter as well as the commonalities. Beginning in 1789 and thereafter, the administrative tradition associated with the reform and melioration of slavery was forced, under the extreme pressures of time and circumstance, into dialogue with more radical notions of abolition and citizenship. The legacies of the campaign to vindicate the protective provisions of the Code Noir continued to play a central role in that dialogue. However, increasingly after 1789, it became a dialogue that could no longer unfold on the terms dictated by elite white administrators or planters.

RACIAL EQUALITY AND THE AUTHORITY OF HISTORY

The August 1791 slave revolt is sometimes used as a chronological marker to distinguish between the "French Revolution in Saint-Domingue" (1789–1791) and the Haitian Revolution proper (1791–1804).[55] This distinction usefully draws attention to the radicalism of the slave insurgency that broke out in the late summer of 1791, and provides a framework for understanding the uniqueness of the Haitian contribution to the age of the Atlantic revolutions. Yet it tends to associate the political mobilization of the *affranchis* and *gens de couleur libres* with the ideological effervescence of the early French Revolution rather than the long eighteenth-century experience of manumission that preceded 1789.[56] That prior history was a factor of at least equal importance in the political consciousness of free blacks and people of color. Similarly, the vacillation and ambivalence that characterized early French revolutionary policy on the rights of free blacks and people of color are often portrayed, in effect, as a function of the relative weight of rival political lobbies in the National Assembly at a given moment: the white planters' lobby versus the advocates of racial equality.[57] The shared formative influence of colonial-era struggles over the regulation of manumission is thereby occluded.

---

[55] See, for example, Gene E. Ogle, "The Trans-Atlantic King and Imperial Public Spheres: Everyday Politics in Pre-Revolutionary Saint-Domingue," in Geggus and Fiering, *The World of the Haitian Revolution*, 89.

[56] See, for example, Gauthier, *L'aristocratie de l'épiderme*. A more comprehensive, eighteenth-century approach is taken in Garrigus, *Before Haiti*.

[57] See Dorigny, "La Société des Amis des Noirs," in Dorigny and Gainot, *La Société des Amis des Noirs*, 31–32, 38–39, 46–52; Gauthier, *L'aristocratie de l'épiderme*, 109–140; Lynn Hunt, *The French Revolution and Human Rights: A Brief Documentary History* (Boston, MA: Bedford Books, 1996), 23–26; and Debien, *Les colons de Saint-Domingue et la Révolution*.

A related difficulty with using the August 1791 slave revolt as a chronological or conceptual dividing line is that the struggle over the granting of full political rights to freed persons in Saint-Domingue unfolded in constant dialogue with the prospect of a slave revolt. The granting of full political rights to free blacks and people of color both generated and reflected a greatly heightened anxiety about the potential for a large-scale black uprising. After the colonial authorities ruthlessly suppressed a free colored uprising led by Vincent Ogé in early 1791, the National Assembly first granted local voting rights in May 1791 to the very small subset of people of color born of free mothers and fathers. The revolutionary legislature then annulled those same rights in September 1791 and finally granted them a second time to all free people of color without limit in April 1792 – after the specter of slave revolt had become a distinct reality. Although the civil rights movement led by free blacks and people of color helped to facilitate the emancipation of the slaves, the slaves' aspirations had already contributed to the cause of racial equality even before the uprising in the Plaine du Nord in August 1791.

For all of these reasons, it is difficult to demarcate a separate domain of action and ideology that we can call the movement for racial equality (as opposed to the slave insurgency) in revolutionary Saint-Domingue. In making sense of the complicated events of 1789–1792, it may help to stand back from the immediacy of the early revolutionary years and place them in their longer-term colonial context. This is not least because the opening salvos in the struggle over racial equality in revolutionary-era Saint-Domingue were experienced in part as extensions of colonial modes of authority and resistance, replays of colonial battles on a larger scale.

The very existence of a numerically significant community of free blacks and people of color in Saint-Domingue was itself, of course, a legacy of the colonial period. Many had gained their first significant experiences in negotiating the challenges of life at the boundary between slavery and freedom in the colonial courts. Whether fending off the claims of creditors in France, asserting a right to use the family name of one's master, challenging the threat of reenslavement, or pursuing professional opportunities in plantation and urban settings alike, the *affranchis* and *gens de couleur* had already acquired a sharp awareness of both the possibilities and the distinct limitations of the manumission regime.[58]

---

[58] These developments are addressed in Garrigus, *Before Haiti*; Rogers, "On the Road to Citizenship," 65–78; and King, *Blue Coat or Powdered Wig*.

That regime had evolved from the "open-door" policy of the 1685 Code Noir to a system of administrative oversight of planter discretion in freeing individual slaves. When colonial administrators began systematically conditioning manumission on service in the maroon-hunting brigades (*maréchaussées*) in the 1770s, free people of color both exploited and challenged the new strategic rationale for emancipation. In 1784 and 1785, the monarchy again imposed a more restrictive policy on manumission, as part of a more general effort to rein in the powers of managers and agents of absentee plantations. By then, many free people of color, particularly those situated in the western and southern provinces, had managed to rise up the colonial social ladder sufficiently to become important coffee growers. However, at no point during the eighteenth century did the *gens de couleur* experience the equal "rights, privileges, and immunities" envisioned in articles 57 and 59 of the Code Noir.

One legacy of these developments was that, at nearly every turn, manumission policy was tightly wound up with colonial policy on the treatment of slaves and the fear of a broad-based slave revolt. Colonial administrators clearly aimed to assert monopolistic control over the manumission process – to wrestle it away from an essentially private and informal domain of interracial and familial relations. Yet their justification for doing so evolved over time, revealing a fundamental ambivalence best captured by Montesquieu's statement that "the republic can be equally endangered by too many freed men and by too many slaves."[59] The revolutionary debates over the rights of *affranchis* and *gens de couleur* can be understood as a dramatization of this perceived policy dilemma, but at the level of political citizenship rather than freedom from slavery per se. The twists and turns of 1791 and 1792, that is, involved the potential advantages and disadvantages of giving full effect to decisions about manumission made many years before. However, the debate over the political and military utility of enforcing political rights for free blacks and people of color at large necessarily proceeded from some of the same strategic assumptions that informed the regulation of individual manumissions.

After 1789, the political thrust of this colonial-era prudentialism became even more difficult to predict, for the freedom of the *affranchis* – a category used in late colonial legislation to group together both long-free colored families and recently manumitted slaves[60] – seemed simultaneously to promote and inhibit the broader goal of maintaining stability on the plantations. Thus it was not simply the white planter elite, gathered in the form of a Parisian political lobby known as the Club Massiac, who opposed the extension of voting rights to free people of color from 1790 to 1792. Drawing on their own eighteenth-century preoccupations with the impact of a "libertine" ex-slave population on the quiescence of the slave community, colonial administrators (in contrast to the position some of their predecessors had taken since the 1760s) reinforced the reactionary racism of most white planters in response to the claims of free colored leaders.[61]

Yet these administrators, along with moderate voices in the National Assembly and the more far-sighted members of the white planter elite, also saw the potential value of using the free colored community as a buffer against slave revolt.[62] The convergence of disparate views around the theme of the well-ordered commonwealth is nicely captured in a letter written on January 20, 1789, from the intendant of Saint-Domingue, Barbé de Marbois, to Naval Minister Castries:

[T]he principle generally accepted by the innovators is that in order to restore matters to a state of regulation and order, it has become indispensable to free ourselves temporarily from the laws that have regulated all relations between those who govern and those who are governed.[63]

Such language was ambiguous enough to comprise both abolitionist proposals and calls for racial equality between whites and free people of color. (Indeed, the statement was broad enough to have encompassed even the fulminations of white planters against the tax and trade policies they associated with ministerial "despotism.") Yet Marbois's statement

---

[60] Garrigus, *Before Haiti*, 167, 170. This use of the term became prominent after about 1770. In the colonial census of 1782, by contrast, the category of "*mulâtres et nègres libres*" was replaced by two more specific groupings: "*gens de couleur, mulâtres*, etc." and (manumitted) "*nègres libres*." Garrigus, "Blue and Brown," 259.

[61] Garrigus, *Before Haiti*, 259–260; Geggus, *Haitian Revolutionary Studies*, 11, 166; Blackburn, *The Overthrow of Colonial Slavery*, 182; Popkin, *You Are All Free*, 69; Fick, *The Making of Haiti*, 118.

[62] Blackburn, *The Overthrow of Colonial Slavery*, 168–169; Dubois, *Avengers of the New World*, 118–119, 130–131, 137; Popkin, *You Are All Free*, 34, 76; Davis, *Inhuman Bondage*, 163–164; Fick, *The Making of Haiti*, 122.

[63] Letter from François Barbé de Marbois, Intendant, to Maréchal de Castries, Naval Minister, Jan. 20, 1789, ANOM, Greffes de Saint-Domingue (Conseil Superieur de Port-au-Prince, 1786–1790), GR//4, Lettre commune n. 55, fol. 85. This passage is underlined in the original, although not necessarily by Marbois.

seems to have been directed especially at the growing political assertiveness of free blacks and people of color in the region surrounding Cap Français. "It is above all in the northern province," continued Marbois, "that the fermentation is felt with a buzz of activity; but even though it has not thus far burst into the open, we can be no less certain that it is nearly general in nature."[64]

The political fermentation of freed persons in this early revolutionary period was based in part on principles that were, on one level, very far from innovative. Awarding citizenship to the freed slave was a practice that dated back to Roman law, at least in the cases of slaves over thirty years of age who were freed by a statutorily recognized mode of manumission. Roman citizenship for the freed person did not entail full political or social equality, of course. The requirement to show deference toward one's former master legitimated various forms of discrimination against the freed slave.[65] In 1789, Moreau de Saint-Méry published a pamphlet that suggests the colonists were conscious of the significance of these ancient precedents in the context of the revolutionary debates over *gens de couleur* citizenship. "In Roman times, it took an entire generation to erase the traces of servitude," he wrote.[66] This observation accurately reflected the role of racial legislation in limiting the scope of freedom for *affranchis* in Saint-Domingue, but it also implied as a normative matter that political equality could wait. Manumission, in Moreau's view, created an "intermediate state between slavery and freedom."[67] (Moreau's pamphlet was a response to the Abbé Grégoire's call for the National Assembly to immediately embrace the cause of racial equality.)[68]

The disparity between the ancient ideal of equal rights incorporated in the Code Noir and the realities of daily life in freedom had a profound impact on the revolutionary strategies of freed persons. This gap – which was perhaps especially acute for the wealthy elites of the southern and western provinces[69] – served to channel the revolutionary debates over political citizenship onto a path that implicated the realization of promises made long ago by Louis XIV. The Sun King's legal (and to some extent moral) authority was consequently set up in tension with that of

---

[64] Ibid.
[65] See Chapter 2.
[66] Moreau de Saint-Méry, *Observations d'un habitant des colonies*, 19.
[67] Ibid.
[68] See also Dubois, *Avengers of the New World*, 84.
[69] Garrigus, *Before Haiti*, 171.

contemporary colonial administrators and the metropolitan revolutionary legislature. The legalism of the free coloreds' campaign for political
equality was doubly savvy from a strategic point of view. It permitted
the *gens de couleur* to portray themselves as faithful adherents to a predefined and authoritative absolutist script, thereby casting their reactionary opponents among the white planters and colonial bureaucracy as the
enemies of law and order.

Moreover, the strategy of balancing an essentially conservative commitment to long-standing principle with a more progressive (but limited)
embrace of the doctrines newly announced in the Declaration of the
Rights of Man had a clear economic dimension. In theory, it allowed free
people of color – some of whom were slaveholders – to advance their own
interests as proprietors without calling into question the legitimacy of
slavery itself. So long as the colonial political order could be said to rest on
a binary and watertight distinction between two and only two classes of
people, freeborn and slave, the more subversive implications of the
campaign for racial equality could perhaps be contained. (In time,
some of the leading advocates for the free colored community, including Julie Raimond and André Rigaud, would loosen their commitment
to a strict version of the two-class principle. Yet the evolution of their
views on this point was closely connected to the unfolding of the slave
revolt and its complicated interaction with the agendas of free people
of color.)[70]

This carefully calibrated fusion of royal law with revolutionary principle informed the *cahier de doléances* (petition or list of grievances)
that a group of leading *gens de couleur* submitted in connection with
the convocation of the Estates General. Although Louis XVI had con-
voked the Estates General in May 1788, the representatives of the clergy,
nobility, and the Third Estate did not actually assemble in Versailles until
one year later, on May 5, 1789. By June 17, the Third Estate had proclaimed itself as the National Assembly, and shortly thereafter vowed
not to disband until a constitution for France had been promulgated.
The submission of a *cahier* in September 1789 by Vincent Ogé and other
leaders of the free colored community was itself a distinctive assertion
of political will. The message was that the legislative and constitutional
claims of this community – comprised of self-styled "free Citizens and

---

[70] As early as October 1789, some free people of color were not averse to criticizing white
planter opposition to their admission to the National Assembly as an example of "slavery"
and a reflection of the complicity of the slave system with racial segregation. See Gauthier,
L'aristocratie de l'épiderme, 42–43; and Dubois, *Avengers of the New World*, 80–81.

Proprietors of Color" – were no less worthy of the Assembly's attention than the roughly six hundred others then clamoring for satisfaction in the metropole.[71]

In its very first article, the *cahier* summoned up a vision of limited racial equality that would remain the official policy of French revolutionary administrators in Saint-Domingue until the decisions of Sonthonax and Polverel in 1793.[72] "The residents of the French colonies are uniquely and generally divided into two classes: free men, and men who are born and who live in slavery."[73] (In declining to embrace an abolitionist position, the petition of the *gens de couleur* was similar to the overwhelming majority of *cahiers de doléances*, relatively few of which went so far as to criticize black slavery.[74]) The class of free men was defined to include "not only all Whites, but also all Creoles of Color, including free Blacks, Mulattos, Quarteroons, and others."[75] Reflecting their understanding of the Code Noir and the Declaration of the Rights of Man as mutually reinforcing documents, the free colored delegates demanded that the National Assembly make the Declaration "common to them along with the whites; and as a consequence that articles 57 and 59 [of the Code Noir] be renewed and enforced as per their form and tenor."[76] Far from superseding the terms of the Code Noir, in other words, the Declaration merely recapitulated them while requiring that they be applied across the racial board, at least where citizenship was concerned.[77]

The *cahier* was an important statement of the political agenda of the free people of color, but their message was not entirely consistent or uniform. In certain contexts, the leading free colored advocates were prepared, at this early stage of the French Revolution, to recognize that their claims of right could not be entirely separated from the issue of the legitimacy of slavery itself. Thus, in a November 23, 1789, letter elaborating on their demands for representation in the National Assembly, Raimond, Ogé, and three other free colored spokespersons criticized the

---

[71] *Cahier contenant les plaintes, doléances & reclamations des citoyens-libres & proprietaires de couleur, des Îles & Colonies françaises* (Paris: n.p., 1789), 1.

[72] See Dubois, *Avengers of the New World*, 144 (quoting Sonthonax).

[73] *Cahier contenant les plaintes*, 1.

[74] Tarrade, "Les colonies et les principes de 1789," 18.

[75] *Cahier contenant les plaintes*, 1.

[76] Ibid., 1–2.

[77] For another example of the invocation of articles 57 and 59 of the Code Noir by free colored leaders in Paris at this time, see the December 2, 1789, *Supplique et Pétition des Citoyens de couleur des Isles et Colonies françaises*, quoted in Gauthier, *L'aristocratie de l'épiderme*, 55. The Abbé Grégoire's use of this same appeal is documented in ibid., 76–77.

white colonists for "throwing off to the side and reducing to the level of beasts of burden those thousands of individuals who are condemned to groan under the shameful weight of slavery."[78] Far from being the natural allies of the *gens de couleur*, the white colonists had, by their obstinance and prejudice, shown themselves to be the "natural enemies" of the free colored community.[79] Locked at the time in a bitter battle over the representation issue with the Club Massiac, the leading *gens de couleur* activists were thus prepared to cast some doubt on the long-term viability of the two-class principle, even if the gesture remained largely hypothetical and abstract at this stage.[80]

Moreover, the legalism of their approach did not prevent the free colored advocates from making selective rather than doctrinaire use of the Code Noir. Indeed, the *cahier* did not shy away from seeking the repeal of certain provisions that were especially baleful to *affranchis* and *gens de couleur*, most notably the article 58 requirement that freed persons show a "singular respect" to their former masters.[81] Because both property and liberty were absolute rights (as the Declaration of the Rights of Man indicated), the colonial measures requiring slaveholders to gain prior administrative approval for or pay taxes on manumissions ought similarly to be revoked.[82] In short, the *cahier* aimed to pick and choose from among those aspects of colonial statutory and administrative law that they deemed consistent with their political and social aspirations. Admitting free colored representatives to serve in the "heart" of the National Assembly, via elections held by the colonial provincial assemblies, was the crowning demand of this petition. And it was ultimately the one issue on the free colored agenda that would most directly contribute to destabilizing the strict binary division of the colonial social order into free persons and the enslaved.

Ogé's biography captures the trajectory that led from the assertion of rights enshrined in the Code Noir and the Declaration of the Rights of Man to the social experience of revolt. Ogé was a merchant from the town of Dondon in the northern province of Saint-Domingue. He spent most of 1789 and 1790 working with his fellow free colored leader Julien Raimond to secure the right of *gens de couleur* to vote for delegates to the

---

[78] Quoted in Gauthier, *L'aristocratie de l'épiderme*, 42–43.
[79] Ibid., 43.
[80] Ibid., 44–45.
[81] *Cahier contenant les plaintes*, 12.
[82] Ibid., 13–14.

colonial (and thus metropolitan) assemblies.[83] On March 28, 1790, the Colonial Committee of the National Assembly issued a set of ambiguous instructions that left open whether free people of color could participate as "persons" in local elections in Saint-Domingue. These instructions elaborated on the terms of a National Assembly decree, dated March 8, that effectively vested the colonies with the authority to determine the status of persons within their boundaries. The colonial administrators refused to interpret the phrase "all persons" in the March 28 instructions in favor of racial equality, and Oge's subsequent lobbying efforts in Paris were essentially rebuffed.[84] He then left France in late 1790 and passed through London, where he visited (and is said to have received support from) the abolitionist Thomas Clarkson. Upon arriving in Saint-Domingue, Ogé joined forces with Jean-Baptiste Chavannes and raised an army of more than three hundred free coloreds; they demanded that the governor permit *gens de couleur* to elect delegates in the provincial assemblies. The uprising was brutally repressed by the colonial militias, and in early 1791 Ogé and Chavannes were executed on the wheel in the public square of Cap Français. Their severed heads were prominently displayed on pikes to serve as an example for other free coloreds who sought to take the equal-rights provisions of the Code Noir at face value.[85]

Notwithstanding such intimidation, the campaign for racial equality based on a synthesis of royal and revolutionary legal principles was carried forward in 1791 by Raimond. Raimond was a wealthy and educated free colored owner of slaves whose family lived in the parish of Aquin, in the southern province of Saint-Domingue. In 1784, with the permission (and tacit approval) of the naval minister, the marquis de Castries, Raimond left Saint-Domingue to begin the work of lobbying the Colonial Ministry in Versailles on behalf of the *gens de couleur*.[86]

---

[83] Dubois, *Avengers of the New World*, 80–85.

[84] Blackburn, *The Overthrow of Colonial Slavery*, 179–180; Tarrade, "Les colonies et les principes de 1789," 25; Davis, *The Problem of Slavery in the Age of Revolution*, 140.

[85] See Geggus, *Haitian Revolutionary Studies*, 11; Dubois, *Avengers of the New World*, 87–88; and John D. Garrigus, "'Thy Coming Fame, Ogé! Is Sure': New Evidence on Ogé's 1790 Revolt and the Beginnings of the Haitian Revolution," in John D. Garrigus and Christopher Morris, eds., *Assumed Identities: The Meanings of Race in the Atlantic World* (Arlington: Texas A&M University Press, for the University of Texas at Arlington, 2010), 19–45.

[86] Gauthier, *L'aristocratie de l'épiderme*, 21; Dubois, *Avengers of the New World*, 60. See also John Garrigus, "Opportunist or Patriot? Julien Raimond (1744–1801) and the Haitian Revolution," *Slavery & Abolition*, 28, no. 1 (2007): 1–21; idem, *Before Haiti*, 234.

By the end of the Old Regime, the vast array of discriminatory laws that had long disabled free people of color, particularly in the aftermath of the Seven Years' War, remained on the books, but many had fallen into desuetude; and beginning in the early 1780s, the registration of new racial laws was actively discouraged by de Castries.[87] Raimond's rise to prominence and the assertiveness of his lobbying efforts support Dominique Rogers's thesis that the free people of color were "bold enough to ask for political rights in 1789, not because their social status was deteriorating ... but because their heightened social integration gave them new confidence."[88]

In a 1791 pamphlet that reflected this confidence, Raimond simultaneously made the case for ending free colored exclusion from the colonial assemblies and documented the history of racially discriminatory legislation in Saint-Domingue. Putting politics, history, and law together to promote a more universalist civic regime in the colony, Raimond tapped freely into the rhetoric of the Enlightenment and the new republicanism. Laws were to be held as just or unjust depending on their accordance with the "law of nature."[89] Colonial legislation that failed to pass the review of either natural law or the Declaration of the Rights of Man was illegitimate, Raimond insisted. Accordingly, he denounced the National Assembly for acting inconsistently with its own Declaration in decreeing that a French citizen who settles in the colonies and marries a free woman of color would thereby be degraded in status on the pretext that the woman had been permanently stained by her slave ancestry.[90]

If natural law and the Declaration were not themselves sufficient to persuade the revolutionary legislators to fully vindicate the principle of equal citizenship, Raimond was prepared to add a third element into the legal mix. In the 1685 edict, Raimond wrote, Louis XVI had "granted to freed persons, properly understood, the right of citizens." Indeed, he had done more than this: He had required the unmarried colonist who "abused" his slave to marry her and thus "legitimate" her children. Emancipated by the fact of her marriage, the woman and her children were "elevated to the condition of her husband."[91] The pièce de résistance

---

[87] Rogers, "On the Road to Citizenship," 70.
[88] Ibid., 75–76.
[89] Raimond, *Observations sur l'origine et le progrès du préjugé*, 26.
[90] Ibid. Raimond does not specify the statute in question.
[91] Ibid., 27–28.

followed: "Will the National Assembly be less just than a despot?"[92] This cunning contrast between the absolutist past and the moral authority of the French revolutionary delegates did not require a starry-eyed view of Louis XIV. Raimond was entirely happy to characterize the late Bourbon king as a tyrant. An attachment to the principles of royal higher law was not the same thing as personal fealty to the memory of a long-since deceased ruler of the French nation. By the same token, commitment to the ideals of the French Revolution did not require unwavering support for the actions of their spokespersons.

Raimond's rhetorical savvy and his pragmatism about the legal sources of racial equality were of a piece. Framing the opposition to racial equality as the true departure from law and order was a shrewd way to defend the free colored cause. Raimond's argument can be seen as a gloss on Edmund Burke's famous denunciation of the French Revolution. Published in November 1790, Burke's *Reflections on the Revolution in France* had targeted the French revolutionaries' supposed hostility to long-established institutions and traditional customs, which, on Burke's reading, were the true guarantors of English liberties.[93] In effect, Raimond was saying that the revolutionary pursuit of racial equality was a movement to preserve an organic continuity with a now distant past – albeit a past that existed more in the letter than in the implementation of the law.

Even as they invoked the authority of the Code Noir in their efforts to turn the tide of metropolitan opinion, advocates for racial equality also conjured up memories of another form of colonial tradition. The role that *affranchis* and *gens de couleur* had historically played in manning the maroon-hunting brigades in Saint-Domingue was never more politically salient than in the unstable colonial world of 1789. Abolitionist agitation in Paris was more limited in scope than the white planter lobby imagined. However, along with the effervescence of free colored activism and the Ogé revolt, it sufficed to place the stability of the plantation economy on the National Assembly's agenda, thanks to the considerable influence of the Club Massiac.[94]

Concern about the maintenance of slavery, however, not only cut across racial lines; it also provided the activist *gens de couleur* in Paris

---

[92] Ibid., 28 (also quoted in Dubois, *Avengers of the New World*, 60). The original reads: "L'assemblée nationale seroit-elle moins juste qu'un déspote?"

[93] Edmund Burke, *Reflections on the Revolution in France* (London: J. Dodsley, 1790).

[94] See Tarrade, "Les colonies et les principes de 1789"; Dubois, *Avengers of the New World*, 82–83; Geggus, *Haitian Revolutionary Studies*, 10–11.

and their allies with a powerful weapon in the fight to advance their claims of racial parity. Metropolitan abolitionists, who shared only part of the free coloreds' agenda, were certainly not averse to sounding the note of slave revolt.[95] The Abbé Grégoire, for example, frequently held the risk of a coordinated black uprising before the planters' eyes. He also connected this risk to the issue of *marronage* and pointed to the role that the free people of color had played in containing fugitive slaves in the colonial era. Yet his references to the potential for a black rebellion were part of an argument that slaves had a natural right to rise up against the oppression of their masters.[96] As Marcel Dorigny has demonstrated, the leading French abolitionists evoked the path of a slow and peaceful extinction of slavery on the merits.[97] They advocated, that is, for the gradual transformation of the colonial economies from slave-based into free-labor systems.[98] As the Society declared in April 1788, "[w]e do not seek to provoke those revolutions that, led by force, can never bring about persuasion. We desire to follow the march of universal reason."[99] Strategic use of the prospect of a violent slave insurrection was a factor in this campaign, but not its central message. The Society had simply not been founded to call for the immediate end of the plantation economy, contrary to the accusations of proslavery apologists who so regularly and successfully conflated forecasts of a slave revolt with actual incitement to violence.[100]

The precautionary invocation of black rebellion was sounded with rather more credibility by representatives of the free colored community and even by some white planters: persons whose eyes and ears were closely attuned to the nuances of events on the ground in Saint-Domingue. The more politically astute of these individuals instinctively recognized that the traditional role of the *gens de couleur* in repressing slave resistance was a powerful complement to the Code Noir in the law-and-order theme of the movement for racial equality. Thus Raimond argued that free people of color were in a unique position to counteract the possibility of a black uprising. In a pamphlet dated May 12, 1791,

[95] Gauthier, *L'aristocratie de l'épiderme*, 23.

[96] Ibid., 68–69, 72–73, 74–75, 78; Dubois, *Avengers of the New World*, 83.

[97] Dorigny, "Le mouvement abolitionniste français," 101–104.

[98] Dorigny, "La Société des Amis des Noirs," in Dorigny and Gainot, *La Société des Amis des Noirs*, 38.

[99] Quoted in Dorigny, "Le mouvement abolitionniste français," 102.

[100] Ibid., 104; Dorigny, "La Société des Amis des Noirs," in Dorigny and Gainot, *La Société des Amis des Noirs*, 38; Gauthier, *L'aristocratie de l'épiderme*, 23.

defending the rights of the free people of color from Moreau de Saint-Méry's polemic against the Société des Amis des Noirs, Raimond wrote: "The slaves? Even though in a state of ignominy, we alone knew how to contain them."[101] Granting the demands of the free colored movement for equal citizenship was, if nothing else, a practical means of averting more widespread social unrest in the colony. Especially after the August 1791 slave revolt, this argument resonated among some in the western and southern provinces of Saint-Domingue (although it carried less weight in the northern part). Because *gens de couleur* had served for decades in the colonial *maréchaussée*, they were indeed seen in these regions as ideal recruits for fighting insurgents.[102] The Marquis de Rouvray, for example, a leading representative of the white planters, essentially adopted the Raimond argument for his own proslavery purposes: "Must one give in to the threats of an inferior cast, and admit it to the rights of the polity, as the price [to be paid] for the evils that it brings upon us?" asked de Rouvray. "Yes ... tactics (*la politique*) must silence the voice of resentment here," he replied.[103]

De Rouvray faced an uphill battle in defending this stance to the majority of his colleagues in the northern province. In Paris, however, the mix of legalistic and instrumental tacks in Raimond's strategy eventually carried the day. The violent crackdown on Ogé's rebellion also led to a decisive turn in metropolitan opinion in favor of the *gens de couleur* and away from the white planter lobby.[104] On May 15, 1791, three days after Raimond's critique of Moreau de Saint-Méry was published, the National Assembly voted to grant political rights to all "people of color born of free fathers and mothers."[105]

---

[101] Julien Raimond, *Réponse aux considérations de M. Moreau, dit de Saint-Méry, député à l'Assemblée nationale, sur les colonies* (Paris: L'Imprimerie du Patriote français, 1791), preface (unpaginated). See also Dubois, *Avengers of the New World*, 83; and Gauthier, *L'aristocratie de l'épiderme*, 300.

[102] Dubois, *Avengers of the New World*, 118.

[103] Pamphile de Lacroix, *Mémoires pour servir à l'histoire de la révolution de Saint-Domingue* (Paris: Pillet aîné, 1819), 128. See also Dubois, *Avengers of the New World*, 118.

[104] On the impact of Ogé's rebellion in France, particularly as mediated by Raimond's advocacy, see Garrigus, *Before Haiti*, 255–259; James, *The Black Jacobins*, 75–76; and Gauthier, *L'aristocratie de l'épiderme*, 199–210.

[105] The text of the decree is reprinted in Dubois and Garrigus, *Slave Emancipation in the Caribbean*, 84. See also Olivier Le Cour Grandmaison, *Les citoyennetés en Révolution (1789–1794)* (Paris: Presses Universitaires de France, 1992), 226–229; and Shanti Marie Singham, "Betwixt Cattle and Men: Jews, Blacks, and Women, and the Declaration of the Rights of Man," in Van Kley, *The French Idea of Freedom*, 134.

The May 15 decision was the culmination of several days of vehement debate prompted by a proposal from the four Assembly committees involved with colonial policy. That proposal, reported to the floor of the Assembly by Pascal-François Delattre, a deputy from the Somme in northern France, would have reconfirmed the March 1790 commitment to vest the colonies with the authority to determine the "status of persons" within their boundaries.[106] (The decree respecting free people of color initially took the form of a compromise amendment that the deputy Jean-François Rewbell offered to this proposal, which was considered by supporters of the *gens de couleur* to be an inflammatory and reactionary concession to the demands of the white planters.) In the course of this debate, the equal-rights provisions of the Code Noir were invoked as a set of background legal norms that compelled recognition of a preexisting state of affairs. The issue, Robespierre told the Assembly, was not whether to "accord political rights" to the free people of color, but rather whether to "conserve" rights they already enjoyed prior to the Revolution. "[T]he old laws" (*"les lois anciennes"*) had never been abrogated by any of the prior revolutionary legislation bearing on personal status in the colonies. (In October 1790, the National Assembly voted to disband the so-called Saint-Marc Assembly, a group of autonomist planters who had sought to defy the authority of the colonial administration in Saint-Domingue; they were exiled by ship to France for doing so. Robespierre's point was, in part, that this prior revolutionary-era measure had done nothing to change the status quo legislated by Louis XIV.)[107] Moreover, those same "old laws" vested free people of color with "the same rights as white colonists." It therefore followed that the *gens de couleur*, by the authority of the Code Noir rather than the good graces of the National Assembly, were equally entitled to the status of "active citizens" as all other free persons.[108]

[106] Pascal-François Delattre, *Rapport fait au nom des comités réunis de Constitution, de la Marine, d'Agriculture et de Commerce, & des Colonies, à la séance du 7 mai 1791, sur les colonies* (Paris: De l'Imprimerie nationale, 1791). See also Gauthier, *L'aristocratie de l'épiderme*, 280–281; and Popkin, *You Are All Free*, 36. The debates of May 12–15, 1791 have been reconstructed, most recently, in Piquet, *L'émancipation des Noirs*, 71–95; and Gauthier, *L'aristocratie de l'épiderme*, 277–307.

[107] For a concise summary of these earlier measures, see Moïse, *Dictionnaire historique de la Révolution Haïtienne*, 126–129.

[108] *Archives parlementaires de 1787 à 1860: Recueil complet des débats législatifs et politiques des chambres françaises*, Series 1 [hereafter *Archives parlementaires*] (Paris: Paul Dupont, 1887), 8: 7–8. In a May 12 speech, the deputy Jean-Denis Lanjuinais cited the Code Noir as the source of the "civil liberty" already enjoyed by the free people of color (quoted in Gauthier, *L'aristocratie de l'épiderme*, 291).

Lying in wait to respond, Moreau de Saint-Méry (then serving in Paris as a deputy to the Assembly from Martinique) intoned that the reform at issue would wreak "the greatest terrors" on the colonies.[109] Rather than help suppress a potential slave revolt, in other words, the granting of political rights to even a small subset of free people of color would bring about that very result. In making this argument, Moreau was eventually joined by the Abbé Maury and other sympathizers of the Club Massiac.[110]

On May 13, one day after this debate over the proposed extension of political rights to free persons of color, the National Assembly voted to accept the colonial committee's proposal to recommit the issue of slavery's status to the colonial assemblies. "[T]he legislature shall make no law on the status of unfree persons in the colonies except at the specific and unprompted request of the colonial assemblies," read the decree.[111] The same day witnessed Robespierre's famous speech in which he declared, "Perish the colonies rather than a principle!" – words first uttered by the physiocrat Dupont de Nemours and then restated by Robespierre in slightly different form.[112] On May 15, Robespierre resumed the line of argument he had commenced two days before, insisting that free people of color were not individuals whom the Assembly had "found deprived of liberty, but whom you have found free and whom you must maintain as free."[113]

In advocating for the May 15 decree, Robespierre did not strike an exclusively positive law note. His remarks also included appeals to "the most sacred rights of humanity" and the "precious and imprescriptible rights" that belonged to the freed persons of the colonies.[114] Yet the reliance on (unenforced) Old Regime legal standards was striking, and it was not limited to this most quintessential of Jacobin spokespersons. In explaining the reasons for its May 15 decree two weeks later, the National Assembly observed that "[e]ven under the Old Regime and under the most despotic of governments, the edict of 1685 had given the freedmen

---

[109] *Archives parlementaires*, 8:9.

[110] Ibid., 95–97.

[111] Quoted in Dubois and Garrigus, eds., *Slave Revolution in the Caribbean*, 84. See also the discussion of this decree in Moïse, *Dictionnaire historique de la Révolution Haïtienne*, 130. The substitution of the phrase "unfree persons" for slaves was the only concession that Robespierre could extract in the text of this constitutional measure. Popkin, *You Are All Free*, 37.

[112] Ardouin, *Études sur l'histoire d'Haïti*, 1:199 fn.1.

[113] *Archives parlementaires*, 8:94.

[114] Ibid.

all the rights that the other citizens enjoyed."[115] The strategic importance of the free people of color as a barrier against slave revolt remained a prominent theme throughout. The Assembly's May 29 *éxposé des motifs* thus underscored the need to erect a unified front among "all free citizens born of free parents … and to create the power best suited to resisting internal troubles."[116]

In practical terms, Rewbell's amendment enfranchised only a few hundred individuals. Yet the decree was enough to cause the colonial deputies to withdraw from the National Assembly in protest the next day. When news of the measure reached Saint-Domingue one month later, it was met with vigilant resistance on the part of the colonists to what they perceived as an act of unjustified interference in their domestic social order.[117] The governor announced that he would refuse to promulgate the new decree, setting off a civil war between whites and *gens de couleur* that proved utterly explosive and irreversible in its effects. For it was in the context of this civil war that the slave revolt of the night of August 22–23, 1791 began in the northern plains surrounding Cap Français.[118]

In the western province, well-armed free people of color, led by Louis-Jacques Beauvais and André Rigaud, were engaged in a tense conflict with white colonists over the interpretation of the May 15 decree. (In addition

---

[115] Quoted in Dubois and Garrigus, *Slave Revolution in the Caribbean*, 85.

[116] Quoted in Moïse, *Dictionnaire historique de la Révolution Haïtienne*, 132.

[117] David Geggus, "Racial Equality, Slavery, and Colonial Secession during the Constituent Assembly," *American Historical Review* 94, no. 5 (December 1989), 1296, 1303. May 15, 1791 also witnessed the Assembly's adoption by acclamation of a decree explicitly prohibiting metropolitan interference with the slave regime. Moreau de Saint-Méry was instrumental to the passage of this decree, which met with opposition from the Abbé Grégoire and also prompted Robespierre's famous "Perish the colonies!" intervention of May 14. See Geggus, "Racial Equality, Slavery, and Colonial Secession," 1296; Davis, *The Problem of Slavery in the Age of Revolution*, 143; and Blackburn, *The Overthrow of Colonial Slavery*, 188. That two such contrasting decrees could be passed in tandem highlights the contradictory influences weighing on metropolitan policy at this time. But the legislation of May 15, 1791 also suggests the possibility of a *quid pro quo* between defenders and opponents of the white colonists. For the text of the noninterference decree and the remarks of Moreau de Saint-Méry and the Abbé Grégoire, see *Archives Parlementaires*, 25:638–743. For the celebrated remarks of Robespierre, see *Archives Parlementaires*, 26:60. As numerous scholars have pointed out, the latter's intervention as a whole was considerably more moderate and pragmatic about colonial affairs than its legendary reputation would suggest. See, *inter alia*, Debien, *Les colons de Saint-Domingue et la Révolution*, 286.

[118] Geggus, *Haitian Revolutionary Studies*, 11. See also Fick, *The Making of Haiti*, 91–105; Blackburn, *The Overthrow of Colonial Slavery*, 191–193; and Hurbon, *L'insurrection des esclaves de Saint-Domingue*.

to the urban coastal centers of Port-au-Prince, Léogane, Saint Marc, and Petit Goâve, the western province included the many medium-sized coffee plantations located along the mountainous interior regions that rose above these towns. Some two thousand such plantations, owned mostly by free people of color, were situated in the western and southern provinces combined.[119] Sugar production in the west was limited to the smaller plains around Port-au-Prince, the Artibonite valley, and a plain known as the Cul-de-Sac that surrounded the village of Croix-des-Bouquets.[120] The coffee farms of the southern peninsula were diversified mostly by indigo production.) The *gens de couleur* in this area used the August 1791 revolt to form a confederation with a group of insurgent slaves who came to be known as the "Swiss." The military example set by these "Confederates" was considered alarming enough to inspire some hastily organized strategic compacts that cut across racial lines. Thus, on September 7, 1791, a colonist named Hanus de Jumecourt cobbled together an alliance between the activist free people of color and the administrators of the western provincial towns of Croix-des-Bouquets and Mirabalais, based on a promise to enforce the May 15 decree.[121]

At the urging of the white planters of Croix-des-Bouquets, who were more moderate and conciliatory in their politics than their largely autonomist counterparts in Port-au-Prince, a similar agreement soon followed between the white colonists and *gens de couleur* of the capital.[122] (Planters and administrators in the even-more recalcitrant southern province would also attempt to follow this pattern, although with less impact than their western counterparts.)[123] The free colored planter Pierre Pinchinat took the leading role in producing the Port-au-Prince concordat, dated September 11, 1791.[124] That document testified to the strength of white anxieties about the pivotal role that free people of color could play in either containing or promoting the prospect of an all-out slave revolt, which by then had fully overtaken the plantations of the northern plain.[125] The purpose of the agreement, the two sides declared, was to

[119] Blackburn, *The Overthrow of Colonial Slavery*, 168.

[120] Popkin, *You Are All Free*, 39.

[121] Ardouin, *Études sur l'histoire d'Haïti*, 1:208–209; Bell, *Toussaint Louverture*, 31; Dubois, *Avengers of the New World*, 119–120.

[122] Ardouin, *Études sur l'histoire d'Haïti*, 1:209–210.

[123] Ibid., 1:213; Dubois, *Avengers of the New World*, 119–120; Geggus, *Haitian Revolutionary Studies*, 13; Bell, *Toussaint Louverture*, 31–32.

[124] Ardouin, *Études sur l'histoire d'Haïti*, 1:211.

[125] Ibid., 1:210.

"stop the progress and the consequences of an insurrection that threatens equally all parts of the colony."[126]

Notwithstanding the potential for all-out warfare that the events in the north threatened, however, the Port-au-Prince concordat also reflected the continuing determination of the *gens de couleur* to consolidate their place in the new political order by invoking the still unfinished business of the Code Noir. The "citizens of color" opened their statement of demands by noting that "the law made in their favor in 1685 had been scorned and violated by the advance of a ridiculous prejudice, and by the abusive practices and ministerial despotism of the Old Regime."[127] As a result, free people of color had been able to enjoy only "very imperfectly" the benefits bestowed on them by the equal-rights provisions of the Code Noir.[128] On its face, the reference to the "ministerial despotism" of the Old Regime suggests that these *gens de couleur* saw themselves in much the same terms that white slaveholders had conventionally used to describe the effects of the fiscal, commercial, and plantation-management policies of colonial administrators. In the context of 1791, the phrase had the clear purpose of castigating the perpetrators of racially discriminatory legislation that prevented the free people of color from enjoying their long-standing rights as equal subjects of the absolute monarchy.

The purpose of their lobbying before the National Assembly, the *gens de couleur* explained, had been to seek the "recognition" of those preexisting rights, "for so long misunderstood, but no less sacred for that."[129] The effect of the decree of May 15, 1791, among other measures, was to bring about just this "recognition." By flouting their responsibilities under the recent decrees, the white planters and their allies in the colonial administration had become the party of lawlessness. The "punctual and literal execution of all articles of the decrees and instructions of the National Assembly sanctioned by the king is alone capable of achieving [the] desirable reunion" of the "citizens of all classes."[130]

The formal "reunion" of free people of color and whites did not eliminate the animosities that existed between these two groups. However, at least temporarily, it permitted the suppression of armed hostilities between the two groups and proved successful at containing the spread

---

[126] *Concordat de MM. les citoyens blancs de Port-au-Prince avec MM. les citoyens de couleur* (N.p.: n.p., 1791), 1.
[127] Ibid., 1–2.
[128] Ibid., 2.
[129] Ibid., 2.
[130] Ibid., 10–11. See also Dubois, *Avengers of the New World*, 120.

of the slave revolt to the western and southern provinces.[131] In the north, meanwhile, where a colonial tradition of free black and free colored military experience was strongest, most *gens de couleur* had initially fought against the insurgent slaves. (The exceptions were those who came from the parishes of Ogé and Chavannes, whose execution the *gens de couleur* of Port-au-Prince had singled out as the "fatal cause of all the misfortunes that now afflict the northern province.")[132]

The situation changed everywhere when the National Assembly, on September 24, 1791, reversed course and voted to withdraw the May 15 measure. A delegation consisting of Edmond de Saint-Léger, Frédéric Ignace de Mirbeck, and Philippe Roume de Saint-Laurent – the first of three civil commissions eventually sent by revolutionary France to Saint-Domingue – was sent to deliver the new decree and to announce a general amnesty for "acts of revolution." This was shortly before news of the August 1791 slave revolt had begun to reach France, so the change of course could not have been intended as an adaptation to the events of August 22–23. Whatever the National Assembly may have been attempting to achieve by this decision to commit the rights of free people of color to the colony's "internal" regime, the decision upset the tenuous political settlements achieved in key zones between *gens de couleur* and whites. Free coloreds in the north began to fight alongside the slave rebels, and in all three regions of the colony, conflict between whites and *gens de couleur* intensified, thereby inducing the opportunistic arming of slaves by all sides.[133] (Already in August, the free colored leaders of the Port-au-Prince area had begun to include slaves in their fighting units.)[134] When the civil commissioners arrived in Saint-Domingue in late November, their efforts to give effect to the September 24 decree were overshadowed by the unfolding chaos and jurisdictional conflicts.[135]

The use of both free coloreds and slaves to contain the conflicts ignited by the August 1791 insurgency built on the precedent set by the militarization of manumission in late colonial Saint-Domingue. As Laurent Dubois writes, "service in the [French Caribbean] republican army was in

[131] Ardouin, *Études sur l'histoire d'Haïti*, 1:212.
[132] *Concordat de MM. les citoyens blancs*, 8; Geggus, *Haitian Revolutionary Studies*, 13. On the strength of the free colored/free black military tradition in the north, see King, *Blue Coat or Powdered Wig*; and Garrigus, "Saint-Domingue's Free People of Color and the Tools of Revolution," 56–58.
[133] Geggus, *Haitian Revolutionary Studies*, 13.
[134] Ardouin, *Études sur l'histoire d'Haïti*, 1:209–212.
[135] Bell, *Toussaint Louverture*, 32.

many ways the continuation of pre-revolutionary service in militias and the *maréchaussée*."[136] As discussed in Chapter 2, the overriding purpose of the *maréchaussée* was to apprehend fugitive slaves (a task that, by its violent and confrontational nature, merged quite often into the process of punishment, which the Code Noir purported to legislate in detail). Commanded by whites, the *maréchaussée* units were traditionally staffed by poor free people of color, although some *gens de couleur* came also to serve in leadership positions as both cavaliers (mounted patrolmen) and brigadiers. Beginning in 1775, as we have seen, the colony began permitting slaves to win their liberty through ten years of service in the *maréchaussée*, which simultaneously opened up a new avenue of manumission and sharply reduced the incentives for free people of color to support the slave-hunting brigades.[137] Separate from the *maréchaussée*, free colored militia units provided an alternative – and relatively more prestigious – means of advancement: Their job was the defense of the colony from foreign invasion, although neither the *maréchaussée* nor the militia was a source of patriotic pride for *gens de couleur* in the southern province.[138] Historians dispute the legacy of the colonial *maréchaussée* and militia units as precedents for the arming of slaves during the revolutionary period.[139] Whatever the relationship between these specific developments may have been, however, it is clear that by the winter and spring of 1791–1792, metropolitan legislators fully appreciated what colonial administrators had internalized in prior years: the close connection between the rights of freed persons and the containment of slave resistance.

Jacques-Pierre Brissot de Warville, who cofounded the Société des Amis des Noirs with the financier and onetime Genevan banker Etienne Clavière, is a case in point. A journalist with strong ties to the British abolitionist community who represented the city of Paris in the French assembly (reconvened as the Legislative Assembly on October 1, 1791 following the dissolution of the National Assembly), Brissot was perhaps the most outspoken and

---

[136] Dubois, "Citizen Soldiers," 235.

[137] Garrigus, *Before Haiti*, 201. See Chapter 2.

[138] Garrigus, *Before Haiti*, 85.

[139] See Geggus, "The Arming of Slaves in the Haitian Revolution," 211. Geggus agrees with Dubois that, as a result of the enlistment of slaves in the colonial *maréchaussée*, armed blacks were an increasing presence in Saint-Domingue and other French Caribbean colonies, but he expresses skepticism that the *maréchaussée* set an important precedent for the use of slave soldiers to combat the Saint-Domingue slave revolt during the 1790s.

well-known French abolitionist at this time.[140] His embrace of the strategic
case for fully enfranchising free blacks and people of color reveals the decisive impact of local developments in Saint-Domingue on the agenda of the
abolitionist movement in Paris. In a December 1791 speech to the Legislative
Assembly on the "causes of the troubles of Saint-Domingue" – the news of
the August 1791 slave revolt had arrived in Paris some two months earlier –
Brissot argued that a plantation colony required "numerous and faithful
guardians to prevent [slave] revolts, and the men of color are, in the nature
of things, the only defenders against revolts."[141] Several months later, in
March 1792, Brissot delivered another address to the Legislative Assembly,
in which he elaborated at length on the "political necessity of revoking the
decree of September 24, 1791, in order to put an end to the troubles of
Saint-Domingue."[142] In this speech, Brissot intoned that the "civil war in
Saint-Domingue has given way to the war of the slaves, or rather three
kinds of war are currently tearing apart this unfortunate island: a war of
blacks against whites, a war of mulattos against whites, and a war of whites
amongst themselves." All three of these conflicts, Brissot stated, were attrib-
utable at their source to a single cause, namely, the "injustice committed
towards the people of color."[143]

Justice and stability were joined at the hip in this prognosis, but it was
not essentially a moral case that Brissot was making. "I do not speak here
of justice and principles," he declared to the revolutionary legislators; "I
appeal simply to your interests and those of the colonies."[144] The recognition of free colored rights was the "only remedy" to "all of the evils"
then afflicting Saint-Domingue, because only the *gens de couleur* and
affranchis could play the necessary mediating role upon which the colony's peace rested: "People of color and free blacks are far more numerous than whites; they form nearly two thirds of the free population of
Saint-Domingue; they reproduce more quickly than whites; ... [and] they

---

[140] There is a large literature on Brissot. In addition to the various studies by Robert
Darnton, see Dorigny and Gainot, *La Société des Amis des Noirs*, 21–26, 296–298;
Bénot, *La Révolution française et la fin des colonies*; and Popkin, *You Are All Free*,
passim.

[141] Jacques-Pierre Brissot, *Discours de J.P. Brissot, député, sur les causes des troubles de
Saint-Domingue, prononcé à la séance du premier décembre 1791* (Paris: Imprimerie
nationale, 1791), 59, also quoted in Popkin, *You Are All Free*, 46.

[142] Jacques-Pierre Brissot, *Discours sur la nécessité politique de révoquer le décret du 24
septembre 1791, pour mettre fin aux troubles de Saint-Domingue* (Paris: L'Imprimerie
du Patriote Français, 1791), 1.

[143] Ibid., 1.

[144] Ibid., 33.

make it less necessary for troops to defend the island." "Feared by the blacks," the free coloreds were also "the best guardians of them."[145] The Legislative Assembly had only to render these guardians their rights, and "all these terrors [affecting the colony] would disappear."[146] By this time, of course, the slave revolt that colonial administrators and pre-revolutionary antislavery writers such as Raynal and Mercier had long anticipated was well under way. Consistent with the mission statement of the Société des Amis des Noirs, Brissot had no need to invoke the futuristic prospect of a black rebellion in order to paint a persuasive picture of the role of racial equality in the maintenance of empire.

Brissot's speech was followed, one month later, by a decree of April 4, 1792, declaring a state of emergency in Saint-Domingue and granting full political rights for all free persons in the colony, regardless of the status of their parents. In its very title, the decree announced that it was a response to the breakdown in social order that Brissot had associated with the September 24 measure: "Law concerning the colonies and the means of appeasing the troubles there."[147] The "germs of discord" that had developed in Saint-Domingue had brought about the "danger of a total subversion," the decree began. "Only the reunited efforts of citizens could preserve their properties from the horrors of pillage and fire."[148] The Legislative Assembly therefore saw fit to "recognize and declare that free people of color and free blacks must enjoy, along with the white colonists, equality of political rights."[149]

For all of its transparently pragmatic self-presentation, the new measure was also accompanied by a very Jacobin anxiety about "conspiratorial" plots against the French nation unfolding on both sides of the hemisphere. The first use of the guillotine and the declaration of war with Austria were only days away, and in the months and years ahead talk of international designs on the liberties of the French nation would prove to be one of the animating forces of revolutionary ideology. In the colonial context, the rhetoric of conspiracy had itself a long history, going back at least to the days of Macandal's 1757 revolt. Yet in the April 4 decree, the Legislative Assembly had made clear that the Saint-Domingue planters – many of whom had already fled as *émigrés* from the revolution to

---

[145] Ibid.
[146] Ibid., 34.
[147] *Loi rélative aux colonies, & aux moyens d'y appaiser les troubles* (Paris: L'Imprimerie Royale, 1792). See also Dubois, *Avengers of the New World*, 130.
[148] *Loi rélative aux colonies*, 1–2.
[149] Ibid., 2.

the United States and other safe harbors of the Atlantic world – were themselves a target of newfound revolutionary suspicion. "[C]itizens having properties in the American colonies" – a category that included many free people of color as well as whites – were barred from serving on the delegation to be selected to enforce the new decree in the colonies.[150]

In a sense, the decree of April 4 can be seen as the endpoint of the long road traveled by articles 57 and 59 of the Code Noir since 1685: the revolutionary fulfillment of a long forgotten royal promise. Thenceforth, the prudential tacks of militarized citizenship for freed persons and the restraint of planter brutality would operate in tandem. And the Code Noir would continue to follow them on their newly joined path.

Thus, when a second civil commission consisting of Léger-Félicité Sonthonax, Etienne Polverel, and Jean Antoine Ailhaud arrived in Saint-Domingue on September 18, 1792, to enforce the new regime of full political equality, it met with the staunch opposition of the white planter community. These delegates would very quickly begin to ally themselves with the free people of color and against the white planters.[151] Pierre François Page and Augustin Jean Brulley, white planters from la Grande Rivière-d'Ennery in the northern province, would eventually denounce Sonthonax and Polverel before the metropolitan legislature in the summer of 1793. As representatives of the white colonists, they charged the commissioners with renewing the tradition of "ministerial despotism" and promoting the political aspirations of the free colored community pursuant to a distorted interpretation of the Code Noir.[152] Although the 1685 edict may have given free blacks and people of color "an active part in the government," said Page and Brulley, it likely did more to oppress than to liberate the freed person. The Code Noir summoned free blacks and people of color to serve in the militia companies, according to Page and Brulley, but mandated that those companies be kept separate from the white militias. Further, freed persons could be reenslaved under the 1685 law for committing the "least offense."[153]

Neither such rule can be found in the 1685 Code Noir. It is difficult to tell whether this discussion reflects simple ignorance of the text or a broad understanding of the Code to include subsequent eighteenth-century regulations. Page and Brulley were not about to trouble themselves with

---

[150] Ibid., 6.
[151] Dubois, *Avengers of the New World*, 144–147.
[152] Pierre François Page and Augustin Jean Brulley, *Développement des causes des troubles et désastres des colonies françaises* (N.p.: n.p., 1793).
[153] Ibid., 105–106.

such considerations, however. For they went on to make clear that whatever the Code Noir may have said to induce hopes of equal citizenship for the *affranchi*, the reality was that free blacks and people of color had never been accorded an "active part in the government" during the colonial period.[154]

On this last point, at least, Page and Brulley were hardly wrong. Particularly in the period following the Seven Years' War, the gains that free people of color had managed to secure through the institutions and processes of manumission in Saint-Domingue met with a powerful backlash. It is nonetheless something of a curious irony to see these two leading voices of the white planter reaction highlighting the regressive aspects of French colonial law, while their prominent free colored counterparts pushed in just the opposite direction, evoking an optimistic (albeit facially conservative) vision of the same regime that Page and Brulley described as oppressive. Several years into the French and Haitian Revolutions, the legal politics of the Code Noir had morphed into an especially peculiar form of ideological contestation, pointing backward when one would have expected a turn to the future, and implicitly condemning the status quo ante when a robust defense of it might have seemed the order of the day. The insurgency of the slaves, and the long struggle for emancipation that followed, would only add to these apparent incongruities, stretching the limits of the Code Noir until the point at which the contradictions between the Old and New Regimes could finally no longer be resolved through the medium of law.

[154] Ibid., 106.

6

To Restore Order and Tranquility

The granting of full political equality to the *gens de couleur* and the arrival of a new civil commission, consisting of Sonthonax, Polverel, and Ailhaud, marked the end of the first stage of the Haitian Revolution.[1] The next stage would feature the emancipation of the slaves of Saint-Domingue in 1793 and 1794. Running through both of these developments was the profound impact of the August 1791 slave revolt. Accordingly, this chapter begins with a discussion of the role of law in the political culture of the insurgency during its formative stage, from late 1791 to the middle of 1792 (prior to the arrival of Sonthonax and Polverel in September 1792). The second part of the chapter turns to the proclamations of Sonthonax and Polverel in 1793, which paved the way for the National Convention's decision to abolish slavery in all of the French colonies in February 1794.

As a republican government took shape in Paris and sought to extend its power into the colonies in connection with the struggle over racial equality, the republic would assume an initially hostile stance toward the slave insurgency. In short order, that hostility gave way to a stance of pragmatic accommodation, as the policies of revolutionary administrators, originating in the metropole, devolved into the same search for local stability that had underwritten the gains of free blacks and people of color in April 1792. Two of the principal leaders of the insurgency in the north, Jean-François Papillon and Georges Biassou, were critical players in the pursuit of an arrangement that would meet the needs of revolutionary administrators and insurgent slaves somewhere in between the

[1] See Dubois, *Avengers of the New World*, 137–138.

255

poles of their respective positions. Their stance evolved over time, but in the course of articulating it, Jean-François and Biassou invoked notions of legality and legitimacy that derived from another complicated mixture of Old Regime and revolutionary standards: a different fusion of the Code Noir and the Declaration of the Rights of Man. Past experiences of planter brutality and visions of future racial equality mixed uncomfortably in the documents that testify to these negotiations. Although the available evidence is extremely limited, it appears that Jean-François and Biassou drew on both of these images in response to the pressures placed on them by their followers in the insurgent camps. The slave insurgency, or at least that part of it led by Jean-François and Biassou, worked its way forward by means of law as well as violence, uncertain of its final destination but resolute in insisting that the days of the radical abuse of slaves were over in Saint-Domingue. This was, to be sure, a vernacular and informal understanding of law, but one that was marked by unmistakable traces of the legal baggage of the Old Regime, especially the protective provisions of the Code Noir.

As for Sonthonax and Polverel, it has become conventional for historians of the Haitian Revolution to identify the decisions of 1793–1794 with something that they call "the abolition of slavery." Examples include such titles as *Léger-Félicité Sonthonax: The First Abolition of Slavery* and *The Emancipation of Blacks in the French Revolution, 1789–1795*, or Jeremy Popkin's recent book on the impact of the *journée* of June 20, 1793: *You Are All Free: The Haitian Revolution and the Abolition of Slavery*.[2] On that June day, Sonthonax and Polverel first extended an offer of emancipation to slaves in the area of Cap Français who agreed to assist in suppressing a rebellion of white sailors led by the republican governor François-Thomas Galbaud du Fort. This was, we intuitively sense (and Popkin persuasively demonstrates), a momentous span of days and months, when the ultimate fate of slavery in Saint-Domingue, and elsewhere in the Atlantic world, was decided. There is much truth to the identification of 1793–1794 with the end of slavery. Slavery was indeed abolished in Saint-Domingue in this period, first by a series of local proclamations issued by the civil commissioners on colonial territory, and then by the National Convention's ratification of those local edicts in Paris in February 1794.

---

[2] Dorigny, *Léger-Félicité Sonthonax: La première abolition de l'esclavage*; and Piquet, *L'émancipation des noirs*. I mean to cite these books only as examples; in their respective understandings of the events of 1793–1794, they differ with one another.

However, the actual processes of abolition – the details of the arrangements by which it was put into effect – were a far more ambiguous and conflicted phenomenon than is suggested by the teleological notion of the "abolition of slavery." It is not simply that the events at issue were highly contingent moments, like so many forks in the road. For that is, arguably, the nature of all historical change. Although tremendously important contributions to modern notions of human rights, the decisions of 1793–1794 were also continuations of the regulatory dynamics of the law of slavery: part of a long-term transformation in the regime of the Code Noir.

THE CODE NOIR OF THE SLAVES

In thinking about the slave insurgents' understanding of the Code Noir, the first note that must be struck is one of caution and uncertainty. The first and second civil commissions consisted of three persons each, whose instructions and views on the question of slavery can be ascertained with more or less confidence based on the written record. The insurgents, by contrast, were a massive group that potentially encompassed the colony's entire slave population of roughly 465,000. To be sure, their leaders – or, at least, the individuals who purported to speak for the masses of slave insurgents in the northern province – comprised a delimited and relatively identifiable circle of individuals. This consisted, in the revolt's early stages, of Biassou, Jean-François, Jeannot Bullet (executed by Jean-François on November 1, 1791), and Boukman Dutty (who was killed in the opening months of the revolt).[3] They were joined somewhat later (the precise moment is still unclear) by the elusive and agile Toussaint Louverture, who would ultimately rise to a position of general leadership over the insurgency. In the western province, which remained relatively untouched by the slave revolt until early 1792, a young slave named Hyacinthe assumed initial leadership of the insurgents. (The west was also home to an important free colored army that answered to a planter named Pierre Pinchinat.) In the south, a group of slave insurgents who styled themselves the "kingdom of the Platons" organized under the leadership of two blacks named Armand and Martial. In late 1791, the free

[3] On the early deaths of Jeannot and Boukman, see Yves Benot, "The Insurgents of 1791, Their Leaders, and the Concept of Independence," in Geggus and Fiering, *The World of the Haitian Revolution*, 107–108; and Dubois and Garrigus, *Slave Emancipation in the Caribbean*, 104–106.

colored Romaine la Rivière, who hailed from the Spanish side of the island, set himself up at the head of a mixed group of slaves and *gens de couleur* in the mountains above Léogane.[4] A fourth leader named Jean Kina attracted the allegiance of several hundred slaves who remained loyal to the white colonists of the south and later (in 1793) joined the British cause.[5] The influence of these southern factions on the course of events was generally overshadowed by that of free colored forces under the leadership of the redoubtable Louis-Jacques Bauvais and André Rigaud, the latter of whom became Louverture's principal rival for control of the colony in the late 1790s.

Nearly all of the documents upon which historians have relied to depict the ideologies of the slave insurgents in 1791 and the years thereafter were signed by one or more of these individuals (and apparently penned, as often as not, by white or free colored personal secretaries taking dictation).[6] These leaders, both slave and free colored, did not necessarily speak for the entire universe of persons who purportedly comprised their respective constituencies in Saint-Domingue. To begin with, the forces they oversaw were only subsets of the slave population, and not necessarily large subsets at that. Hyacinthe's army in the western province, for example, was ten to fifteen thousand strong as of the spring of 1792.[7] This was a significant fighting force at the time, to be sure, but nothing close to the size of the total slave population of the western and southern provinces (which was more than half of the colony's overall slave population of 465,000). Moreover, within the armed groups themselves, there is evidence of disagreement over the tactics and policies pursued by their leaders. Jean-François and Biassou, for example, were challenged by their supporters over the legitimacy of an offer to lay down the northern insurgents' arms in exchange for the emancipation of some fifty insurgent notables (an episode discussed in greater detail later).[8] If these disagreements did not rise to the level of an outright conflict of interest, they nonetheless speak to fissures within and between subcultures of the slave insurgency that belie efforts to generalize about the movement as a whole.[9]

[4] See Fick, *The Making of Haiti*, 137–156; Moïse, *Dictionnaire historique de la Révolution Haïtienne*, 285; Dubois, *Avengers of the New World*, 108.
[5] On Kina, see Geggus, *Haitian Revolutionary Studies*, 137–151.
[6] Geggus, "Print Culture and the Haitian Revolution," 83, 88–89, 95.
[7] Dubois, *Avengers of the New World*, 136.
[8] Ibid., 126–128; Popkin, *You are All Free*, 48; Geggus, *Haitian Revolutionary Studies*, 13.
[9] Cf. Geggus, "Print Culture and the Haitian Revolution," 91–93.

Entire interpretations about the subsequent instability and divisiveness of post-revolutionary Haitian society have been erected on the foundation of these and similar considerations. It is not my purpose to participate in that debate.[10] Rather, the point is simply to underscore the difficulty of engaging in meaningful generalizations about the slave insurgents' own understandings of the purposes and nature of their uprising, as well as their perceptions of Old Regime institutions such as the Code Noir.

With these evidentiary and interpretive limitations in mind, I want to suggest a provisional outline of certain strands of thought that may have informed the political culture of the insurgents between August 1791 and the abolition of slavery in 1793. This outline is based on some of the most recent findings of Haitian revolutionary scholarship and on a small number of primary sources that seem to represent the demands and views of at least some slave insurgents in the northern province. To the extent that these sources reflect simply the views of a few insurgent leaders in a particularly circumscribed area of the colony, my analysis in these pages may not have any larger implications for something that we can call the "political culture" of the Haitian Revolution. Indeed, depending on the authenticity of the documents at issue, it may well be that their teachings have even less to offer us.[11] This does not necessarily place us in territory radically different from other aspects of the Haitian Revolution for which the documentary record is far richer, or from the study of any other historical event, for that matter.[12] Yet it does rule out the possibility of such confident pronouncements as the following: The insurgents' "intent was to achieve some kind of negotiated settlement with the white world that would improve their situation, not to try to isolate themselves and the island altogether."[13] Perhaps negotiation was indeed their intent.

---

[10] See, for example, Trouillot, *Silencing the Past*, 37–40, 66–69 (emphasizing the divisions between creole and bossale slave revolutionary forces in 1802–1803); idem, *Haiti: State against Nation*, 43–45; Fatton, *The Roots of Haitian Despotism*, 49–55. Cf. Nicholls, *From Dessalines to Duvalier* (emphasizing divisions between black and mulatto ideologists in Haiti going back to the colonial and revolutionary periods).

[11] See Geggus, "Print Culture and the Haitian Revolution," 88–92. See also Popkin, *You Are All Free*, 17–18 n.26.

[12] As Simon Schama has written, "if in the end we must be satisfied with nothing more than broken lines of communication to the past ... that perhaps is still enough to be going on with." Simon Schama, *Dead Certainties (Unwarranted Speculations)* (New York: Alfred Knopf, 1991), 326.

[13] Popkin, *You Are All Free*, 17. Popkin goes on to cite to a first-person account describing the slave insurgents of 1791 in nearly opposite terms, as seeking to achieve complete domination over the whites. Ibid., 46–47. Other historians of the revolution have opined on the insurgencies' "original intent" in the same style of omniscient narration that is

Just as plausibly, they may have had neither of these mutually exclusive categories – compromise or isolation – in mind. Did certain subgroups or regions within the insurgency favor one approach and others a different tack?[14] We simply cannot be certain about any of these points, and it is a reassuring myth to pretend otherwise.

My own interpretive voice plays a more significant role in describing the worldview of certain circles within the slave insurgency than it does in portraying, for example, the mindset of Sonthonax or Julien Raimond, who left behind voluminous written traces of their understanding of events. Yet silence or confessions of indeterminacy on a subject matter as important as the insurgents' own understanding of the world of the law to which they and their ancestors had long been subject are poor substitutes for omniscient narration. Part of the interpretation that follows rests on the assumption that, at least in certain areas of the colony, slaves did in fact have knowledge of the Code Noir and of the political and legal debates it had spawned over the course of the eighteenth century. Because the legacy of colonial-era battles over planter brutality is important to this interpretation, let us return for a moment to the pre-revolutionary period.

A review of the early history of the Code Noir's circulation reveals an effort by the colonial judiciary to publicize the provisions of the monarchy's edict in the face of seemingly widespread settler indifference. In 1688, the Conseil Souverain of Petit Goâve (the predecessor of the Port-au-Prince tribunal) found that the registration and publication of Louis XIV's edict in the high courts had failed to prevent violations by "several persons" (the specific violations and individuals at issue were left anonymous). Citing the court's failure to publish the Code at the parish level, these individuals, whether through "malice or ignorance," had evidently pleaded lack of knowledge of the law in their defense. The Sovereign Council responded by ordering that the edict be posted on the doors of all parish churches and read throughout the colony at the rise of Sunday mass.[15] This early testament to the difficulty of enforcing

---

traditional in narrative history. See, for example, Bell, *Toussaint Louverture*, 36–42. On the omniscient tone of voice and the historiography of slavery, see Brown, *The Reaper's Garden*, 10.

[14] See Benot, "The Insurgents of 1791," 108. Benot suggests here that Jeannot, Boukman, and a third leader named Paul (Bélin) belonged to a more radical wing of the insurgency, whereas Jean-François and Biassou comprised a more moderate faction.

[15] "Arrêt du Conseil du Petit-Goâve," Sept. 29, 1688, LC, 1:476.

the Code Noir was a preview of many later struggles over the balance of power between masters and judges in Saint-Domingue. However, it also suggested that planters' very indifference to the Code generated a form of judicial-administrative resistance that served to publicize knowledge about the law of slavery.

The question, of course, is just how far this publicity extended, and whether it specifically encompassed the Code's protective provisions. Prior to the 1788 Maguero and Lejeune cases discussed in Chapter 4, a mere handful of cases actually resulted in the prosecution of masters for the brutalization or murder of their slaves pursuant to articles 26, 42, and 43 of the Code Noir. Two of these cases transpired in 1724 and 1726.[16] In the 1730s and 1740s, a number of domestic slaves from Saint-Domingue, brought by their masters to France, sued in French courts for their freedom on the basis of the doctrine that slavery had long since been abolished on metropolitan soil. Some of these cases originated in claims of physical abuse, including the most well-known freedom lawsuit of the eighteenth century: that of Jean Boucaux. Arrested before he could escape from his master, Boucaux succeeded in having his case heard by the Parlement of Paris in 1738, to much publicity. Another such case, involving a slave named Catherine ("Catin") Morgan who succeeded in escaping from her owner, was tried in Nantes in 1747.[17] Although these cases may well speak more to metropolitan than colonial legal politics, they were followed with great interest in Saint-Domingue.

The next significant example of slave invocations of the protective regimen of the Code Noir involves a pair of interlocking matters dating back to the early 1770s. At that time, a trial judge investigating the atrocities of a planter named Dessources found that he could not proceed to impose the letter of the Code Noir in light of an intervening Conseil Supérieur ruling that refused to permit punishment of a master for the torture and mutilation of his slaves. Instead, the magistrates in the Dessources case settled for an order returning the defendant's slaves to him on the condition that the death or sale of any of them would trigger further proceedings.[18]

---

[16] "Arrêt du Conseil du Petit Goâve," January 3, 1724, ANOM, F/3/90, fols. 123–125 (convicting a master of burning the feet and legs of a female slave who died from the wounds; the punishment included a fine and three months' imprisonment); "Arrêt du Conseil de Léogane," September 2, 1726, ANOM, F/3/90, f. 187 (condemning a slave driver to three years of galley labor for killing a slave "in a fit of anger").

[17] Johnson, "The Reinvention of Slavery in France," 98, 266, 279.

[18] See Chapter 4.

In March 1780, a colonist was sentenced to corporal punishment and lifetime galley service for "coldly and unnecessarily" slitting the throats of two fugitive slaves arrested by him.[19]

The earliest of these cases would have been distant memories by 1789. The proceedings of the 1770s were relatively high-profile matters and may well have engendered significant discussion outside of the immediate legal and plantation circles involved. The lifetime sentence of a colonist for the murder of two fugitive slaves in 1780 was an extraordinary event for any year. Yet our understanding of how these prior events may have reverberated in the broader political culture of Saint-Domingue is necessarily limited by the sparseness of the legal and other documentation that evidences them.

By contrast, there is good reason to believe that, in the ten years just prior to the Revolution, knowledge about the protective provisions of the Code did indeed circulate among at least certain parts of the slave community. The monarchy's controversial plantation-management reforms of 1784–1785, which aimed to reinvigorate and amplify the Code's rules regarding the punishment and abuse of slaves, reflected and incorporated the same administrative anxiety about publicity that had attended the Code from its very beginning. The new ordinances required that they be "read, published, and posted everywhere it is needed."[20] Although the Conseil Supérieur in Cap Français refused to register the 1784 ordinance (at the cost of finding itself suspended and merged with the high court in Port-au-Prince), the colonists' vehement protests were themselves a very effective form of advertisement for the new regulatory regime. As with prior administrative and judicial efforts to bring the Code Noir to bear on the ground in Saint-Domingue, the issue is not whether the new laws were actually enforced – the answer to that question is generally no – but rather what message they communicated. Insofar as the ordinances communicated a royal judgment that the planters and their representatives had exceeded the proper limits of their authority over slaves, that message managed to reach the slave community in at least some form. As David Geggus has discovered, the controversy over the plantation-management

---

[19] "Arrêt du Conseil du Port-au-Prince," March 11, 1780, ANOM, F/3/90, f. 51. This punishment was in derogation of a 1673 ordinance that freed whites in the French islands from liability for killing fugitive slaves: "Ordonnance du Gouverneur-Général des Isles," August 28, 1673, LC, 1:268–269.

[20] "Ordonnance du Roi," Dec. 3, 1784, LC, 6:667; "Ordonnance du Roi," Dec. 23, 1785, LC, 6:928. The phrase appeared at the end of both ordinances, except that in the 1785 ordinance, a requirement of registration by the high courts was added.

reforms prompted a wave of strike action by slaves.[21] Thus, we have at least some direct evidence that the protective regimen of the Code Noir – as modified in 1784–1785 – became associated with a tradition of slave protest against the conditions of their forced labor.

But how exactly might this tradition have developed? What were its channels of communication and influence? Where in the colony was it most likely to have taken shape? And what messages were conveyed by that tradition? These are difficult questions to answer, but the prosecution of Nicolas Lejeune in 1788 is probably an important part of the answer to all of them. The Lejeune affair arrived as a jolt to the colonists' and administrators' sense of self, and was consciously litigated in the courts as a *cause célèbre*. It witnessed exceptional forms and levels of involvement by slave complainants who were willing to take the risk of seeking to enforce the dispensations of article 26. And it occurred, not years or decades, but mere months before the beginning of the French Revolution.

It is possible, but highly unlikely, that Lejeune's prosecution would have entirely escaped the attention of wider segments of the urban slave communities in Cap Français and Port-au-Prince. After 1772, both the Conseil Supérieur and *sénéchaussée* of Cap Français were located in Government House, near the corner of the rue du Conseil and the rue du Gouvernement. Beginning in January 1787, when the northern high court was suspended and merged with its counterpart in Port-au-Prince, the *sénéchaussée* alone held forth in Government House.[22] (The building was so named because it also housed the offices of the governor and intendant, a separate Palais de Justice having never been built.)[23] It was here, in Cap Français, that Nicolas Lejeune was indicted, tried, and then acquitted in absentia in the spring of 1788, and here also where the Conseil Supérieur heard earlier cases involving the legitimacy of punishing masters for acts of brutality committed against their slaves.

The former headquarters of the Jesuits until their expulsion in 1763, Government House overlooked a public square known as the place Montarcher, at whose center sat an immaculate stone fountain braced on each of four corners by very tall Ionic columns. The ever-opinionated

[21] Geggus, "Saint-Domingue on the Eve of the Haitian Revolution," 12.

[22] Moreau de Saint-Méry, *Description topographique*, 1:321, 383. All further references to this title in the remainder of this chapter are to the original Philadelphia edition rather than the modern Paris edition.

[23] Ibid., 359.

FIGURE 6.1. This aerial view of Cap Français, showing the city surrounded by mountains to the north and west and by its harbor to the south, was originally published in Médéric Louis-Élie Moreau de Saint-Méry, *Recueil de vues des lieux principaux de la colonie française de Saint-Domingue, gravées par les soins de M. Ponce* (Paris: Moreau de Saint-Méry, 1791). Courtesy of the John Carter Brown Library at Brown University.

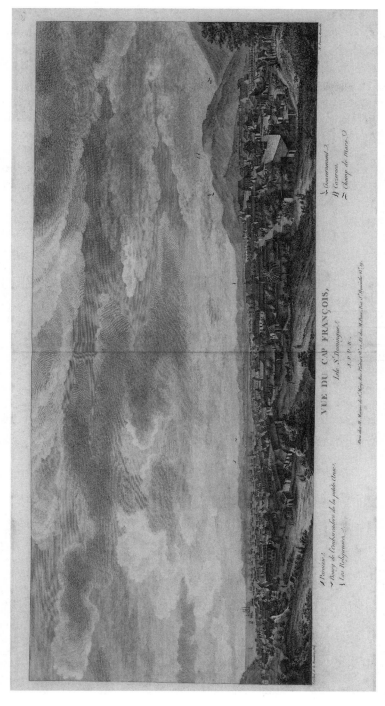

Perroteau 1

Bourg de l'embarcadere de la petite Anse 2

Les Religieuses 3

VUE DU CAP FRANÇOIS,

Isle St. Domingue 4

I. P. D. R.

A. Gouvernement 2

B) Cazernes.

Z Champ de mars. 9

Paris chez M. Moreau de S. Mery Rue Pelican N°11 & chez M. Ponce Rue d'Enfer N°69

FIGURE 6.2. This view of Cap Français from the foot of the mountains to its north, also published in Moreau's 1791 *Recueil de vues*, shows Government House in the right background. Courtesy of the John Carter Brown Library at Brown University.

Moreau de Saint-Méry found that the modest scale of the square contrasted awkwardly with the grand classical ambitions of the fountain.[24] Yet he also described the rue du Gouvernement as a bustling street lined end to end with the houses of merchant-ship captains and traders.[25] Walking along this street, Moreau wrote, one could hear the sounds of all of France, from Gascony and Provence in the south to Normandy and Dunkerque in the north. White merchants, however, were not the only persons to regularly find themselves within sight and earshot of the judicial and administrative headquarters of Cap Français. The neighborhood was also frequented by "sturdy negroes who, armed with heavy round sticks, beat out rhythms on the barrels in which coffee beans were packed."[26] Just north of the place Montarcher, the public theater (*la Comédie*) could be found, where performances of the latest plays and comedies from France – including an opera version of Raynal's *Histoire des deux indes* – were held before audiences that included both whites and free people of color (seated in segregated fashion).[27] The political center of Cap Français was very much a public space, in which persons of different racial backgrounds would inevitably cross paths with one another and be able to take in the news of major developments emanating from within Government House.

The *sénéchaussée* made use of a small auditorium for its hearings. A bevy of clerks, notaries, prosecutors, private attorneys, litigants, and assorted other creatures of the law came and went throughout the day.[28] Inside the much grander hearing room of the Conseil Supérieur, a wooden balustrade divided the room into equal halves. On one side sat the judges, adorned in black, along a semicircular enclosure; on the other were

[24] Ibid.

[25] Ibid., 321.

[26] Ibid., 322.

[27] Ibid., 359–361. Free people of color were prohibited from attending the theater from its founding in 1740 until 1766, when a new facility was opened. Thereafter, they attended both evening balls and dramatic performances along with whites, albeit from secondary loge-level seating located above and behind the seats reserved exclusively for whites. (A similar arrangement applied to the theater in Port-au-Prince.) Jean Fouchard, *Le théâtre à Saint-Domingue* (Port-au-Prince, Haïti: Imprimerie de l'État, 1955), 179–183; idem, *Plaisirs de Saint-Domingue: notes sur la vie sociale, littéraire et artistique* (Port-au-Prince, Haïti: H. Deschamps, 1988), 87, 91, 94–96, 103. Raynal's *Histoire* was adapted as *L'héroïne américaine* and staged in Cap Français in 1787. Jean Fouchard, *Artistes et répertoire des scènes de Saint-Domingue* (Port-au-Prince, Haïti: H. Deschamps, 1988), 172; Jill Casid, *Sowing Empire: Landscape and Colonization* (Minneapolis: University of Minnesota Press, 2005), 221.

[28] Moreau de Saint-Méry, *Description topographique*, 1:383–385.

PLACE ET FONTAINE MONTARCHER,

DEVANT LE GOUVERNEMENT,

au Cap-François, Isle S.ᵗ Domingue.

FIGURE 6.3. This engraving of Place Montarcher (published in Moreau's *Recueil de vues*) shows Government House in the background and, yet farther behind, the mountains overlooking Cap Français. From 1772 to 1787, both the Conseil Supérieur and trial court of Cap Français were located in Government House. Courtesy of the John Carter Brown Library at Brown University.

located benches for the attorneys arguing cases before the high court and for the viewing public. The spectacle of this auditorium, Moreau declared, would have been "genuinely beautiful" but for the fact that it was insufficiently elevated.[29] A separate room nearby, which gave on to a

[29] Ibid., 378, 389.

balcony overlooking the place Montarcher, housed the high court's deliberation and criminal chambers.[30]

In Port-au-Prince, the Conseil Supérieur held forth in distinctly less impressive surroundings. The original courthouse, located on the rue Royale in the old part of the town, was destroyed along with much of the rest of Port-au-Prince in an earthquake in 1770. A new building was eventually constructed on the same street, not far from the site of the old Port-au-Prince fish market. The auditorium featured two banks of seats, upper and lower. Oral arguments were suspended by administrative ordinance in January 1787; thereafter, cases were decided on the basis of the parties' briefs. At the end of the Old Regime, the court's archives could be found rotting in an insect-infested adjacent room. The overall structure, situated as it was very close to the city's prisons, was generally neglected and decrepit, making the Port-au-Prince high court, in Moreau's view, an especially undignified setting for judicial business.[31] However lacking in decorum and propriety, the tribunal's location made it, too, a kind of urban crossroads, accessible from and opening onto the outside world.

In addition to these considerations of legal geography, several other factors likely lent the Lejeune prosecution a public profile beyond the narrow circle of persons immediately concerned. One such factor is that Lejeune, by taking flight from the arms of justice, made himself subject to the contempt of court (*contumace*). *Contumace* was an elaborately regulated matter in Old Regime French law. It figured in numerous articles of the *Ordonnance criminelle* promulgated under Louis XIV in 1670, the code that governed the investigation and trial of criminal cases in France for most of the eighteenth century. Under the 1670 ordinance, a defendant who failed to appear in court within fifteen days of his summons would be called to account by the public cry of a trumpet for eight consecutive days. The ordinance required that a single cry be sounded in each of three places for the eight-day duration: the public square; in front of the courthouse where the case was being tried; and in front of the defendant's residence.[32] (Technically, the cry served as a secondary form of summons; a judgment of contumacy would later follow, assuming the accused still failed to appear.) We cannot be certain, of course, that Lejeune was treated to such a public display of his contumacy, though

---

[30] Ibid., 379. For visual renderings of the *sénéchaussée* and Conseil Supérieur courtrooms (based on Moreau's *Description*), see Ogle, "Policing Saint Domingue," 234–235.

[31] Moreau de Saint-Méry, *Description topographique*, 2:345–347.

[32] Ordonnance criminelle, arts. 7–9 (1670).

the sources indicate that he was in fact found in contempt.[33] Several years before the Lejeune case, in 1782, the colony's high courts had called for the strict enforcement of the 1670 criminal ordinance, specifically the provisions concerning *contumace*.[34] It seems likely, given the high stakes of the prosecution, that Lejeune was publicly singled out in some form for his flight from justice. If that singling out took the traditional form prescribed in law, Lejeune's misdeeds would have been sounded not only in Plaisance – where the defendant's slaves were no doubt already aware that their master had departed the scene – but also in the public square of Cap Français, where the proceedings were being heard.

If there were opportunities for slaves to learn about the contests over the meaning and limits of the Code Noir during the late colonial era, they would have unfolded in connection with these urban spaces, where the world of the law intersected with the traffic of the public squares.[35] The city was a place of countless small-scale disputes, involving market-place regulation, the maintenance of order, and other opportunities for urban conflict, which involved slaves, free people of color, and whites alike. In seeking to resolve their tussles with other city residents, primarily free people of color, the slaves of Cap Français did not shy away from making claims before the local magistrate, a *sénéchal* who, in the capacity of *juge de police*, had jurisdiction over such matters. (Free people of color returned the favor to slaves.)[36] As Gene Ogle has written, these demonstrations of legal initiative suggest that "at least some of the colony's slaves saw its judicial officers as figures whose authority potentially superceded that of their masters."[37]

The criminal law was the context in which this lesson would have been conveyed most forcefully, however. Urban slaves were more likely than their plantation counterparts to have been exposed to the influence of judicial tales about planter brutality: stories that told of the unchecked

---

[33] Letter from François Barbé de Marbois, intendant, and Alexandre de Vincent de Mazarade, governor, to César-Henri de la Luzerne, naval minister, Aug. 29, 1788, ANOM, F/3/90, fol. 265.

[34] ANOM, CSD, F/3/275, fol. 649.

[35] The public squares were important for another reason as well: It was here that slaves found guilty of capital "crimes" were put to death by the Executioner of High Justice, a post that, after 1741, was reserved primarily to slaves convicted of theft by breaking and entering. These latter slaves were thus in a unique position to learn about the colonial legal system. See Ogle, "Policing Saint Domingue," 98.

[36] Moreau de Saint-Mery, *Description topographique*, 1:489. This passage is discussed in Ogle, "Policing Saint Domingue," 231–232.

[37] Ogle, "Policing Saint Domingue," 232.

power of masters but also referenced an alternative social order that had been legislated by Louis XIV and never implemented in the colony. The phenomenon of slave royalism, to the extent that it derived from the Code Noir's provisions criminalizing the torture and mutilation of slaves by their masters, was probably an urban phenomenon at its origins. In the two major cities of Saint-Domingue, where the Lejeune prosecution and its reverberations brought these articles of the Code Noir to life, at least some slaves may have learned to identify royal law with the cause of protection from the excesses of domestic sovereignty.

Although this kind of exposure would have been heavily concentrated in the urban, largely domestic slave communities of Cap Français and Port-au-Prince, it was not necessarily limited to them. From the repeated efforts of colonial administrators to limit slaves from traveling beyond the confines of their plantations without a written pass from their master, we know that slaves from the northern plain found their way on a regular basis to Cap Francais.[38] They did so both illicitly and legally: Moreau notes that market Sundays brought roughly fifteen thousand blacks to the place Clugny in Cap Français, where the *marché des nègres* was formally situated as of 1766.[39] (Georges Biassou himself was almost certainly one of these slaves who frequented Cap Français more or less regularly, for he spent his early years on the plantations of Haut du Cap. From those hillsides overlooking the Cap Français harbor, it was but a forty-minute walk to the northern capital.[40]) The commercial activity spawned by the slave markets also served to link the plantations together in an informal network of trade and communication.[41] The slave markets were also linked to "disorderly" Sunday gatherings in the taverns (*cabarets*) of Cap Français, where slaves met to sell wine and liquor to one another. In 1736, these assemblies prompted a local magistrate to observe that an unregulated tavern culture posed a "most dangerous" risk to the "welfare and security" of the colony.[42]

---

[38] Moreau de Saint-Méry, *Description topographique*, 1:451, 487; "Arrêt du Conseil du Cap," Feb. 7, 1707, LC, 2:90–91.

[39] Moreau de Saint-Méry, *Description topographique*, 1:441. In 1686, the Conseil d'Etat amended article seven of the Code Noir to permit slaves in the French colonies to hold markets on Sundays and holidays. "Arrêt du Conseil d'État," Oct. 13, 1686, LC, 1:447–448. See also Popkin, *You Are All Free*, 67.

[40] Jane Landers, *Atlantic Creoles in the Age of Revolutions* (Cambridge, MA: Harvard University Press, 2010), 55.

[41] See "Arrêt de Règlement du Conseil du Cap," Nov. 7, 1736, LC, 3:460–461 (barring merchants from using unsupervised slaves to go from plantation to plantation selling goods).

[42] "Ordonnance du Juge de police du Cap," June 22, 1736, ANOM, CSD, F/3/269, fols. 513–514. On the late-night gatherings of slaves in the taverns of Cap Français, see Moreau de Saint-Méry, *Description topographique*, 1:487.

Finally, there is some evidence that, by the early revolutionary period, if not earlier, slaves had come into direct contact with the writings of the Abbé Raynal and the colonial jurist Hilliard d'Auberteuil, two authors who had made much of the problem of planter brutality in Saint-Domingue. In 1802, Jean-Félix Carteau, a white planter exile from Saint-Domingue, claimed that that he had seen Raynal's and Hilliard d'Auberteuil's books – which "took pity on the condition of [the negroes]" – in the hands of some blacks on the eve of the 1791 slave revolt.[43] Suggesting that the slaves in question had secretly purchased the texts from abolitionist Bordeaux sea captains, Carteau described the implications as follows:

Few slaves knew how to read, but only one was needed in a work gang (*atelier*) in order to read to the others, when the conspiracy was taking shape, in order to prove to them how much their grievances were being voiced in France, and how much it was hoped that they would shake off the harsh yoke of their ruthless masters. The mulattos and free blacks had learned how to read, and undoubtedly they assisted the blacks on this occasion.

Carteau also noted that abolitionist engravings, apparently depicting the sufferings of slaves, had circulated among the blacks of Saint-Domingue during this period.[44] This information should be treated with a grain of salt, as it was cited to support the highly politicized claim that the "friends of the blacks" had "contributed in principle to the uprising of the slaves."[45] That thesis had long been a staple of reactionary white opponents of the free colored campaign for political rights and the slave insurgency alike. However, such critics rarely, if ever, associated Hilliard d'Auberteuil (as opposed to Raynal) with the cause of the Society of the Friends of the Blacks. An advocate for colonial autonomy, the creole lawyer had criticized planter brutality and arbitrariness as a threat to the efficiency of the plantation system. He was not someone easily confused with an abolitionist. Moreover, various accounts have placed Raynal's work in the hands of Toussaint Louverture prior to the August 1791 uprising.[46] Thus, Carteau's claim is difficult to dismiss out of hand. If

[43] Jean-Félix Carteau, *Soirées bermudiennes, ou Entretiens sur les événemens qui ont opéré la ruine de la partie française de l'isle de Saint-Domingue* (Bordeaux: Pellier Lawalle, 1802), 75–76, also quoted in Geggus, "Print Culture and the Haitian Revolution," 85. Carteau misspelled Hilliard's name as "Hiriart" in this passage.

[44] Carteau, *Soirées bermudiennes*, 76.

[45] Ibid., 75.

[46] Geggus, "Print Culture and the Haitian Revolution," 85; Dubois, *Avengers of the New World*, 172. The book in question is Raynal's *Histoire des deux indes*, but it is worth recalling that Raynal's name also appeared on the title page of the 1785 *Essai sur l'Administration de Saint-Domingue*. Most likely written by Malouet, that work

true, it means that at least some slaves had access to a body of work that underscored the prevalence of planter abuses in Saint-Domingue.

These are some of the paths by which urban slaves in the two principal cities of Saint-Domingue, and plantation slaves in the surrounding areas, may have learned of and discussed the desultory colonial history of efforts to enforce the protective provisions of the Code Noir. Yet the most persuasive evidence that slaves did in fact absorb at least some of the lessons of that history comes from the revolutionary period itself. This evidence consists primarily of three letters written between late 1791 and mid-1792 by two leaders of the insurgency – Jean-François and Biassou, joined by Gabriel Aimé Belair in July 1792 – to the civil commissioners Saint-Léger, Mirbeck, and Roume.[47] On December 12, 1791, Jean-François and Biassou, describing the insurgency as a "revolution that has made us, along with the whites, its sad victims," offered to put down the rebellion and return the insurgents to their plantations in exchange for the liberty of the "principal chiefs."[48] On December 21, they wrote to urge the commissioners to "outlaw" the "barbarous" and "harsh mistreatment" that slaves had long endured at the hands of their masters in Saint-Domingue.[49] Finally, in July 1792, Jean-François and Biassou (with Belair) reiterated the problem of radical abuse on the plantations but joined it with a call for "general liberty" for the slaves, citing to the 1789 Declaration of the Rights of Man.[50]

highlighted the risks that a system of "two governments" – unrestrained planters versus powerless royal administrators – posed to the long-term stability of the colony. On Hilliard d'Auberteuil and Malouet, see Chapter 3.

[47] The third signatory of the July 1792 letter is indicated only as "Belair." According to David Geggus, this was not Toussaint Louverture's nephew Charles Belair, but rather Biassou's officer Gabriel Aimé Belair. In seeking to reconstruct the insurgents' intentions, historians have sometimes made use of an anonymous fourth letter that dates to September 1791, written by a white captive named Claude Boisbrun and dictated by the free colored secretary to Jeannot. In that letter, the anonymous insurgents demanded an end to slavery in Saint-Domingue. Geggus, "Print Culture and the Haitian Revolution," 89 and n.29.

[48] The letter appears in full in Dubois and Garrigus, *Slave Revolution in the Caribbean*, 100–101. On Biassou's career, see Landers, *Atlantic Creoles in the Age of Revolutions*, 55–94.

[49] Dubois and Garrigus, *Slave Revolution in the Caribbean*, 102.

[50] Piquionne, "Lettre de Jean-Francois, Biassou, et Belair, juillet 1792." An English translation appears in Nick Nesbitt, ed., *Toussaint L'Ouverture: The Haitian Revolution* (London: Verso, 2008), 5–8. David Geggus has concluded that this letter is a forgery and that its most likely author was the Abbé Delahaye, the Dondon parish priest. See Geggus, "Print Culture and the Haitian Revolution," 89, 91; idem, "Slave Resistance and Emancipation: The Case of Saint-Domingue," in *Who Abolished Slavery? Slave Revolts and Abolitionism: A Debate with João Pedro Marques*, ed. Seymour Drescher and Peter C. Emmer (New York: Bergahn Books, 2010), 114; idem, *Haitian Revolutionary Studies*,

These letters figure centrally in an ongoing debate among historians of the Haitian Revolution over the nature of the slave insurgents' ideologies. In the view of most scholars, a distinctly royalist worldview dominated the political culture of the early insurgency.[51] Monarchy provided the slaves with something that the "shadowy" new world of revolutionary authority could not: a comprehensible and familiar ideology of legitimacy and hierarchy.[52] Some significant anecdotal and visual evidence supports this interpretation. Well before they joined the Spanish or British sides of the international military conflict over Saint-Domingue, the slave insurgents in the northern province had begun to display the symbols of their fidelity to the cause of king and church.[53] They seem to have freely adorned the white cocarde (the color white signaling the standard of the Bourbon dynasty). Jean-François described the scarlet tunic worn by some of his men as "the king's uniform," which was also adorned with the royal fleur-de-lis (the same mark that had been branded on the bodies of fugitive slaves found to have escaped from their plantations).[54] The death of Boukman, the reputed organizer of the famous August 21, 1791, vodou ceremony at Bois Caïman that inspired the slave revolt, was greeted by his supporters with the statement that he been killed "in the most just of causes, the death of his king."[55]

However, the exact nature and sources of this ideology remain subjects of great dispute. Some have interpreted this royalism to mean that, at its outset, the insurgents had only the limited purpose of ending brutality on the plantations and returning the slaves to work under a more lenient and flexible regime.[56] Others have found that the insurgents, motivated

267 n. 49. Other scholars (myself included) have found the letter sufficiently credible to draw inferences from it about the goals and nature of the early insurgency. For a persuasive defense of the document's probable authenticity, see Popkin, *You Are All Free*, 50. Without citing any evidence, Nick Nesbitt has asserted that Toussaint Louverture signed the name of his then fourteen-year-old nephew Charles Belair to this letter in place of his own. See Nesbitt, *Toussaint L'Ouverture*, 5.

[51] Dubois, *Avengers of the New World*, 106; Bell, *Toussaint Louverture*, 84–85; Ogle, "The Trans-Atlantic King," 89–91; Geggus, *Haitian Revolutionary Studies*, 142–143.

[52] Geggus, *Haitian Revolutionary Studies*, 142.

[53] Ibid.

[54] Ibid.; Dubois, *Avengers of the New World*, 106.

[55] Dubois, *Avengers of the New World*, 106. According to Geggus, the evening of August 21 is the most likely date of the Bois Caïman ceremony, though it is traditionally understood to have taken place on Aug. 14. Geggus, *Haitian Revolutionary Studies*, 87.

[56] See, for example, Popkin, *You Are All Free*, 17; Bell, *Toussaint Louverture*, 32–33, 36, 4; João Pedro Marques, "Slave Revolts and the Abolition of Slavery: An Overinterpretation," trans. Richard Wall, in Drescher and Emmer, *Who Abolished Slavery?* 14–15, 20, 24; John Thornton, "Africa and Abolitionism," in Drescher and Emmer, *Who Abolished Slavery?*

to question not just the conditions of their treatment but also the legitimacy of slavery and racial subordination *tout court*, creatively fused royalism with republican demands and thereby transformed both.[57] It is entirely possible, and indeed likely, that some slaves observed republican language in use through interactions with white colonists or through stories traded in the colony's port towns, where news from France was most easily available.

There is almost certainly some truth to both of these arguments. However, in seeking to assimilate the insurgents' tactics and statements to the poles of either royalist authoritarianism or republican egalitarianism, or even to a creative synthesis of the two, the debate over the aims of the slave revolt has turned at times into a parade of (occasionally anachronistic) abstractions.[58] The overarching terms in which this debate is framed may be part of the problem.

The royalism of the early slave insurgency was a phenomenon of remarkably diverse origins and manifestations.[59] Yet our knowledge of it comes largely filtered through the accounts of white colonists and metropolitan observers, for whom the subject was highly useful political and racial fodder. Consider the example of Jean-Philippe Garran de Coulon, the president of the commission that would later investigate the conduct of Sonthonax and Polverel, and author of an official report on the causes of the Saint-Domingue revolt published in 1797. In Garran de Coulon's view, the royalism of the slaves boiled down to a matter of ignorance. Not having known any other form of government, whether in their ancestral African homelands or Saint-Domingue, the slaves had no other ideological options but the royalist one.[60] Garran de Coulon was by no means a reactionary, and in the late 1790s he opposed the growing clamor of

100; Geggus, "Slave Resistance and Emancipation: The Case of Saint-Domingue," in Drescher and Emmer, *Who Abolished Slavery?* 114.

[57] See Dubois, *Avengers of the New World*; 105, 107; idem, "Our Three Colors: The King, the Republic and the Political Culture of Slave Revolution in Saint-Domingue," *Historical Reflections* 29 (2003): 83–102; idem, "An enslaved Enlightenment," 10–12.

[58] This is particularly true of Geggus's recent argument that Dubois minimizes the "authoritarian" strands of the Haitian revolutionary leaders. See Geggus, "The Caribbean in the Age of Revolution," 95–100. (It is not clear whether this critique involves Dubois's work on Guadeloupe or Saint-Domingue.)

[59] Ogle, "The Trans-Atlantic King," 89.

[60] Jean-Philippe Garran de Coulon, *Rapport sur les troubles de Saint-Domingue, fait au nom de la Commission des colonies, des Comités de salut public, de législation et de marine, réunis* (Paris: Imprimerie nationale, 1797–1798), 2:209, also quoted in Dubois, *Avengers of the New World*, 108. See also Bell, *Toussaint Louverture*, 32–33, 36, 42.

voices calling for a forcible restoration of slavery in Saint-Domingue. Like many white colonists, however, he saw more absence than presence in the royalism of the slaves.

A related difficulty involves balancing the influences of African and French colonial conceptions of kingship. There seems little question that practices associated with African (and particularly Congolese) kingship left a profound imprint on the colony's enslaved.[61] Well over one half of the slave population of Saint-Domingue had arrived in the eight years just prior to the August 1791 slave revolt. Between 1783 and 1791, roughly 300,000 slaves were transported to Saint-Domingue.[62] The views and experiences of kingship that these slaves brought with them to Hispaniola likely had a privileged place in their understanding of royal authority in the colonies. At the same time, we know far less about the role of kingship traditions other than the Congolese in the political culture of the slave insurgency. The diversity of the slaves' African backgrounds precluded the possibility that one tradition could speak for or transplant the others.[63] Furthermore, the very idea of singling out something that we can call an "African" political ideology, separate and distinct from ideas grounded in European thought or Caribbean experience, is itself questionable.[64]

One way out of these interpretive dilemmas is to suggest that a royalism oriented around the distant French king provided a generic umbrella under which slaves of differing African traditions could be accommodated, represented, and ultimately united in opposition to a common goal.[65] Yet as Robin Blackburn has observed, the royalism of the insurgent slaves is "not easily interpreted as fidelity to a particular king."[66] Thus, if the Bourbon brand proved to have a distinctive appeal for the insurgents, it is not simply because the diversity of their widely varying African backgrounds enabled them to find common ground in the figure of Louis XVI.

Another approach is to break the concept of royalism into smaller, less abstract terms and then revisit the primary sources in question, and

---

[61] See Thornton, "'I am the Subject of the King of Congo'"; idem, "African Soldiers in the Haitian Revolution"; Popkin, *You Are All Free*, 130.

[62] These figures are derived from Voyages: The Trans-Atlantic Slave Trade Database, available at www.slavevoyages.org. I thank Emma Rothschild for drawing them to my attention.

[63] Ogle, "The Trans-Atlantic King," 90.

[64] Dubois, "An enslaved Enlightenment," 13.

[65] Ogle, "The Trans-Atlantic King," 90–91.

[66] Blackburn, "Epilogue," in Geggus and Fiering, *The World of the Haitian Revolution*, 395.

the events to which they relate, from a more grounded, if still tentative, approach. By situating the limited evidence at hand in relation to the political and legal conflicts over the reform of slavery in the 1780s, it may be possible to see that Biassou and Jean-François were engaged in something more concrete than an effort to vindicate an authoritarian, egalitarian, or African agenda. In particular, they may have had recourse to a pragmatic and vernacular reading of the protective regimen of the Code Noir, understood not in a narrowly textual sense but as an expression of the idea that the king had limited the master's authority over the slave. As Garran de Coulon observed, "the royal government" did little to actually protect slaves from physical abuse during the colonial period, "but its protection, weak as it was, was the only one that [slaves] could invoke against the tyranny of their masters."[67] That Old Regime tradition of protection in principle, though not in fact, revealed its true significance only in the revolutionary period.

Stated differently, the ideology of at least some insurgent leaders in the north appears to have incorporated a legal component, albeit one that was not expressed in legalistic terms.[68] The insurgent leaders joined in – and so extended – the permanent debate about the meaning of the Code Noir that had marked the entire colonial history of Saint-Domingue.

LAW IN THE CAMPS OF JEAN-FRANÇOIS AND BIASSOU, 1791–1792

This reassertion of the Code Noir arose in the context of a series of exchanges between the civil commissioners and the insurgent leaders in the north over the question of amnesty. Upon arriving in Saint-Domingue in November 1791, the second civil commission announced that the National Assembly had decreed a general amnesty for "acts of revolution" that had been extended to encompass the uprisings in France's overseas colonies. In their initial exchanges with the commissioners (late November and early December), Jean-François and Biassou demanded to be included in that amnesty and offered to bring the insurgency under control and return the slaves to their plantations. In exchange, the colonists would agree to the granting of several hundred "liberties" for the insurrection's leaders and amnesty for all those fighting in their camps.

---

[67] Garran de Coulon, *Rapport sur les troubles*, 2:209–210. See also Popkin, *You Are All Free*, 130.

[68] Cf. Dubois, "An enslaved Enlightenment," 13.

(Toussaint Louverture, who was closely involved in these negotiations, may have persuaded Jean-François and Biassou to reduce the number of liberties demanded from several hundred to fifty – a demand that was made only orally and in secret.) The commissioners' efforts to negotiate an early end to the slave revolt along these lines were frustrated by recalcitrant colonists in the planter-dominated northern assembly, who refused to brook any notion of compromise with "rebel negroes" short of an unconditional and apologetic return to the status quo ante. Their steadfastness was apparently matched by the determination of the more radical insurgent chiefs, Jeannot first among them, to push for an all-out end to slavery, although the written evidence of this campaign is of dubious provenance. For their part, the followers of Jean-François and Biassou appear to have gotten wind of the settlement negotiations, possibly as a result of news reports deliberately published in the colonial newspaper to foster dissent among the insurgent camps. The constituents of Jean-François and Biassou responded to the news of the settlement talks by pressing their leaders to go beyond self-serving measures and take a more aggressive stance toward the problem of planter brutality.[69]

The traces left by the Code Noir on these competing demands and pressures are captured in the insurgents' December 1791 correspondence with the civil commissioners.[70] On December 12, Jean-François and Biassou wrote to the commissioners to express their commitment to "the reestablishment of order." However, the idea of trying to seek out and punish the "authors" responsible for this "disturbed equilibrium" was counterproductive and hopeless, they said. Only the emancipation of the insurgents' commanders could succeed in bringing about a closure that would otherwise require much time and "the ruin of the property owners." Even so, there were risks in proceeding along those lines, the two leaders wrote. "False rumors will make the slaves obstinate, for example, the idea that the king has granted them three free days per week." In order to help quell the anticipated resistance, it would be necessary for the civil commission to put on a display of French military force.[71]

---

[69] Dubois, *Avengers of the New World*, 125–127; Popkin, *You Are All Free*, 48; Geggus, "Print Culture and the Haitian Revolution," 89, 91; idem, *Haitian Revolutionary Studies*, 125; Benot, "The Insurgents of 1791," 108; Bell, *Toussaint Louverture*, 32–33, 36, 42.

[70] By December 1791, Ailhaud had already abandoned his post in the south and returned to France. Thus, only Sonthonax and Polverel were involved in the negotiations with Jean-François and Biassou at this time.

[71] Letter from Jean-François and Biassou to the Civil Commissioners, Dec. 12, 1791, in Dubois and Garrigus, *Slave Revolution in the Caribbean*, 100–101.

Showcasing Jean-François's and Biassou's creativity in casting their own demands for emancipation as a question of the "general welfare,"[72] the letter was perhaps most revealing for its reference to the rumor that Louis XVI had decided to grant the slaves three free days a week.[73] That rumor had apparently originated with the Bois Caïman ceremony, but in a sense it reached back much further, for it evoked not just the king's grace and mercy generally, but the more benevolent dispositions of the Code Noir specifically. The purported promise was both an improvement upon, and an extension of, article 6 of the Code, which barred plantation labor on Sunday and other Catholic holy days. Robin Blackburn's observation that "[i]n the first year or two [of the insurgency] very tangible objectives – such as three free days a week, the freedom of this person or that, the fate of this garden or plot – had more purchase and meaning than French legal categories" therefore misses the mark.[74] Although *revolutionary* legal categories such as "citizenship," "equality," and "liberty" were still about two years off into the horizon insofar as their direct application to slaves was concerned, the remnants of *Old Regime* legal rules and traditions, modified or otherwise, were very much in play at this time. (Another persistent rumor – that the king had already agreed to liberate the slaves altogether – was clearly more difficult to reconcile with the text of the Code Noir.)[75]

The point is further suggested in a second letter that Jean-François and Biassou wrote two weeks later, on December 21, to the civil commissioners. More clearly than any other document of the period, this letter underscored the gap that separated the principal leaders from the masses who lent the insurrection its power. Jean-François and Biassou began, somewhat unconvincingly, by asserting that "in our role as chiefs we have a great deal of power" over the insurgent slaves. At the same time, although it was still possible to prevent widespread bloodshed,

---

[72] Ibid., 100.

[73] Bell, *Toussaint Louverture*, 33, 85; Dubois, *Avengers of the New World*, 106; Popkin, *You Are All Free*, 130. Historians have not been able to trace this rumor to any printed text that might have circulated in Saint-Domingue during this period. See Geggus, "Print Culture and the Haitian Revolution," 85. Bell writes that the abolition of the whip was also part of the Bois Caïman legend (*Toussaint Louverture*, 85). On the Bois Caïman ceremony itself, see Geggus, *Haitian Revolutionary Studies*, 81–92.

[74] Blackburn, "Epilogue," in Geggus and Fiering, *The World of the Haitian Revolution*, 395.

[75] On the role of rumors in the political culture of the slave insurgency, see Geggus, *Haitian Revolutionary Studies*, 12; idem, "Print Culture and the Haitian Revolution," 85, 87; Dubois, *Avengers of the New World*, 106–107.

"there are many things that still hold them back," the leaders professed. Two items in particular stood out. First, the insurgents were concerned about being treated to a replay of the Ogé affair of late 1790 and early 1791, in which the authorities of Cap Français pretended to extend an olive branch to Ogé before hastening to execute him once he voluntarily surrendered.[76]

Second, the "negro slaves" had evidently expressed lingering grievances about the prevalence of planter brutality in Saint-Domingue. Jean-François and Biassou accordingly evoked

[t]he bad treatment of their masters, most of whom torture their slaves by mistreating them in all sorts of ways, taking away their two hours [of midday rest], their holidays, and Sundays, leaving them naked, without any help even when they are sick, and letting them die of misery. Yes, sirs, how many barbarous masters there are who enjoy being cruel to these miserable slaves, or else managers or administrators who, to stay in their employers' good graces, afflict a thousand of the same cruelties on the slaves as they pretend to carry out their responsibilities.

It is difficult not to see in this passage some reference to the 1784–1785 plantation-management ordinances, which specifically targeted the phenomenon of brutality by managers and overseers rather than masters, and the 1788 Lejeune affair, among other relics of the long eighteenth-century debate over the proper reach of the Code Noir.[77] Yet whatever the specific underlying referents may have been, the passage clearly drew upon (without actually citing) an array of rules from the 1685 royal edict: These rules prohibited masters from working their slaves on Sundays and Catholic holidays; required masters to provide adequate clothing, food, and maintenance for their slaves and to care for sick slaves under their control; and barred the unauthorized torture and killing of slaves.[78]

---

[76] Letter from Jean-François and Biassou to the Civil Commissioners, Dec. 12, 1791, in Dubois and Garrigus, *Slave Revolution in the Caribbean*, 102. The letter described Ogé's execution as a form of "treason" (*trahison*), but that term is perhaps better translated as "betrayal" here.

[77] As David Geggus observes, the main impact of the 1784–1785 plantation-management reforms may have been to provide "a plausible basis for the royalist ideology that the slave insurgents would adroitly use in 1791." Geggus, "Saint-Domingue on the Eve of the Haitian Revolution," 12. On the significance of the 1784–1785 reforms to the political culture of the insurgents, see also Dubois, "An enslaved Enlightenment," 13; idem, *Avengers of the New World*, 1–6; Ogle, "The Trans-Atlantic King," 89–90; and Carolyn Fick, "Emancipation in Haiti: From Plantation Labour to Peasant Proprietorship," *Slavery and Abolition* 21, no. 2 (2000): 13–14.

[78] Code Noir, arts. 6, 22, 24–27, 42–43 (1685).

The December 21 letter grouped these provisions together and rendered them in a manner that seems to express a vernacular slave understanding of the king's protective regime in Saint-Domingue. Of course, Jean-François and Biassou were not necessarily giving the commissioners an unvarnished and transparent version of their constituents' sentiments. Both here and in the December 12 letter, their choice of words revealed a complex interchange between personal and group aspirations, between the leaders' own quest for individual emancipation and the pursuit of the slaves' "general will."[79] Yet there was little incentive for Jean-François and Biassou themselves to dwell on the specific theme of planter brutality at such length unless they were doing so as part of a genuine effort to persuade the commissioners to take practical steps that would bring the overwhelming mass of the insurgents into the fold of compromise. After all, the two leaders were not attempting to bargain for a future in which they themselves would be returned to plantations. To the contrary, the agreement they pursued entailed that Jean-François and Biassou would take advantage of their liberties to find new homes in foreign countries (as both eventually did, in Spain and Florida, respectively).[80]

So it seems highly likely that the emphasis on planter brutality was a negotiating tool dictated by real and widespread concerns emanating from within the northern insurgent camps loyal to Jean-François and Biassou. Indeed, the December 21 letter concluded by exhorting Saint-Léger, Mirbeck, and Roume to "look favorably on these unfortunates by clearly outlawing such harsh mistreatment, abolishing the terrible plantation prisons (*cachots*), where the stays are miserable, and trying to improve the condition of this class of men so necessary to the colony." Whether such reforms would in fact have succeeded in persuading the insurgents to "take up their work once again and ... return to order," as Jean-Francois and Biassou promised they would, is of course another matter. (The resistance to Toussaint Louverture's later efforts to implement a regime of forced labor in Saint-Domingue suggests something of the depth and persistence of this issue.)[81]

The ideology that emerges from these letters – if it can be called an ideology – is not usefully subsumed under the abstract rubric of "royalism." Although generally consistent with the broad outlines of a

---

[79] This phrase was used in the December 12 letter. Jean-François and Biassou to the Civil Commissioners, Dec. 12, 1791, in Dubois and Garrigus, *Slave Revolution in the Caribbean*, 100.

[80] Popkin, *You Are All Free*, 48; Geggus, "Print Culture and the Haitian Revolution," 92.

[81] Jean-François and Biassou to the Civil Commissioners, Dec. 12, 1791, in Dubois and Garrigus, *Slave Revolution in the Caribbean*, 102. I discuss the Louverture episode in the conclusion of this book.

monarchical worldview, the letters (particularly that of December 21) seem more directly concerned to draw on the power of a specific legal tradition. That legal tradition was, of course, long associated in Saint-Domingue with the benevolent authority of the king. It was the king, and not the National or Legislative Assembly, who had prohibited the torture and mutilation of slaves, had mandated their proper nourishment and maintenance by planters, had restricted overseers and managers from overworking and abusing their slaves, and so forth. Yet royal authority per se was not necessarily an essential component of the vernacular understanding of these protective rules and policies reflected in the correspondence of Jean-François and Biassou. Although the person of the king figured in the December 12 letter, he was entirely absent from the missive of December 21.

This discrepancy would grow into an actual gap as the rapidly changing context of the insurgency continued to unfold. An exchange of white for black prisoners was eventually agreed. Nonetheless, the negotiations between the civil commissioners and the leadership cohort of Jean-François and Biassou ultimately broke down.[82] The first half of 1792 witnessed a steady radicalization of the terms of the slave insurgency in the north. (As we saw in the previous chapter, the decree of April 4, 1792, granting full political equality to the free blacks and people of color was a response to this radicalization.) Even as their demands became more expansive, and their embrace of republican ideology more pronounced, however, the insurgent leaders' emphasis on the conditions of enslavement endured, and with it the vernacular reading of the Code Noir that had emerged in the negotiations of December 1791.

In July 1792, Biassou and Jean-François, joined by Biassou's officer Gabriel Aimé Belair, renewed their dialogue with the civil commissioners and the planters' colonial assembly in Cap Français.[83] They began as they had ended their December communications, on the note of planter brutality. Yet rather than connect this theme to a strategy for a two-track compromise (liberty for the chiefs and a return to plantation labor for the

[82] Popkin, *You Are All Free*, 48–50; Dubois, *Avengers of the New World*, 128; Bell, *Toussaint Louverture*, 35.

[83] This letter was first published on February 9, 1793, in the newspaper *Le Créole Patriote* by Claude Milscent. A colonist born in Saint-Domingue, Milscent was active in efforts to repress *marronage* during the late colonial period. Milscent left Saint-Domingue for France in June 1790 and became a sympathizer of the insurgency. He was executed under the Terror in 1794. A second version of the letter was printed by Colonel Cambefort, by whom the letter may have been received and who directed the military campaign against the insurgents. Piquionne, "Lettre de Jean-François, Biassou, et Belair," 216–218; Geggus, "Print Culture and the Haitian Revolution," 89.

masses), the insurgent leaders used it to build a case for general liberty. The opening passage on the abuses of enslavement reads as follows:

For too long, Gentlemen, by way of abuses which cannot too strongly be deemed to have taken place because of our lack of understanding and our ignorance, we have been victims of your greed and your avarice. Under the barbarous lashes of your whip we accumulated treasures for you that you enjoy in this colony. The human species suffered to see the barbarities to which you treated these men like you (yes, men) over whom you have no other right than that of the strongest and most barbarous.[84]

This overture managed at once to evoke a long-standing history of planter atrocities and to deny that any "right" of ownership in human beings could exist. The emphasis on the conditions of enslavement was consistent with the school of administrative thought and practice that, going back to the 1780s, had aimed to preserve slavery by eliminating its most egregious aspects. To this extent, the letter can be read as part of an Old Regime tradition that hearkened back to the importance of enforcing the protective provisions of the Code Noir. Because the insurgent leaders now held the law of slavery itself to be an illegitimate exercise of authority over others, however, that meliorative tradition was clearly an inadequate substitute for the demands that the insurgent leaders were now putting forth.

Jean-François, Biassou, and Belair made clear that their position on this issue of principle left no room for compromise. "We are unable to see or find the right that you pretend to have over us ... being all children of a same father created in the same image. We are thus equal to you in natural law." In addition to summoning the authority of natural law, they appealed to the secular scripture embodied in the Declaration of the Rights of Man, "which says that men are born free and equal in rights."[85] Perhaps reflecting the struggles that must have ensued within the insurgent camp over the propriety of negotiating for the liberty of only a narrow range of persons, the three insurgent leaders proceeded to disavow any further interest in the pragmatic option of a quid pro quo.[86] (Their refusal to countenance such a resolution was not necessarily shared by other insurgent leaders. Toussaint Louverture, for one, supported an effort, essentially contemporaneous with this letter, to end

---

[84] Piquionne, "Lettre de Jean-François, Biassou, et Belair," 207. I have modernized the punctuation of this letter but have otherwise sought to preserve its informal grammar and style.

[85] Ibid., 207–208.

[86] Ibid., 208.

the uprising along lines similar to those contemplated by the December 1791 negotiations.)[87]

This letter may well mark the point at which the slave revolt turned into an attack on the institution of slavery itself.[88] Yet it is important to recall that, its republican language notwithstanding, the letter did not in fact call for an end to plantation labor. While insisting that emancipation and amnesty be extended to all of the former slaves, the leaders offered in exchange to disarm their followers, return them "to the plantations to which they belonged," and subject them to a system of fixed terms of wage-based labor.[89] As Jeremy Popkin notes, this was clearly a more radical position than the fig leaf extended in December 1791, but it was also more restrained than the uncompromising abolitionist stance that seems to have been taken by Jeannot, Boukman, and the more radical wing of the insurgency in the immediate aftermath of the August 1791 uprising.[90]

Together, these documents from December 1791 and July 1792 reveal important aspects of the political culture of the slave insurgents associated with Jean-François and Biassou. They suggest, first, that a sense of legality and legitimacy was important to these insurgents, both as way of making sense of their past and as a language for asserting claims about the shape of their future. Second, the Code Noir was a central, although not exclusive, reference point of this language. As the July 1792 letter indicates, the vernacular legal vocabulary of the insurgents grouped around Jean-François and Biassou also encompassed the Declaration of the Rights of Man. By mid-1792, their movement had begun to coalesce around an understanding that a new and more far-reaching form of justice might be possible. The vision of law reflected in these documents summoned royal authority in support of a more humane plantation-labor regime, but did not necessarily require the person of the king to effectuate that regime on the ground. Garran de Coulon's observation that the authority of the king was the sole power the slaves could "invoke against the tyranny of their masters" therefore captured only one aspect of the new landscape of authority created between late 1791 and mid-1792.[91] It was nonetheless an important aspect, for even with the more radical framework

[87] Geggus, *Haitian Revolutionary Studies*, 125.
[88] Bell, *Toussaint Louverture*, 42.
[89] Piquionne, "Lettre de Jean-François, Biassou, et Belair," 209–210.
[90] Popkin, *You Are All Free*, 51; Benot, "The Insurgents of 1791," 108.
[91] Garran de Coulon, *Rapport sur les troubles*, 2:209–210, also quoted in Dubois, *Avengers of the New World*, 107.

expressed in July 1792, elements of Old Regime colonial administrative thought persisted. That power was made concrete only in the handful of cases when, under the Old Regime, slaves had been able to invoke their right to indirectly challenge their masters' infractions of the Code Noir in court. However, the letters of Jean-François and Biassou suggest that an authority so often eclipsed in everyday plantation life under the Old Regime had a significant symbolic afterlife.

The role of law and legality in the insurgents' representation of their demands had two important tactical advantages. It enabled these insurgents both to impugn the planters as lawless and predatory and to diminish the power of local colonial administrators as unworthy of the magnanimity of their royal sponsor.[92] Further, it permitted Jean-François and Biassou to express the insurgent agenda in gradualist and reformist terms, rather than in the rhetoric of a total and cataclysmic overthrow of the plantation system evoked by white planters. To some extent, this reformism, with its progressive emphasis on the conditions of treatment and labor, was a mirror image of the gradualist position of the leading French abolitionists of the day. Yet it also shared overtones with the ideas of colonial administrators, such as Malouet, who sought to prolong the life of the plantation economy by reorganizing slavery along more temperate and sustainable lines. At the same time, in pursuing their demands, Jean-François and Biassou were no longer operating within the world of an imagined, hypothetical uprising long contemplated by the strategic critics of the planters' domestic sphere. This was especially true by the middle of 1792, for by that time the insurgent leaders were in a position to see that the troops whose imminent arrival in the colony had long been threatened were not forthcoming.[93] The old debate within administrative and planter circles over brutality and moderation was now unfolding in a context in which slave insurgents held the upper hand.

In their July 1792 peace offering, Jean-François and Biassou called for the proposed settlement to be submitted to the approval of the Spanish government.[94] After the Spanish and British intervened in Saint-Domingue in 1793 and 1794, military considerations drew the slave insurgents associated with Jean-François and Biassou even further into the orbit of European royalism, the better to procure arms and the protection of

[92] Cf. Blackburn, "Epilogue," in Geggus and Fiering, *The World of the Haitian Revolution*, 395.

[93] Popkin, *You Are All Free*, 51.

[94] Piquionne, "Lettre de Jean-François, Biassou, et Belair," 209.

a rival great power. Nonetheless, in the course of the initial encounters between the civil commissioners and the principal heads of the insurgency, between late 1791 and mid-1792, royalism per se turns out to have played a relatively small role, and colonial legal imagery a correspondingly larger role. As it turns out, the legal heritage of the Old Regime was actively at work on both sides of those encounters.

THE CODE OF SONTHONAX AND POLVEREL

A second civil commission, consisting of Sonthonax, Polverel, and Jean-Antoine Ailhaud, arrived in Saint-Domingue in September 1792 with a mission to restore order in the colony pursuant to the terms of the April 4, 1792, decree.[95] The trio was sent, that is, to enforce the new regime of "equality of political rights" across the entire class of free persons, not to extend that regime.[96] The April 4 decree specifically authorized the commissioners, first, to disband the existing colonial assemblies (from which free people of color had been excluded) and to convene new assemblies chosen by the newly expanded electorate. Second, the commissioners were vested with the power to arrest and deport the "authors of the troubles of Saint-Domingue" to France for trial. Suppression of the slave insurgency as well as restoration of damaged plantation infrastructure were part and parcel of this mandate. The April 4 decree appropriated six million livres for subsistence needs and the reconstruction effort, and it ordered the dispatch of an armed force of "sufficient" size to ensure that no further disruptions to the plantation economy would ensue.[97]

Consistent with these mandates, the commissioners' initial public statements upon arriving in Saint-Domingue professed a commitment to the "two-class" theory of colonial society that Ogé, Raimond, and other free colored leaders had endorsed in 1790 and 1791. Only free persons and slaves could exist on the territory of Saint-Domingue. "We declare that slavery is necessary for the agriculture and the prosperity of the colonies," Sonthonax assured an assembly of colonists gathered in the church of Cap Français to welcome the new commissioners. A few months later, Sonthonax wrote to Brissot that an immediate abolition "would surely lead to the massacre of all the whites." Contrary to the conspiracy

[95] *Loi relative aux colonies*, 2.
[96] Ibid.
[97] Ibid., 3–5.

theories of white planters that would later engulf Sonthonax and Polverel in controversy, there is no indication that the second civil commission was intent on bringing a sudden end to slavery in the colony.[98]

To be sure, the new administrators, Sonthonax especially, had drunk deeply from the well of republican ideology in their formative political years.[99] Members of the correspondence committee of the Jacobin Club, both men were in touch with Brissot's circle and were receptive to the proposals for gradual emancipation emanating from the Société des Amis des Noirs.[100] Indeed, in September 1790, Sonthonax himself had published two anonymous newspaper editorials that called for the abolition of slavery and the extension of political rights to former slaves.[101] Yet such proposals were generally understood not to prejudice the continued viability of the plantation economy; indeed, they were formulated precisely to facilitate that objective. The thrust of the gradual emancipation school was sometimes difficult to disentangle from an earlier tradition of administrative reform proposals, stemming from the 1780s, that countenanced the reorganization rather than transformation of slave labor.

This point is important to stress, because historians have sometimes interpreted the commissioners' decisions in this period, particularly the emancipation proclamations of August and September 1793, as essentially desperate acts inspired by the sudden needs of the moment – pragmatic accommodations to a set of immediate and contingent circumstances.[102] These they certainly were. After an initial hostile encounter with the slave insurgency, the policies of Sonthonax and Polverel devolved very quickly into an approach of pragmatic accommodation. And that adjustment was no doubt partly the reflection of contingent circumstances. The fate of slavery in Saint-Domingue would be decided under circumstances

---

[98] Dubois, *Avengers*, 144; Popkin, *You Are All Free*, 102; Marcel Dorigny, "Sonthonax et Brissot: Le cheminement d'une filiation politique assumée," in Dorigny, *Léger-Félicité Sonthonax*, 31–32. See also Stein, *Léger Félicité Sonthonax*, 47.

[99] Stein, *Léger Félicité Sonthonax*, 20–25.

[100] Popkin, *You Are All Free*, 87–89; Dubois, *Avengers of the New World*, 161.

[101] Benot, *La révolution française et la fin des colonies*, 125–126; Geggus, "Slave Resistance and Emancipation," 115; Popkin, *You Are All Free*, 87; Dorigny, "Sonthonax et Brissot," 33–35. The editorials were published in Prudhomme's weekly newspaper *Les Révolutions de Paris* on Sept. 25 and Oct. 1, 1790. Sonthonax admitted to the authorship of these contributions in the course of his trial before the National Convention in 1795.

[102] For an older example, see "Aux origines de l'abolition de l'esclavage," 36 (1st trimester, 1949): 26, 36 (3rd and 4th trimesters, 1949): 356 n.2. More recently, see Popkin, *You Are All Free*, 1, 15.

dictated not solely by metropolitan legislators and colonial adminis-trators representing a republican empire. It was also a reaction to the demands of a movement for free colored enfranchisement and a slave insurgency whose scope and ultimate direction were far from clear in the fall of 1791 and would remain so for several years. Military strategy and political deliberation were inseparable in this context. Given such contingent exigencies, co-optation of and pragmatic accommodation to the slave revolt may seem like the inevitable and necessary responses of a metropole lacking true alternatives.

The specific manner of this accommodation, however, was anything but a foregone conclusion, and its terms were not invented out of thin air. The evolving reaction of the second civil commission to the slave revolt in Saint-Domingue reflected both the ambiguities and limitations of a colo-nial tradition preoccupied with the strategic implications of manumission and planter brutality. On certain points, that tradition was unambiguous, as in the case of articles 57 and 59 of the Code Noir, which were in effect the original source of authority for the commissioners' presence in Saint-Domingue. On this issue, there could be no negotiation with the white colonists, including the recalcitrant majority who failed to appreciate the stabilizing effect that an equalization of rights with the free people of color could have. At the same time, as the naval minister's instructions to the new commissioners stated, the free people of color were themselves to be reminded of their obligation to show respect toward "those who ele-vated them from the state of servitude" – another duty that derived from the Code Noir (and from Roman law long before it).[103]

Understood as a framework for organizing the management of a plantation-labor force, however, there was much about the Code Noir that could be bent in this direction or that without twisting the entire apparatus out of recognizable shape (as it had been twisted in the context of discriminatory legislation that chipped steadily away at the rights of the *gens de couleur*). Indeed, that had been the essence of the Code Noir's story for more than a century: much more brutality and far greater reg-ulation of manumission than its authors had envisioned. Yet that same flexibility in the joints could militate in more progressive and ameliora-tive directions while still adhering to the basic principle that a rule of law for a plantation economy needed, above all, to be workable. The regime of the Code Noir contained many provisions that could be extended,

[103] The instructions are quoted in Popkin, *You Are All Free*, 95.

adapted, or revived in just this way. Sonthonax, Polverel, and Ailhaud came to salvage what could be retained of that regime. In time, they would effectively dispense with some of the colonial absolutist template, but in their efforts to supplant it with a new legal framework, they drew, both explicitly and implicitly, on the legacy of the old.

Upon their arrival in Cap Français in September 1792, the new civil commissioners were faced not only with the problem of how to enforce the April 4 decree in the face of white planter obstinacy. They also confronted the more radical agenda of the slave insurgents that Jean-François and Biassou had communicated to the first civil commission in July 1792. Notwithstanding the republican commitments of that letter, the insurgents loyal to Jean-François and Biassou had by the spring of 1793 become allied to the authority of the Spanish king and his representatives in the eastern part of Hispaniola. (Toussaint Louverture joined them in early June.)[104] This alliance, which came with an infusion of arms and the promise of a continued supply of more, significantly raised the stakes of the slave insurgency and made it more imperative than ever that the civil commissioners manage to end the "troubles" of Saint-Domingue.

Their initial response was to meet the insurgency on its original terms: that is, by offering an improvement in the conditions of slavery. This strategy corresponded well with the traditional teachings of local administrative experience in light of the radical abuse of slaves, and it was entirely consistent with the stated mission of the civil commissioners to preserve a two-caste system in Saint-Domingue. In the west, Polverel was, in principle, better positioned to carry out this mission, given the potential for significant free colored support in suppressing the slave insurrection. In the north, where Sonthonax presided, matters were even further complicated by the onset of a dramatic struggle for power in Cap Français between the civil commission and the newly appointed governor, General François-Thomas Galbaud, who sought to champion the cause of the displaced northern planters.[105] In the south, the commissioners' authority was (along with the April 4, 1792, decree) rejected from the start; there, the white colonists were already actively seeking a protective alliance with the British.[106]

The story of the second civil commission is, in essence, one of a move from the regulation of planter brutality to the embrace of emancipation in the space of a single summer. Galbaud's riot in Cap Français, the onset

---

[104] Geggus, *Haitian Revolutionary Studies*, 125.
[105] The best study of this conflict is now Popkin, *You Are All Free*.
[106] Fick, *The Making of Haiti*, 158.

of international military conflict with Spain and Britain, and the gathering strength of the slave insurrection under Biassou and Jean-François's leadership all combined to force the hand of the commissioners. After an apparent illness led to Ailhaud's early departure from the colony, Polverel did his best to assert a semblance of control over the southern province in addition to his western base.[107] Together, and also in competition with one another, Sonthonax and Polverel would dispense with the two-caste principle.[108] Yet the path they followed toward this radical departure from script was also a continuation of the colonial administrative search for the well-ordered plantation society.

On May 5, 1793, Sonthonax and Polverel issued the first in their historic string of proclamations. Styled as an intervention into the "discipline of slaves," the pronouncement introduced the civil commissioners as having been "delegated to the French leeward islands to restore order and public tranquility there" – a formulaic but nonetheless revealing phrase that would appear at the head of nearly all of the proclamations to follow.[109] Sonthonax and Polverel sought to use their opening salvo to convince the slave insurgents that the new administration would use its metropolitan-backed power to protect the slaves from the long-standing abuses of their masters. Already in February and March 1793, Sonthonax had written to the National Convention (as the French legislature had become known following the proclamation of a Republic in September 1792) to insist that time was running out for France to assert control of matters in Saint-Domingue. Absent rapid action on a plan to "fix the lot of the slaves," the colony might be forever lost to France.[110]

The commissioners began their May 5 proclamation by noting that "it is not among the slaves that one ought to search for the causes of their insurrections. It is neither for themselves, nor by themselves that they rebel; they are simply ceding to foreign impulsions."[111] This rhetoric was merely the latest installment in a long line of statements that, since the beginning of the August 1791 slave revolt, refused to recognize

---

[107] Ailhaud's early exit led Sonthonax and Polverel to promote Olivier Ferdinand Delpeche, the commission's secretary, to take his place.

[108] For an interesting comparison of the "two paths" followed by Sonthonax and Polverel, see Jacques de Cauna, "Polverel et Sonthonax, deux voies pour l'abolition de l'esclavage," in Dorigny, *Léger Félicité Sonthonax*, 47–53.

[109] Etienne Polverel and Léger-Félicité Sonthonax, "Proclamation relative à la discipline des esclaves," May 5, 1793 in "Aux origines de l'abolition," 36 (1st trimester, 1949): 35. The phrase was sometimes used without the adjective "public."

[110] Stein, *Léger Félicité Sonthonax*, 83; Dubois, *Avengers of the New World*, 154–155.

[111] Polverel and Sonthonax, "Proclamation," May 5, 1793, in "Aux origines de l'abolition," 36 (1st trimester, 1949): 35.

even a relative autonomy and volition on the part of the slave insurgents. The sources of the slave revolt were believed to lie elsewhere. As David Geggus has written, the many suspects included "[r]oyalist counterrevolutionaries, the Amis des Noirs, secessionist planters, the remnants of Ogé's band, and the free coloreds in general."[112] (Garran de Coulon pointedly criticized this pattern of thought and its various conspiratorial offshoots in 1797, noting that the slaves had "need for no other instigator than the irresistible attraction [of liberty] for all living beings who [labor] under the chains of tyranny.")[113] The administrators' focus on the conditions of slave treatment was not itself a conspiratorial thesis, but by localizing the supposed sources of slave resistance, it made radical abuse the central normative issue and directed attention away from the overall question of slavery's basic legitimacy.

The equation of planter brutality with the supposed "causes" of colonial unrest nonetheless resonated deeply within the eighteenth-century regime of the Code Noir. To put an end to the "insurrections of slaves," Sonthonax and Polverel declared, it was necessary to inquire into the conduct and thinking of "free persons" rather than scrutinize the actions of the enslaved. The ease with which slaves spread their "projects of revolt" testified to the planters' poor management and oversight practices. "The slaves are treated with inhumanity" because plantation owners flouted laws mandating "good treatment" and requiring a certain number of overseers proportional to the size of their slave populations.[114]

Unlike Viefville des Essars, however, for whom this status quo demanded abolition of the Code Noir, Sonthonax and Polverel insisted that there was no need for new laws to supersede the existing regimen.[115] The body of their proclamation proceeded to reprise the provisions of the Code Noir and the protested 1784–1785 plantation-management ordinances. Article 15 of the new proclamation, for example, reiterated the terms of articles 42 and 43 of the Code by banning the "inhumane" discipline of slaves, whether by way of mutilation or homicide. (Torture was not mentioned in this provision, which was promulgated at a time when the practice of judicial torture had been fully abolished in French criminal law.)[116]

---

[112] Geggus, *Haitian Revolutionary Studies*, 12.
[113] Garran de Coulon, *Rapport sur les troubles*, 2:194, also quoted in part in Dubois, *Avengers of the New World*, 105.
[114] Polverel and Sonthonax, "Proclamation," May 5, 1793, in "Aux origines de l'abolition," 36 (1st trimester, 1949): 36.
[115] Ibid., 39.
[116] Ibid. (Art. 15).

In some respects, the Code Noir was literally dressed up in a new exterior. Thus, the fleurs-de-lis were to be replaced by the letter "M" (presumably standing for *marron*) as a marker branded on the skin of the fugitive slave.[117] Even in their efforts to relax the 1685 regime, Sonthonax and Polverel signaled their intent to re-create the old order, exempting from the fugitive-slave penalties any insurgents who quit the "rebel" camps and returned to their plantations within a month.[118] The full proclamation was ordered published in creole translation and posted and read aloud to assemblies of slaves on all of the plantations.[119]

THE CONDITIONS OF LIBERTY

If any single development pushed Sonthonax and Polverel to go beyond this reformist platform, it was the deadlock between them and Governor Galbaud's restorationist campaign. In June 1793, the commissioners moved to imprison Galbaud in a ship off the coast of Le Cap. This resulted in all-out conflict between Galbaud's supporters (a group that consisted largely of white sailors), free people of color (who saw in Galbaud a threat to their recently restored liberties), and insurgent slaves released from the city's prisons in the midst of the enveloping disorder.[120] On the morning of June 20, Cap Français burned for the second time in as many years. It was in this context that Sonthonax and Polverel made their first critical turn in the direction of general emancipation. On the afternoon of the same day, with the city still smoldering, the commissioners issued a standing offer of liberty and equal citizenship to "all Negro warriors who will fight for the Republic."[121]

---

[117] Ibid., 42 (art. 34).

[118] Ibid., 42 (art. 35).

[119] Ibid., 42 (art. 40). This was not the only proclamation that Sonthonax published in creole in 1793. Others included the August 29 emancipation proclamation (discussed later). See Geggus, "Print Culture and the Haitian Revolution," 83. The full creole text of the August 29 proclamation is reproduced in Jean Barnabé, "Les proclamations en créole de Sonthonax et Bonaparte: graphie, histoire, et glottopolitique," in *De la Révolution française aux révolutions créoles et nègres*, ed. Michel Martin and Alain Yacou (Paris: Éditions Caribéennes, 1989), 147–149.

[120] Popkin, *You Are All Free*, 1–2, 20, 189–216; Dubois, *Avengers of the New World*, 158. See also Elizabeth Colwill, "Gendering the June Days: Race, Masculinity, and Slave Emancipation in Saint Domingue," *Journal of Haitian Studies* 15, nos. 1–2 (2009): 103–123; and idem, "Fêtes de l'hymen, fêtes de la liberté: Matrimony, Emancipation, and the Creation of New Men," in Geggus and Fiering, *The World of the Haitian Revolution*, 125–155.

[121] Popkin, *You Are All Free*, 1–3, 211–213; Bell, *Toussaint Louverture*, 53–54. In mid-May, thus even before the culmination of the standoff with Galbaud, the commissioners

The opportunistic limits of this offer were suggested two days later, when Sonthonax and Polverel wrote to Biassou seeking to entice the insurgent leader away from the Spanish side. While promising liberty for Biassou and his troops in exchange for their support, the commissioners held out the prospect of improvements for slaves on the plantations.[122] Not surprisingly, Toussaint Louverture and other insurgent leaders initially interpreted the offer of June 20 as a desperate and cynical gamble on the part of the beleaguered commissioners.[123]

Still, a breach had been broken, and the emancipation of slave recruits to the republican cause on June 20, 1793, opened the regulatory floodgates that had been constructed over the course of the Old Regime in response to the manumission of individual slaves by their masters. The *journée* of June 21, 1793, was, in a sense, the culmination of a trend that had begun in late colonial times with the militarization of manumission in the 1770s. The critical differences were twofold. First, slave military labor was now needed on a far vaster scale and more immediate basis than was true in colonial times. Second, the emancipation of slave recruits in 1793 served primarily to arm the republican administrators in their explosive conflicts with the white civilian population (both *grand* and *petit blanc*), rather than to provide manpower for the pursuit of fugitive slaves.

It is therefore correct to argue, as Jeremy Popkin recently has, that the French revolutionary abolition of slavery in 1793–1794 was the consequence of a civil war among Saint-Domingue's free population, rather than a straightforward extension of the Declaration of the Rights of Man or the inevitable product of the slave insurgency.[124] Less convincing, however, is Popkin's assertion that the emancipation proclamations of Sonthonax and Polverel (and their subsequent ratification by the National Convention) were "the result of a crisis that had little to do with slavery."[125] As we have seen, a reformist preoccupation with the treatment of slaves both predated and postdated Sonthonax and Polverel's initial offer of freedom. The *journée* of June 20, 1793, was a critical moment in the story of the extension of general liberty in Saint-Domingue, but only one such moment on a road that originated in the regime of the Code Noir, which itself outlived

---

had begun to emancipate slaves who had been armed by their owners and municipal authorities in Saint-Domingue. Geggus, *Haitian Revolutionary Studies*, 125.

[122] Dubois, *Avengers of the New World*, 159.

[123] Popkin, *You Are All Free*, 3, 20; Geggus, *Haitian Revolutionary Studies*, 127.

[124] Popkin, *You Are All Free*, 7–8, 11–15, 19–20.

[125] Ibid., 20.

the pivotal events of June 20.[126] The watershed of June 20 undoubtedly reflected the commissioners' pragmatic mission to "restore order and public tranquility" in Saint-Domingue. Yet the disorder to which it responded involved not simply the specter of intraracial (white-versus-white) conflict, or even conflict between whites and free people of color, but also the broader instability fostered by the slave insurgency.

Polverel's proclamation of August 27, 1793, nicely demonstrates this point. After the immediate crisis in Le Cap had passed, the civil commissioners ordered Galbaud and his collaborators deported to France to stand judgment before the National Convention for their insubordination. Most of Galbaud's remaining sympathizers promptly fled on ships for the coastal towns of the United States, including Baltimore, Philadelphia, and Charleston. This effectively emptied the Cap Français region of its autonomist white planter population as well as its royalist officers and *petits blancs* hostile to the commissioners.[127] Having consolidated their control of the northern capital by recruiting an emergency force of black republican soldiers and cementing an alliance with the free people of color, the commissioners turned their attention to the problem of how best to deal with the slave insurgency. Ongoing conflict in the northern and western provinces, fueled by Spanish support for the insurrection, helped persuade the commissioners that more far-reaching measures were needed to secure the loyalty of the vast majority of black rebels.[128]

Polverel's August 27 proclamation proposed to entice both "insurgent" and "noninsurgent" slaves to the French republican side by offering them the fruits of the plantations abandoned by émigré planters. It was, in effect, a conditional offer of emancipation – consisting of "freedom, equality, and lands in property" – designed to revive the disrupted plantation economy of the western province while also strengthening the fragile military position of the republican forces.[129] By bearing arms for France or cultivating lands abandoned by their former masters, slaves could demonstrate that they were worthy of citizenship and a share of the plantation

---

[126] For the reactions of contemporary witnesses to the June 20 proclamation as a transformative moment, see Colwill, "Fêtes de l'hymen, fêtes de la liberté," 130, 149 n.25. Colwill dates the proclamation to June 20 rather than June 21.

[127] Dubois, *Avengers of the New World*, 159; Geggus, *Haitian Revolutionary Studies*, 13.

[128] "Aux origines de l'abolition," 36 (1st trimester, 1949): 47 n.1; Dubois, *Avengers of the New World*, 161.

[129] Etienne Polverel, "Proclamation relative à la distribution du revenu des propriétés confisquées des émigrés entre les guerriers et les cultivateurs," Aug. 27, 1793, in "Aux origines de l'abolition," 36 (1st trimester, 1949): 46.

revenues.[130] A separate provision promised an "irrevocable" grant of liberty to those "armed negroes currently in a state of insurrection" who agreed to turn over possession of the lands under their control, swear an oath to the French Republic, and fight for the republican forces until the end of the "external war and internal troubles."[131] The warrior and the cultivator became the ideal personality types (to borrow Max Weber's phrase) of the new republican imperial order.[132]

That new order would depart from the regime of slavery enshrined in the Code Noir, but would do so by perpetuating its concern with the conditions of plantation discipline. Thus cultivators could enjoy the benefits of liberty and citizenship only so long as they continued to work the plantations to which they were attached.[133] Somewhat apologetically, Polverel explained that he and Sonthonax had been forced to reiterate the provisions of the Code Noir and the 1784 plantation-management ordinance in their May proclamation because their commission did not include the authority to go beyond existing laws. A new decree of the National Convention, however, had since vested the commissioners with the power to make any "provisional" changes to the plantation-labor regime deemed necessary to "maintain the internal peace of the colonies."[134] Polverel's August 27 proclamation affirmed that he and Sonthonax intended to use these expanded powers to enact new regulations that, "in regard to the

[130] Ibid. The emancipation provision was enshrined in article 1 of the proclamation. The specific revenue shares are set forth at ibid., 52 ff. Women cultivators were to receive half of the male share of the profits (an inequality they protested at the time, to no avail). Ibid., 52; Peabody, "Négresse, Mulâtresse, Citoyenne," 66. "Cultivators" aged seventy and older and those unable to work due to sickness were guaranteed a share of the revenues but excluded from the ability to own property. Polverel, "Proclamation," Aug. 27, 1793, in "Aux origines de l'abolition," 36 (1st trimester, 1949): 53.

[131] Polverel, "Proclamation," Aug. 27, 1793, in "Aux origines de l'abolition," 36 (1st trimester, 1949): 54. The bearing of arms on behalf of the Republic was not made a condition of that liberty, but was a prerequisite for being able to own property. Alternatively, insurgents who surrendered could opt to meet the requirements for the status of cultivator. Polverel did not specify the legal status of insurgents who refused to hand over control of the territories in their possession or to take up the roles of either cultivator or warrior. Presumably these individuals would have remained "enslaved" in the eyes of the Republic simply by reason of not being able to satisfy any of the conditions for emancipation set forth in the proclamation.

[132] Max Weber, *Economy and Society: An Outline of Interpretive Sociology*, ed. Guenther Roth and Claus Wittich, trans. Ephraim Fischoff et al. (Berkeley: University of California Press, 1978), 1:626. See also article eight of the Aug. 27 proclamation, providing that all vacant plantations belong in common to warriors and cultivators of the western province. "Aux origines de l'abolition," 36 (1st trimester, 1949): 49.

[133] Polverel, "Proclamation," Aug. 27, 1793, in "Aux origines de l'abolition," 36 (1st trimester, 1949): 48.

[134] The decree was dated March 5, 1793. Ibid., 48 & n.1.

slaves, will temper the rigor of the excessive punishments indicated by the Code Noir." The effect of this softening of the plantation-labor regime would be to raise those "Africans" who chose to remain with the masters' plantations "almost to the level of free men."[135] "Almost," that is, but not quite, for just as colonial-era regulations had imposed conditions and limits on the liberties of manumitted slaves even when mobilizing them for security purposes, Polverel and Sonthonax would do the same.

The new regime entailed two additional consequences, said Polverel. It would demolish the nefarious prejudices of those who doubted that the "African race" could be persuaded to work without the compulsion of slavery.[136] In addition, it would persuade the colonists – whose lands were now made subject to profit-sharing arrangements with their former slaves – that free labor was more profitable than slavery. Thus "enlightened as to their true interests," the colonists would come around to the view that "cultivation by free hands … is less costly and more productive than cultivation by slaves."[137]

The prudential standard of the "true interests" of masters, once used by colonial administrators to persuade planters of the merits of treating their slaves with humanity, was now used to argue for a distinctly unsentimental and economic view of plantation labor.[138] Yet even in this new form, a pragmatic preoccupation with the conditions of treatment, propelled by worries about the threat of the unfolding slave insurgency, remained a potent factor in the analysis. Its modernizing appeal to the sensibility of the free market notwithstanding, Polverel's August 27 proclamation was squarely aimed at securing the allegiance of the ex-slave leaders Biassou, Jean-François, Macaya, and Toussaint, all then fighting under the Spanish flag.[139]

As a technique for organizing and regulating the conditions of plantation labor, then, slavery was very much at issue in the proclamations of the civil commissioners. Their policies reflected an administrative impulse to contain the subversive repercussions of the slave revolt while echoing the Old Regime anxiety about the destabilizing effects of "excessive" manumissions. Sonthonax's proclamation of August 29, 1793, was no

---

[135] Ibid., 48.

[136] Ibid., 47.

[137] Ibid. On this theme, see also Dorigny, *Anti-esclavagisme, abolitionnisme, et abolitions*, 17–19 (discussing Adam Smith and the physiocrats' views on the inefficiency of slave labor); idem, "La Société des Amis des Noirs," in Dorigny and Gainot, *La Société des Amis des Noirs*, 36.

[138] See Chapter 3.

[139] "Aux origines de l'abolition," 36 (1st trimester, 1949): 47 n.1.

exception to this pattern, even though it has come to overshadow all
the other pronouncements of the civil commissioners as a result of its
ostensible radicalism and precedential impact. In fact, both Polverel and
Sonthonax were preceded in their respective proclamations by an event
that remains relatively obscure in the historical literature: an assembly
of some fifteen thousand old and new citizens, the so-called Commune
of Cap Français, which enthusiastically voted on August 25, 1793, for a
general emancipation. Robin Blackburn has suggested that this unher-
alded popular vote in Le Cap inspired both Sonthonax and Louverture to
come out simultaneously in favor of general liberty a few days later. (On
August 29, Louverture issued a proclamation from Camp Turel in which
the hitherto obscure insurgent leader announced that "I want Liberty and
Equality to reign in Saint-Domingue" and invited his fellow insurgents to
join him in that cause.)[140] If so, Polverel seems to have been no less moved
by the vote, and the competition between the two civil commissioners
to be seen as the pioneer of general liberty in Saint-Domingue became a
three-way race involving Louverture.

One might just as easily interpret this rivalry as a competition to
"restore order and tranquility" in the French colony – the introduc-
tory formula used to open all of the civil commissioners' pronouncements, Sonthonax's August 29 proclamation included.[141] Indeed, in early
September, as he moved to introduce an unconditional form of general
liberty in the western province, Polverel himself insisted that Sonthonax
had been forced to act under the pressure of "unexpected events," a transparent reference to the conflict with Galbaud, the destruction of Cap
Français, and the threat posed by Jean-François's army. In freeing the
slaves of the northern province, Polverel opined, Sonthonax "himself ...
was not free."[142]

These were perhaps the words of an outmaneuvered rival. There was,
however, much in the text of Sonthonax's proclamation itself that complicated the stirring dose of republican idealism with which it began: "*Men
are born and remain free and equal in rights*: this, citizens, is the Gospel
of France; it is well past time that it be proclaimed in all departments

---

[140] See Blackburn, "Epilogue," in Geggus and Fiering, *The World of the Haitian Revolution*,
395. Dubois puts this event at Aug. 24 rather than Aug. 25. On the Camp Turel declaration and its context, see Geggus, *Haitian Revolutionary Studies*, 127–128; Bell,
Toussaint Louverture, 18–19; Dubois, *Avengers of the New World*, 176–177.

[141] Léger-Félicité Sonthonax, "Proclamation relative à l'émancipation générale dans la
province du Nord," Aug. 29, 1793, in "Aux origines de l'abolition," 36 (3rd and 4th
trimesters, 1949): 348.

[142] Ibid., 356.

of the Republic."[143] Sonthonax was now patently misleading in describing the scope of the commissioners' mandate as a gradual preparation for the "general emancipation of the slaves."[144] Indeed, the contradiction with the commissioners' initial embrace of the two-caste principle was too blatant to ignore entirely. Sonthonax conceded that, upon arriving in Saint-Domingue and finding the colony's white population divided by a "schism," the commissioners had committed to the view that "slavery is necessary to cultivation."[145]

This awkward attempt to square the commissioners' original mandate from the Convention with the subsequent evolution of their policies in Saint-Domingue was itself framed in the language of precautionary calculation. "If, by the greatest of imprudences, we had attempted [in the fall of 1792] to rupture the links between masters and slaves," Sonthonax argued, the result would have been a complete bloodbath. The slaves, driven by a "just fury," would have immediately set upon their "executioners" without regard to distinctions between the "innocent" and the "guilty." By contrast, the only remaining white residents of Saint-Domingue as of August 1793 were all "friends of the law and of French principles."[146]

According to both Polverel and Sonthonax, however, this change of circumstances would have been of no consequence without the expanded administrative powers given the commissioners by the National Convention's decree of March 5, 1793. Sonthonax cited that decree, which licensed any provisional measures necessary to preserve the colony's "internal peace," as the basis for his proclamation.[147] He framed the project of emancipation, accordingly, in terms of a provisional reform of the "*police and discipline*" of the plantations – which is to say, the framework traditionally associated with the administration of the Code Noir in colonial times. "This police and discipline will be changed: a new order of things will be reborn, and the old servitude will disappear."[148]

The spirit of the late colonial Old Regime was present in this formulation, and in the substantive provisions of the proclamation. Sonthonax was not altogether unjustified in describing the new order as a dramatic

---

[143] Ibid., 348 (emphasis in the original).

[144] Ibid.

[145] Ibid., 349.

[146] Ibid., 349–350. Cf. Michelle Vovelle, "Sonthonax: sa place dans l'histoire des abolitions," in Dorigny, *Léger-Félicité Sonthonax*, 163 (contrasting the "prudent strategies" of the Society with Sonthonax's anticipatory vision).

[147] Sonthonax, "Proclamation," Aug. 29, 1793, in "Aux origines de l'abolition," 36 (3rd and 4th trimesters, 1949): 351.

[148] Ibid., 350 (emphasis in the original).

departure from the status quo, even if his portrayal of freedom as a gift from the French nation was abstract to the point of obfuscation.[149] It is difficult to deny the manifest radicalism of the first part of article 2: "All blacks and persons of mixed-blood, currently enslaved, are declared free to enjoy all rights attached to the status of French citizen."[150] By simultaneously emancipating the slaves of the northern province and making them citizens, Sonthonax was clearly acting on a scale far greater than the piecemeal enfranchisement of manumitted slaves contemplated by articles 57 and 59 of the Code Noir. (Those articles were provisionally abrogated along with the rest of the 1685 edict in the August 29 proclamation).[151]

At the same time, it is difficult to overlook the conditional nature of this grant of liberty and citizenship. Even as it liberated and enfranchised the slaves, article 2 made clear that they "will however be subjected to a regime" of plantation discipline. The bulk of Sonthonax's proclamation was dedicated to elaborating on the terms of that discipline.[152] "Negroes currently attached to their former masters' plantations will be required to remain there; they will be employed in the cultivation of the land."[153] The proclamation required these "former slave-cultivators" to remain on their plantations for the space of a year, unless they received the permission of a justice of the peace to work elsewhere.[154] Thereafter, official permission would still be required for cultivators to travel beyond the limits of their localities.[155] The responsibility to "maintain order" on the plantations now essentially resided in the justices of the peace, who were vested with the power to replace an owner's choice of overseer in the event of complaints from the cultivators.[156]

---

[149] Ibid., 351. The exact phrase is "[d]evenus citoyens par la volonté de la Nation Française." As Madison Smartt Bell notes, Sonthonax was indeed "completely sincere" in his abolitionism (*Toussaint Louverture*, 140).

[150] Sonthonax, "Proclamation," Aug. 29, 1793, in "Aux origines de l'abolition," 36 (3rd and 4th trimesters, 1949): 351.

[151] Ibid., 355 (art. 37). It is only partly valid to say, as Laurent Dubois does, that this was the "most radical" aspect of Sonthonax's proclamation (*Avengers of the New World*, 165), for the principle of citizenship for the freed slave dated back to Roman law.

[152] Sonthonax, "Proclamation," Aug. 29, 1793, in "Aux origines de l'abolition," 36 (3rd and 4th trimesters, 1949): 351.

[153] Ibid., 352 (art. 8).

[154] Ibid., 352 (art. 11).

[155] Ibid., 355 (art. 36).

[156] Ibid., 353, 354. Other significant provisions included the following: The whip was to be superseded by the rod, and punishments thenceforth to be meted out by way of salary cuts (art. 27); revenues were to be shared on a one-third basis for the owners, a second third to be used by the owner for costs of business, and a final third for the cultivators (art. 12); women were to be paid one-third less than men (arts. 16–17); within 15 days,

If there were echoes of the 1784 plantation-management reforms in some of these provisions, it is because neither Sonthonax nor Polverel had found a way to conceptualize the new regime without relying on the stabilizing function served by guarantees of continued plantation labor. Although Polverel gave greater emphasis than Sonthonax to the need for the ex-slaves to own a part of the property they worked,[157] the two commissioners were united on the necessity for a new system of "police and discipline" to replace the old.

When Polverel followed up with his own emancipation proclamation for the western province on September 4, 1793, he lectured the ex-slaves in terms that recalled the colonial concern with the libertinage of manumitted slaves.[158] The freed persons, Polverel intoned, would only find happiness in "property and work," not "disorder, idleness, and brigandage."[159] Indeed, the old specter of interracial sexual promiscuity and corruption hung over the emancipation decisions of the civil commissioners. In July, the commissioners had issued a proclamation encouraging insurgent slave "warriors" to free their wives and children through marriage, an incentive already long enshrined in article 9 of the Code Noir;[160] and Sonthonax's August 29 proclamation included a provision that appears to have targeted women prostitutes for imprisonment.[161]

By the late fall of 1793, a regime of "general liberty" based on the sharing of plantation revenues and the "discipline" of cultivators had been extended, at least formally, to all three provinces of the colony.[162] However, the British landing at Jérémie in September added a major additional wildcard to the situation in the south and west. From Jérémie, the British quickly expanded their control into the northern part of the southern peninsula, and the free colored leader André Rigaud retained

---

all men who were neither property owners nor registered to work on a plantation or in domestic service would be arrested and imprisoned, as would women with no "known means of existence" (a seeming allusion to prostitution) (arts. 33 and 34).

[157] Etienne Polverel, "Proclamation relative à la liberté générale différée," Sept. 4 1793, in "Aux origines de l'abolition," 36 (3rd and 4th trimesters, 1949): 356–357.

[158] Cf. Holt, *The Problem of Freedom*, 56 (noting that the drafters of the apprenticeship system for Jamaican slaves emancipated in 1834 "did regard the slaves as children needing to be reeducated as wage laborers and resocialized as citizens").

[159] Etienne Polverel, "Proclamation relative à la liberté générale différée," Sept. 4 1793, in "Aux origines de l'abolition," 36 (3rd and 4th trimesters, 1949): 358.

[160] Code Noir, art. 9 (1685). See Colwill, "Fêtes de l'hymen, fêtes de la liberté," 125–155; and Peabody, "Négresse, Mulâtresse, Citoyenne," 64.

[161] Sonthonax, "Proclamation," Aug. 29, 1793, in "Aux origines de l'abolition," 36 (3rd and 4th trimesters, 1949): 355 (art. 34).

[162] For Polverel's October 31, 1791, proclamation extending "general liberty" to the west and south, see "Aux origines de l'abolition," 36 (3rd and 4th trimesters, 1949): 372 ff.

effective control of the area surrounding Les Cayes.[163] The British occupation of Saint-Domingue, which would ultimately reach into parts of both the southern and western provinces and last for four years, dramatically raised the stakes of the civil commissioners' strategy of trading conditional freedom for military reinforcements. Not surprisingly, given this military context, Polverel's promise to give the freedmen and women an ownership share of the plantations proved incapable of enforcement in the western and southern provinces.[164] More generally, the various qualifications and conditions imposed under the new order would long complicate the lives of those freed under the provisional authority of Sonthonax and Polverel.[165]

The National Convention's emancipation decree of February 4, 1794, was, in substance, merely a ratification of decisions made by Sonthonax and Polverel in the spur of the moment and under the pressure of circumstances. Indeed, in the most immediate sense, the decree was prompted by the arrival in France of three deputies from Saint-Domingue elected under Sonthonax's supervision: a white delegate named Louis Dufay, the free colored representative Jean-Baptiste Mills, and Jean-Baptiste Belley, a former slave turned republican officer.[166] Elected in September, the three men arrived in Paris on January 23, 1794, only to be imprisoned by the Committee on General Security, acting under pressure from Page and Brulley on behalf of the white planter lobby. The Committee on Public Safety then intervened to arrange for the release of the trio. The appearance of the three Saint-Domingue delegates in the National Convention several days later triggered the remarkably brief but surprisingly complex debate that culminated in the famous decree of February 4.[167] This does not mean that the decision itself was without great significance. Toussaint Louverture, for one, believed that the decisions of Sonthonax and Polverel in the New World would matter little

---

[163] See David P. Geggus, *Slavery, War, and Revolution: The British Occupation of Saint Domingue, 1793–1798* (New York: Oxford University Press, 1982).

[164] Dubois, *Avengers of the New World*, 164.

[165] See Rebecca J. Scott, "'She … Refuses to Deliver Up Herself as the Slave of Your Petitioner': Émigrés, Enslavement, and the 1808 Louisiana Digest of the Civil Laws," *Tulane European and Civil Law Forum* 24 (2009): 115–36; Rebecca J. Scott and Jean M. Hébrard, "Les papiers de la liberté: Une mère africaine et ses enfants a l'époque de la Révolution Haïtienne," *Genèses*, 66 (March 2007): 4–29.

[166] Popkin, *You Are All Free*, 327, 352–353; Dubois, *Avengers of the New World*, 168–169.

[167] Popkin, *You Are All Free*, 352–364. The three men had traveled via a sojourn in the United States before landing in Bordeaux, hence the later than usual date of their arrival in France.

until they were firmly and fully endorsed by the metropole.[168] Further, the Convention's action persuaded many free people of color in the northern province that they had indeed finally arrived at the end of the road envisioned by the Code Noir.[169] For the decree of 16 Pluviôse (as it is known by its French revolutionary calendrical date) sanctioned the abolition not only of slavery, but also of racial discrimination in the French colonies. Equal citizenship across the color line was characterized as the logical corollary of ending slavery: "The National Convention declares slavery abolished in the colonies. In consequence it declares that all men, without distinction of color, domiciled in the colonies, are French citizens and will enjoy all the rights assured under the Constitution."[170]

So simple and emphatic in its language, the decree was nonetheless easily amenable to readings between the lines. The National Convention was clearly responding to the expanding threat of the British invasion. The deputy who stood to move that the Convention abolish slavery did so immediately after Dufay's speech defending Sonthonax's "wise and enlightened policy of creating new citizens for the Republic in order to oppose our enemies."[171] Securing these "new men" their rights would make them "more attached to their duties: first and foremost [of which] will be to fight for your country, which they regard as theirs."[172] The decree was thus the equivalent of an offer of alliance to the black insurgents and to the slave populations of territories still controlled by royalist planters and the British.[173] As Robin Blackburn notes, the act of 16 Pluviôse may not have been pure *realpolitik*, for it carried the great strategic risk of alienating the United States.[174] Voices of principle were not altogether absent from the scene. Some of the more radical Montagnards in the Convention had spoken out against slavery during the first half of 1793. Yet by the time Dufay, Belley, and Mills arrived in Paris, the planter lobby had succeeded to a striking degree at inserting slavery as a kind of wedge issue between the Montagnards and Brissot's party, the

---

[168] Bell, *Toussaint Louverture*, 100.

[169] Ibid., 132.

[170] *Archives parlementaires*, 84:284. An English translation of the decree is reproduced in Bell, *Toussaint Louverture*, 100; and (with a slightly different rendering) in Dubois and Garrigus, *Slave Revolution in the Caribbean*, 132.

[171] *Archives parlementaires*, 84:278 (also quoted in Dubois, *Avengers of the New World*, 170).

[172] *Archives parlementaires*, 84:282.

[173] Blackburn, "Epilogue," in Geggus and Fiering, *The World of the Haitian Revolution*, 397.

[174] Ibid.

Girondins.[175] The brevity of the Convention's debate over the measure makes it difficult to assess the motives of all of the delegates who voted for it.[176] However, it seems fair to say that in its purpose and, ultimately, in its effect, the decree of 16 Pluviôse was largely strategic and precautionary in nature.

That effect was not immediate. As of April 1794, by which time news of the decree would have reached Saint-Domingue, many of the insurgents who would have been freed under the combined effect of the Sonthonax/Polverel proclamations and the National Convention's decree were still withholding their support for the French republican cause.[177] By May 5, however, when Toussaint Louverture declared for France, the National Convention began to achieve its objectives.[178] Louverture likely allied with France for a combination of pragmatic and idealistic reasons: a deteriorating relationship with the Spanish side; a corresponding concern that the safety of his family (then living in an area of the central plateau controlled by the Spanish) would be better secured if they were living in French-controlled territory; internecine conflict with Jean-François and Biassou; a sense that the local balance of power in Saint-Domingue was shifting to France; and last but not least, a genuine commitment to the cause of general liberty.[179]

Toussaint Louverture's conversion to the republican cause, far more than the decree of 16 Pluviôse, would prove to be the single most decisive development for the future course of the Haitian Revolution. It eventually enabled him to consolidate control over all regions of colony. Further, it ultimately placed him in the position of being able to serve not merely as a military leader, but as a lawgiver in his own right. In that role, he would continue and in some ways intensify the search for a well-ordered commonwealth in Saint-Domingue.

[175] Popkin, *You Are All Free*, 334.
[176] Ibid., 364.
[177] Bell, *Toussaint Louverture*, 97.
[178] Ibid., 101.
[179] Ibid., 99–101. See also Geggus, *Haitian Revolutionary Studies*, 127–135.

Conclusion

The revolutionary transformation of the Code Noir did not end with the departure of Sonthonax and Polverel from Saint-Domingue in June 1794, to face trial in France concerning their conduct over the preceding two years. (Polverel died before the trial was over; Sonthonax was eventually acquitted of all charges in October 1795 and returned to the colony as head of a new civil commission in May 1796.) In the later 1790s, after control of Saint-Domingue had passed to Toussaint Louverture, the difficulties of reconciling a workable plantation economy with a meaningful commitment to liberty for the former slaves continued to complicate the effort to embed a rule of law in Saint-Domingue. The colony's first black lawgiver would manage to creatively address, but not entirely transcend, those difficulties.

The story of Louverture's rise to power between 1794 and 1800, well told in several recent accounts, need only briefly be summarized here.[1] Critical to understanding the nature of the regime that Louverture would eventually consolidate is that this period was thoroughly dominated by war. Louverture's apprenticeship in the exercise of colonial administrative power was overwhelmingly military in nature and consisted of two overlapping phases: a stage of foreign military occupation and then a period of internal struggle for power between various factions seeking to inherit the mantle of French control. Louverture's decision to join the French republican forces, sometime between April and July 1794, made it possible for Sonthonax and Polverel to force a Spanish departure from

[1] See Bell, *Toussaint Louverture*, 135–265; Dubois, *Avengers of the New World*, 171–250; and Geggus, *Haitian Revolutionary Studies*, 14–25.

Santo Domingo in July 1795. By the middle of 1798, that same alliance led to the eviction of the British – although not before Louverture succeeded in pressuring Sonthonax himself to depart the scene for one final time in August 1797. His European rivals all subdued, the black leader devoted most of 1799 and 1800 to vanquishing the forces of his free colored rival André Rigaud in the south. Rigaud himself fled in July 1800, and by the fall of that year, Louverture was in a position to exercise uncontested internal authority over the entirety of Hispaniola, subject only to the continued external claims of French sovereignty.

Seeking to consolidate that authority and to secure the gains of the black revolution by restoring its debilitated economy, Louverture turned to law and the regulation of the colony's labor system.[2] In so doing, he managed to step into the shoes of Sonthonax in a further sense, for the legal regime that Louverture enacted beginning in October 1800 was a continuation of Sonthonax and Polverel's spartan restrictions on the liberty of the freed persons.[3] Agricultural cultivation was the "prop of governments" and the "mechanism of all states," Louverture declared in the preliminary discourse of his October 12 regulation. Just as it was unacceptable for a soldier in the field of battle to abandon his post without incurring the severest of punishments, so too was it necessary to persuade the cultivator that the "security of liberty" required him to remain on his plantation and attend diligently to his work.[4] Accordingly, the regulation provided that those cultivators then in a state of "idleness," that is, who failed to report to their plantations and resume working for their respective shares of the collective profits within eight days, would be punished "with the same severity as rank-and-file soldiers."[5]

At one level, this rhetoric hearkened back to an old colonial tradition of decrying the libertinage and unruliness of freed persons in Saint-Domingue, particularly those residing in the colony's cities and towns. Furthermore, the threat of military-style retribution was a variation on

---

[2] See the outstanding study by Moïse, *Le projet national de Toussaint Louverture*.

[3] David Geggus, "Toussaint Louverture and the Haitian Revolution," in Weisberger et al., *Profiles of Revolutionaries*, 127; Cauna, "Polverel et Sonthonax," 52; Carolyn Fick, "Emancipation in Haiti," 24; and Popkin, *You Are All Free*, 378. The Haitian historian Vertus Saint-Louis has analyzed Louverture's militarization of the colony's agricultural system in "Régime militaire et Règlements de culture en 1801"; and *Aux origines du drame d'Haïti: Droit et commerce maritime (1794–1806)* (Port-au-Prince, Haïti: L'Imprimeur II, 2006), 149–171.

[4] Toussaint Louverture, "Règlement de culture," Oct. 12, 1800, in Moïse, *Le projet national de Toussaint Louverture*, 132–134. This book reprints the entire text of the regulation.

[5] Ibid., 135–136.

Montesquieu's theme of the importance of the fear of punishment to the maintenance of slavery. There was, to be sure, a more immediate context for Louverture's policy. Many of the plantations had lain fallow during the long period of foreign military occupation and, indeed, ever since the outset of the slave insurgency. In 1798, a group of ex-slaves loyal to Louverture's nephew Moïse had refused to obey the French general Gabriel Marie Théodore Joseph d'Hédouville's orders to work the plantation fields, in protest against the continued assertion of French military authority and the imprisonment of Moïse. (Indeed, that very protest occasioned calls by former slaves for Louverture to assume control of the entire colony.)[6] However, the underlying anxiety about the fragility of a well-ordered commonwealth in Saint-Domingue was still there, as was the colonial ambivalence about whether the freed person should indeed be allowed to be free. Moreover, the regulation unmistakably echoed Sonthonax and Polverel's administrative-reformist vision of a post-emancipation plantation economy.

Louverture's project was arguably distinct from earlier precedents and traditions in at least three respects. First, reflecting the impact of the military conflicts of the preceding six years and the attendant exile of many of the colony's white planters, the old preoccupation with the threat of arbitrary planter brutality was replaced by a newfound confidence in the fixed promise of lawlike military severity: brutality in the form of the rule of law rather than the unconstrained passions of colonial slavery. Second, and most obviously, Louverture's program was that of a black lawgiver, the culmination of a larger movement by nonwhites to assert control over the transformation of the regime of the Code Noir begun in 1789 and 1791. A call to restore the discipline of plantation labor did not necessarily have the same cultural meaning coming from such a lawgiver as it did when voiced by a French commanding general or civil commissioner. Third, as Claude Moïse has shown, Louverture gravitated toward a more self-conscious and pronounced understanding of the distinction between "individual" and "general" liberty than any of his predecessors. For Louverture, to be free in 1800 did not mean freedom to dispose of one's individual physical labor as one wished. It meant, instead, to do what was necessary to preserve the collective freedom of the former slaves as a society still vulnerable to the threat of colonial enslavement.[7]

---

[6] Malick Ghachem, "The Colonial Vendée," in Geggus and Fiering, *The World of the Haitian Revolution*, 169–170.

[7] Moïse, *Le projet national de Toussaint Louverture*, 69. See also Carlo Avierl Celius, "Le Contrat social haïtien," *Pouvoirs dans la Caraïbe* 10 (1998): 27–70.

These differences notwithstanding, the new regime was entirely capable of eliciting protest from those subject to its yoke. In the fall of 1801, Moïse led a second rebellion of his followers, this time directed against his uncle Louverture and the exigencies of the new plantation-labor rules.[8] By that time, Louverture had had occasion to extend his legal-economic reforms with a second landmark enactment: a new constitution for Saint-Domingue, promulgated in July 1801.

The 1801 Constitution was the culmination of Louverture's effort to secure a stable colonial commonwealth in Saint-Domingue. In principle, slavery was held incompatible with the fundamental principles of the new polity: "There can be no slaves on this territory; servitude is forever abolished here. All men who are born here live and die free and French." The use of the adjective "French" in this article suggested that Louverture's vision for Saint-Domingue entailed a continued attachment to France, although some contemporaries (Napoleon included) were convinced the 1801 Constitution was the functional equivalent of an assertion of independence. Whatever the exact nature of the external framework Louverture had in mind, it was qualified by the overriding principle that "the law is the same for all, whether it punishes or protects."[9]

Other aspects of the Constitution, however, suggest that the idea of uniform punishment took priority over equal protection in Louverture's constitutional vision. Borrowing from a long-standing colonial legal valorization of local custom, Louverture subjected all provisions relating to agriculture and trade to the domestic imperatives of the Saint-Domingue economy. In order to extirpate the supposed "vice" of cultivators who strayed from their plantations, a practice that the Constitution condemned as "contrary to public order," Louverture incorporated by reference the punitive provisions of his October 1800 regulation. "[B]eing essentially agricultural," Saint-Domingue "could not suffer the least interruption in the work" of its plantations. Another

---

[8] Dubois, *Avengers of the New World*, 247–248.

[9] Constitution of Saint-Domingue, July 1801, in Moïse, *Le projet national de Toussaint Louverture*, 104. Bell suggests that Louverture was walking a tightwire between the great powers of the Atlantic world and was concerned to strike a pose that would prove palatable to the French, British, and Americans all at once. Bell, *Toussaint Louverture*, 211–212. Claude Moïse posits that Louverture had in mind a "dominion"-type relationship with France, not unlike that which would later characterize the nexus between the United States and Puerto Rico. Moïse, *Le projet national de Toussaint Louverture*, 62–64.

article authorized the renewal of the slave trade into Saint-Domingue, using the phrase "new cultivators" rather than slaves to describe the persons to be imported.[10]

Overall, as Sybille Fischer has observed, the 1801 Constitution seemed "designed to guarantee some continuity with the French colonial past while also developing a language that would make the return of slavery impossible."[11] Whether under the name of "general liberty" or slavery, however, the new regime was given precious little time to prove itself.[12] In November 1801, in another proclamation denouncing idleness as the "source of all disorders" in a "well-ordered state," Louverture added to the burdens of the former slaves by instituting a new system of plantation surveillance geared towards "fixing cultivators to the plantations."[13] This measure coincided with Louverture's suppression of the second Moïse uprising, which would prove to be his final victory as a military leader in revolutionary Haiti. In effect, Louverture's constitutional experiment could demonstrate only that the weight of the colonial era still hung heavy over Saint-Domingue, as it did over those in France who longed to restore the plantation system of old.

The perceived audacity of the 1801 Constitution led Napoleon to dispatch a massive military expedition to subdue Louverture and the black revolution. Lured into a negotiating session with leaders of that expedition, Louverture was arrested and deported to France in June 1802, where he died not long after. Back in Saint-Domingue, an all-out war of extermination between French forces and the armies commanded by Louverture's successor, Jean-Jacques Dessalines, continued into 1803 before culminating in the declaration of Haitian independence on January 1, 1804. Notoriously, one of the first acts of Dessalines' new regime was to order the massacre of most of the whites then remaining in the former French colony: a ruthless act of vengeance for all of the ruthless atrocities committed over the preceding century and more.[14] Another of his acts

---

[10] Constitution of Saint-Domingue, July 1801, in Moïse, *Le projet national de Toussaint Louverture*, 99, 106–107.

[11] Sibylle Fischer, *Modernity Disavowed: Haiti and the Cultures of Slavery in the Age of Revolution* (Durham, NC: Duke University Press, 2004), 230.

[12] Geggus, *Haitian Revolutionary Studies*, 23.

[13] Toussaint Louverture, Proclamation, November 1801, in Moïse, *Le projet national de Toussaint Louverture*, 150, 155, also quoted in Dubois, *Avengers of the New World*, 248–249.

[14] Davis, *Inhuman Bondage*, 172.

was to announce a new constitution for Haiti.[15] Law and violence traveled together until the very end.

The long arc of Haiti's passage from slavery to freedom underscores just how much of our heritage of legal and moral opposition to slavery descends from the ambiguous and highly conflicted pragmatism of the colonial law of slavery itself.[16] This is not an unusual characteristic of legal and moral "progress." We regularly arrive at perceptions of justice and injustice through complicated detours that may have little to do with morality or first principles necessarily, and more to do with situational understandings, local intuitions, fears, strategic concerns about efficiency and self-interest, and the accumulated knowledge of lived experience. Just as often, these pragmatic considerations are then translated into – if they are not already accompanied by – a sense of what our common humanity requires or commends.[17] In the case of slavery, as the eighteenth-century Haitian experience suggests, the impulse to eliminate the domestic sovereignty of masters originated in significant respects in a prior tactical impulse to constrain the brutality of masters toward their slaves in the interests of preserving the stability of the slave system

[15] On Dessalines' 1805 Constitution, which created an imperial head of state that was essentially the mirror image of Napoleon, see Fischer, *Modernity Disavowed*, 231–236, 275–281 (where the Constitution appears in English translation); and Claude Moïse, *Constitutions et luttes de pouvoir en Haïti*, vol. 1, *La faillite des classes dirigeantes (1804–1915)* (Montreal: CIDIHCA, 1988), 29–35.

[16] For a discussion of an American variation on this theme, see Genovese, *Roll, Jordan, Roll*, 49–69 (describing the movement for the "humanitarian reform" of slavery that emerged in the antebellum South). Genovese argues that "[t]he campaign to improve the lot of the slaves predated the abolitionist agitation, as did the campaign to confirm the blacks in perpetual slavery. Abolitionism and the southern reaction to it accelerated forces already in motion." Ibid., 55. Cf. Jordan, *White over Black*, 368 (arguing that the late-eighteenth-century humanitarian reform movement in the American South served to extend the life of slavery by making it more tolerable for slaveowners and abolitionists alike). On the law of the antebellum South, see Morris, *Southern Slavery and the Law*, 161–208; Tushnet, *Slave Law in the American South*; and Andrew Fede, "Legitimized Violent Slave Abuse in the American South, 1619–1865: A Case Study of Law and Social Change in Six Southern States," *American Journal of Legal History* 29, no. 2 (1985): 93–150. See also Johnson, "Inconsistency, Contradiction, and Complete Confusion," 415 ("Over the course of the 19th century, crimes of wanton murder and indiscriminate violence against slaves by slaveholders were increasingly punished in Southern courts, though legal action remained rare and the emergent legal standard – 'moderate force' – elastic.").

[17] Cf. Sen, *The Idea of Justice*, 1–2. In a discussion of Edmund Burke's 1789 speech in Parliament calling for the impeachment of Warren Hastings, the governor of the British East India Company, Sen points to the importance of "plural grounding" in diagnoses of injustice: "using a number of different lines of condemnation, without seeking an agreement on their relative merits."

generally. Furthermore, once that impulse had taken hold, it continued to be shaped by colonial-era ambivalence about the nature and scope of the liberty to be enjoyed by the freed person.

Therein lies an important corrective to those who would argue that modernity marks a sharp rupture with the values and institutions of the slave era.[18] Abolitionism – or at least certain important strands of abolitionist thought – emerged from *within* the legal world of slavery as well as from outside it. Like the colonial contests over the law of slavery, abolitionism entailed an instrumental as well as moral project, which is to say that it too was an effort to moderate the perceived dangers that stemmed from the anxious, crisis-prone world of masters and their captive "enemies."

Lest this point sound too abstract, I hasten to emphasize that it bears a significant relationship to the Haitian experience. The strategic critique of planter brutality that shaped the French colonial law of slavery and left traces on the unfolding of the Haitian Revolution led a very specific afterlife in the Atlantic world. It is an afterlife that figured critically in the law and politics of slavery in the early American republic and the British West Indies (among other places), where the events of the Haitian Revolution were filtered through both of two different lenses: a proslavery or revanchist lens and an abolitionist one.[19]

Although neither has gone unexplored, the proslavery perspective is the more familiar to historians of the American South, who have long noted, in David Brion Davis's summation, that "the Haitian Revolution reinforced the conviction (of slaveholders especially) that slave emancipation in any form would lead to economic disaster as well as the slaughter of whites."[20] As Edward Rugemer has recently shown, this conviction was shaped in significant measure by the American reception of a single book, the British Caribbean planter and parliamentarian Bryan

---

[18] We do not, of course, live "after" the reality of slavery itself, or at least the reality of certain forms of human domination over other humans – such as sexual trafficking – that can reasonably be described as slavery. See Kevin Bales, *Disposable People: New Slavery in the Global Economy* (Berkeley: University of California Press, 1999) (discussing varied forms of contemporary slavery including debt bondage in Pakistan and India and sex slavery in Thailand). For an analysis of the debate over whether the effects of slavery are still with us in the United States, see Ariela Gross, "When is the Time of Slavery? The History of Slavery in Contemporary Legal and Political Argument," *California Law Review* 96 (2008): 309 (discussing the reparations debate in contemporary America). See also Dayan, *Story of Cruel and Unusual* (arguing that modern Eighth Amendment jurisprudence reflects the legacies of the law of slavery).

[19] By far the best work on the impact of the Haitian Revolution in the early American republic is now Ashli White, *Encountering Revolution: Haiti and the Making of the Early Republic* (Baltimore, MD: The Johns Hopkins University Press, 2010).

[20] Davis, *Inhuman Bondage*, 159.

Edwards's *Historical Survey of the French Colony of St. Domingo*.[21]
Edwards's polemical account made the French abolitionist Society of
the Friends of the Blacks the primary culprit in the events that had laid
waste to the plantation society of Saint-Domingue.[22] Southern white anxieties stemmed not only from the suspected influence of Boston and other
northern abolitionists, however, but also from the fear that black and free
colored refugees arriving from Cap Français would spread the Haitian
revolutionary "contagion" throughout the American plantation states.[23]
In response to this fear of "French negroes" (as they were called), nearly
all of the Southern coastal states passed legislation in the 1790s and early
1800s restricting the entry of slaves from other jurisdictions into their
borders.[24] The "lessons" of Haiti were also reflected in laws restricting
manumission and in the rise of colonization schemes.[25]

However, this very fear of a revolutionary contagion imported by
Haitian refugees of color into the American South was equally amenable
to abolitionist treatment. As Lacy Ford has written, with reference to the
impact of the Haitian Revolution, "[i]n the minds of many upper South
whites, a system, however profitable, that provided such a source of vul-
nerability demanded either reform or elimination." Stated differently, the
proslavery and abolitionist spins on the Haitian Revolution were different
sides of the same coin: Both incorporated a form of the commonwealth
critique of slavery, reviving Bodin's old prognostications about the cor-
rupting effects of human bondage on the republic. Further, both involved
initiatives to manage the hazards that slavery posed in a world in which
slave revolution was now a demonstrably real threat. The malleability of

---

[21] Edward Barlett Rugemer, *The Problem of Emancipation: The Caribbean Roots of the American Civil War* (Baton Rouge: Louisiana State University Press, 2008), 43. Edwards's book was published in 1797. For the period prior to 1797, see Ashli White, "Saint-Dominguan Refugees and American Distinctiveness in the Early Years of the Haitian Revolution," in Geggus and Fiering, *The World of the Haitian Revolution*, 248–260; and idem, *Encountering Revolution*.

[22] Rugemer, *Problem of Emancipation*, 44.

[23] Lacy K. Ford, *Deliver Us From Evil: The Slavery Question in the Old South* (New York: Oxford University Press, 2009), 26–27; White, *Encountering Revolution*, 142–145.

[24] This was true of North Carolina, South Carolina, and Georgia. Virginia curiously abstained. Maryland passed a deportation rather than exclusion measure. South Carolina resumed importation of slaves in 1803. Ford, *Deliver Us From Evil*, 85–86, 89; Jordan, *White over Black*, 382. See also Davis, *Inhuman Bondage*, 161 (noting that the Haitian Revolution added pressure on Congress to close off the American slave trade in 1807, the earliest date allowed by the Constitution); and White, *Encountering Revolution*, 149–150.

[25] Davis, *Inhuman Bondage*, 161.

the American debates echoed the structure of argument in the Lejeune case, in which both sides had sought to invoke the perceived hazard of revolt as a kind of trump card in favor of their respective positions.[26]

To be sure, American anxieties about the excesses and instability of slave society long predated the coming of the Haitian Revolution. Thomas Jefferson's discussion of slavery in *Notes on the State of Virginia* (1781) – "[t]he whole commerce between master and slave is a perpetual exercise of the most boisterous passions, the most unremitting despotism on the one part, and degrading submissions on the other"; "I tremble for my country when I reflect that God is just" – is only the most familiar example.[27] In the early republican era, however, Haiti gave a renewed life to these preexisting anxieties and provided a powerful mechanism for channeling them in the form of law and policy.

Thus, Southern state laws restricting the importation of persons of color from Saint-Domingue identified the prospect of domestic unrest with the very bodies of individual Haitian slaves and ex-slaves. Those bodies were seen, quite literally, as carriers of risk, personalized extensions of the dynamics that had led to the overthrow of colonial law in Saint-Domingue. The Haitian Revolution did not simply crystallize the stakes in the strategic critique of slavery for Americans: It was believed to have physically embodied and exported those stakes. And abolitionist agitators did not hesitate to exploit that belief. For example, in 1792, the Reverend Charles Nisbet of Philadelphia, principal of Dickinson College, observed that "[a] Negro war, which may probably break out soon," would promote the antislavery agenda.[28] Nisbet's fellow antislavery Pennsylvanian David Bard warned in 1804, the year Haitian independence was declared, that southerners could anticipate a French invasion funneled through Saint-Domingue.[29] Such sentiments were specifically connected to the phenomenon of planter cruelty, which Americans frequently identified with Caribbean plantation practices.

---

[26] For their part, African Americans in cities such as Philadelphia found it necessary to balance their sympathy for the Haitian Revolution with a need not to be seen as supporting the advocacy of armed rebellion. White, *Encountering Revolution*, 145–146.

[27] Jefferson, "Notes on the State of Virginia," 288–289. See also John Chester Miller, *The Wolf by the Ears: Thomas Jefferson and Slavery* (Charlottesville: University Press of Virginia, 1991), 38–45. For a more general discussion of the preexisting "balance of terror" on which North American slavery rested, see Ford, *Deliver Us From Evil*, 356–357.

[28] Quoted in Merton L. Dillon, *Slavery Attacked: Southern Slaves and Their Allies, 1619–1865* (Baton Rouge: Louisiana State University Press, 1990), 48.

[29] Ibid., 52.

Thus in 1800, shortly after the revelation of Gabriel's conspiracy in Virginia (an alleged plot to commit slave revolt that was believed to have ties to the Saint-Domingue revolutionaries), a northern newspaper urged its readers in verse form to "remember ere too late/The tale of St. Domingo's fate./Tho *Gabriel* dies, a host remain/Oppress'd with slavery's galling chain."[30]

Nor did one have to be a committed abolitionist to believe that the stability of Southern society required efforts to end slavery, and that gradual emancipation was the only risk-free method of achieving that goal. The alternative, of course, was repression – and Haiti demonstrated clearly enough where that road led.[31] Against the danger of revolution à la Saint-Domingue, wrote Thomas Jefferson to James Madison in 1799, "there is no remedy but timely measures on our part, to clear ourselves, by degrees, of the matter on which that lever [leaven?] can work."[32] (By "timely measures," Jefferson was referring to a scheme of gradual emancipation.) Three years later, in 1802, Governor James Monroe of Virginia concluded on a similar note that, "while this class of people [slaves] exists among us, we can never count with certainty on its tranquil submission."[33] As late as 1814, Jefferson was still passively advocating emancipation "through the generous energy of our minds," as an alternative to having it forced through "the bloody process of St. Domingo."[34]

A similar mix of concerns made headway in early-nineteenth-century Britain and its West Indian colonies. Abolitionists who needed no convincing about the vices of slavery nonetheless couched their appeals in language that any patriotic Briton could appreciate. Conservative in nearly every other respect, the abolitionist and lawyer James Stephen

---

[30] Ibid., 61 (emphasis in the original). See also Jordan, *White over Black*, 378–379.

[31] Dillon, *Slavery Attacked*, 67.

[32] Thomas Jefferson to James Madison, Feb. 5, 1799, in *The Writings of Thomas Jefferson*, ed. Paul Leicester Ford (New York: G.P. Putnam's, 1896), 7:343 (also quoted in Tim Matthewson, "Jefferson and Haiti," *Journal of Southern History* 61, no. 2 (1995): 224). See also Thomas Jefferson to St. George Tucker, Aug. 28, 1797, in Ford, *Writings of Thomas Jefferson*, 7:168 (relating Jefferson's views on the "mode of emancipation" and stating that "the first chapter of this history, which has begun in St. Domingo ... may prepare our minds for a peaceable accommodation between justice, policy & necessity").

[33] Quoted in Dillon, *Slavery Attacked*, 68.

[34] Quoted in Ford, *Deliver Us From Evil*, 70. See also Abruzzo, *Polemical Pain*, 98–100. For the British West Indian variation on this theme, see Fergus, "'Dread of insurrection,'" 772–775. As its title suggests, Matthew J. Clavin's *Toussaint Louverture and the American Civil War: The Promise and Peril of a Second Haitian Revolution* (Philadelphia: University of Pennsylvania Press, 2010) traces the competing abolitionist and proslavery narratives of the Haitian Revolution in the United States up through the 1860s.

was a fervent critic of slavery, who fixed on the precedent of Saint-Domingue in his 1802 work *The Crisis of the Sugar Colonies.* Addressing himself "not to the *conscience* of a British Statesman, but to his *prudence* alone," Stephen argued that without a dramatic shift in course, Britain would not be able to avert the fate of the French Caribbean empire.[35] On the other end of the ideological spectrum, fears stirred by the declaration of Haitian independence in 1804 led the hitherto pro-slavery newspaper *The Times* of London suddenly to come out in favor of abolition.[36]

The commonwealth critique of slavery, which had grown roots in Haiti during the colonial period, had come full circle. Haiti itself was now one of the most potent sources and symbols of the strategic case for abolition in the post-revolutionary Atlantic world.

My story has come to an end, and I am all too aware of how much more there is to say about the legacies of Haiti's experience under the law of slavery.[37] From our present-day vantage point, it is difficult to avert one's eyes from what has transpired in Haiti since 1789 or 1804. As I write this conclusion, it is almost exactly one year to the day since the January 2010 earthquake, and the view of Haiti since that terrible event has become especially unavoidable. I must leave to others the task of making sense of the complexities of Haiti's contemporary predicament.[38]

But the "fierce urgency of now" is also a function of history.[39] And the political chaos that marked the bicentennial only a few years before – involving what some have characterized as the legitimate removal of a dictator, and what others have called a coup d'état – confirms that the memories, antagonisms, and scars of Haiti's distant past are not yet resolved. The Haitian Revolution is not yet "over," in contrast to what

---

[35] Quoted in Adam Hochschild, *Bury the Chains: Prophets and Rebels in the Fight to Free an Empire's Slaves* (Boston: Houghton Mifflin, 2005), 301–302.

[36] See Geggus, "The Caribbean in the Age of Revolution," 89; and Morgan, "Ending the Slave Trade," 117–120 (discussing the "mixed" impact of the Haitian Revolution on British antislavery).

[37] See, among other works, Trouillot, *Haiti: State Against Nation*; Nicholls, *From Dessalines to Duvalier*; and Fatton, *The Roots of Haitian Despotism.*

[38] See Erica Caple James, *Democratic Insecurities: Violence, Trauma, and Intervention in Haiti* (Berkeley: University of California Press, 2010); and Paul Farmer, *Haiti after the Earthquake* (New York: PublicAffairs, 2011). Laurent Dubois's *Haiti: The Aftershocks of History* (New York: Metropolitan, 2012) was not yet available as this book went to press.

[39] Martin Luther King, Jr., Address at the March on Washington, Aug. 28, 1963, available at http://www.mlkonline.net/dream.html (last viewed December 31, 2010).

François Furet famously said of the French Revolution.[40] It is beyond argument that slavery is a large part of the explanation for these persisting wounds and vulnerabilities. Yet how exactly we understand slavery – how exactly we make sense of the Old Regime – is a matter that has become more complex, rather than less, with the passing of time.

At some point in the not-too-distant future, the legalized slavery that so indelibly marked the trajectories of the plantation Americas will cease to belong to the world of living memory and will become solely an object of "history." When that happens, slavery's place in the field of Atlantic political and legal contestation will recede, to be replaced by other, more recent institutional pasts. For the time being, however, and now with far greater urgency than before, Haiti continues to search for a stable and coherent society whose efforts to build a viable government and economy are no longer overwhelmed by the legacies of slavery. Although profoundly troubled by the long arm of the slave era, Haiti is not alone in this regard. Its experience is the touchstone for understanding the persistent effects, both domestic and international, of the "boisterous passions" that governed master-slave relations in the Atlantic world, and of the strategic ethics that have accompanied democratization in societies where chattel bondage once reigned.[41]

[40] Furet, *Interpreting the French Revolution*, 1–79.
[41] Jefferson, "Notes on the State of Virginia," 288.

Bibliography

Note: The abbreviation "LC" as used in the footnotes refers to Moreau de Saint-Méry's six-volume *Loix et constitutions* collection, the full reference for which appears under "Printed Primary Sources" below. All other abbreviations used in the footnotes are defined below under "Archival and Manuscript Sources."

Archival and Manuscript Sources

Archives de la Chambre de Commerce de Marseille, France

Série H. Article 14.
Série H. Article 44.

Archives nationales d'outre-mer, Aix-en-Provence, France (ANOM)

1. Correspondance générale Saint-Domingue (CGSD)
   C/9A/1. 1664–1688.
   C/9A/160. 1788.
2. Collection Moreau de Saint-Méry, Fonds ancien, Série F.
   F/3/90. Police des Noirs.
   F/3/153. Documents sur l'inoculation, la justice à l'Ile de France, mémoires sur Saint-Domingue. Législation, XVIIIè siècle.
   F/3/271. Code de Saint-Domingue. 1741–1755. ⎫
   F/3/272. Code de Saint-Domingue. 1756–1765. ⎪
   F/3/273. Code de Saint-Domingue. 1776–1775. ⎬ (CSD)
   F/3/274. Code de Saint-Domingue. 1776–1779. ⎪
   F/3/275. Code de Saint-Domingue. 1780–1782. ⎭

Printed Primary Sources

Anon. "Aux origines de l'abolition de l'esclavage: Proclamations de Polverel et de Sonthonax, 1793–1794." *Revue d'histoire des colonies*, 36 (1st trimester, 1949): 24–55, and 36 (3rd and 4th trimesters, 1949): 348–423.

Cahier contenant les plaintes, doléances & reclamations des citoyens-libres & proprietaires de couleur, des Îles & Colonies françaises. Paris: n.p., 1789.

Catéchisme révolutionnaire, ou L'histoire de la Révolution française, par demandes et par réponses: à l'usage de la jeunesse républicaine, et de tous les peuples qui veulent devenir libres. Paris: Debarle, 1793–1794.

Code Noir (1685).

Code Noir (1724).

Concordat de MM. les citoyens blancs de Port-au-Prince avec MM. les citoyens de couleur. N.p.: n.p., 1791.

"Esclavage." In *Répertoire universel et raisonné de jurisprudence civile, criminelle, canonique et bénéficiale*, edited by Joseph Nicolas Guyot, 7:71–77. Paris: Visse, 1784.

Le Code Noir. Edited by Robert Chesnais. Paris: L'Esprit frappeur, 1998.

Loi relative aux colonies, & aux moyens d'y appaiser les troubles. Paris: L'Imprimerie Royale, 1792.

Ordonnance criminelle (1670).

"Nègres." In *Répertoire universel et raisonné de jurisprudence civile, criminelle, canonique et bénéficiale*, edited by Joseph Nicolas Guyot, 12:57–58. Paris: Visse, 1784.

Relation d'une conspiration tramée par les nègres dans l'îsle de S. Domingue. N.p.: n.p., 1758.

Archives parlementaires de 1787 à 1860: Recueil complet des débats législatifs et politiques des chambres françaises. Series 1 (1787–1799), vols. 8 (Paris: Paul Dupont, 1881), 25–26 (Paris: Paul Dupont,1887), 84 (Paris: Centre National de la Recherche Scientifique, 1962).

Bodin, Jean. *The Six Bookes of a Commonweale: A facsimile reprint of the English translation of 1606 Corrected and supplemented in light of a new comparison with the French and Latin texts.* Translated by Richard Knolles and Kenneth Douglas McRae. Edited by Kenneth Douglas McRae. Cambridge, MA: Harvard University Press, 1962.

Les six livres de la république. 6 vols. Lyon: G. Cartier, 1593. Reprint, Paris: Fayard, 1986.

On Sovereignty: Four Chapters from "The Six Books of the Commonwealth." Edited and translated by Julian H. Franklin. Cambridge, UK: Cambridge University Press, 1992.

Brissot, Jacques-Pierre. *Discours de J.P. Brissot, député, sur les causes des troubles de Saint-Domingue, prononcé à la séance du premier décembre 1791.* Paris: Imprimerie nationale, 1791.

Discours sur la nécessité politique de révoquer le décret du 24 septembre 1791, pour mettre fin aux troubles de Saint-Domingue. Paris: L'Imprimerie du Patriote Français, 1791.

Burke, Edmund. *Reflections on the Revolution in France*, London: J. Dodsley, 1790.

Carteau, Jean-Félix. *Soirées bermudiennes, ou Entretiens sur les événemens qui ont opéré la ruine de la partie française de l'isle de Saint-Domingue.* Bordeaux: Pellier Lawalle, 1802.

Commission des Colonies. *Débats entre les accusateurs et les accusés dans l'affaire des colonies.* 11 vols. Paris: Imprimerie Nationale, 1795.

Condorcet, Marie Jean Antoine Nicolas de Caritat, marquis de. *Réflexions sur l'esclavage des nègres.* Neuchâtel, Switzerland: La Société Typographique, 1781.

Delattre, Pascal-François. *Rapport fait au nom des comités réunis de Constitution, de la Marine, d'Agriculture et de Commerce, & des Colonies, à la séance du 7 mai 1791, sur les colonies.* Paris: De l'Imprimerie nationale, 1791.

Dubuisson, Paul-Ulric. *Nouvelles considérations sur Saint-Domingue, en réponse à celles de M. H. D.* Paris: Cellot & Jombert, 1780.

Garran de Coulon, Jean-Philippe. *Rapport sur les troubles de Saint-Domingue, fait au nom de la Commission des colonies, des Comités de salut public, de législation, et de marine.* 4 vols. Paris: Imprimerie nationale, 1797–99.

Hilliard-d'Auberteuil, Michel René. *Considérations sur l'état présent de la colonie de Saint-Domingue: ouvrage politique et législative.* 2 vols. Paris: Grange, 1776–1777.

Jefferson, Thomas. "Notes on the State of Virginia." In *Thomas Jefferson: Writings,* edited by Merrill D. Peterson, 123–325. New York: Library of America, 1984.

The Writings of Thomas Jefferson. Edited by Paul Leicester Ford. Vol. 7. New York: G.P. Putnam's, 1896.

Locke, John. *Two Treatises of Government.* Edited by Peter Laslett. Cambridge Texts in the History of Political Thought. Cambridge, UK: Cambridge University Press, 1988.

Malouet, Pierre-Victor. *Mémoires de Malouet, publiés par son petit-fils le Baron Malouet.* 2nd ed. Paris: E. Plon et cie, 1874.

Mémoire sur l'esclavage des nègres. Neuchâtel, Switzerland: n.p., 1788.

Montesquieu, Charles-Louis de Secondat, baron de. *The Spirit of the Laws.* Edited and translated by Anne M. Cohler, Basia Carolyn Miller, and Harold Samuel Stone. Cambridge Texts in the History of Political Thought. Cambridge. UK: Cambridge University Press, 1989.

Moreau de Saint-Méry, Médéric-Louis-Elie. *Description topographique, physique, civile, politique, et historique de la partie française de l'isle Saint-Domingue.* New ed. Edited by Blanche Maurel and Étienne Taillemite. 3 vols. Paris: Librairie Larose for the Société de l'histoire des colonies françaises, 1958.

Description topographique, physique, civile, politique, et historique de la partie française de l'isle Saint-Domingue. 2 vols. Philadelphia, PA: Dupont, 1797–1798.

Discours de M. Moreau de Saint-Méry au Roi, prononcé dans l'Hôtel de Ville de Paris, le 17 juillet 1789. N.p.: n.p., 1789.

ed. *Loix et constitutions des colonies françaises de l'Amérique sous le vent.* 6 vols. Paris: by the author, 1784–90.

Observations d'un habitant des colonies sur le Mémoire en faveur des gens de couleur, ou sang-mêlés, de Saint-Domingue & des autres Isles françaises de l'Amérique, adressé à l'Assemblée Nationale, par M. Grégoire, Curé d'Embermésnil, Député de Lorraine. N.p.: n.p., 1789.

Page, Pierre François, and Augustin Jean Brulley. *Développement des causes des troubles et désastres des colonies françaises*. N.p.: n.p., 1793.

Piquionne, Natalie. "Lettre de Jean-François, Biassou et Belair, juillet 1792." *Chemins critiques*, 3 (1997): 206–220.

Raimond, Julien. *Observations sur l'origine et le progrès du préjugé des colons blancs contre les hommes de couleur*. Paris: Belin, 1791.

Réponse aux considérations de M. Moreau, dit de Saint-Méry, député à l'Assemblée nationale, sur les colonies. Paris: L'Imprimerie du Patriote français, 1791.

Raynal, abbé Guillaume-Thomas-François [Pierre-Victor Malouet]. *Essai sur l'administration de Saint-Domingue*. N.p.: n.p., 1785.

Smith, Adam. *Lectures on Jurisprudence*. Edited by R. L. Meek, D. D. Raphael, and P. G. Stein. Vol. 5, *The Glasgow Edition of the Works and Correspondence of Adam Smith*. Oxford: Oxford University Press, 1978.

Tocqueville, Alexis de. *Writings on Empire and Slavery*. Edited and translated by Jennifer Pitts. Baltimore, MD: The Johns Hopkins University Press, 2001.

Viefville des Essars, Jean-Louis, baron de. *Discours et Projet de Loi pour l'affranchissement des Nègres, ou l'Adoucissement de leur Régime, et Réponse aux Objections des colons*. Paris: L'Imprimerie Nationale, [1789] [copy in "Mélanges sur l'Amérique" collection, vol. 4., no. 7, John Carter Brown Library, Providence, Rhode Island].

Secondary Sources

Abolition de l'Esclavage: Mythes et réalités créoles. Paris: Comité des Fêtes de Vᵉ Arrondissement, avec le concours du Centre cultural du Panthéon, 1998.

Abruzzo, Margaret. *Polemical Pain: Slavery, Cruelty, and the Rise of Humanitarianism*. Baltimore, MD: The Johns Hopkins University Press, 2011.

Adelman, Jeremy, ed. *Colonial Legacies: The Problem of Persistence in Latin American History*. New York: Routledge, 1999.

Agamben, Giorgio. *State of Exception*. Trans. Kevin Attell. Chicago, IL: University of Chicago Press, 2005.

Alexander, Gregory. *Commodity and Propriety: Competing Visions of Property in American Legal Thought, 1776–1970*. Chicago: The University of Chicago Press, 1999.

Amat, Roman d', and R. Limouzin-Lamothe, eds. *Dictionnaire de Biographie Française*. Vol. 65. Paris: Librairie Letouzey et Ané, 1966.

Anderson, Duane. "The Legal History of the Reign." In *The Reign of Louis XIV: Essays in Celebration of Andrew Lossky*, edited by Paul Sonnino, 73–93. Atlantic Highlands, NJ: Humanities Press International, 1990.

Appiah, Kwame Anthony. *The Honor Code: How Moral Revolutions Happen*. New York: W.W. Norton, 2010.

Ardouin, Beaubrun. *Études sur l'histoire d'Haïti, suivies de la vie du général J.-M. Borgella*. 2nd ed. 11 vols. Port-au-Prince, Haïti: F. Dalencour, 1958.

Armitage, David. *The Declaration of Independence: A Global History.* Cambridge, MA: Harvard University Press, 2007.

"The Declaration of Independence and International Law." *The William and Mary Quarterly* 59, no. 1 (Jan. 2001): 39–64.

"John Locke, Carolina, and the *Two Treatises of Government.*" *Political Theory* 32, no. 5 (2004): 602–627.

Armitage, David, and Sanjay Subrahmanyam, eds. *The Age of Revolutions in Global Context, ca. 1760–1840.* New York: Palgrave Macmillan, 2010.

Aubert, Guillaume. "'The Blood of France': Race and Purity of Blood in the French Atlantic World." *The William and Mary Quarterly* 61, no. 3 (July 2004): 439–478.

Auguste, Claude B., and Marcel B. Auguste. *L'Expédition Leclerc, 1801–1803.* Port-au-Prince: Henri Deschamps, 1985.

Bailyn, Bernard. *The Ideological Origins of the American Revolution.* Enl. ed. Cambridge, MA: The Belknap Press of Harvard University Press, 1992.

Baker, Keith Michael. "Enlightenment and Revolution in France: Old Problems, Renewed Approaches." *Journal of Modern History* 53, no. 2 (June 1981): 281–303.

"Political languages of the French Revolution." In *The Cambridge History of Eighteenth-Century Political Thought.* Edited by Mark Goldie and Robert Wokler, 626–659. New York: Cambridge University Press, 2006.

"Sovereignty." In *A Critical Dictionary of the French Revolution.* Edited by François Furet and Mona Ozouf. Translated by Arthur Goldhammer. Cambridge, MA: Harvard University Press, 1989.

"Transformations of Classical Republicanism in Eighteenth-Century France." *Journal of Modern History* 73, no. 1 (March 2001): 32–53.

Bales, Kevin. *Disposable People: New Slavery in the Global Economy.* Berkeley: University of California Press, 1999.

Barnabé, Jean. "Les proclamations en créole de Sonthonax et Bonaparte: graphie, histoire, et glottopolitique." In *De la Révolution française aux révolutions créoles et nègres*, edited by Michel Martin and Alain Yacou, 130–150. Paris: Éditions Caribéennes, 1989.

Bart, Jean. "Esclavage et servage tardif." In *Les abolitions de l'esclavage: De L. F. Sonthonax à V. Schoelcher, 1793–1794–1848: Actes du colloque international tenu à l'Université de Paris VIII les 3, 4, et 5 février 1994*, edited by Marcel Dorigny, 26–29. Paris: Presses Universitaires de Vincennes et Éditions UNESCO, 1995.

Bell, Madison Smartt. *Toussaint Louverture: A Biography.* New York: Pantheon, 2007.

Bender, Thomas, ed. *The Antislavery Debate: Capitalism and Abolitionism as a Problem in Historical Interpretation.* Berkeley: University of California Press, 1992.

Benot, Yves. "The Insurgents of 1791, Their Leaders, and the Concept of Independence." In *The World of the Haitian Revolution*, edited by Norman Fiering and David Geggus, 99–110. Bloomington: University of Indiana Press, 2009.

"Le procès Sonthonax ou les 'débats entre les accusateurs et les accusés dans l'affaire des colonies' (an III)," In *Léger-Félicité Sonthonax: La première abolition de l'esclavage: La Révolution française et la Révolution de Saint-Domingue*, edited by Marcel Dorigny, 55–63. Paris: Société française d'histoire d'outre-mer, 1997.

La Révolution française et la fin des colonies. Paris: Éditions la Découverte, 1989.

Blackburn, Robin. "Epilogue." In *The World of the Haitian Revolution*, edited by Norman Fiering and David Geggus, 393–402. Bloomington: University of Indiana Press, 2009.

"Haiti, Slavery, and the Age of the Democratic Revolution." *The William and Mary Quarterly* 63, no. 4 (2006): 643–674.

The Making of New World Slavery: From the Baroque to the Modern, 1492–1800. New York: Verso, 1997.

The Overthrow of Colonial Slavery, 1776–1848. New York: Verso, 1988.

Bloch, Marc. *La société féodale*. 2 vols. Paris: Éditions Albin Michel, 1968.

Breathett, George. "Catholicism and the Code Noir in Haiti." *The Journal of Negro History* 73, no. 1 (1988): 1–11.

Brown, Christopher Leslie, and Philip D. Morgan, eds. *Arming Slaves: From Classical Times to the Modern Age*. New Haven: Yale University Press, 2006.

Moral Capital: Foundations of British Abolitionism. Chapel Hill: University of North Carolina Press, 2006.

Brown, Vincent. *The Reaper's Garden: Death and Power in the World of Atlantic Slavery*. Cambridge, MA: Harvard University Press, 2008.

"A Vapor of Dread: Observations on Racial Terror and Vengeance in the Age of Revolution." In *Revolution! The Atlantic World Reborn*. Ed. Thomas Bender, Laurent Dubois, and Richard Rabinowitz, 177–198. New York: D. Giles, for the New York Historical Society, 2011.

Caenegem, R. C. van. *An Historical Introduction to Private Law*. Translated by D. E. L. Johnston. Cambridge, UK: Cambridge University Press, 1992.

An Historical Introduction to Western Constitutional Law. Cambridge, UK: Cambridge University Press, 1995.

Cajuste, Pierre Richard. "Un livre d'histoire, un livre actuel: Une interview avec le professor Vertus Saint-Louis." *Haïti en Marche*, May 3, 2006.

Cardoso, Ciro Flamarion. *La Guyane française: 1715–1817: Aspects économiques et sociaux: contribution à l'étude des sociétés esclavagistes d'Amérique*. Petit Bourg, Guadeloupe: Ibis Rouge Éditions, 1999.

Casid, Jill. *Sowing Empire: Landscape and Colonization*. Minneapolis: University of Minnesota Press, 2005.

Cauna, Jacques de. "Polverel et Sonthonax, deux voies pour l'abolition de l'esclavage." In *Léger-Félicité Sonthonax: La première abolition de l'esclavage: La Révolution française et la Révolution de Saint-Domingue*, edited by Marcel Dorigny, 47–54. Saint-Denis, France: Société française d'histoire d'outre-mer et Association pour l'étude de la colonisation européenne, 2005.

Celius, Carlo Avierl. "Le Contrat social haïtien." *Pouvoirs dans la Caraïbe* 10 (1998): 27–70.

Chesnais, Robert. Introduction to *Le Code Noir*, 5–6. Edited by Robert Chesnais. Paris: L'esprit frappeur, 1998.

Clavin, Matthew J. *Toussaint Louverture and the American Civil War: The Promise and Peril of a Second Haitian Revolution*. Philadelphia: University of Pennsylvania Press, 2010.

Cobban, Alfred. *A History of Modern France*. Vol. 1, *Old Régime and Revolution, 1715–1799*. New York: Pelican Books, 1957. Reprint, New York: Penguin Books, 1990.

———. *The Social Interpretation of the French Revolution*. Cambridge, UK: Cambridge University Press, 1964.

Cohen, William B. *The French Encounter with Africans: White Response to Blacks, 1530–1880*. Bloomington: Indiana University Press, 1980.

Cole, Joshua. "Intimate Acts and Unspeakable Relations: Remembering Torture and the War for Algerian Independence." In *Memory, Empire, and Postcolonialism: Legacies of French Colonialism*, edited by Alec G. Hargreaves, 125–141. Lanham, MD: Lexington Books, 2005.

Colwill, Elizabeth. "Fêtes de l'hymen, fêtes de la liberté: Matrimony, Emancipation, and the Creation of New Men." In *The World of the Haitian Revolution*, edited by David Patrick Geggus and Norman Fiering, 125–155. Bloomington: Indiana University Press, 2009.

———. "Gendering the June Days: Race, Masculinity, and Slave Emancipation in Saint Domingue." *Journal of Haitian Studies* 15, nos. 1–2 (2009): 103–123.

Darnton, Robert. *The Forbidden Bestsellers of Pre-Revolutionary France*. New York: W.W. Norton, 1995.

Davis, David Brion. "The Comparative Approach to American History: Slavery." In *Slavery in the New World: A Reader in Comparative History*, edited by Laura Foner and Eugene D. Genovese, 60–68. Englewood Cliffs, NJ: Prentice-Hall, 1969.

———. *Inhuman Bondage: The Rise and Fall of Slavery in the New World*. New York: Oxford University Press, 2006.

———. *The Problem of Slavery in the Age of Revolution, 1770–1823*. Ithaca, NY: Cornell University Press, 1975.

———. *The Problem of Slavery in Western Culture*. Ithaca, NY: Cornell University Press, 1966.

———. *Slavery and Human Progress*. New York: Oxford University Press, 1984.

Davis, Natalie Zemon. "Judges, Masters, Diviners: Slaves' Experience of Criminal Justice in Colonial Suriname." *Law and History Review* 29, no. 4 (Nov. 2011): 925–984.

Dayan, Colin [Joan]. *Haiti, History, and the Gods*. Berkeley: University of California Press, 1995.

———. *The Story of Cruel and Unusual*. Cambridge, MA: MIT Press, 2007.

Debbasch, Yvan. "Au coeur du 'gouvernement des esclaves': La souveraineté domestique aux Antilles françaises (XVIIᵉ – XVIIIᵉ siècles)." *Revue française d'Histoire d'Outre-mer* 72, no. 266 (1985): 31–54.

———. *Couleur et liberté: Le jeu du critère ethnique dans un ordre juridique esclavagiste*. Annales de la Faculté de Droit et des Sciences Politiques et Économiques de Strasbourg, vol. 16. Paris: Librairie Dalloz, 1967.

Debien, Gabriel. *Les colons de Saint-Domingue et la Révolution: Essai sur le club Massiac (Août 1789 – Août 1792)*. Paris: Armand Colin, 1953.

Les engagés pour les Antilles (1634–1715). Paris: Librairie Larose, for la Société de l'histoire des colonies françaises, 1952.

Les esclaves aux Antilles françaises (XVIIᵉ–XVIIIᵉ siècles). Basse-Terre: Société d'histoire de la Guadeloupe, 1974.

Études antillaises (XVIIIᵉ siècle). Paris: Armand Colin, 1956.

Degler, Carl N. *Neither Black nor White: Slavery and Race Relations in Brazil and the United States*. New York: Macmillan, 1971. Reprint, Madison: University of Wisconsin Press, 1986.

Delesalle, Simone, and Lucette Valensi. "Le mot 'nègre' dans les dictionnaires français d'Ancien Régime: histoire et lexicographie." *Langue française* 15 (Sept. 1972): 79–104.

Dillon, Merton L. *Slavery Attacked: Southern Slaves and Their Allies, 1619–1865*. Baton Rouge: Louisiana State University Press, 1990.

Dorigny, Marcel. ed. *Les abolitions de l'esclavage: De L. F. Sonthonax à V. Schoelcher, 1793–1794–1848: Actes du colloque international tenu à l'Université de Paris VIII les 3, 4, et 5 février 1994*. Paris: Presses Universitaires de Vincennes et Éditions UNESCO, 1995.

Anti-esclavagisme, abolitionnisme, et abolitions: Débats et controverses en France de la fin du XVIIIe siècle aux années 1840. Québec: Les Presses de l'Université Laval, 2008.

"Le mouvement abolitionniste français face à l'insurrection de Saint-Domingue ou la fin du mythe de l'abolition graduelle." In *L'insurrection des esclaves de Saint-Domingue (22–23 août 1791)*, edited by Laënnec Hurbon, 97–113. Paris: Éditions Karthala, 2000.

ed. *Léger-Félicité Sonthonax: La première abolition de l'esclavage: La Révolution française et la Révolution de Saint-Domingue*. Paris: Société française d'histoire d'outre-mer, 1997.

"Sonthonax et Brissot: Le cheminement d'une filiation politique assumée." In *Léger-Félicité Sonthonax: La première abolition de l'esclavage: La Révolution française et la Révolution de Saint-Domingue*, edited by Marcel Dorigny, 29–40. Saint-Denis, France: Société française d'histoire d'outre-mer et Association pour l'étude de la colonisation européenne, 2005.

Dorigny, Marcel, and Bernard Gainot. *La Société des Amis des Noirs, 1788–1799: Contribution à l'histoire de l'abolition de l'esclavage*. Paris: Éditions UNESCO, 1998.

Drescher, Seymour. *Abolition: A History of Slavery and Antislavery*. New York: Cambridge University Press, 2009.

Dilemmas of Democracy: Tocqueville and Modernization. Pittsburgh: University of Pittsburgh Press, 1968.

"History's Engines, British Mobilization in the Age of Revolution." *The William and Mary Quarterly* 66, no. 4 (Oct. 2009): 737–756.

"Tocqueville and the Revolution of 1848." In *Profiles of Revolutionaries in Atlantic History, 1700–1850*, edited R. William Weisberger et al., 286–299. Boulder, CO: Social Science Monographs, 2007.

Drescher, Seymour, and Peter C. Emmer, eds. *Who Abolished Slavery? Slave Revolts and Abolitionism: A Debate with João Pedro Marques*. New York: Bergahn Books, 2010.

Dubois, Laurent. "An Atlantic Revolution." *French Historical Studies* 32, no. 4 (2009): 655–661.

Avengers of the New World: The Story of the Haitian Revolution. Cambridge, MA: Harvard University Press, 2004.

"Avenging America: The Politics of Violence in the Haitian Revolution." In *The World of the Haitian Revolution*, edited by David Patrick Geggus and Norman Fiering, 111–124. Bloomington: University of Indiana Press, 2009.

"Citizen Soldiers: Emancipation and Military Service in the Revolutionary French Caribbean." In *Arming Slaves: From Classical Times to the Modern Age*, edited by Christopher Leslie Brown and Philip D. Morgan, 233–254. New Haven, CT: Yale University Press, 2006.

A Colony of Citizens: Revolution and Slave Emancipation in the French Caribbean, 1787–1804. Chapel Hill, NC: University of North Carolina Press, for the Omohundro Institute of Early American History and Culture, 2004.

"An enslaved Enlightenment: Rethinking the Intellectual History of the French Atlantic." *Social History* 31, no. 1 (2006): 1–14.

"The Road to 1848: Interpreting French Anti-Slavery." *Slavery and Abolition* 22, no. 3 (2001): 150–157.

"Our Three Colors: The King, the Republic and the Political Culture of Slave Revolution in Saint-Domingue." *Historical Reflections* 29 (2003): 83–102.

Dubois, Laurent, and John D. Garrigus. *Slave Revolution in the Caribbean, 1789–1804: A Brief History with Documents*. Boston, MA: Bedford/St. Martin's, 2006.

Duchet, Michèle. *Anthropologie et histoire au siècle des lumières*. Paris: Maspero, 1971. Reprint, Paris: Albin Michel, 1995.

"Malouet et le problème de l'esclavage." In *Malouet, 1740–1814: actes du colloque des 30 novembre et 1er décembre 1989*, edited by Jean Ehrard and Michel Morineau, 63–70. Riom: La Revue d'Auvergne, for the Association riomoise du bicentenaire de la Révolution française et la Société des amis du Centre de recherches révolutionnaires et romantiques, 1990.

Ehrhard, Jean. *Lumières et esclavage: L'esclavage colonial et la formation de l'opinion publique en France au XVIIIᵉ siècle*. Brussels: Éditions Andre Versaille, 2008.

Elicona, Anthony Louis. *Un colonial sous la Révolution en France et en Amérique: Moreau de Saint-Méry*. Paris: Jouve et Compagnie, 1934.

Farmer, Paul. *Haiti after the Earthquake*. New York: PublicAffairs, 2011.

Fatton, Robert, Jr. *The Roots of Haitian Despotism*. Boulder, CO: Lynne Rienner, 2007.

Fede, Andrew. "Legitimized Violent Slave Abuse in the American South 1619–1865: A Case Study of Law and Social Change in Six Southern States." *American Journal of Legal History* 29, no. 2 (1985): 93–150.

Fergus, Claudia. "'Dread of insurrection': Abolitionism, Security, and Labor in Britain's West Indian Colonies, 1760–1823." *The William and Mary Quarterly* 66, no. 4 (Oct. 2009): 757–780.

Feugère, Anatole. *Un précurseur de la Révolution: L'Abbé Raynal (1713–1796)*. Angoulême: Imprimerie ouvrière, 1922. Reprint, Geneva: Slatkine Reprints, 1970.

Fick, Carolyn E. "The French Revolution in Saint-Domingue: A Triumph or a Failure?" In *A Turbulent Time: The French Revolution and the Greater Caribbean*, edited by David Barry Gaspar and David Patrick Geggus, 51–75. Bloomington: Indiana University Press, 1997.

    The Making of Haiti: The Saint Domingue Revolution from Below. Knoxville: The University of Tennessee Press, 1990.

Fieldhouse, D. K. *The Colonial Empires: A Comparative Survey from the Eighteenth Century*. London: Weidenfeld and Nicolson, 1966.

Fiering, Norman, and David Geggus, eds. *The World of the Haitian Revolution*. Bloomington: University of Indiana Press, 2009.

Fischer, Sibylle. *Modernity Disavowed: Haiti and the Cultures of Slavery in the Age of Revolution*. Durham, NC: Duke University Press, 2004.

Ford, Lacy K. *Deliver Us From Evil: The Slavery Question in the Old South*. New York: Oxford University Press, 2009.

Foucault, Michel. *Discipline and Punish: The Birth of the Prison*. Translated by Alan Sheridan. New York: Vintage Books, 1979.

Fouchard, Jean. *Artistes et répertoire des scènes de Saint-Domingue*. Port-au-Prince, Haïti: H. Deschamps, 1988.

    Plaisirs de Saint-Domingue: notes sur la vie sociale, littéraire et artistique. Port-au-Prince, Haïti: H. Deschamps, 1988.

    Le théâtre à Saint-Domingue. Port-au-Prince, Haïti: Imprimerie de l'État, 1955.

Fox, Edward Whiting. *History in Geographic Perspective: The Other France*. New York: W. W. Norton, 1971.

François, Augustin, baron de Silvestre. *Notice biographique de M. Moreau de Saint-Méry ... lue à la Société royale d'agriculture*. Paris: Imprimerie de Mme. Huzard, 1819.

Franklin, Julian H. *Jean Bodin and the Rise of Absolutist Theory*. Cambridge, UK: Cambridge University Press, 1973.

Frostin, Charles. *Les révoltes blanches à Saint-Domingue aux XVIIᵉ et XVIIIᵉ siècles (Haïti avant 1789)*. Paris: Éditions de l'École, 1975.

Furet, François. *Interpreting the French Revolution*. Translated by Elborg Forster. Cambridge, UK: Cambridge University Press, 1981.

Furet, François and Mona Ozouf, eds. *A Critical Dictionary of the French Revolution*. Trans. Arthur Goldhammer. Cambridge, MA: Harvard University Press, 1989.

Garrigus, John D. *Before Haiti: Race and Citizenship in French Saint-Domingue*. New York: Palgrave Macmillan, 2006.

    "Blue and Brown: Contraband Indigo and the Rise of a Free Colored Planter Class in French Saint-Domingue." *The Americas* 50, no. 2 (1993): 233–263.

    "Catalyst or Catastrophe? Saint-Domingue's Free Men of Color and the Battle of Savannah, 1779–1782." *Revista/Review Interamericana* 22, nos. 1–2 (1992): 109–125.

    "Opportunist or Patriot? Julien Raimond (1744–1801) and the Haitian Revolution." *Slavery & Abolition*, 28, no. 1 (2007): 1–21.

"Saint-Domingue's Free People of Color and the Tools of Revolution." In *The World of the Haitian Revolution*, edited by David Patrick Geggus and Norman Fiering, 49–64. Bloomington: Indiana University Press, 2009.

"'Sons of the Same Father': Gender, Race, and Citizenship in French Saint-Domingue, 1760–1792." In *Visions and Revisions of Eighteenth-Century France*, edited by Christine Adams, Jack R. Censer, and Lisa Jane Graham, 137–153. University Park: The Pennsylvania State University Press, 1997.

"'Thy Coming Fame, Ogé! Is Sure': New Evidence on Ogé's 1790 Revolt and the Beginnings of the Haitian Revolution." In *Assumed Identities: The Meanings of Race in the Atlantic World*, edited by John D. Garrigus and Christopher Morris, 19–45. Arlington: Texas A&M University Press, for the University of Texas at Arlington, 2010.

"White Jacobins/Black Jacobins: Bringing the Haitian and French Revolutions Together in the Classroom." *French Historical Studies* 23, no. 2 (Spring 2000): 259–275.

Gaspar, David Barry, and David Patrick Geggus, eds. *A Turbulent Time: The French Revolution and the Greater Caribbean*. Bloomington: Indiana University Press, 1997.

Gauthier, Florence. *L'aristocratie de l'épiderme: Le combat de la Société des Citoyens de Couleur 1789–1791*. Paris: CNRS Éditions, 2007.

Gayarré, Charles. *History of Louisiana: The French Domination*. 4th ed. Vol. 1. New Orleans, F. F. Hansell & Bro., 1903.

Geertz, Clifford. *Local Knowledge: Further Essays in Interpretive Anthropology*. New York: Basic Books, 1983.

Geggus, David. "The Arming of Slaves in the Haitian Revolution." In *Arming Slaves: From Classical Times to the Modern Age*, edited by Christopher Leslie Brown and Philip D. Morgan, 209–232. New Haven, CT: Yale University Press, 2006.

"The Caribbean in the Age of Revolution." In *The Age of Revolutions in Global Context*, edited by David Armitage and Sanjay Subrahmanyam, 83–100. New York: Palgrave Macmillan, 2010.

"The French Slave Trade: An Overview." *William and Mary Quarterly* 58, no. 1 (Jan. 2001): 119–138.

"Gabriel Debien (1906–1990)." *Hispanic American Historical Review* 71, no. 1 (1991): 140–142.

Haitian Revolutionary Studies. Bloomington: Indiana University Press, 2002.

ed. *The Impact of the Haitian Revolution in the Atlantic World*. Carolina Lowcountry and the Atlantic World Series, edited by Rosemary Brana-Shute. Columbia: University of South Carolina Press, 2002.

"Print Culture and the Haitian Revolution: The Written and the Spoken Word." In *Liberty! Égalité! Independencia: Print Culture, Enlightenment, and Revolution in the Americas, 1776–1838*, 79–96. Worcester, MA: American Antiquarian Society, 2007.

"Racial Equality, Slavery, and Colonial Secession during the Constituent Assembly." *American Historical Review* 94, no. 5 (December 1989): 1290–1308.

"Saint-Domingue on the Eve of Revolution." In *The World of the Haitian Revolution*, edited by David Patrick Geggus and Norman Fiering, 3–20. Bloomington: Indiana University Press, 2009.

"Slave Resistance and Emancipation: The Case of Saint-Domingue." In *Who Abolished Slavery? Slave Revolts and Abolitionism: A Debate with João Pedro Marques*, edited by Seymour Drescher and Peter C. Emmer, 112–119. New York: Bergahn Books, 2010.

Slavery, War, and Revolution: The British Occupation of Saint Domingue, 1793–1798. New York: Oxford University Press, 1982.

"Sugar and Coffee Cultivation in Saint Domingue and the Shaping of the Slave Labor Force." In *Cultivation and Culture: Labor and the Shaping of Slave Life in the Americas*, edited by Ira Berlin and Philip D. Morgan, 73–98. Charlottesville: University Press of Virginia, 1993.

"Thirty Years of Haitian Revolution Historiography." *Revista Mexicana del Caribe* 3, no. 5 (1998): 179–197.

"Toussaint Louverture and the Haitian Revolution." In *Profiles of Revolutionaries in Atlantic History, 1700–1850*, edited R. William Weisberger et al., 115–135. Boulder, CO: Social Science Monographs, 2007.

Genovese, Eugene D. *Roll, Jordan, Roll: The World the Slaves Made.* New York: Vintage, 1976.

Géraud-Lloca, Edith. "La coutume de Paris outre-mer: l'habitation antillaise sous l'Ancien Régime." *Revue historique de droit français et étranger* 60, n. 2 (1982): 207–259.

Ghachem, Malick W. "The Colonial Terror." Paper read at the Wednesday colloquium of the Dubois Institute for African and African American Research, Harvard University, December 10, 2003.

"The Colonial Vendée," in *The World of the Haitian Revolution*, edited by David Patrick Geggus and Norman Fiering, 156–176. Bloomington: Indiana University Press, 2009.

The Haitian Revolution, 1789–1804: An Exhibition at the John Carter Brown Library (May to September 2004). Providence, RI: The John Carter Brown Library, 2004.

"Montesquieu in the Caribbean: The Colonial Enlightenment between *Code Noir* and *Code Civil*." In *Postmodernism and the Enlightenment: New Perspectives in Eighteenth-Century French Intellectual History*, edited by Daniel Gordon, 7–30. New York: Routledge, 2001. Originally published in *Historical Reflections/Réflexions Historiques* 25, no. 2 (Summer 1999): 183–210.

"Sovereignty and Slavery in the Age of Revolution: Haitian Variations on a Metropolitan Theme." PhD diss., Stanford University, 2002.

Giacomel, Robert. *Le code noir: autopsie d'un crime contre l'humanité.* Nîmes: C. Lacour, 2003.

Gisler, Antoine. *L'esclavage aux Antilles françaises (XVIIe- XIXe siècle).* Rev. ed. Paris: Éditions Karthala, 1981.

Grandmaison, Olivier Le Cour. *Les citoyennetés en Révolution (1789–1794).* Paris: Presses Universitaires de France, 1992.

Gross, Ariela. "When is the Time of Slavery? The History of Slavery in Contemporary Legal and Political Argument." *California Law Review* 96 (2008): 283–321.

Harouel, Jean-Louis. "Le Code Noir." In *Abolition de l'Esclavage: Mythes et réalites créoles*, 23–27. Paris: Comité des Fêtes du Vᵉ Arrondissement, avec le concours du Centre culturel du Panthéon, 1998.

Hartog, Hendrik. *Man and Wife in America: A History*. Cambridge, MA: Harvard University Press, 2000.

Hathaway, Oona A. "The Promise and Limits of the International Law of Torture." In *Torture: A Collection*, edited by Sanford Levinson, 199–212. New York: Oxford University Press, 2004.

Haudrère, Philippe. "Code Noir." In *Dictionnaire de l'ancien régime*, edited by Lucien Bély, 274–275. Paris: Presses Universitaires de France, 1996.

Hirschman, Albert O. *The Passions and the Interests: Political Arguments for Capitalism before Its Triumph*. Princeton, NJ: Princeton University Press, 1977.

Hobsbawm, Eric. *The Age of Revolution, 1789–1848*. London: Weidenfeld & Nicholson, 1962; reprinted New York: Vintage, 1996.

Hochschild, Adam. *Bury the Chains: Prophets and Rebels in the Fight to Free an Empire's Slaves*. Boston: Houghton Mifflin, 2005.

Holt, Thomas C. *The Problem of Freedom: Race, Labor, and Politics in Jamaica and Britain, 1832–1938*. Baltimore, MD: Johns Hopkins University Press, 1991.

Horwitz, Morton J. *The Transformation of American Law, 1780–1860*. Cambridge, MA: Harvard University Press, 1979.

Hroděj, Philippe, ed. *L'esclave et les plantations: De l'établissement de la servitude à son abolition: Un hommage à Pierre Pluchon*. Rennes: Presses Universitaires de Rennes, 2008.

Hunt, Lynn. "Forgetting and Remembering: The French Revolution Then and Now." *American Historical Review* 100, no. 4 (October 1995): 1119–1135.

——— *The French Revolution and Human Rights: A Brief Documentary History*. Boston, MA: Bedford Books, 1996.

——— "The French Revolution in Global Context." In *The Age of Revolutions in Global Context*, edited by David Armitage and Sanjay Subrahmanyam, 20–36. New York: Palgrave Macmillan, 2010.

——— *Inventing Human Rights: A History*. New York: W.W. Norton, 2007.

Hurbon, Laënnec, ed. *L'insurrection des esclaves de Saint-Domingue (22–23 août 1791)*. Paris: Éditions Karthala, 2000.

James, C. L. R. *The Black Jacobins: Toussaint L'Ouverture and the San Domingo Revolution*. 2nd ed., rev. New York: Random House, 1963.

James, Erica Caple. *Democratic Insecurities: Violence, Trauma, and Intervention in Haiti*. Berkeley: University of California Press, 2010.

Jaubert, Pierre. "Le Code noir et le droit romain." In *Histoire du droit social: mélanges en homage à Jean Imbert*, edited by Jean-Louis Harouel, 321–331. Paris: Presses Universitaires de France, 1989.

Jennings, Lawrence C. *French Anti-Slavery: The Movement for the Abolition of Slavery in France, 1802–1848*. New York: Cambridge University Press, 2000.

Johnson, Ilona Vernez. "The Reinvention of Slavery in France: From the Jean Boucaux Affair to the Eve of the Haitian Revolution." PhD diss., Pennsylvania State University, 1999.

Johnson, Walter. "Inconsistency, Contradiction, and Complete Confusion: The Everyday Life of the Law of Slavery." *Law and Social Inquiry* 22, no. 2 (1997): 405–433.

Jordan, Winthrop. *White Over Black: American Attitudes Toward the Negro, 1550–1812*. Baltimore, MD: Penguin Books, 1969.

Joucla, Henri. *Le Conseil Supérieur des Colonies et ses Antécédents*. Paris: Les Éditions du Monde Moderne, 1927.

Kahn, Paul. *Sacred Violence: Torture, Terror, and Sovereignty*. Ann Arbor: University of Michigan Press, 2008.

King, Preston. *The Ideology of Order: A Comparative Analysis of Jean Bodin and Thomas Hobbes*. London: George Allen & Unwin, 1974.

King, Stewart R. *Blue Coat or Powdered Wig: Free People of Color in Pre-Revolutionary Saint-Domingue*. Athens: University of Georgia Press, 2001.

"The Maréchaussée of Saint-Domingue: Balancing the Ancien Regime and Modernity." *Journal of Colonialism and Colonial History* 5, n. 2 (Fall 2004).

Lacroix, Pamphile de. *Mémoires pour servir à l'histoire de la révolution de Saint-Domingue*. Paris: Pillet aîné, 1819.

Landers, Jane G. *Atlantic Creoles in the Age of Revolutions*. Cambridge, MA: Harvard University Press, 2010.

Langbein, John H. "The Legal History of Torture." In *Torture: A Collection*, edited by Sanford Levinson, 93–104. New York: Oxford University Press, 2004.

Torture and the Law of Proof: Europe and England in the Ancien Régime. New ed. Chicago, IL: University of Chicago Press, 2006.

Langley, Lester D. *The Americas in the Age of Revolution, 1750–1850*. New Haven, CT: Yale University Press, 1996.

Laurent, Gérard. "Les Volontaires de St. Domingue." *Conjonction* 131 (Nov. 1976): 39–57.

Lebeau, Auguste. *De la condition des gens de couleur libres sous l'Ancien Régime*. Poitiers: A. Masson, 1903.

Levinson, Sanford. "Slavery and the Phenomenology of Torture." *Social Research* 74 (2007): 149–168.

Torture: A Collection. New York: Oxford University Press, 2004.

Lewis, Gordon K. *Main Currents in Caribbean Thought: The Historical Evolution of Caribbean Society in its Ideological Aspects, 1492–1900*. Lincoln: University of Nebraska Press, 2004.

Lokke, Carl L. *France and the Colonial Question: A Study of Contemporary French Opinion, 1763–1801*. New York: Columbia University Press, 1932.

Lowell, A. Lawrence. "The Judicial Use of Torture, Part I." *Harvard Law Review* 11, no. 4 (1897): 220–233.

Madiou, Thomas. *Histoire d'Haïti*. 2nd ed. 3 vols. Port-au-Prince, Haïti: Edmond Chenet and the Départment de l'instruction publique, 1922–1923.

Mann, Bruce H. "Revolutionary Justice: Law and Society in the American Revolution." Inaugural lecture as holder of the Carl F. Schipper, Jr. Professorship of Law, Harvard Law School, May 13, 2009, available at http://www.law.harvard.edu/news/spotlight/faculty-research/lectures.html (last viewed May 10, 2010).

Marques, João Pedro. "Slave Revolts and the Abolition of Slavery: An Overinterpretation." In *Who Abolished Slavery? Slave Revolts and Abolitionism: A Debate with João Pedro Marques*, edited by Seymour Drescher and Peter C. Emmer, translated by Richard Wall, 3–89. New York: Bergahn Books, 2010.

Matthewson, Tim. "Jefferson and Haiti." *Journal of Southern History* 61, no. 2 (1995): 209–248.

Maurel, Blanche, and Étienne Taillemite. Introduction to *Description topographique, physique, civile, politique et historique de la partie française de l'isle Saint-Domingue*, by Médéric-Louis-Elie Moreau de Saint-Méry. Edited by Blanche Maurel and Étienne Taillemite. 3 vols. Paris: Librairie Larose for the Société de l'histoire des colonies françaises, 1958.

McClellan, James E., III. *Colonialism and Science: Saint Domingue in the Old Regime*. Baltimore, MD: The Johns Hopkins University Press, 1992.

McCusker, John J. *Money and Exchange in Europe and America, 1600–1775*. Chapel Hill: University of North Carolina Press, for the Institute of Early American History and Culture, 1978.

McPherson, James M. *Tried by War: Abraham Lincoln as Commander in Chief*. New York: Penguin Press, 2008.

Meadows, R. Darrell. "Social Networks and Transatlantic Migration: Saint-Domingue Refugees during the French and Haitian Revolutions." Working Paper No. 01–19, International Seminar on the History of the Atlantic World, 1500–1825, Harvard University, Cambridge, MA.

Meyer, Jean. "Des origines à 1763." In Jean Meyer, Annie Rey-Goldzeiguer, and Jean Tarrade. *Histore de la France coloniale*. Vol. 1, *La conquête*. Paris: Armand Colin, 1991.

Miller, John Chester. *The Wolf by the Ears: Thomas Jefferson and Slavery*. Charlottesville: University Press of Virginia, 1991.

Moïse, Claude. *Constitutions et luttes de pouvoir en Haïti*. Vol. 1, *La faillite des classes dirigeantes (1804–1915)*. Montréal: Les Éditions du CIDIHCA, 1988.

——— ed. *Dictionnaire historique de la Révolution Haïtienne (1789–1804)*. Montréal: Les Éditions du CIDIHCA, 2003.

——— *Le projet national de Toussaint Louverture et la Constitution de 1801*. Montréal: Les Éditions du CIDIHCA, 2001.

Moore, Lara Jennifer. *Restoring Order: The École des Chartes and the Organization of Archives and Libraries in France, 1820–1870*. Duluth, MN: Litwin Books, 2008.

Morgan, Philip D. "Ending the Slave Trade: A Caribbean and Atlantic Context." In *Abolitionism and Imperialism in Britain, Africa, and the Atlantic*, edited by Derek R. Peterson, 101–128. Athens: Ohio University Press, 2010.

Morris, Thomas D. *Southern Slavery and the Law, 1619–1860*. Chapel Hill: University of North Carolina Press, 1996.

Mousnier, Roland. *Les institutions de la France sous la monarchie absolue, 1598–1789*. Vol. 2, *Les organes de l'État et la Société*. Paris: Presses Universitaires de France, 1980.

Muthu, Sankar. *Enlightenment Against Empire*. Princeton, NJ: Princeton University Press, 2003.

Nash, Gary. "Sparks from the Altar of '76: International Repercussions and Reconsiderations of the American Revolution." In *The Age of Revolutions in Global Context*, edited by David Armitage and Sanjay Subrahmanyam, 1–19. New York: Palgrave Macmillan, 2010.

Nesbitt, Nick. *Universal Emancipation: The Haitian Revolution and the Radical Enlightenment*. Charlottesville: University Press of Virginia, 2008.

ed. *Toussaint L'Ouverture: The Haitian Revolution*. London: Verso, 2008.

Nicholas, Barry. *An Introduction to Roman Law*. Oxford: Oxford University Press, Clarendon Press, 1962.

Nicholls, David. *From Dessalines to Duvalier: Race, Colour and National Independence in Haiti*. Rev. ed. New Brunswick, NJ: Rutgers University Press, 1996.

Ogle, Gene E. "'The Eternal Power of Reason' and 'The Superiority of Whites': Hilliard d'Auberteuil's Colonial Enlightenment." *French Colonial History* 3 (2003): 35–50.

"Policing Saint Domingue: Race, Violence, and Honor in an Old Regime Colony." PhD diss., University of Pennsylvania, 2003.

"The Trans-Atlantic King and Imperial Public Spheres: Everyday Politics in Pre-Revolutionary Saint-Domingue." In *The World of the Haitian Revolution*, edited by David Patrick Geggus and Norman Fiering, 79–96. Bloomington: Indiana University Press, 2009.

Olivier-Martin, François. *Histoire du droit français des origines à la Révolution*. Paris: Domat Montchrestien, 1948. Reprint, Paris: CNRS Editions, 1995.

Olwell, Robert. *Masters, Slaves, & Subjects: The Culture of Power in the South Carolina Low Country, 1740–1790*. Ithaca, NY: Cornell University Press, 1998.

Onuf, Peter S. *Jefferson's Empire: The Language of American Nationhood*. Charlottesville: University Press of Virginia, 2000.

Pagden, Anthony. *Lords of All the World: Ideologies of Empire in Spain, Britain, and France, c. 1500 – c. 1800*. New Haven, CT: Yale University Press, 1995.

Palmer, Robert. *The Age of the Democratic Revolution: A Political History of Europe and America, 1760–1800*. 2 vols. Princeton, NJ: Princeton University Press, 1959, 1964.

Palmer, Vernon Valentine. "The Origins and Authors of the Code Noir." *Louisiana Law Review* 56, no. 2 (Winter 1995): 363–407.

Parry, J. H. *The Spanish Seaborne Empire*. New York: Alfred Knopf, 1981; reprint, Berkeley: University of California Press, 1990.

Patterson, Orlando. *Freedom*. Vol. 1, *Freedom in the Making of Western Culture*. New York: Basic Books, 1991.

Slavery and Social Death: A Comparative Study. Cambridge, MA: Harvard University Press, 1982.

"Three Notes of Freedom: The Nature and Consequences of Manumission." In *Paths to Freedom: Manumission in the Atlantic World*, edited by Rosemary Brana-Shute and Randy J. Sparks, 15–30. Charleston: University of South Carolina Press, 2009.

Peabody, Sue. "Négresse, Mulâtresse, Citoyenne: Gender and Emancipation in the French Caribbean, 1650–1848." In *Gender and Slave Emancipation in the Atlantic World*, edited by Pamela Scully and Diana Paton, 56–78. Durham, NC: Duke University Press, 2005.

"There are No Slaves in France": The Political Culture of Race and Slavery in the Ancien Régime. Oxford, UK: Oxford University Press, 1996.

Peters, Edward. *Torture.* Exp. ed. Philadelphia: University of Pennsylvania Press, 1996.

Peterson, Derek R., ed. *Abolitionism and Imperialism in Britain, Africa, and the Atlantic.* Athens: Ohio University Press, 2010.

Peytraud, Lucien. *L'esclavage aux Antilles françaises avant 1789, d'après des documents inédits des Archives coloniales.* Paris: Hachette, 1897.

Phillips, Ulrich Bonnell. *American Negro Slavery: A Survey of the Supply, Employment and Control of Negro Labor As Determined by the Plantation Regime.* New York: D. Appleton, 1918.

Phillips, William D., Jr. " Manumission in Metropolitan Spain and the Canaries in the Fifteenth and Sixteenth Centuries." In *Paths to Freedom: Manumission in the Atlantic World*, edited by Rosemary Brana-Shute and Randy J. Sparks, 31–50. Charleston: University of South Carolina Press, 2009.

Piquet, Jean-Daniel. *L'émancipation des Noirs dans la Révolution française (1789–1795).* Paris: Éditions Karthala, 2002.

Pluchon, Pierre. ed. *Histoire des Antilles et de la Guyane.* Toulouse: Privat, 1982.

Vaudou, sorciers, empoisonneurs: De Saint-Domingue à Haïti. Paris: Éditions Karthala, 1987.

Pocock, J. G. A. *The Machiavellian Moment: Florentine Political Thought and the Atlantic Republican Tradition.* Princeton: Princeton University Press, 1975.

Popkin, Jeremy D. "The French Revolution's Other Island." In *The World of the Haitian Revolution*, edited by David Patrick Geggus and Norman, 199–222. Bloomington: Indiana University Press, 2009.

You Are All Free: The Haitian Revolution and the Abolition of Slavery. New York: Cambridge University Press, 2010.

Price, Richard, ed. *Maroon Societies: Rebel Slave Communities in the Americas.* 3rd ed. Baltimore, MD: The Johns Hopkins University Press, 1996.

Quarles, Benjamin. *The Negro in the American Revolution.* Chapel Hill: University of North Carolina Press, 1996.

Raphanaud, Gaston. *Le baron Malouet, ses idées, son oeuvre, 1740–1814.* Paris: A. Michalon, 1907.

"Raynal, abbé Guillaume-Thomas-François." In *Biographie universelle, ancienne et moderne.* Vol. 37. Paris: Michaud, 1824.

Regnault de Beaucaron, Charles Edmond. *Souvenirs anecdotiques et historiques d'anciennes familles champenoises et bourguignonnes.* Paris: Plon-Nourrit et cie, 1906.

Souvenirs de famille; voyages, agriculture, précédés d'une Causerie sur le passé. Paris: Plon-Nourrit et cie, 1912.

Rey, Alain, ed. *Dictionnaire historique de la langue française.* 3 vols. Paris: Le Robert, 1998.

Rioux, Jean-Pierre. *Dictionnaire de la France coloniale.* Paris: Flammarion, 2007.

Rogers, Dominique. "On the Road to Citizenship: The Complex Route to Integration of the Free People of Color in the Two Capitals of Saint-Domigue." In *The World of the Haitian Revolution,* edited by David Patrick Geggus and Norman Fiering, 65–78.

Roux, Marie, marquis de. *Louis XIV et les provinces conquises: Artois, Alsace, Flandres, Roussillon, Franche-comté.* Paris: Les Éditions de France, 1938.

Rugemer, Edward Barlett. *The Problem of Emancipation: The Caribbean Roots of the American Civil War.* Baton Rouge: Louisiana State University Press, 2008.

Rushforth, Brett. *Bonds of Alliance: Indigenous and Atlantic Slaveries in New France.* Chapel Hill: University of North Carolina Press, for the Omohundro Institute of Early American History and Culture, 2012.

Sahlins, Peter. *Unnaturally French: Foreign Citizens in the Old Regime and After.* Ithaca, NY: Cornell University Press, 2004.

Saint-Louis, Vertus. *Aux origines du drame d'Haïti: Droit et commerce maritime (1794–1806).* Port-au-Prince, Haïti: L'Imprimeur II, 2006.

"Régime militaire et Règlements de culture en 1801." *Chemins critiques* 3, nos. 1–2 (1993): 183–227.

Sala-Molins, Louis. *Le code noir, ou le calvaire de Canaan.* Paris: Presses Universitaires de France, 1987.

Dark Side of the Light: Slavery and the French Enlightenment. Trans. John-Conteh Morgan. Minneapolis: University of Minnesota Press, 2006.

Sarat, Austin, Lawrence Douglas, and Martha Merrill Umphrey, eds. *The Limits of Law.* Stanford, CA: Stanford University Press, 2005.

Savage, John. "Between Colonial Fact and French Law: Slave Poisoners and the Provostial Court in Restoration-Era Martinique." *French Historical Studies* 29, no 4 (2006): 565–594.

Schama, Simon. *Citizens: A Chronicle of the French Revolution.* New York: Knopf, 1989.

Dead Certainties (Unwarranted Speculations). New York: Alfred Knopf, 1991.

Rough Crossings: Britain, the Slaves, and the American Revolution. London: BBC Books, 2005.

Schmidt, Nelly. *Réformateurs coloniaux et abolitionnistes de l'esclavage, 1820–1851.* Paris: Karthala, 2000.

Scott, David. *Conscripts of Modernity: The Tragedy of Colonial Enlightenment.* Durham, NC: Duke University Press, 2004.

Scott, Rebecca J. "The Atlantic World and the Road to Plessy v. Ferguson." *Journal of American History* 94, no. 3 (2007): 726–733.

"Public Rights, Social Equality, and the Conceptual Roots of the Plessy Challenge." *Michigan Law Review* 106 (2008): 777–804.

"'She … Refuses to Deliver Up Herself as the Slave of Your Petitioner': Émigrés, Enslavement, and the 1808 Louisiana Digest of the Civil Laws." *Tulane European and Civil Law Forum* 24 (2009): 115–136.

Scott, Rebecca J., and Jean M. Hébrard. "Les papiers de la liberté: Une mère africaine et ses enfants a l'époque de la Révolution Haïtienne." *Genèses*, 66 (March 2007): 4–29.

Seeber, Edward D. *Anti-Slavery Opinion in France during the Second Half of the Eighteenth Century*. Baltimore, MD: Johns Hopkins University Press, 1937.

Sen, Amartya. *The Idea of Justice*. Cambridge, MA: Harvard University Press, 2009.

Shammas, Carole. "Anglo-American Household Governance in Comparative Perspective." *William and Mary Quarterly* 52, no. 1 (Jan. 1995): 104–144.

Silverman, Lisa. *Tortured Subjects: Pain, Truth, and the Body in Early Modern France*. Chicago, IL: University of Chicago Press, 2001.

Singham, Shanti Marie. "Betwixt Cattle and Men: Jews, Blacks, and Women, and the Declaration of the Rights of Man." In *The French Idea of Freedom: The Old Regime and the Declaration of Rights of 1789*, edited by Dale Van Kley, 114–153. Stanford, CA: Stanford University Press, 1994.

Sonenscher, Michael. *Before the Deluge: Public Debt, Inequality, and the Intellectual Origins of the French Revolution*. Princeton, NJ: Princeton University Press, 2007.

Spieler, Miranda. "The Legal Structure of Colonial Rule during the French Revolution." *William and Mary Quarterly* 66, no. 2 (Apr. 2009): 365–408.

Staël, Germaine de. *Considérations sur la Révolution française*, edited by Jacques Godechot. Paris: Tallandier, 2000.

Stannard, David E. *American Holocaust: The Conquest of the New World*. Oxford: Oxford University Press, 1992.

Stein, Robert Louis. *Léger Félicité Sonthonax: The Lost Sentinel of the Republic*. Rutherford, NJ: Fairleigh Dickinson University Press, 1985.

Steinfeld, Robert J. *The Invention of Free Labor: The Employment Relation in English and American Law and Culture, 1350–1870*. Chapel Hill: The University of North Carolina Press, 1991.

Taillemite, Étienne. "La Fayette et l'abolition de l'esclavage." In *L'esclave et les plantations: De l'établissement de la servitude à son abolition: Un hommage à Pierre Pluchon*, edited by Philippe Hrodĕj, 229–239. Rennes: Presses Universitaires de Rennes, 2008.

Tarrade, Jean. "De l'apogée économique à l'effrondrement du domaine colonial (1763–1830)." In *Histoire de la France coloniale*. Vol. 1, *La conquête*, by Jean Meyer, Annie Rey-Goldzeiguer, and Jean Tarrade. Paris: Armand Colin, 1991.

"L'esclavage est-il réformable? Les projets des administrateurs coloniaux à la fin de l'Ancien Régime." In *Les abolitions de l'esclavage de L. F. Sonthonax à V. Schoelcher, 1793, 1794, 1848: Actes du colloque international tenu à l'Université de Paris VIII les 3, 4, et 5 février 1994*, edited by Marcel Dorigny, 133–141. Saint-Denis: Presses Universitaires de Vincennes; Paris: Éditions UNESCO, 1995.

"Les colonies et les principes de 1789: les Assemblées révolutionnaires face au problème de l'esclavage." In *La Révolution française et les colonies*, edited by Jean Tarrade, 9–33. Paris: Librairie L'Harmattan, pour la Société française d'histoire d'outre-mer, 1989.

Thibau, Jacques. *Le temps de Saint-Domingue: L'esclavage et la Révolution française*. Paris: J.-C. Lattès, 1989.

Thornton, John K. "Africa and Abolitionism." In *Who Abolished Slavery? Slave Revolts and Abolitionism: A Debate with João Pedro Marques*, edited by Seymour Drescher and Peter C. Emmer, 93–102. New York: Bergahn Books, 2010.

"African Soldiers in the Haitian Revolution." *Journal of Caribbean History* 25 (1993): 59–80.

"'I am the Subject of the King of Congo': African Ideology in the Haitian Revolution." *Journal of World History* 4 (1993): 181–214.

Tocqueville, Alexis de. *The Ancien Régime and the French Revolution*. Edited by Jon Elster. Translated by Arthur Goldhammer. Cambridge Texts in the History of Political Thought. New York: Cambridge University Press, 2011.

Writings on Empire and Slavery. Edited and translated by Jennifer Pitts. Baltimore, MD: The Johns Hopkins University Press, 2001.

Todd, David. "A French Imperial Meridian, 1814–1870." *Past and Present* 210, no. 1 (Feb. 2011): 155–186.

Tournerie, Jean-André. "Un projet d'école royale des colonies en Touraine au XVIIIᵉ siècle." *Annales de Bretagne et des pays de l'Ouest* 99, no. 1 (1992): 33–60.

Trouillot, Michel-Rolph. *Haiti: State against Nation: The Origins and Legacy of Duvalierism*. New York: Monthly Review Press, 1989.

Silencing the Past: Power and the Production of History. Boston, MA: Beacon Press, 1995.

Tully, James, ed. *Meaning and Context: Quentin Skinner and his Critics*. Princeton, NJ: Princeton University Press, 1988.

Tushnet, Mark. *Slave Law in the American South: State v. Mann in History and Literature*. Lawrence: University of Kansas Press, 2003.

Vaissière, Pierre de. *Saint-Domingue: La société et la vie créole sous l'ancien régime (1629–1789)*. Paris: Perrin et Cie, 1909.

Van Kley, Dale, ed. *The French Idea of Freedom: The Old Regime and the Declaration of Rights of 1789*. Stanford, CA: Stanford University Press, 1994.

Veyne, Paul. "Les esclaves." In *Histoire de la vie privée*, edited by Philippe Ariès and Georges Duby. Vol. 1, *De l'empire romain à l'an mil*, edited by Paul Veyne, 61–79. Paris: Éditions du Seuil, 1985.

Vignols, Léon. *Les esclaves coloniaux en France au XVIIᵉ et XVIIIᵉ siècles et leur retour aux Antilles*. Rennes: Oberthur, 1927.

Vonglis, Bernard. "La double origine du Code noir." In *Les Abolitions dans les Amériques*, edited by Liliane Chauleau, 101–107. Fort-de-France: Société des amis des archives et de la recherche sur le patrimoine culturel des Antilles, 2001.

Vovelle, Michel. *La mentalité révolutionnaire: Société et mentalités sous la Révolution française*. Paris: Éditions sociales, 1985.

"Sonthonax: sa place dans l'histoire des abolitions." In *Léger-Félicité Sonthonax: La première abolition de l'esclavage: La Révolution française et la Révolution de Saint-Domingue*, edited by Marcel Dorigny, 159–167. Saint-Denis, France: Société française d'histoire d'outre-mer et Association pour l'étude de la colonisation européenne, 2005.

Watson, Alan. "The Origins of the Code Noir Revisited." *Tulane Law Review* 71, no. 4 (March 1997): 1041–1072.

    Roman Slave Law. With a foreword by A. Leon Higginbotham, Jr. Baltimore, MD: The Johns Hopkins University Press, 1987.

    Slave Law in the Americas. Athens: The University of Georgia Press, 1989.

Weber, Max. *Economy and Society: An Outline of Interpretive Sociology*. Edited by Guenther Roth and Claus Wittich. Translated by Ephraim Fischoff et al. Vol. 2. Berkeley: University of California Press, 1978.

Weisberger, R. William, Dennis P. Hupchick, and David L. Anderson, eds. *Profiles of Revolutionaries in Atlantic History, 1700–1850*. Boulder, CO: Social Science Monographs, 2007.

White, Ashli. *Encountering Revolution: Haiti and the Making of the Early Republic*. Baltimore, MD: Johns Hopkins University Press, 2010.

    "Saint-Dominguan Refugees and American Distinctiveness in the Early Years of the Haitian Revolution." In *The World of the Haitian Revolution*, edited by David Patrick Geggus and Norman Fiering, 248–260. Bloomington: Indiana University Press, 2009.

Whitman, James Q. *Harsh Justice: Criminal Punishment and the Widening Divide between American and Europe*. New York: Oxford University Press, 2003.

Woloch, Isser. "On the Latent Illiberalism of the French Revolution." *American Historical Review* 95, no. 5 (1990): 1452–1470.

Wucker, Michele. *Why the Cocks Fight: Dominicans, Haitians, and the Struggle for Hispaniola*. New York: Hill and Wang, 1999.

Index

Index